The Old Farmer's Almanac

Calculated on a new and improved plan for the year of our Lord

1997

Being 1st after LEAP YEAR and (until July 4)
221st year of American Independence

FITTED FOR BOSTON AND THE NEW ENGLAND STATES, WITH SPECIAL
CORRECTIONS AND CALCULATIONS TO ANSWER FOR ALL THE UNITED STATES.

Containing, besides the large number of Astronomical Calculations
and the Farmer's Calendar for every month in the year, a variety of

NEW, USEFUL, AND ENTERTAINING MATTER.

ESTABLISHED IN 1792

by Robert B. Thomas

*"Labor to keep alive in your breast
that little spark of celestial fire
called conscience."*

– GEORGE WASHINGTON

CONTENTS

The Old Farmer's Almanac • 1997

page 10

page 82

page 94

page 176

page 88

page 166

page 118

Charts, Tables, and Departments

34

☞ How to Use This Almanac

Better traction.

Better turning.

Better cutting.

Better riding.

Better looking.

Simply Better.

Some things are just better than others. Like our tractors. With sure-footed traction, the durability of steel construction, a Free-Floating™ mowing deck, a smooth, car-like ride, and an extremely tight turning radius, you won't find a better way to mow your lawn. And that means a better investment for you. So don't settle for something good, get a Simplicity tractor. It's better.

Call 1-800-987-LAWN for the dealer nearest you.

MANUFACTURING, INC.®

Ask the right questions when shopping for a tractor.

Shopping for the right tractor to care for your yard can be confusing. There are many brands, and, at first glance, they seem similar. A tractor is an investment that should last for years. To truly get your money's worth, go beyond the shiny paint to compare the design, features, and quality of different models by asking these questions:

How well is it made?

Ask about the design and manufacture of the tractor to assess its quality and durability. To assure longevity, look for all-steel construction, including the hood. And check the tractor's frame design. For maximum durability, look for a channel frame design, welded for added strength. Different gauges of steel support critical stress areas, making a channel frame more rugged than the single-piece stamped frame usually found on less expensive units.

How well does it cut?

There are three keys to a great cut: the mowing deck, the turning radius and the traction. Examine how the mowing deck is mounted on the tractor. Look for an axle-mounted mowing deck that "floats" freely, adjusting to changes in terrain. This deck mounting system follows the contours of your yard, reducing scalping and providing a smooth, even cut. Another sign of a great cut is the ability to manicure around landscaping, minimizing the trimming required after mowing. Look for a tractor with a tight turning radius to complete the job efficiently, one

that's capable of mowing around trees and shrubs in one pass. Finally, just like in a car, look for features that improve traction. Good traction ensures that the tractor's wheels will not slip when climbing steep inclines or mowing wet, slippery areas.

How easy is it to use and maintain?

Remember, a tractor should make your yard chores easier and less tiring. The design and ergonomics of a unit make a difference. Are controls conveniently located? How simple are key operator tasks, such as adjusting the cutting height or engaging the mower deck? Is the seat comfortable, and easily adjustable for different operators? Make sure that routine maintenance is truly routine. For example, you should be able to detach the mower deck easily, without special tools.

What if the tractor needs service, or you need advice?

After you take your tractor home, you may have a question or need a part. Your best assurance that the tractor you select will continue to work for you into the future is to buy it from a knowledgeable, servicing dealer.

Finally, remember that the best way to make a confident, informed decision about a tractor is to take a test drive. Make sure your retailer can accommodate a demonstration of the product, including how it handles and cuts.

Pᴛᴏ ATRONS

Who, exactly, *are* you nine million Almanac readers?

They tell us there will be about nine million people who will read this 205th edition of *The Old Farmer's Almanac* over the next few months. That's figuring some four readers per copy — a conservative estimate. Of course, there haven't always been that many readers. The real circulation surge of the Almanac has taken place just in the last ten years. There were only 3,000 folks, for instance, who bought Robert B. Thomas's first edition in the fall of 1792. However, our old records indicate that the circulation tripled the next year and then steadily increased until it reached 170,000 during the Civil War years. In this century, the Almanac experienced a decline during the Depression, the only decline in its history. So when our family-owned company, Yankee Publishing Inc., headquartered here in Dublin, New Hampshire, took over from Little-Brown in Boston in 1939, we inherited a circulation of only 88,000. But the circulation arrow has been pointing up ever since.

So who are you 1997 Almanac readers, now nine million strong? We have always thought we had a pretty good *general* idea — we figured you probably live in your own home in a small town or in the country, it's likely you enjoy gardening, and for sure, you are plenty smart enough to know

that a quarter Moon looks like a half circle and that the Earth is closest to the Sun during the coldest month of the year. We suspect most of you also know that if the wind is in the east, there's no point trying to induce a fish to bite.

Those were just "gut instincts." We didn't *really* know you. So during this past year, for the first time in our long history, we hired a professional reader-survey company to find out *exactly* who you are.

As it turned out, our instincts were not far off. Eighty-two percent of you *do* own your own homes, and most of you *do* live outside urban areas. Yes, the majority of you love your gardens and, to be precise, spend 5.5 hours each week in them. As to smart, well, you surely are. We know that not just because the study proves you are better educated than the average person, but also because you are more likely to own your own business and more likely to be better-off financially. That sort of thing requires smarts. Also, roughly three-quarters of you have purchased five or more books in the past year.

It was interesting to learn, too, that your attitudes are anything but simplistic. For example, you are more likely than the general population to believe in the experience and wisdom of our older people. Yet you feel it is the energy and ideas of our young people that represent the best hope for solving the country's problems. Over 60 percent of you are very troubled by how difficult it is to get straight, dependable answers in today's world, but on the other hand, 81 percent of you feel you live in a country that stands for what is the very best in today's world.

We suspected you were good citizens, but we didn't realize *how* good. Now we know. About 80 percent of you vote in

(continued on page 8)

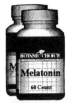

every general election, for instance — way above the national average. And you are much more involved in the life of your communities than the average person is. This covers doing volunteer work, raising money for good causes, writing letters to newspaper editors, being active in civic issues, etc. In other words, you are the sort of people who *care*.

Perhaps our biggest surprise was to learn that almost half of you own your own computers. And that you're twice as likely as members of the general population to subscribe to an online service such as the Internet's World Wide Web on which, as it so happens, the Almanac now has a site (http://www.almanac.com).

Our biggest disappointment? Well, we learned that only 19 percent of you actually use the very expensive (about $43,187 this year) hole we always have punched in the upper left-hand corner of the Almanac. So instead of hanging your copy on the wall somewhere handy, as was done in the old days, over 50 percent of you keep it on a bookshelf during the year. That's fine. But does it mean you don't care about the hole anymore?

All in all, we have to say that as a result of this survey we are more pleased and proud than ever to know you — all nine million of you. With this edition and in the years ahead, we can only hope you won't ever think we have let you down.

J. D. H. (JUNE 1996)

However, it is by our works and not our words that we would be judged. These, we hope, will sustain us in the humble though proud station we have so long held in the name of,

Your obedient servant,

THE 1997 EDITION OF
THE OLD FARMER'S ALMANAC
Established in 1792 and published every year thereafter
ROBERT B. THOMAS *(1766-1846)*
FOUNDER

EDITOR *(12th since 1792)*: Judson D. Hale Sr.
MANAGING EDITOR: Susan Peery
EXECUTIVE EDITOR: Tim Clark
ART DIRECTOR: Margo Letourneau
SOLAR PROGNOSTICATOR: Dr. Richard Head
WEATHER GRAPHICS: ©Accu-Weather, Inc., 1996
ASTRONOMER: Dr. George Greenstein
COPY EDITOR: Lida Stinchfield
ASSOCIATE EDITORS: Mare-Anne Jarvela, Debra Sanderson
ASSISTANT EDITORS: Anna Larson, Maude Salinger, Mary Sheldon
ARCHIVIST: Lorna Trowbridge
CONTRIBUTING EDITORS: Jamie Kageleiry;
Bob Berman, *Astronomy;* Castle Freeman Jr., *Farmer's Calendar;* Sarah Hale, *Reference*
PRODUCTION DIRECTOR: Susan Gross
PAGE PRODUCTION MANAGER: David Ziarnowski
PRODUCTION ASSISTANT: Clare Innes
SENIOR PRODUCTION ARTISTS: Lucille Rines, Christopher Simard

GROUP PUBLISHER: John Pierce
PUBLISHER *(23rd since 1792)*: Sherin Wight
ADMINISTRATIVE ASSISTANT: Sarah Duffy
ADVERTISING PRODUCTION / CLASSIFIED: Donna Stone
MAIL ORDER MARKETING MANAGER: Deb Walsh
DIRECT SALES MANAGER: Cindy Schlosser
SPECIAL MARKETS DIRECTOR: Ronda Knowlton

ADVERTISING MARKETING REPRESENTATIVES:
Mail Order Advertising
NORTHEAST & WEST: Robert Bernbach, 914-769-0051;
MIDWEST: Dwight Early & Sons, 708-466-0001
General Advertising
NATIONAL MARKETING DIRECTOR: Russ Weller, 847-480-8844;
MIDWEST: Media Marketers, 312-236-4830;
WEST: Frank Strazzulla, 818-366-5388; SOUTHEAST: Carl Crombach, 706-754-3025; EAST: Peter Uhry, 203-637-5478
NEWSSTAND CIRCULATION: P.S.C.S.
DISTRIBUTION: Curtis Circulation Company

EDITORIAL, ADVERTISING, AND PUBLISHING OFFICES:
P.O. Box 520, Dublin, NH 03444
Phone: 603-563-8111 • Fax: 603-563-8252
Internet Address: http://www.almanac.com

YANKEE PUBLISHING INC., MAIN ST., DUBLIN, NH 03444

Joseph B. Meagher, *President;* Judson D. Hale Sr., *Senior Vice President;* Brian Piani, *Vice President and Chief Financial Officer;* Jody Bugbee, John Pierce, and Joe Timko, *Vice Presidents.*

The Old Farmer's Almanac will not return any unsolicited manuscripts that do not include a stamped and addressed return envelope.

The Old Farmer's Almanac publications are available at special discounts for bulk purchases for sales promotions or premiums. Contact Special Markets, 603-563-8111.

CONSUMER
TASTES *and* TRENDS
FOR 1997

by Jamie Kageleiry

What's Good for You in 1997

Fidgeting

■ The National Institutes of Health compared **fidgety and calm people**. The people who paced the room, moved their arms and legs a lot, and changed positions often (the types who make us **nervous at meetings**), burned anywhere from 138 to 685 calories a day more than the nonfidgeters. (There was no word on how well they slept at night.)

Eggs

■ A lot of **dietary doomsayers** have, well, egg on their faces these days. A University of Washington study recently found that most people, even those with elevated cholesterol levels, can **safely eat two eggs a day** — as long as they go easy on total fat consumption. Only ten percent of cholesterol-sensitive people need to be careful about eating eggs.

Laughing

■ Laugh, and your immune and neuroendocrine systems laugh with you. An hour spent laughing, discovered Dr. Lee Berk at the Loma Linda School of Public Health in California, not only **lowers levels of stress hormones**, but appears to strengthen the immune system. Six-year-old kids have it best: Researchers estimate they laugh an average of 300 times per day. (Adults chuckle only between 15 and 100 times a day, but hey, we have taxes to pay.)

Junk Food

■ Junk food usually contains artificial flavors, which, the National Center for Health Statistics has found, contain salicylates, chemical cousins of aspirin. Aspirin **reduces the risk of heart attacks**. Ergo, junk food is good for you! (Don't load up on extra Twinkies hoping to live forever — the ordinary American diet already provides the salicylates equivalent to one baby aspirin, the recommended daily amount to ward off a heart attack.)

What's Bad for You in 1997

The Stress on Stress

■ It used to be that few people believed the **mind could influence the body**. Now too many people think that *everything* that goes wrong in our bodies is **caused by our minds**, from infertility to colds to cancer. Doctors and psychologists are

beginning to see that stress, though it can play a role, has become overused as a reason for illness.

Daylight Saving Time

■ Psychologists in British Columbia, Canada, say that **Daylight Saving Time can be dangerous.** On the Monday following the spring switch, there are almost eight percent more traffic accidents than the previous or following Monday, according to the study published in the *New England Journal of Medicine.* People are still sleepy from that lost hour, apparently. Then when Oc-

tober rolls around and we **get that extra hour of sleep,** traffic accidents drop on the first Monday (then return to average the next Monday).

Electric Lights

■ Those who study such things have found that even normal levels of **indoor lighting can reset the human biological clock,** creating a sort of permanent jet lag. "Exposure to artificial light after sunset in industrial countries has shifted the clocks of most people by four or five hours," reports Dr. Charles Czeisler of Boston. That means most people in the United States are actually on Hawaii time. "Thomas Edison had a **bigger effect on the human body clock** than anyone realized," says Czeisler. "Every time we turn on a light, we are inadvertently taking a drug that affects how we will sleep."

Home, Sweet Home, 1997

■ **Bamboo furniture is back.** World War II-vintage pieces are **hot collectibles.** Watch for bamboo on flatware handles, picture frames, boxes, and benches. Some designers are even trying to make a kind of fiberglass from it to use in house siding and car fenders.

■ **Neutrals will remain popular** for paint and furniture colors. But look for the earthy colors (the greens, off-whites, taupes, and grays) to be deeper, more saturated. **The "khaki family"** (rich yellows and greens) will be the most popular. "We're seeing the khaki-ing of America," James Martin of the Color People in Denver told the *Wall Street Journal.* "Not shabby, but comfortable. That is what people are after." Stripes of all types will be popular on curtains and upholstery.

■ **Generation X'ers keep a clean house.** According to a new survey, conducted for the Manhattan-based **Soap and Detergent Association,** 55 percent of 20-somethings said neatness was *very important,* up six percentage points from when the same question was asked on a similar survey in 1975.

(continued)

Good News

■ Super Seniors

We've all heard people say that we **start to lose brain cells** the minute we hit 20, and it's downhill from there. But data shows that in healthy people in their eighties and nineties, not only is brain-cell loss relatively modest, but the mind  can also recruit other circuits to get a task done. In fact, one out of ten people continues to increase mental abilities in the later decades. And not only have they become brainier, but **people over 65 are now living longer** and are less at risk of developing disabling chronic disease.

■ A Surefire Way to Halt Hiccups

According to the magazine *Physician and Sportsmedicine,* here's what you should do: Briefly **apply ice cubes to the sides of your neck**, at the level of the larynx. That's it! No standing on your head, no one yelling "Boo!" It works by interrupting the reflex nerve signals that cause the spasmodic contractions of the diaphragm that we call hiccups.

Bad News

■ Old Unfaithful

What's the world coming to when you can't even set your watch by the **eruptions of Yellowstone's Old Faithful?** In the 1950s the average interval between geyser eruptions was 62 minutes. Recently, the interval has averaged 77 minutes, with wide variation. "One day, it might just quit permanently," noted a park scientist (to the dismay of tourism officials). Increased seismic activity siphons off the underground pressure so that Old Faithful is literally losing steam.

The Most Creative Way We've Heard to Lower the Federal Deficit

The Internal Revenue Service in Kentucky has been recycling unused tax forms into toilet paper. Since the program started in 1993, it has saved more than $55,000; the IRS has saved an additional $25,000 on trash pickup.

Aside from the patriotic aspect of lowering the deficit and the bonus of providing a gift for that hard-to-please person, isn't this sweet revenge?

Moose Encounters

■ Auto accidents involving moose in Canada are way up — **that's bad**. Moose are attracted by road salt, so researchers developed a repellent called Wolfin, an extract of wolf urine, to keep moose off the highways **(that's good)**. However, not only does Wolfin cost more than Chanel No. 5, but some moose are actually attracted to the smell **(that's bad)**. Then researchers found that covered drainage ditches, which trap the salty water and keep it away from the moose, reduce moose accidents by 80 percent **(that's good)**. But . . . it's time-consuming to dig ditches. It took dozens of workers *five years* to complete a ten-kilometer stretch in Ontario. **(And that's bad.)**

(continued)

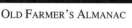

12 Great Reasons to Own a Mantis Tiller

1.Weighs just 20 pounds. Mantis is a joy to use. It starts easily, turns on a dime, lifts nimbly over plants and fences.

2. Tills like nothing else. Mantis bites down a full 10" deep, churns tough soil into crumbly loam, prepares seedbeds in no time.

3. Has patented "serpentine" tines. Our patented tine teeth spin at up to 240 RPM— twice as fast as others. Cuts through tough soil and vegetation like a chain saw through wood!

4. Weeds faster than hand tools. Reverse its tines and Mantis is a precision power weeder. Weeds an average garden in 20 minutes.

5. Digs planting furrows. With the Planter/Furrower, Mantis digs deep or shallow furrows for planting. Builds raised beds, too!

6. Cuts neat borders. Use the Border Edger to cut crisp edges for flower beds, walkways, around shrubs and trees.

7. Dethatches your lawn. Thatch on your lawn prevents water and nutrients from reaching the roots. The Dethatcher quickly removes thatch.

8. Aerates your lawn, too. For a lush, healthy carpet, the Aerator slices thousands of tine slits in you lawn's surface.

9. Trims bushes and hedges! Only Mantis has an optional 24" or 30" trimmer bar to prune and trim your shrubbery and small trees.

10. The Mantis Promise Try any product that you buy directly from Mantis with **NO RISK!** If you're not completely satisfied, send it back to us within one year for a complete, no hassle refund.

11. Warranties. The entire tiller is warranted for two full years. The tines are quaranteed forever against breakage.

12. Fun to use. The Mantis Tiller/Cultivator is so much fun to use gardeners everywhere love their Mantis tillers.

Learn more about Mantis today!
For free details, call
TOLL FREE 1-800-366-6268.

Best New Way to Save Money, 1997

■ **That Spam Sparkle**
Don't throw away your left-over Spam! Joey Green, the author of

Polish Your Furniture with Panty Hose, says you can use it to **polish your furniture** and save yourself a few bucks. Green also suggests using mouthwash as a deodorant and peanut butter as shaving cream (but not vice versa).

Worst New Way to Save Money, 1997

■ **That Ring of Impermanence**
Rent-a-Centers nationwide are seeing **brisk rentals of**

engagement rings at $12.99 to $24.99 a week. Some couples rent their sparklers only for the wedding; others rent just until they're sure they're engaged to the right person.

Pet News

■ **Premiums for Your Pooch**
Gumbo couldn't stop eating tennis balls. In one year, reported the *Wall Street Journal*, the black Labrador was taken to the vet for **tennis-ball-removal surgery** five times at $800 a throw (so to speak). But Gumbo's owner, Meleah Larocca, didn't panic. Gumbo was covered by a major-medical insurance plan.

VPI Insurance Group in California says that the number of Americans insuring their pets (for premiums ranging up to $151 a year, with a $40 per visit deductible) has **doubled in the last few years.**

Sally Schrieber, an actuary in Britain, where 700,000 dogs and cats are insured, reports that:

■ **Cats are less costly to treat than dogs (they're smaller).**

■ **Mongrels are healthier than purebreds.**

■ **The bigger the dog, the more often it gets sick.**

(P.S. Mrs. Larocca finally took Gumbo to a behavioral therapist — not covered in her policy — and Gumbo hasn't eaten a tennis ball in six months.)

The Differences Between Men and Women, 1997

■ **Men and boys** buy **80 percent of the CD-ROM** games on the market.

■ **Hotel gender gap?** Women, according to the Novotel hotel chain, use more towels (4) per hotel stay than men (2). But men, defying the cliché, carry more luggage. For a typical two-night stay, **men average two bags; women only one.**

When ordering from room service, men favor hamburgers, women go for club sandwiches; both sexes order beer over other beverages.

Hotel staffers **unanimously agree** that men leave rooms neater than women.

(continued)

The Hot Collectibles in 1997

■ The Seventies

Though stores are featuring groovy new vases and lamps that **look strangely familiar,** flea-market coups are the best: striped vases (if you can work all that orange and gold into your current color scheme), macramé wall hangings, and Barcaloungers.

■ Offices of Yesteryear

Typewriters, pens, inkwells, anything that is **becoming obsolete** is also becom-

ing collectible. Real prizes: aluminum desks from the 1920s, amoeba-shaped desks from the 1960s.

■ Toys

Besides the continued popularity of toys from baby boomers' youths (**Barbie dolls, Lincoln logs, Matchbox cars**), tiny tin toys that came as prizes in boxes of Cracker Jacks (worth up to $150) or other popcorn snacks have become hot properties.

New for '97, or Why Didn't We Think of That Before?

Lidded Ice Cube Tray

■ No more **messy sloshing** between sink and freezer: Randall Dale of North Carolina thought up an ice tray with a snap-tight lid on a continuous plastic hinge. The patent office granted him Patent No. 5,397,097.

Tuna Can Squeezer

■ It's not just for tuna cans — anything drainable in a can is game. Joseph Casapulla's **liquid extractor** sits on the edge of your sink and holds your open can upside down while squeezing the lid, making all the liquid ooze out.

Glow-in-the-Dark Bowling

■ "You might think of it as a big roll of Scotch tape that you **lay down on top of the bowling lane,**" inventor Brent Perrier told *The New York Times*. "It glows like a son of a gun and it gives a whole different look to the bowling center."

Greenhouse Refrigerators

■ Martin Nix of Seattle has come up with a way to turn old refrigerators into greenhouses. He takes out the condenser, compressor, and motor, then cuts a hole in the top and installs a skylight, a solar-powered fan, and **a reflector to capture more light**. (He also suggests installing a south-facing window on the side of the fridge.) Mr. Nix says it's especially great for tomatoes.

And to think the U.S. Patent Office almost closed 100 years ago because it was thought that there could be no more useful inventions.

(continued)

Food Trends

Convenience, Comfort, and Home Cooking

How to Live Long While Eating Well

A Harvard study has found that rural Greek villagers who lived the longest ate the typical Greek diet — lots of legumes, cereals and bread, fruits and vegetables, small amounts of meat and dairy, moderate alcohol, and a high ratio of monosaturated fat (such as olive oil) to saturated fat (such as butter). Olive oil makes vegetables taste so good that the Greeks eat lots of them (up to a pound a day, sautéed in olive oil).

The average American coffee drinker has 3.5 cups a day — down a bit since 1993. Over half of all coffee is consumed at breakfast.

■ **CONVENIENCE** shows up all over the place. Take-out was popular before; it's through the roof now. Even **the fanciest of restaurants offer it**. Grocery stores are offering hot meals to go, and supermarket chains are offering online (or fax or phone) grocery ordering for customers. Home delivery will be common as soon as stores figure out how to make it profitable.

Another nod to convenience: Girl Scouts cookies may now be **ordered over the phone** in New York City.

■ **COMFORT:** Cheesecake and deep-fried foods are back in vogue. **Also in the comfort department:** a resurgence of hot chocolate. Tea continues its upswing.

■ **HOME COOKING:** "We're selling nostalgia," says Marc Phillips, owner of Phillips Farms in New Jersey, who saw **sales of homemade jam skyrocket** when he switched to an authentic two-piece canning-jar lid. And one of the biggest winners in the gourmet-food business has been "Mrs. Stimpert's Pickles," which sell at $25 for a 64-ounce jar in Bloomingdale's.
Homemade pies will be the most popular desserts in a year or so, and emblematic of

moderating tastes, milk chocolate will replace the luxurious dark as the chocolate of choice.

Americans use 68 more spices now than ten years ago, and continue to experiment with the **more exotic cuisines**, especially Asian, Mediterranean (including Turkish), and North African.

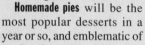

Quince will be popular, as will kale. Look for wider supermarket selections of Asian vegetables such as Chinese eggplant, bok choy, and lemongrass.

French food (pâté, frog legs) is in vogue again in city restaurants.

(continued)

☞ Catalog Emporium

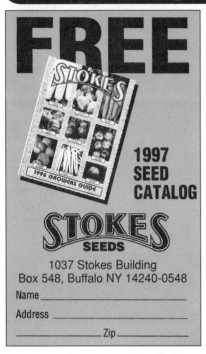

In Case You Were Wondering

According to the newly released *Statistical Abstract of the United States:*

■ One in three Americans is still exercising after age 75.

■ Rock-music sales are twice those of country and ten times those of jazz.

■ Eight percent of American households have herb gardens.

■ Forty-two million Americans play amateur softball on 200,000 adult teams and 62,000 kids' teams.

■ In the last recorded year (1993), two billion books were sold in the United States, more than half of them paperbacks.

■ Estimated number of Santas hired by all malls in the country: 7,460.

Here's to Your Health

■ **Cancer fighters:** The *Wall Street Journal* recently reported that "the seeds of current [cancer] research promise a bumper crop of insights in the next decade. The outcome is more likely to be the ensemble of players at a dinner table than the solo actors in a pill bottle."

A Swedish team has discovered that substances in human breast milk may protect against cancer. An abundant protein called "alpha-lactalbumin" somehow "stimulates cancer cells to commit suicide," leaving normal, mature cells unharmed. The discovery could lead to the design of effective antitumor agents.

Researchers have found that people who consume the most fruits and vegetables (such as Seventh-Day Adventists) have about half the cancer cases of those who consume the least.

■ **(Don't read this next paragraph while you're eating . . .)**
"We just have to get past what I call the Yuck Factor," says surgeon Dr. John Church, who is launching a "maggot therapy program" in Oxford, England. This is not therapy for maggots, but therapy *using* maggots. For centuries, physicians have noticed that maggot-infested wounds healed faster than those without. "Maggots thrive off dead meat and bacteria," explained the doctor, "and can get into the nooks and crannies that antibiotics can't reach."

■ **Chronic Fatigue Syndrome** may be linked to a common abnormality in the way the body regulates blood pressure, often called "hypotension," according to a recent study at Johns Hopkins Hospital in Baltimore. Many sufferers of the disease have responded to a treatment of increased salt and fluid intake along with standard blood pressure-regulating drugs.

(continued)

Agricultural News

■ **"Biotechnology,"** wrote *The New York Times* recently, "is leading to a revolution in farming by allowing genetic characteristics to be transferred selectively from one species to another." For example, a **petunia gene fortifies soybeans** so that a powerful and inexpensive herbicide called Roundup may be sprayed on soybean fields to control weeds. Without the petunia protection, the soybeans would die from the herbicide. Experts say that by early next century, at least half the country's cropland will grow plants harboring at least one foreign gene.

Some futurists believe that advances in biotechnology will yield **cows that produce low-fat milk** (you were hoping for chocolate?), disease-resistant potatoes (grown by crossing them with a chicken gene), and leaner pork.

Organic Trend

A consumer trend is showing its impact on farms: Sales of organic produce have doubled in the last five years, and sales of milk from organically fed cows are rising.

The Mood

■ **Manners?** Parents are concerned that **society has become less civil**, so they're enrolling children in etiquette classes and seeking advice from books and child-development experts. Even institutions like MIT are offering "Charm Schools" to teach table manners,  telephone and E-mail etiquette, how to ask for dates, and other niceties.

■ **Divorce rates** are down; sociologists say "the traditional American family is making a comeback." **Another indication** that our lightning-speed society is yearning for gentler times: Poetry, both classic and homegrown, is suddenly wildly popular. "Salons" (where people gather just to talk) are springing up everywhere. Even the Internet, which has zoomed us to the future, is used mostly for visiting and "chatting."

■ **Though the economy is** in good shape, our recession-born frugality has stuck: **now *everyone* goes to flea markets** and even brags about used cars. Wal-Mart is gaining converts in ritzy suburbs. It's another part of the "getting back to basics" trend. Even our national savings rate has improved noticeably in the past year.

Many of those who have been "downsized" out of corporate culture have decided it was **the best thing that ever happened** to them: They've opened inns or started small businesses and found a happy life in the slow lane.

Make no mistake: Most Americans these days are still in the fast lane. And anything that helps two-earner families to run their

(continued)

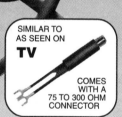

lives will continue to be popular. But we get the sense that **people are at least trying to slow down**. A new study has shown that not only can "all work and no play" make you dull and unhappy, but it can also actually make you fail at the job in which you're striving.

■ **Where futuristic nightmares** were painted of technology creating one giant anonymous mass, high tech has instead **allowed consumers to become individuals:** each customer at a Ritz-Carlton hotel now has his or her own personal preferences recorded in a computer for the next stay; Levi's will make a pair of jeans that will fit only you (for $65 plus shipping); a news service will scan sources and compile a report on what *you* are interested in.

Fashion Trends

■ **It's back to the seventies** in women's fashions. It's a nice take-off: **flared pants aren't elephantine**, but slim and slightly flared, often called "boot-leg." Jackets are longer and slimmer, often belted. Other fashion trends for women:

Suits in tartans and windowpane plaid.

Velvet, suede, and chenille (anything with texture).

Long coats (many with big hoods) and cardigans.

The military look: Jackets with epaulets and belts; long, straight skirts; shades of army fatigue, olive green, tan. Many of these clothes can be found in thrift stores and army-navy stores.

Other popular colors: Brown, white, black (as usual) with splashes of eggplant (a restrained plum/purple), light blue, and even wild print and striped fabrics in dresses (especially short A-line shifts) and jumpsuits (the 1970s again).

Clunky footwear, from combat-type boots to thick-soled Oxfords, flattering with the long skirts and flared trousers. And Hush Puppies (in a rainbow spectrum of colors) are back!

■ **Men will also have some military-style choices:** casual jackets with patch pockets and epaulets (if we didn't know better, we'd call them leisure suits). **Look for Hawaiian print shirts** this spring and summer. For suits, pleated pants are out, flat-front trousers are in.

■ **For children,** the news is **uniforms for school.** More and more public schools are adopting dress codes.

■ **Feel funny wearing fur?** Horsefeathers! Turkey feathers, that is — according to Celeste Massullo, a manufacturer of **luxurious coats, parkas, and jackets** made of feathers from turkeys and ostriches. Each hand-sewn garment looks like fox and sells for $600 to $2,600.

(continued on page 31)

INTRODUCING
THE OLD FARMER'S ALMANAC
GENERAL STORE

You've imagined it, you've asked for it, and now, here it is – The Old Farmer's **Almanac General Store.** An old-fashioned general store where you can sit back in a comfortable rocking chair, drink an ice cold Stewart's root beer, play a game of checkers, and find a slew of wonderful products that you thought had disappeared forever—like ice cream makers, rock candy on a stick, salt-glazed stoneware, farm tables, homemade pickles, wooden toys, classic quilts, fine country dinnerware, cast iron cookware, sturdy overalls, weather barometers, and durable garden tools that you can pass down to your grandchildren.

We've opened four stores so far but since there may not be a store near you, we're offering a sampling of country items for your home that you can order simply by calling **1-888-632-2212.** When you call, you'll get to speak to one of our friendly folks in the store. They will answer your questions, take your order, and even tell you what's new because we have a lot more than what you'll see here – about 2,500 different products in all. We will also arrange to ship your selections anywhere in the United States, gift wrap them if you like or even put it all together in a country gift basket – so just give us a call!

Coffee Mug >>>>>>>

We like our coffee mugs sturdy and functional, and these are. Our stoneware mugs, made in Texas, are personalized with our insignia and glazed with a special process that never wears out. We also found the best coffee in case you're interested. It's ground by the folks at the "Country Coffee Company". Try a 4 oz. sampler of the house blend for just $3.95!

◄ Mug - $10.00 {Set of Two - $18.00} ►

<<<<<For The *Birds!*

Out of *77* birdhouses and bird feeders we carry, this one is a favorite – of the birds, that is. With red wood sides and a tin roof, they are handcrafted in Kentucky from material salvaged from 100 year-old barns that were to be destroyed. Thank you for helping us keep this part of America alive.

◄ Birdhouse - $55.00 ►

*P*ickled Veggies >>>>>

Summer Sensation, the people's choice, is hand-packed by "The Pickle Cottage" in Bucklin, Kansas. This colorful garden mixture of summer's best vegetables is pure poetry in a jar. Pickled in a spicy dill brine, the crisp vegetables delight all the senses. Let their country signature accent your kitchen.

◄ Pint - $9.50 / Half Gallon - $19.95 ►

To Order Call 1-888-632-2212

Apple Butter ❯❯❯❯❯❯❯❯❯❯❯
Peach Butter And, Yes, Pumpkin Butter Too!

Made by "The House of Webster" in Rogers, Arkansas, these delightful spreads are great on just about everything. We recommend the apple butter on cinnamon rolls, the peach butter on wheat toast and you must try the pumpkin butter on gingerbread! Each jar is 19 ounces and is made with wholesome, natural ingredients. Regularly priced at $4.95 each. Try all three {one of each} for a special price.

All Three Only $12.95

THE OLD FARMER'S ALMANAC GENERAL STORE™

Annie, Amos & Jacks ›

Annie has become a favorite little friend of everyone who works in the store, and little girls love her too. And of course, we also have her partner, Amos, who sports denim trousers and a cap. Both are 12" high and together, they like playing an old-fashioned game of Jacks. {Jacks also available for $7.50.}

Annie & Amos – $22.00 each

«Peppermint Pig

Cracking the hard candy Peppermint Pig and sharing it with family and friends has proudly become a yuletide tradition symbolizing the coming of good health, happiness and prosperity. The first Peppermint Pigs were made in Saratoga Springs, New York in the early 1880's. To this day, they are made nowhere else. The complete story of this unique Christmas tradition is enclosed in a red gift box with the 8 oz. Peppermint Pig, a velvet pouch and a small silver hammer. {Available October 1}

Gift Boxed Peppermint Pig – $14.95

*L*ike to visit us? We'd love to see you in one of our new stores. They are located in the Mall Of America in Bloomington, Minnesota; Fox Valley Center in Aurora, Illinois; Circle Center Mall in Indianapolis, Indiana; and Collin Creek Mall in Plano, Texas. Hope to see you soon!

So Long, Farewell, Adios

Cash

■ Most futurists agree that within ten to 20 years, our **culture will become "cashless."** We will have one "smart" card that registers all transactions. Or even better, **our fingerprint** will be enough to access our credit and bank accounts and pay whatever bill is at hand, even for a cup of coffee.

Cursive Writing

■ Many educators, parents, and purists in general fear that handwriting is becoming a lost art. Most children are going right **from printing to computer keyboards.** But historians lament that without knowing cursive writing, future generations will never appreciate their grandparents' love letters, not to mention the Constitution.

Male Gynecologists

■ Though 72 percent of the physicians in the field are now men, **demand by women for female doctors** is exceeding supply. And women are now flooding into the profession in unprecedented numbers — last year women accounted for 60 percent of all ob-gyn residents and are more aggressively recruited (and better paid) than their male counterparts.

Diarrhea

■ Two researchers at the Woods Hole (Massachusetts) Oceanographic Institute have identified the lineage of a **parasite that afflicts millions of people** with diarrhea. Finding out where this bug comes from, they report, will make it much easier to develop medicines against it.

Demographica

■ **The aging of the population** is showing up all over the country: In 1996 Mickey Mouse became eligible for Social Security, and the first baby boomers turned 50. With so many **vigorous 50-year-olds in the marketplace,** advertisers and retailers will be targeting a "50 to 65" group that, while more affluent, is only a little less active and travel-oriented than those under 50.

Family patterns (contrary to popular perception) **are more stable** than ten years

ago. The typical 1990s family has one or two children, and both parents work outside the home. The average number of children women will have in their lifetime is now 2.0, the highest number since 1972. Not coincidentally, one of the country's fastest-growing industries is child care. Thirty percent of the ten million preschoolers needing care attend organized child-care facilities.

Though the **nation's population grew by 2.4 million,** New York State's population dropped by 17,000 last year, the first such drop since the 1970s. Perhaps they've all gone to the Northwest, now the number one destination for people choosing to move. Oregon has double the number of people moving in than out.

** OREGON or BUST!**

Some Like It Hot (And Some Don't)

Scientists have known that fewer babies (about 20 percent) are conceived in July and August. But not until 1995's hot summer was the relationship of conception to temperature solidly tracked. "After unseasonably hot summers," said researcher David Lam (who looked at 50 years' weather reports and birth records) in *Parenting Magazine*, "we found up to 26 percent fewer births the next spring." □ □

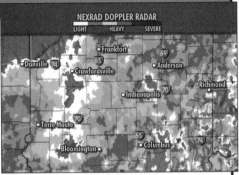

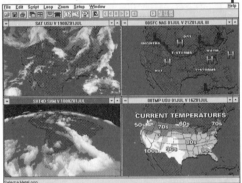

How to Use This Almanac

Anywhere in the U.S.A.

Annually, for the interest and pleasure of our readers, *The Old Farmer's Almanac* provides a variety of astronomical data calculated for the upcoming year. The data covers a wide range of phenomena — the rising and setting times of the Sun and Moon; the declination of the Sun; the astronomical age and placement of the Moon and its monthly phases; the rising and setting times of the visible planets; solar and lunar eclipses; dates and times of meteor showers; rising and setting times of the bright stars; and a monthly summary of astronomical highlights.

The Left-Hand Calendar Pages

(Pages 54-80)

Much of the data is contained in the Left-Hand Calendar Pages (pages 54-80). For the enlightenment of our readers, part of a sample page is reproduced below, with an explanatory text summarizing the individual entries.

☞ **Please note** that all the times given in this edition of the Almanac are calculated for **Boston, Massachusetts.** However, Key Letters accompany much of the data. They are provided so that readers may correct the Boston times to those of their own localities. Several examples are given below to clarify this procedure. (**Eastern Standard Time is used throughout the Almanac.** One hour should be added for Daylight Saving Time between April 6 and October 26.)

Sample Left-Hand Calendar Page
(from November 1996 — page 54)

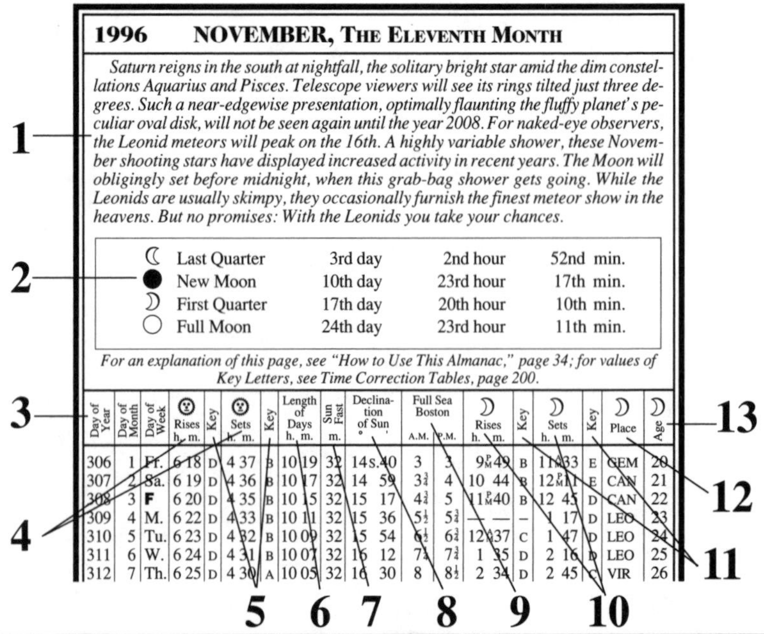

1996 NOVEMBER, The Eleventh Month

Saturn reigns in the south at nightfall, the solitary bright star amid the dim constellations Aquarius and Pisces. Telescope viewers will see its rings tilted just three degrees. Such a near-edgewise presentation, optimally flaunting the fluffy planet's peculiar oval disk, will not be seen again until the year 2008. For naked-eye observers, the Leonid meteors will peak on the 16th. A highly variable shower, these November shooting stars have displayed increased activity in recent years. The Moon will obligingly set before midnight, when this grab-bag shower gets going. While the Leonids are usually skimpy, they occasionally furnish the finest meteor show in the heavens. But no promises: With the Leonids you take your chances.

☾	Last Quarter	3rd day	2nd hour	52nd min.
●	New Moon	10th day	23rd hour	17th min.
☽	First Quarter	17th day	20th hour	10th min.
○	Full Moon	24th day	23rd hour	11th min.

For an explanation of this page, see "How to Use This Almanac," page 34; for values of Key Letters, see Time Correction Tables, page 200.

Day of Year	Day of Month	Day of Week	☉ Rises h. m.	Key	☉ Sets h. m.	Key	Length of Days h. m.	Sun Fast m.	Declination of Sun ° '	Full Sea Boston A.M.	Full Sea Boston P.M.	☽ Rises h. m.	Key	☽ Sets h. m.	Key	☽ Place	☽ Age
306	1	Fr.	6 18	D	4 37	B	10 19	32	14 s. 40	3	3	9 P.M. 49	B	11 A.M. 33	E	GEM	20
307	2	Sa.	6 19	D	4 36	B	10 17	32	14 59	$3\frac{3}{4}$	4	10 44	B	12 P.M. 11	E	CAN	21
308	3	**F**	6 20	D	4 35	B	10 15	32	15 17	$4\frac{3}{4}$	5	11 P.M. 40	B	12 45	D	CAN	22
309	4	M.	6 22	D	4 33	B	10 11	32	15 36	$5\frac{1}{2}$	$5\frac{3}{4}$	— —	–	1 17	D	LEO	23
310	5	Tu.	6 23	D	4 32	B	10 09	32	15 54	$6\frac{1}{2}$	$6\frac{3}{4}$	12 A.M. 37	C	1 47	D	LEO	24
311	6	W.	6 24	D	4 31	B	10 07	32	16 12	$7\frac{1}{4}$	$7\frac{3}{4}$	1 35	D	2 16	D	LEO	25
312	7	Th.	6 25	D	4 30	A	10 05	32	16 30	8	$8\frac{1}{2}$	2 34	D	2 45	C	VIR	26

1. The text heading the calendar page is a summary of the sky sightings for the month. These astronomical highlights appear on each month's calendar page.

2. The dates and times of the Moon's phases for the month. (For more details, see Glossary, page 42.)

3. The days of the year, month, and week are listed on each calendar page. The traditional ecclesiastical calendar designation for Sunday — the Dominical Letter — G/F for 1996, E for 1997 — is used by the Almanac. (For further explanation, see Glossary, page 42.)

4. Sunrise and sunset times (EST) for Boston for each day of the month.

5. Key Letter columns. The letters in the two columns marked "Key" are designed to correct the sunrise/sunset times given for Boston to other localities. Note that each sunrise/sunset time has its Key Letter. The values (that is, the number of minutes) of these Key Letters are given in the **Time Correction Tables**, page 200. Simply find your city, or the city nearest you, in the tables, and locate the figure in the appropriate Key Letter column. Add, or subtract, those minutes to the sunrise or sunset time given for Boston. (Because of the complexities of calculation for different locations, times may not be precise to the minute.)

Example:

To find the time of sunrise in Harrisburg, Pennsylvania, on November 1, 1996:

Sunrise, Boston, with Key Letter D (p. 34)	6:18 A.M., EST
Value of Key Letter D for Harrisburg (p. 202)	+19 minutes
Sunrise, Harrisburg	6:37 A.M., EST

Use the same process for sunset. (Add one hour for Daylight Saving Time between April 6 and October 26.)

6. Length of Days. This column denotes how long the Sun will be above the horizon in Boston for each day of the month. To determine the length of any given day in your locality, follow the procedure outlined in #5 above to determine the sunrise and sunset times for your city. Then, add 12 hours to the time of sunset, subtract the time of sunrise, and you will have the length of day.

Example:

Sunset, Camden, New Jersey, Nov. 1	4:56
Add 12 hours	+ 12:00
	16:56
Subtract sunrise, Camden, Nov. 1	– 6:30
Length of day, Camden, Nov. 1 (10 hrs., 26 min.)	10:26

– Beth Krommes

7. The Sun Fast column is designed to change sundial time into clock time in Boston. A sundial reads natural, or Sun, time, which is neither Standard nor Daylight time except by coincidence. Simply *subtract* the minutes given in the Sun Fast column to get Boston clock time, and use Key Letter C in the Time Correction Tables (page 200) to correct the time for your city. (Add one hour for Daylight Saving Time between April 6 and October 26.)

Example:

To change sundial time into clock time in Macon, Georgia, on November 1, 1996:

Sundial reading, Nov. 1	12:00
Subtract Sun Fast (p. 34)	– 32 minutes
Clock time, Boston	11:28 A.M., EST
Use Key C for Macon (p. 202)	+ 50 minutes
Clock time, Macon	12:18 P.M., EST

8. This column denotes the declination of the Sun (angular distance from the celestial equator) in degrees and minutes, at *noon,* EST.

9. The times of daily high tides in Boston, for morning and evening, are recorded in this column. ("3" under "Full Sea Boston, A.M." on November 1 means that the high tide that morning will be at 3:00 — with the number of feet of high tide shown for some of the dates on the Right-Hand Calendar Pages. Where a dash is shown under Full Sea, it indicates that time of high water has occurred on or after midnight and so is recorded on the next date.) Tide corrections for some localities can be found in the **Tide Correction Tables** on page 206.

10. Moonrise and moonset times (EST) for Boston for each day of the month. (Dashes indicate that moonrise or moonset has occurred on or after midnight and so is recorded on the next date.)

11. Key Letter columns. These columns designate the letters to be used to correct the moonrise/moonset times for Boston to other localities. As explained in #5, the same procedure for calculating "Sunrise/sunset" is used *except* that an additional correction factor based on longitude (see table below) should be used. For the longitude of your city, consult the Time Correction Tables, page 200.

Longitude of city	Correction minutes
58°- 76°	0
77°- 89°	+1
90°-102°	+2
103°-115°	+3
116°-127°	+4
128°-141°	+5
142°-155°	+6

Example:

To determine the time of moonrise in Boise, Idaho, on November 1, 1996:

Moonrise, Boston, with Key Letter B (p. 34)	9:49 P.M., EST
Value of Key Letter B for Boise (p. 200)	+ 58 minutes
Correction for Boise longitude 116° 12'	+ 4 minutes
Moonrise, Boise	10:51 P.M., MST

Use the same procedure for moonset. (Add one hour for Daylight Saving Time between April 6 and October 26.)

12. The Moon's Place denoted in this column is its *astronomical* place, i.e., its *actual* placement, in the heavens. (This should not be confused with the Moon's *astrological* place in the zodiac, as explained on page 164.) **All calculations in this Almanac, except for the astrological information on pages 161-164, are based on astronomy, not astrology.**

In addition to the 12 constellations of the astronomical zodiac, five other abbreviations appear in this column: Auriga (AUR), a northern constellation between Perseus and Gemini; Cetus (CET), which lies south of the zodiac, just south of Pisces and Aries; Ophiuchus (OPH), a constellation primarily north of the zodiac, but with a small corner between Scorpius and Sagittarius; Orion (ORI), a constellation whose northern limit first reaches the zodiac between Taurus and Gemini; Sextans (SEX), which lies south of the zodiac except for a corner that just touches it near Leo.

13. The last column lists the Moon's age, i.e., the number of days since the previous new Moon. (The lunar month is 29.53 days.)

Further astronomical data may be found on page 48, which lists the eclipses for the upcoming year, the principal meteor showers, and dates of the full Moon over a five-year period.

The Visible Planets (pages 46-47) lists the rising and setting times for Venus, Mars, Jupiter, and Saturn for 1997; page 50 carries the rising and setting and transit times of the Bright Stars for 1997. Both feature Key Letters, designed to convert the Boston times given to those of other localities (see #5 and #11 above).

Also, on page 205, can be found "The Twilight Zone," a chart that enables you to calculate the length of time of dawn and dark in your area.

THE RIGHT-HAND CALENDAR PAGES
(Pages 55-81)

These pages are a combination of astronomical data; specific dates in mainly the Anglican church calendar, inclusion of which has always been traditional in American and English almanacs (though we also include some other religious dates); tide heights at Boston (the Left-Hand Calendar Pages include the daily times of high tides; the corrections for your locality are on page 206); quotations; anniversary dates; appropriate seasonal activities; and a rhyming version of the weather forecasts for New England. (Detailed forecasts for the entire country are presented on pages 120-149.)

The following details some of the entries from the Right-Hand Calendar Pages, together with a sample (the first part of November 1996) of a calendar page explained. Also, following the Almanac's tradition, the Chronological Cycles and Eras for 1997 are listed.

– Beth Krommes

MOVABLE FEASTS AND FASTS FOR 1997

Septuagesima Sunday .... Jan. 26
Shrove Tuesday .... Feb. 11
Ash Wednesday .... Feb. 12
Palm Sunday .... Mar. 23
Good Friday .... Mar. 28
Easter Day .... Mar. 30
Rogation Sunday .... May 4

Ascension Day .... May 8
Whitsunday-Pentecost .... May 18
Trinity Sunday .... May 25
Corpus Christi .... May 29
1st Sunday in Advent.............. Nov. 30

THE SEASONS OF 1996-1997

Fall 1996 ...... Sept. 22, 1:00 P.M., EST
Winter 1996 .. Dec. 21, 9:06 A.M., EST
Spring 1997 .. Mar. 20, 8:55 A.M., EST
Summer 1997 June 21, 3:20 A.M., EST
Fall 1997 ...... Sept. 22, 6:56 P.M., EST
Winter 1997 .. Dec. 21, 3:07 P.M., EST

CHRONOLOGICAL CYCLES FOR 1997

Golden Number (Lunar Cycle) 3
Epact.. 21
Solar Cycle 18
Dominical Letter .... E
Roman Indiction.............................. 5
Year of Julian Period 6710

Era	Year	Begins
Byzantine	7506	Sept. 14
Jewish (A.M.)*	5758	Oct. 1
Roman (A.U.C.)..........	2750	Jan. 14
Nabonassar.................	2746	Apr. 24
Japanese	2657	Jan. 1
Grecian (Seleucidae)...	2309	Sept. 14 (or Oct. 14)
Indian (Saka)..............	1919	Mar. 22
Diocletian...................	1714	Sept. 11
Islamic (Hegira)*........	1418	May 8
Chinese (Lunar)	4695	Feb. 7
(Ox)		

Year begins at sunset

DETERMINATION OF EARTHQUAKES

☞ Note, on right-hand pages 55-81, the dates when the Moon (☾) "rides high" or "runs low." The date of the high begins the most likely five-day period of earthquakes in the Northern Hemisphere; the date of the low indicates a similar five-day period in the Southern Hemisphere. You will also find on these pages a notation for Moon on the Equator (☾ on Eq.) twice each month. At this time, in both hemispheres, is a two-day earthquake period.

NAMES AND CHARACTERS OF THE PRINCIPAL PLANETS AND ASPECTS

☞ Every now and again on these Right-Hand Calendar Pages, you will see symbols conjoined in groups to tell you 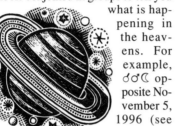 what is happening in the heavens. For example, ♂♂☾ opposite November 5, 1996 (see below), means that Mars ♂ and the Moon ☾ are on that date in conjunction ♂ or apparently near each other.

Here are the symbols used . . .

☉	Sun	♂	Mars
○ ● ☾	Moon	♇	Pluto
☿	Mercury	♃	Jupiter
♄	Saturn	♂	Conjunction, or in
♀	Venus		the same degree
♅	Uranus	☊	Ascending Node
⊕	Earth	☋	Descending Node
♆	Neptune	☍	Opposition, or
			180 degrees

EARTH AT APHELION AND PERIHELION 1997

☞ The Earth will be at Perihelion on January 1, 1997, when it will be 91,400,005 miles from the Sun. The Earth will be at Aphelion on July 4, 1997, when it will be 94,512,258 miles from the Sun.

SAMPLE RIGHT-HAND CALENDAR PAGE
(from November 1996 — page 55)

Day of the month. Day of the week. For detailed regional forecasts, see pages 120-149.

The Dominical Letters for 1996 were G until Leap Day (February 29) and F thereafter. The letter for 1997 is E because the first Sunday of the year falls on the fifth day of January.

Conjunction — closest approach — of Mars and the Moon.

24th Sunday after Pentecost. (Events in the church calendar generally appear in this typeface.)

Morning tide at Boston, shown to be at 1:45 A.M. on the left-hand page, will be 10.1 feet. The 2 P.M. tide will be 11.1 feet.

St. Hilda, seventh-century British abbess, founder of the Whitby Monastery. Her wise counsel and advice were sought by rulers and commoners. (Certain religious feasts and civil holidays appear in this typeface.)

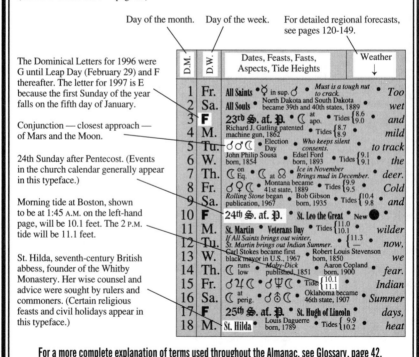

For a more complete explanation of terms used throughout the Almanac, see Glossary, page 42.

Whenever My Ex-Husband Dates This One Skinny Blonde, I Have A Secret Trick I Play On Him.

by Leslie McClennahan

Did you ever notice that when you're fat, men don't look you in the eye? They look across your shoulder. There's no eye contact.

My name is Leslie McClennahan. I'm a real person. I live near Goose Creek, South Carolina. Up until two years ago, I was never looked in the eye. By anyone.

I was falling asleep by 8 o'clock most evenings. When I did go out for an evening, my husband was ashamed of me. And said so to my face. When I walked, my thighs brushed together. I couldn't even cross my legs. I was fat. Not just "overweight." Fat. I was 5'5" tall and weighed 205 pounds.

About 18 months ago, my husband Darrell left a "Dear Leslie" letter on my dresser and broke off our relationship.

I went for counseling. I knew that my weight was the source of my troubles. But I'd tried 14 different diets. One by one. And I failed at all of them.

My counselor listened carefully and recommended an entirely different program. This wasn't a "diet." It was a unique new weight-loss program researched by a team of bariatric physicians — specialists who treat the severely obese. The program itself was developed by Robert Johnson, M.D. of Charleston, South Carolina.

I entered the program on October 2nd. Within the first four days, I lost only three pounds. So I was disappointed. But during the three weeks that followed, my weight began to drop. Rapidly. Within the next 193 days, I went from 205 pounds to 124 pounds. To me it was a miracle. This was the first time in my life I'd ever lost weight *and kept it off!*

The reason the program worked was simple. I was *always* eating. I could eat *six times every day.* So I never felt deprived. Never hungry. I could snack in the afternoon. Snack before dinner. I could even snack at night while I was watching TV.

How can you eat so much and still lose weight?

The secret is not in the amount of food you eat. It's in the *prescribed combination* of foods you eat in each 24–hour cycle.

Nutritionally dense portions of special fiber, unrefined carbohydrates, and certain proteins that generate a calorie-burning process that continues all day long ... a complete 24–hour fat-reduction cycle. Metabolism is evened out, so fat is burned away around the clock. Not just in unhealthy spurts like many diets. That's why it lets you shed pounds so easily. Without hunger. Without nervousness.

And it's all good wholesome food. No strange foods. You'll enjoy a variety of meats, chicken, fish, vegetables, potatoes, pasta, sauces — plus your favorite snacks.

This new program must be the best kept secret in America. Because, up until now, it's *only been available to doctors.* No one else. In fact, The Charleston Program has been used by 207 doctors in the U.S. and Canada to treat more than 6,250 patients. So it's doctor-tested. And proven. This is the first time it's been available to the public.

There are other benefits too...

- There are no amphetamines. No drugs of any kind.

- No pills. No powders. No chalky-tasting drinks to mix.

- There's no strenuous exercise program.

- You don't count calories. Just follow the program. It's easy.

- There are no daily charts or records to keep.

- You eat foods you enjoy. Great variety. Great taste.

- You can dine out.

- There's much less fluid retention.

But *here's* the best part...

Once you lose the weight, you'll *keep it off.* Permanently! Because you're not hungry all the time.

Let's face it. We all have "eating lifestyles." Our eating habits usually include three meals a day. Plus two or three snacks. We all love snacks. Especially at night.

But most diets try to change all that.

And *that's why they fail!*

The Charleston Program is different. It lets you *continue your normal eating lifestyle.* You can eat six times a day. You can snack when you wish. So, when you lose the weight, you can keep it off. For good. Permanently.

Here are some *other patients* from South Carolina who entered Dr. Johnson's program with me.

Marie C. is a 42-year-old textile worker who went from 167 to 139 pounds.

As I got into the program, I began to feel better, to develop more energy. Now my husband has trouble keeping up with me — in every way!

Dr. Karl D. is a 36-year-old man who went from 237 to 168 in only *six months!*

...words cannot describe how good I feel. I'm not hungry or tired at all. I feel alive again!

Josette C. is a 33-year-old woman who went from 165 to 119 in four months.

My husband has started looking at me the way he did before we got married. It's wonderful.

And then there's *me.*

Whenever I see my ex-husband, Darrell, and his blonde girlfriend, I have this secret trick I play on him. I know the restaurant where the two of them go with several other couples. I love to go there with a date — I have plenty now — stroll past his table and softly whisper, "Hello, Darrell."

I know through the "grapevine" that they all keep asking about me ... Am I still single? ... Does he still care about me? ... Are we still seeing each other? And, each time he has to explain ... I love it.

Obviously, I'm excited about the program. This is the first time it's been available outside of a clinical setting. Dr. Johnson has asked Green Tree Press, Inc. to distribute it.

We'll be happy to send you the program to examine for 35 days. Show it to your doctor. Try it. There's *no obligation.* In fact, your check won't be cashed for 31 days. You may even postdate it 31 days in advance, if you wish.

Choose a day and start the program. If you don't begin losing weight within five days — and continue losing weight — we'll promptly return your *original uncashed check.* No delays. No excuses.

Or keep it longer. Try it for six months. Even then, if you're not continuing to lose weight on a regular basis, you'll receive a full refund. Promptly. And without question. This is the fairest way we know to prove to you how well this new program works.

To order, just send your name, address and postdated check for $12.95 (plus $3.00 shipping/handling) to The Charleston Program, c/o Green Tree Press, Inc., Dept. 115, 3603 West 12th Street, Erie, PA 16505.

AN IMPORTANT REMINDER

As your weight begins to drop, do not allow yourself to become too thin.

It's also very important to consult your physician before commencing any weight-loss program. Show him this program. And be sure to see him periodically if you intend to take off large amounts of weight.

©1996 *Green Tree Press, Inc.*

HOLIDAYS AND OBSERVANCES, 1997

(*) Recommended as holidays with pay for all employees
(**) State observances only

Jan. 1 (*) New Year's Day
Jan. 19 (**) Robert E. Lee's Birthday
 (Ark., Fla., Ga., La., S.C., Tenn., Tex.)
Jan. 20 (*) Martin Luther King Jr.'s
 Birthday *(observed)*
Feb. 2 Groundhog Day
Feb. 11 (**) Mardi Gras *(Ala., La.)*
Feb. 12 (**) Abraham Lincoln's Birthday
Feb. 14 Valentine's Day
Feb. 17 (*) Presidents Day
Feb. 22 George Washington's Birthday
Mar. 2 (**) Texas Independence Day
Mar. 15 (**) Andrew Jackson Day *(Tenn.)*
Mar. 17 (**) St. Patrick's Day; Evacuation
 Day *(Boston and Suffolk Co., Mass.)*
Apr. 2 (**) Pascua Florida Day
Apr. 13 (**) Thomas Jefferson's Birthday
 (Ala., Okla.)
Apr. 21 (**) Patriots Day *(Me., Mass.)*
Apr. 25 Arbor Day *(except Alaska,
 Ga., Kans., Va., Wyo.)*
May 1 May Day
May 8 (**) Truman Day *(Mo.)*
May 11 Mother's Day
May 17 Armed Forces Day
May 19 Victoria Day *(Canada)*
May 26 (*) Memorial Day *(observed)*
June 5 World Environment Day
June 11 (**) King Kamehameha I Day
 (Hawaii)
June 14 Flag Day
June 15 Father's Day
June 17 (**) Bunker Hill Day *(Boston and
 Suffolk Co., Mass.)*
June 20 (**) West Virginia Day
July 1 Canada Day
July 4 (*) Independence Day

July 24 (**) Pioneer Day *(Utah)*
Aug. 1 (**) Colorado Day
Aug. 11 (**) Victory Day *(R.I.)*
Aug. 16 (**) Bennington Battle Day *(Vt.)*
Aug. 26 Women's Equality Day
Sept. 1 (*) Labor Day
Sept. 9 (**) Admission Day *(Calif.)*
Sept. 12 (**) Defenders Day *(Md.)*
Oct. 9 Leif Eriksson Day
Oct. 13 (*) Columbus Day *(observed)*;
 Thanksgiving *(Canada)*; (**) Native
 Americans Day *(S. Dak.)*
Oct. 18 (**) Alaska Day
Oct. 31 Halloween; (**) Nevada Day
Nov. 4 Election Day; (**) Will Rogers
 Day *(Okla.)*
Nov. 11 (*) Veterans Day; (**) Admission
 Day *(Wash.)*
Nov. 19 (**) Discovery Day *(Puerto Rico)*
Nov. 27 (*) Thanksgiving Day
Dec. 10 (**) Wyoming Day
Dec. 25 (*) Christmas Day
Dec. 26 Boxing Day *(Canada)*

RELIGIOUS OBSERVANCES

Epiphany	Jan. 6
First day of Ramadan	Jan. 10
Ash Wednesday	Feb. 12
Palm Sunday	Mar. 23
Good Friday	Mar. 28
Easter Day	Mar. 30
First day of Passover	Apr. 22
Orthodox Easter	Apr. 27
Islamic New Year	May 9
Whitsunday-Pentecost	May 18
Rosh Hashanah	Oct. 2
Yom Kippur	Oct. 11
First day of Chanukah	Dec. 24
Christmas Day	Dec. 25

HOW THE ALMANAC WEATHER FORECASTS ARE MADE

Our weather forecasts are determined by the use of a secret formula devised by the founder of this Almanac in 1792, enhanced by the most modern scientific calculations based on solar activity. We believe nothing in the universe occurs haphazardly; there is a cause-and-effect pattern to all phenomena, including weather. It follows, therefore, that we believe the weather is predictable. It is obvious, however, that neither we nor anyone else has as yet gained sufficient insight into the mysteries of the universe to predict weather with anything resembling total accuracy.

GLOSSARY

Aph. – Aphelion: Planet reaches point in its orbit farthest from the Sun.

Apo. – Apogee: Moon reaches point in its orbit farthest from the Earth.

Celestial Equator: The circle in the celestial sphere halfway between the celestial poles. It can be thought of as the plane of the Earth's equator projected out onto the sphere.

Celestial Sphere: An imaginary sphere projected out into space, with an observer on Earth as its center. It represents the entire sky; all celestial objects other than the Earth are imagined as being on its inside surface. It is used for describing the positions and motions of stars and other heavenly objects.

Conj. – Conjunction: Time of apparent closest approach to each other of any two heavenly bodies. **Inf. – Inferior:** Conjunction in which the planet is between the Sun and the Earth. **Sup. – Superior:** Indicates that the Sun is between the planet and the Earth.

Declination: Measurement of angular distance of a celestial object perpendicularly north or south of the celestial equator — analogous to latitude on Earth. The Almanac gives the Sun's declination at noon EST.

Dominical Letter: Used for the ecclesiastical calendar and determined by the date on which the first Sunday of the year falls. If Jan. 1 is a Sunday, the Letter is A; if Jan. 2 is a Sunday, the Letter is B; and so on to G. In leap year the Letter applies through February and then takes the Letter before.

Eclipse, Lunar: Occurs when the Moon, at full phase, enters the shadow of the Earth. There are three kinds. **Total:** The Moon passes completely into the umbra (central dark part) of the Earth's shadow. **Partial:** Only part of the Moon passes through the umbra. **Penumbral:** The Moon passes through only the penumbra (an area of partial darkness that surrounds the umbra).

Eclipse, Solar: Occurs when the Moon passes between the Earth and the Sun, and all three bodies are aligned in the same plane. **Annular:** The Moon appears silhouetted against the Sun, with a ring of sunlight showing around it.

Epact: A number from 1 to 30 to harmonize the lunar year with the solar year; used for the ecclesiastical calendar. Indicates the Moon's age at the instant Jan. 1 begins at the meridian of Greenwich, England.

Eq. – Equator: A great circle of the Earth equidistant from the two poles.

Equinox, Autumnal: Sun appears to cross the celestial equator from north to south. **Vernal:** Sun appears to cross the celestial equator from south to north.

Era, Chronological: A system of reckoning time by numbering the years from an important occurrence or a particular point of time.

Evening Star: A planet that is above the horizon at sunset and less than 180 degrees east of the Sun in right ascension.

Golden Number: The year in the 19-year cycle of the Moon, so called because of its importance in determining Easter. (The Moon repeats its phases approximately every 19 solar years.) To find the Golden Number of any year, add one (1) to that year, then divide the result by 19. The remainder is the Golden Number. When there is no remainder, the Golden Number is 19.

Gr. El. – Greatest Elongation: Greatest apparent angular distance of a planet from the Sun as seen from the Earth.

Julian Period: A period of 7,980 years, beginning at 4713 B.C. and providing a chronological foundation for the modern study of ancient history. It is a system of astronomical dating that allows the difference between two dates to be calculated more easily than with conventional civil calendars. To find the Julian year, add 4,713 to any year. The system was devised by 16th-century scholar Joseph Scaliger and named in honor of his father.

Moon's Age: The number of days since the previous new Moon.

Moon on Equator: Day of month when the Moon is on the celestial equator.

Moon's Phases, First Quarter: Right half of Moon illuminated. **Full Moon:** Moon reaches opposition. The entire disk of the Moon is illuminated as viewed from Earth. **Last Quarter:** Left half of Moon illuminated. **New Moon:** Sun and Moon in conjunction. The entire disk of the Moon is darkened as viewed from Earth.

Moon's Place, Astronomical: The actual position of the Moon within the constellations on the celestial sphere. **Astrological:** The position of the Moon within the astrological zodiac according to calculations made over 2,000 years ago. Because of precession of the equinoxes and other (continued on page 44)

Sand, cat-hairs, dust and dust-mites...
Nothing gets by the 8-lb. ORECK XL!

The favorite vacuum of over 50,000 hotels

and more than 1 million professional and private users. Now you can use this powerful vacuum to clean your home better than ever before.

Exclusive Filter System assures hypo-allergenic cleaning with Germastat®.

Ideal for those who suffer from dust-related or allergic discomforts. There's virtually no after dust. Its unique top-fill action carries the litter up through the handle and deposits it on the inside top of the bag. Yesterday's dirt can't seep out. And the metal-tube top-fill performance works without hoses to crack, leak or break... ever.

The lightest full-size vacuum

available. It weighs just 8 pounds. So stairs are a snap. It's super-powerful, with amazing cleaning power: the fast, double helical brushes revolve at an incredible 6,500 times a minute.

ORECK's Helping Hand® handle orthopedic-ally designed on the principles of ergonomics is available. To put it simply: no need to squeeze your hand or bend your wrist. A godsend for people with hand or wrist problems.

Exclusive New Microsweep® gets bare floors super clean, without any hoses, attachments or adjustments.

A full 10-year Guarantee against breakage or burnout of the housing PLUS a full 3-year Warranty on the extended life motor. We'll let you try the ORECK XL in your home for 15 days. If you don't love it, you don't keep it.

Made in the USA

FREE with purchase

Super Compact Canister

The 4-lb. dynamo you've seen on TV. The motor's so powerful it lifts a 16-lb. bowling ball! Hand-holdable and comfortable. Cleans under refrigerators... car seats... books... ceilings... even typewriter, computer and piano keys. With 8 accessories. Yours FREE when you purchase an ORECK XL upright. Offer limited, so act now.

FOR FREE INFORMATION, CALL NOW TOLL-FREE

1-800-286-8900

and ask for Ext.98044
No salesperson will visit.

ORECK CORPORATION
100 Plantation Road, New Orleans, LA 70123

Best Fishing Days, 1997

(and other fishing lore from the files of *The Old Farmer's Almanac*)

Probably the best fishing time is when the ocean tides are restless before their turn and in the first hour of ebbing. All fish in all waters — salt or fresh — feed most heavily at that time.

Best temperatures for fish species vary widely, of course, and are chiefly important if you are going to have your own fishpond. Best temperatures for brook trout are 45° to 65° F. Brown trout and rainbows are more tolerant of higher temperatures. Smallmouth black bass do best in cool water. Horned pout take what they find.

Most of us go fishing when we can get time off, not because it is the best time. But there are best times:

☞ One hour before and one hour after high tide, and one hour before and one hour after low tide. (The times of high tides are given on pages 54-80 and corrected for your locality on pages 206-207. Inland, the times for high tides would correspond with the times the Moon is due south. Low tides are halfway between high tides.)

☞ "The morning rise" — after sunup for a spell — and "the evening rise" — just before sundown and the hour or so after.

☞ Still water or a ripple is better than a wind at both times.

☞ When there is a hatch of flies — caddis or mayflies, commonly. (The fisherman will have to match the hatching flies with *his* fly — or go fishless.)

☞ When the breeze is from a westerly quarter rather than north or east.

☞ When the barometer is steady or on the rise. (But, of course, even in a three-day driving northeaster the fish isn't going to give up feeding. His hunger clock keeps right on working, and the smart fisherman will find something he wants.)

☞ When the Moon is between new and full.

Moon Between New & Full, 1997

Jan. 8-23	July 4-19
Feb. 7-22	Aug. 3-18
Mar. 8-23	Sept. 1-16
April 7-22	Oct. 1-15
May 6-22	Oct. 31-Nov. 14
June 5-20	Nov. 29-Dec. 13
Dec. 29-31	

Glossary *(continued)*

factors, this does not denote the Moon's actual position in the heavens.

Moon Rides High or Runs Low: Day of month at which the Moon is highest above or farthest below the celestial equator.

Moonrise & Moonset: The time of the Moon's rising above or descending below the horizon.

Morning Star: A planet that is above the horizon at sunrise and less than 180 degrees west of the Sun in right ascension.

Node: Either of the two points on opposite sides of the celestial sphere where the Moon's orbit intersects the ecliptic.

Occn. – Occultation: Eclipse of a star or planet by the Moon or another planet.

Opposition: Time when the Sun and Moon or planet appear on opposite sides of the sky (elongation 180 degrees).

Perig. – Perigee: Moon reaches point in its orbit closest to the Earth.

Perih. – Perihelion: Planet reaches point in its orbit closest to the Sun.

R.A. – Right Ascension: The coordinate on the celestial sphere for measuring the east-west positions of celestial bodies; analogous to longitude on the Earth.

Roman Indiction: A cycle of 15 years established Jan. 1, A.D. 313, as a fiscal term. Add 3 to the number of years in the Christian era and divide by 15. The remainder is Roman Indiction — no remainder is 15.

Solar Cycle: A period of 28 years, at the end of which the days of the month return to the same days of the week.

Solstice, Summer: Point at which the Sun is at its maximum (23.5°) north of the celestial equator. **Winter:** Point at which the Sun is at its maximum (23.5°) south of the celestial equator.

Stat. – Stationary: Halt in the apparent movement of a planet against the background of the stars just before the planet comes to opposition.

Sun Fast/Slow: The adjustment needed to reconcile sundial time to standard clock time. This adjustment factor is given in the Left-Hand Calendar Pages.

Sunrise & Sunset: Visible rising and setting of the Sun's upper limb across the unobstructed horizon of an observer whose eyes are 15 feet above ground level.

Twilight: Begins or ends when stars of the sixth magnitude appear or disappear at the zenith; or when the Sun is about 18 degrees below the horizon.

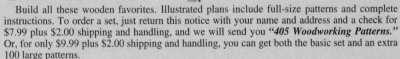

THE VISIBLE PLANETS, 1997

The times of rising or setting of the planets Venus, Mars, Jupiter, and Saturn on the 1st, 11th, and 21st of each month are given below. The approximate time of rising or setting of these planets on other days may be found with sufficient accuracy by interpolation. For an explanation of Key Letters (used in adjusting the times given here for Boston to the time in your town), see page 35 and pages 200-204. Key Letters appear as capital letters beside the time of rising or setting. (For definitions of morning and evening stars, see pages 42-44.)

VENUS is a difficult-to-see object low in the morning sky at the beginning of the year and soon becomes too close to the Sun for observation. During early summer it reappears low in the west as an evening star; it slowly becomes brighter and higher through autumn and reaches maximum brilliance in December. Venus is in conjunction with Mercury on January 12, with Jupiter on February 5, and with Mars on October 26 and December 22.

MARS rises before midnight, and is visible for most of the night, throughout the year. It is brightest when at opposition on March 17 and retrogrades into Leo before resuming eastward motion through Virgo in early June and Libra in late August. Then, fading steadily, it speeds through Scorpius, Ophiuchus, Sagittarius, and on into Capricornus by mid-December. Mars is in conjunction with Venus on October 26 and December 22.

Boldface — P.M. Lightface — A.M.		**Boldface — P.M.** Lightface — A.M.	
Jan. 1 ...... rise 5:36 E	July 1 ...... set 8:55 E	Jan. 1 ...... rise 10:47 C	July 1 ...... set 11:20 B
Jan. 11 .... " 5:54 E	July 11 .... " 8:51 D	Jan. 11 .... " 10:22 C	July 11 .... " 10:51 B
Jan. 21 .... " 6:08 E	July 21 .... " 8:42 D	Jan. 21 .... " 9:53 C	July 21 .... " 10:23 B
Feb. 1....... " 6:16 E	Aug. 1..... " 8:29 D	Feb. 1....... " 9:15 C	Aug. 1..... " 9:53 B
Feb. 11.... " 6:18 D	Aug. 11... " 8:15 C	Feb. 11.... " 8:35 C	Aug. 11... " 9:28 B
Feb. 21.... " 6:14 D	Aug. 21... " 8:00 C	Feb. 21.... " 7:48 C	Aug. 21... " 9:03 B
Mar. 1..... " 6:08 D	Sept. 1..... " 7:43 B	Mar. 1..... " 7:06 B	Sept. 1..... " 8:38 B
Mar. 11.... " 5:58 D	Sept. 11... " 7:28 B	Mar. 11... " 6:10 B	Sept. 11... " 8:16 A
Mar. 21.... " 5:47 C	Sept. 21... " 7:15 B	Mar. 21... " 5:11 B	Sept. 21... " 7:57 A
Apr. 1..... " 5:34 B	Oct. 1 ...... " 7:05 A	Apr. 1..... set 5:04 D	Oct. 1 ...... " 7:39 A
Apr. 11.... set 6:30 D	Oct. 11 .... " 6:58 A	Apr. 11.... " 4:17 D	Oct. 11 .... " 7:24 A
Apr. 21.... " 6:55 D	Oct. 21 .... " 6:55 A	Apr. 21.... " 3:32 D	Oct. 21 .... " 7:11 A
May 1 .... " 7:21 D	Nov. 1 .... " 6:57 A	May 1 .... " 2:50 D	Nov. 1..... " 7:00 A
May 11 ... " 7:46 E	Nov. 11.... " 7:02 A	May 11 ... " 2:11 D	Nov. 11... " 6:53 A
May 21 ... " 8:09 E	Nov. 21.... " 7:08 A	May 21 ... " 1:35 C	Nov. 21... " 6:49 A
June 1 ..... " 8:31 E	Dec. 1 ..... " 7:12 A	June 1 ..... " 12:57 C	Dec. 1 ..... " 6:46 A
June 11 ... " 8:45 E	Dec. 11 ... " 7:08 A	June 11 ... " 12:24 C	Dec. 11 ... " 6:46 A
June 21 ... set 8:53 E	Dec. 21 ... " 6:53 A	June 21 ... set 11:50 B	Dec. 21 ... " 6:46 A
	Dec. 31 ... set 6:20 A		Dec. 31 .. set 6:48 A

JUPITER begins the year too close to the Sun for observation. It first appears in March in the eastern morning sky in Capricornus. Rising four minutes earlier each day, it comes up at midnight in June and reaches opposition on August 9, when it rises at sunset and is visible throughout the night. Remaining in Capricornus, it is seen in the southwest at nightfall during the final two months of the year. Jupiter is in conjunction with Venus on February 5.

SATURN can be seen in the western evening sky until early March, when it becomes too close to the Sun for observation. It reappears in the morning sky in late May in Pisces, where it remains throughout the year. It is brightest and visible all night when at opposition on October 9. Saturn remains well up at nightfall and favorably placed for observation for the remainder of the year.

Boldface — P.M.			Lightface — A.M.				Boldface — P.M.			Lightface — A.M.		
Jan. 1	**set**	**5:27**	A	July 1	**rise 9:33**	D	Jan. 1	**set**	**11:03**	C	July 1 ......rise	12:00	B
Jan. 11	"	**4:59**	A	July 11	"	**8:52**	D	Jan. 11	"	**10:26**	C	July 11 ....rise	**11:22**	B
Jan. 21	"	**4:32**	A	July 21	"	**8:10**	D	Jan. 21	"	**9:51**	C	July 21	"	**10:43**	B
Feb. 1	rise	6:31	E	Aug. 1	"	**7:23**	D	Feb. 1	"	**9:13**	C	Aug. 1	"	**10:00**	B
Feb. 11	"	5:59	E	Aug. 11	set 4:42		A	Feb. 11	"	**8:39**	C	Aug. 11	"	**9:21**	B
Feb. 21	"	5:26	D	Aug. 21	"	3:56	A	Feb. 21	"	**8:05**	C	Aug. 21	"	**8:41**	B
Mar. 1	"	5:00	D	Sept. 1	"	3:06	A	Mar. 1	"	**7:38**	C	Sept. 1	"	**7:57**	B
Mar. 11	"	4:27	D	Sept. 11	"	2:22	A	Mar. 11	"	**7:05**	C	Sept. 11	"	**7:17**	B
Mar. 21	"	3:54	D	Sept. 21	"	1:39	A	Mar. 21	"	**6:32**	C	Sept. 21	"	**6:36**	B
Apr. 1	"	3:16	D	Oct. 1	"	12:54	A	Apr. 1	"	**5:56**	C	Oct. 1	"	**5:51**	B
Apr. 11	"	2:42	D	Oct. 11	"	12:14	A	Apr. 11	rise	4:59	C	Oct. 11	set	5:48	C
Apr. 21	"	2:07	D	Oct. 21	set 11:36		A	Apr. 21	"	4:23	B	Oct. 21	"	5:05	C
May 1	"	1:31	D	Nov. 1	**10:57**		A	May 1	"	3:46	B	Nov. 1	"	4:17	C
May 11	"	12:55	D	Nov. 11	**10:22**		A	May 11	"	3:09	B	Nov. 11	"	3:35	C
May 21	"	12:17	D	Nov. 21	"	**9:49**	A	May 21	"	2:33	B	Nov. 21	"	2:53	C
June 1	**rise**	**11:32**	D	Dec. 1	"	**9:18**	B	June 1	"	1:52	B	Dec. 1	"	2:12	C
June 11	"	**10:53**	D	Dec. 11	"	**8:47**	B	June 11	"	1:15	B	Dec. 11	"	1:32	C
June 21	**rise 10:13**		D	Dec. 21	"	**8:18**	B	June 21	rise 12:37		B	Dec. 21	"	12:52	C
				Dec. 31	set 7:49		B					Dec. 31	set 12:14	C

MERCURY can be seen in the east only before sunrise or in the west only after sunset. It is visible mornings between these approximate dates: January 8-February 15, May 23-June 15, September 6-October 2, and December 23-31. The planet is brighter at the end of each period, and best morning viewing conditions in northern latitudes occur during the third week of September. It is visible evenings during these approximate dates: March 21-April 17, July 3-August 12, and November 15-December 12. The planet is brighter at the beginning of each period, and best viewing conditions occur from the end of March to the second week of April.

DO NOT CONFUSE 1) Venus with Jupiter on February 5 and 6 and then again in the southwestern evening sky throughout November and December. In all cases Venus is the brighter of the two. 2) Mercury with Saturn in May in the morning sky. Mercury will always be the lower of the two. 3) Mars with the star Spica the first week of August. Nearly the same brightness, Mars appears orange, while Spica is blue.

Eclipses for 1997

There will be four eclipses in 1997, two of the Sun and two of the Moon. One of the lunar and one of the solar eclipses will not be visible in the United States or Canada; the others will be seen partially in the locations specified below. Lunar eclipses are technically visible from the entire night side of the Earth; solar eclipses are visible only in certain areas.

1. Total eclipse of the Sun, March 8-9. Totality will be visible on March 9 *only* in Siberia; the partial phase will be visible on March 8 in Alaska and extreme western Canada. There, the partial eclipse begins at 5:30 P.M., PST, and 4:30 P.M., Alaska Standard Time. This partial phase ends at 7:15 P.M., PST, and 6:15 P.M., Alaska Standard Time.

2. Partial eclipse of the Moon, March 23-24. The beginning of the umbral phase will be visible in North America except Alaska and northwestern Canada. The end will be visible throughout North America. The Moon enters penumbra on the 23rd at 8:41 P.M., EST (5:41 P.M., PST); the middle of the eclipse occurs at 11:39 P.M., EST (8:39 P.M., PST); the Moon leaves penumbra on the 24th at 2:38 A.M., EST (on the 23rd at 11:38 P.M., PST).

3. Partial eclipse of the Sun, September 1. This eclipse will not be visible in the United States or Canada.

4. Total eclipse of the Moon, September 16. This eclipse will not be visible in the United States or Canada.

Full Moon Days

	1997	1998	1999	2000	2001
Jan.	23	12	1/31	20	9
Feb.	22	11	—	19	8
Mar.	23	12	2/31	19	9
Apr.	22	11	30	18	7
May	22	11	30	18	7
June	20	9	28	16	5
July	19	9	28	16	5
Aug.	18	7	26	15	4
Sept.	16	6	25	13	2
Oct.	15	5	24	13	2
Nov.	14	4	23	11	1/30
Dec.	13	3	22	11	30

Principal Meteor Showers

Shower	Best Hour (EST)	Radiant Direction*	Date of Maximum**	Approx. Peak Rate (/hr.)	Associated Comet
Quadrantid	5 A.M.	N.	Jan. 4	40-150	—
Lyrid	4 A.M.	S.	Apr. 21	10-15	1861 I
Eta Aquarid	4 A.M.	S.E.	May 4	10-40	Halley
Delta Aquarid	2 A.M.	S.	July 30	10-35	—
Perseid	4 A.M.	N.	Aug. 11-13	50-100	1862 III
Draconid	9 P.M.	N.W.	Oct. 9	10	Giacobini-Zinner
Orionid	4 A.M.	S.	Oct. 20	10-70	Halley
Taurid	midnight	S.	Nov. 9	5-15	Encke
Leonid	5 A.M.	S.	Nov. 16	5-20	1866 I
Andromedid	10 P.M.	S.	Nov. 25-27	10	Biela
Geminid	2 A.M.	S.	Dec. 13	50-80	—
Ursid	5 A.M.	N.	Dec. 22	10-15	—

* Direction from which the meteors appear to come.
** Date of actual maximum occurrence may vary by one or two days in either direction.

BRIGHT STARS, 1997

The upper table shows the Eastern Standard Time when each star transits the meridian of Boston (i.e., lies directly above the horizon's south point there) and its altitude above that point at transit on the dates shown. The time of transit on any other date differs from that on the nearest date listed by approximately four minutes of time for each day. For a place outside Boston the local time of the star's transit is found by correcting the time at Boston by the value of Key Letter "C" for the place. (See footnote.)

Star	Constellation	Magni-tude	Jan. 1	Mar. 1	May 1	July 1	Sept. 1	Nov. 1	Alt.
					Time of Transit (EST) Boldface — P.M. Lightface — A.M.				
Altair	Aquila	0.8	**12:49**	8:57	4:57	12:57	**8:49**	**4:49**	56.3
Deneb	Cygnus	1.3	**1:39**	9:47	5:48	1:48	**9:40**	**5:40**	92.8
Fomalhaut	Psc. Austr.	1.2	**3:54**	**12:02**	8:02	4:02	**11:55**	**7:55**	17.8
Algol	Perseus	2.2	**8:05**	**4:13**	**12:13**	8:13	4:09	**12:09**	88.5
Aldebaran	Taurus	0.9	**9:32**	**5:40**	**1:40**	9:40	5:37	1:37	64.1
Rigel	Orion	0.1	**10:10**	**6:18**	**2:19**	10:19	6:15	2:15	39.4
Capella	Auriga	0.1	**10:12**	**6:20**	**2:20**	10:21	6:17	2:17	93.6
Bellatrix	Orion	1.6	**10:21**	**6:29**	**2:29**	10:30	6:26	2:26	54.0
Betelgeuse	Orion	var. 0.4	**10:51**	**6:59**	**2:59**	10:59	6:56	2:56	55.0
Sirius	Can. Maj.	−1.4	**11:41**	**7:49**	**3:49**	11:49	7:45	3:46	31.0
Procyon	Can. Min.	0.4	12:39	**8:43**	**4:43**	**12:43**	8:39	4:39	52.9
Pollux	Gemini	1.2	12:45	**8:49**	**4:49**	**12:49**	8:45	4:45	75.7
Regulus	Leo	1.4	**3:08**	**11:12**	**7:12**	**3:12**	11:08	7:08	59.7
Spica	Virgo	var. 1.0	6:24	2:32	**10:28**	**6:28**	**2:24**	10:25	36.6
Arcturus	Bootes	−0.1	7:15	3:23	**11:19**	**7:19**	**3:15**	11:15	66.9
Antares	Scorpius	var. 0.9	9:28	5:36	1:36	**9:32**	**5:28**	**1:28**	21.3
Vega	Lyra	0.0	11:35	7:43	3:43	**11:39**	**7:36**	**3:36**	86.4

– Beth Krommes

RISINGS AND SETTINGS

The times of the star's rising and setting at Boston on any date are found by applying the interval shown to the time of the star's transit on that date. Subtract the interval for the star's rising; add it for its setting. The times for a place outside Boston are found by correcting the times found for Boston by the values of the Key Letters shown. (See footnote.) The directions in which the star rises and sets shown for Boston are generally useful throughout the United States. Deneb, Algol, Capella, and Vega are circumpolar stars — this means that they do not appear to rise or set, but are above the horizon.

Star	Interval hr. m.	Rising Key	Dir.	Setting Key	Dir.
Altair	6:36	B	EbN	E	WbN
Fomalhaut	3:59	E	SE	D	SW
Aldebaran	7:06	B	ENE	D	WNW
Rigel	5:33	D	EbS	B	WbS
Bellatrix	6:27	B	EbN	D	WbN
Betelgeuse	6:31	B	EbN	D	WbN
Sirius	5:00	D	ESE	B	WSW
Procyon	6:23	B	EbN	D	WbN
Pollux	8:01	A	NE	E	NW
Regulus	6:49	B	EbN	D	WbN
Spica	5:23	D	EbS	B	WbS
Arcturus	7:19	A	ENE	E	WNW
Antares	4:17	E	SEbE	A	SWbW

NOTE: The values of Key Letters are given in the Time Correction Tables (pages 200-204).

The Most Dramatic
NATURAL
EVENT
OF 1997

After decades of disappointing comets, 1996's Hyakutake renewed people's interest in the legendary splendor of comets. This spring another comet of historic proportions will come into view and it promises a fabulous show — even for city dwellers. Keep your fingers crossed.

by Bob Berman

Relatively few people had ever seen a comet until last year. But this worldwide innocence was understandable. Earth had been suffering from a decades-long comet deprivation. In 1974 the now-infamous comet Kohoutek, widely advertised as the "comet of the century," turned out to be the fizzle of the century. The much-awaited return of Halley's comet in 1986 was a big bust, too.

Then came comet Hyakutake. Discovered by a Japanese amateur astronomer on January 30, 1996, it rushed earthward so quickly that it reached naked-eye visibility by the Ides of March. A week later, the world suddenly understood the glory of a great comet. Its 50-degree tail stretched across the heavens. The only problem was the faintness of Hyakutake's tail. The slightest bit of haze, moonlight, or suburban light-pollution rendered all but the first tenth of the tail invisible. From cities, some people said, "Yes, I've seen that little fuzzy blob. What's the big deal?"

As 1997 begins, the scene is set for the world to experience a profound new cometary awakening. Discovered July 23, 1995, by Dr. Alan Hale of New Mexico and Thomas Bopp of Arizona, comet Hale-Bopp has all the characteristics of a giant. Even at the unusually great distance at which Hale-Bopp was first seen, beyond the orbit of Jupiter, it was already bright enough at tenth magnitude to be faintly visible in small amateur instruments. This is a pattern displayed by great historical comets.

Comets begin their careers as tailless blurs, befitting their lowly status as chunks of dirty ice a few miles across. As they fall inward from their original home in the dark, freezing vastness of the outer solar system beyond Neptune, the Sun's heat vaporizes their surface ice layers. The resulting stream of gas and dust is blown millions of miles outward by the solar wind. This thin tail, illuminated by the Sun and also glowing on its own, accounts for the comet's immense size and ineffable beauty.

While most people think of comets and meteors as interchangeable, they are very different creatures of the night. Meteors are pieces of icy rock that are truly minuscule — typically the size of apple seeds. They emerge and vanish in a few seconds at most; moreover, meteors perform in our own atmosphere, less than 80 miles up. Although comets travel at several miles per second, they typically lie tens of millions of miles from Earth at closest approach and do not appear to be in motion during a single night. A morning-sky comet rises ahead of the dawn, but otherwise hangs silent and motionless. An evening-sky comet materializes low in the west when darkness falls and sets within a few hours. Such leisurely changes are very different from the zippy, transient antics of meteors.

Comets have a well-deserved reputation for being frustratingly unpredictable; this comes from our inability to foresee how sunlight will affect their ices. We can always predict *where* comets will appear but have much more trouble knowing how bright they'll become. Still, most astronomers expect that Hale-Bopp will glow brightly enough to be seen even in the light-polluted skies of major cities. Because of its orientation to the Earth, its tail will describe an arc of only about ten degrees, about the size of a clenched fist held at arm's length against the sky.

Uncertainties aside, Hale-Bopp's tail will probably be brighter than Hyakutake's and better able to withstand less-than-optimal viewing conditions. Its geometry is well suited for observers in mid-northern latitudes, such as in the United States, Canada, Europe, and Japan. Unless our previous luck with comets conjures up another celestial bummer, this spring's rare show of heavenly fireworks will be the most dramatic natural event of 1997.

Where and When to See Comet Hale-Bopp

★ This great comet will be at maximum about May 1, but observers will be able to start seeing it with the naked eye much earlier. Watch the eastern sky about an hour before sunrise in mid-January. A clear, unobstructed horizon is necessary, since the comet will be only ten degrees (about the width of a clenched fist at arm's length) above the skyline. During nights when the Moon is skinny or absent in the predawn hours, Hale-Bopp will be obvious as it continues to brighten, rising higher each week until early March, when it will gradually sink lower while becoming more northerly (rising more leftward). **Optimum moonless periods for predawn viewing in the eastern sky will occur January 7-18, February 4-18, and March 6-20.**

Then the action switches to the evening sky, an hour after sunset. Now the comet will be approaching its brightest. **Optimum moonless periods for early evening viewing in the western sky will occur March 28-April 10 and April 26-May 9.** This latter interval should coincide with Hale-Bopp's most luminous appearance.

If You Miss Hale-Bopp in 1997 . . .

★ You blew it: It won't be back for several thousand years, the amount of time it takes to make a giant orbit between the Sun and the comet's outermost point in the universe, about ten times as far from the Sun as the planet Neptune. The comet will approach no closer to Earth than 122 million miles — about 30 million miles more than the Sun's distance from Earth. Hale-Bopp will come within 85 million miles of the Sun.

1996 NOVEMBER, THE ELEVENTH MONTH

Saturn reigns in the south at nightfall, the solitary bright star amid the dim constellations Aquarius and Pisces. Telescope viewers will see its rings tilted just three degrees. Such a near-edgewise presentation, optimally flaunting the fluffy planet's peculiar oval disk, will not be seen again until the year 2008. For naked-eye observers, the Leonid meteors will peak on the 16th. A highly variable shower, these November shooting stars have displayed increased activity in recent years. The Moon will obligingly set before midnight, when this grab-bag shower gets going. While the Leonids are usually skimpy, they occasionally furnish the finest meteor show in the heavens. But no promises: With the Leonids you take your chances.

☾	Last Quarter	3rd day	2nd hour	52nd min.
●	New Moon	10th day	23rd hour	17th min.
☽	First Quarter	17th day	20th hour	10th min.
○	Full Moon	24th day	23rd hour	11th min.

For an explanation of this page, see "How to Use This Almanac," page 34; for values of Key Letters, see Time Correction Tables, page 200.

Day of Year	Day of Month	Day of Week	☼ Rises h. m.	Key	☼ Sets h. m.	Key	Length of Days h. m.	Sun Fast m.	Declination of Sun ° '	Full Sea Boston A.M.	Full Sea Boston P.M.	☽ Rises h. m.	Key	☽ Sets h. m.	Key	Place	☽ Age
306	1	Fr.	6 18	D	4 37	B	10 19	32	14s.40	3	3	9ᴘ49	B	11ᴀ33	E	GEM	20
307	2	Sa.	6 19	D	4 36	B	10 17	32	14 59	3¾	4	10 44	B	12ᴘ11	E	CAN	21
308	3	**F**	6 20	D	4 35	B	10 15	32	15 17	4¾	5	11ᴘ40	B	12 45	D	CAN	22
309	4	M.	6 22	D	4 33	B	10 11	32	15 36	5½	5¾	— —	–	1 17	D	LEO	23
310	5	Tu.	6 23	D	4 32	B	10 09	32	15 54	6½	6¾	12ᴀ37	C	1 47	D	LEO	24
311	6	W.	6 24	D	4 31	B	10 07	32	16 12	7¼	7¾	1 35	D	2 16	D	LEO	25
312	7	Th.	6 25	D	4 30	A	10 05	32	16 30	8	8½	2 34	D	2 45	C	VIR	26
313	8	Fr.	6 27	D	4 29	A	10 02	32	16 47	8¾	9¼	3 35	D	3 16	C	VIR	27
314	9	Sa.	6 28	D	4 28	A	10 00	32	17 04	9½	10	4 37	E	3 50	C	VIR	28
315	10	**F**	6 29	D	4 27	A	9 58	32	17 21	10¼	10¾	5 41	E	4 27	B	VIR	0
316	11	M.	6 30	D	4 26	A	9 56	32	17 37	10¾	11¼	6 46	E	5 09	B	LIB	1
317	12	Tu.	6 32	D	4 25	A	9 53	31	17 54	11½	—	7 50	E	5 58	B	SCO	2
318	13	W.	6 33	D	4 24	A	9 51	31	18 09	12	12¼	8 51	E	6 52	B	OPH	3
319	14	Th.	6 34	D	4 23	A	9 49	31	18 25	1	1	9 49	E	7 53	B	SAG	4
320	15	Fr.	6 35	D	4 22	A	9 47	31	18 40	1¾	2	10 40	E	8 58	B	SAG	5
321	16	Sa.	6 37	D	4 21	A	9 44	31	18 55	2½	2¾	11ᴀ26	E	10 06	C	CAP	6
322	17	**F**	6 38	D	4 20	A	9 42	31	19 09	3½	3¾	12ᴘ07	D	11ᴘ15	C	AQU	7
323	18	M.	6 39	D	4 19	A	9 40	30	19 23	4½	5	12 44	D	— —	–	PSC	8
324	19	Tu.	6 40	D	4 19	A	9 39	30	19 37	5½	6	1 19	D	12ᴀ24	D	AQU	9
325	20	W.	6 42	D	4 18	A	9 36	30	19 51	6¾	7	1 53	C	1 32	D	PSC	10
326	21	Th.	6 43	D	4 17	A	9 34	30	20 04	7½	8	2 27	C	2 39	D	PSC	11
327	22	Fr.	6 44	D	4 17	A	9 33	30	20 17	8½	9	3 02	B	3 46	E	PSC	12
328	23	Sa.	6 45	D	4 16	A	9 31	29	20 29	9¼	10	3 39	B	4 52	E	ARI	13
329	24	**F**	6 46	D	4 15	A	9 29	29	20 41	10¼	10¾	4 20	B	5 55	E	ARI	14
330	25	M.	6 47	D	4 15	A	9 28	29	20 53	10¾	11½	5 05	B	6 55	E	TAU	15
331	26	Tu.	6 49	E	4 14	A	9 25	28	21 04	11½	—	5 53	B	7 51	E	TAU	16
332	27	W.	6 50	E	4 14	A	9 24	28	21 15	12¼	12¼	6 44	B	8 42	E	ORI	17
333	28	Th.	6 51	E	4 14	A	9 23	28	21 26	1	1	7 38	B	9 28	E	GEM	18
334	29	Fr.	6 52	E	4 13	A	9 21	27	21 36	1¾	1¾	8 33	B	10 08	E	GEM	19
335	30	Sa.	6 53	E	4 13	A	9 20	27	21s.46	2½	2½	9ᴘ29	B	10ᴀ44	E	CAN	20

NOVEMBER hath 30 days. 1996

"What do you hunt, Orion,
This starry night?"
"The Ram, the Bull and the Lion,
And the Great Bear," says Orion.
– Robert Graves

D. M.	D. W.	Dates, Feasts, Fasts, Aspects, Tide Heights	Weather ↓
1	Fr.	**All Saints** • ☿ in sup. ☌ • *Must is a tough nut to crack.* •	*Too*
2	Sa.	**All Souls** • North Dakota and South Dakota became 39th and 40th states, 1889 •	*wet*
3	**F**	**23rd S. af. P.** • ☾ at apo. • Tides {8.6 / 9.0 •	*and*
4	M.	Richard J. Gatling patented machine gun, 1862 • Tides {8.7 / 8.9 •	*mild*
5	Tu.	☌ ♂ ☾ • Election Day • *Who keeps silent consents.* •	*to track*
6	W.	John Philip Sousa born, 1854 • Edsel Ford born, 1893 • Tides {9.1 / 9.1 •	*the*
7	Th.	☾ on Eq. • ☾ at ☊ • *Ice in November Brings mud in December.* •	*deer.*
8	Fr.	☌ ♀ ☾ • Montana became 41st state, 1889 • Tides {9.9 / 9.5 •	*Cold*
9	Sa.	*Rolling Stone* began publication, 1967 • Bob Gibson born, 1935 • Tides {10.4 / 9.8 •	*and*
10	**F**	**24th S. af. P.** • **St. Leo the Great** • New ● •	
11	M.	**St. Martin** • **Veterans Day** • Tides {11.0 / 10.1 •	*wilder*
12	Tu.	*If All Saints brings out winter, St. Martin brings out Indian Summer.* • {11.3 / — •	*now,*
13	W.	Carl Stokes became first black mayor in U.S., 1967 • Robert Louis Stevenson born, 1850	*we*
14	Th.	☾ runs low • *Moby-Dick* published, 1851 • Aaron Copland born, 1900 •	*fear.*
15	Fr.	☌ ♃ ☾ • ☌ ♆ ☾ • Tides {10.1 / 11.1 •	*Indian*
16	Sa.	☾ at perig. • ☌ ♅ ☾ • Oklahoma became 46th state, 1907 •	*Summer*
17	**F**	**25th S. af. P.** • **St. Hugh of Lincoln** •	*days,*
18	M.	**St. Hilda** • Louis Daguerre born, 1789 • Tides {9.9 / 10.2 •	*heat*
19	Tu.	Pelé scored 1,000th goal, 1967 • Calvin Klein born, 1942 • {10.1 / 10.1 •	*and*
20	W.	☾ on Eq. • ☾ at ☋ • ☌ ♄ ☾ • Tides {10.3 / 10.0 •	*haze.*
21	Th.	President Harry Truman rode in captured German submarine, 1946 • {10.7 / 10.1 •	*This*
22	Fr.	President John F. Kennedy assassinated, 1963 • Tides {11.0 / 10.1 •	*warm*
23	Sa.	**St. Clement** • Billy the Kid born, 1859 • {11.2 / 10.1 •	*weather's*
24	**F**	**26th S. af. P.** • ☌ ♇ ☉ • Full Beaver ○ •	
25	M.	*Don't talk about yourself; it will be done when you leave.* • {11.2 / 10.0 •	*queer —*
26	Tu.	Ford roadster priced at $260, 1925 • Eric Sevareid born, 1912 • {11.1 / — •	*are*
27	W.	☾ rides high • Anders Celsius born, 1701 • Jimi Hendrix born, 1942 •	*we*
28	Th.	**Thanksgiving Day** • First recorded auto race in U.S., 1895 • {9.5 / 10.5	*in the*
29	Fr.	First Army-Navy football game; Navy 24 – Army 0, 1890 • Tides {9.3 / 10.1	*wrong*
30	Sa.	**St. Andrew** • Mark Twain born, 1835 • {9.1 / 9.7 •	*hemisphere?*

One of the striking differences between a cat and a lie is that a cat has only nine lives. – Mark Twain

Farmer's Calendar

On front porches, doorsteps, and frost-bitten lawns, Halloween jack-o'-lanterns, undiscarded, contemplate with degrees of chagrin their fate: They're stuck in the wrong festival, they have outlived their time and now show faces full of regret to a world for which they are unprepared. The icon of All Hallows Eve, a feast of misrule derived, no doubt, from pagan hell-raising far older than Christianity, ought not to endure to Thanksgiving, that mild and pious exercise in Puritan merrymaking — but it does.

My jack-o'-lantern is never thrown out. I haven't the heart. I simply leave it where it is, on the step. I then watch over the succeeding weeks as it softens and transforms. The manic grin I carved on October 31 sags and settles. It decays into a mask of pain and finally, by the end of November, becomes a hollow rictus of despair. In the features of the pumpkin, spread over a month or more, are all the changes that pass in a few seconds over the face of the man who walks into the wrong bar and finds, where he expected the chamber of commerce dinner, the outlaw Angels in full leather, chains, and hair.

Sad mortality. The eyes drop, the mouth falls at the corners, the skin draws in, the whole pumpkin seems to spread at the equator, flattening, corrupting into a slack and pathetic wreckage — the vegetable equivalent of an idle marchioness come to the end of a long life of self-indulgence.

It's not a pretty sight. Each year as the season turns past Thanksgiving and into the winter storms, I'm relieved to find my poor old friend's decline covered at last with a decent blanket of snow.

1996 DECEMBER, THE TWELFTH MONTH

If the Leonid meteors were disappointing (or were clouded out) last month, December offers a far more reliable display. The Geminid meteors have been the best annual shower since the 1960s. Bright but curiously lacking trails, the Geminids peak on Friday the 13th. More than just the date might make you feel vulnerable: Geminids (most the size of apple seeds) are the densest, heaviest meteors of all. They have a greater likelihood of surviving passage through our atmosphere and making it to the ground than those of any other major shower. The best viewing is shortly after midnight, when you're likely to see one a minute. Winter begins on the 21st, at 9:06 A.M.*, EST.*

☾	Last Quarter	3rd day	0 hour	7th min.
●	New Moon	10th day	11th hour	58th min.
☽	First Quarter	17th day	4th hour	31st min.
○	Full Moon	24th day	15th hour	41st min.

For an explanation of this page, see "How to Use This Almanac," page 34; for values of Key Letters, see Time Correction Tables, page 200.

Day of Year	Day of Month	Day of Week	☼ Rises h. m.	Key	☼ Sets h. m.	Key	Length of Days h. m.	Sun Fast m.	Declination of Sun ° '	Full Sea Boston A.M.	Full Sea Boston P.M.	☽ Rises h. m.	Key	☽ Sets h. m.	Key	☽ Place	☽ Age
336	1	**F**	6 54	E	4 12	A	9 18	27	21s.55	3¾	3¼	10 P.M. 25	C	11 A.M. 17	D	CAN	21
337	2	M.	6 55	E	4 12	A	9 17	26	22 03	4	4¼	11 P.M. 22	C	11 A.M. 47	D	LEO	22
338	3	Tu.	6 56	E	4 12	A	9 16	26	22 12	4¾	5	— —	–	12 P.M. 16	D	LEO	23
339	4	W.	6 57	E	4 12	A	9 15	25	22 19	5¾	6	12 A.M. 20	D	12 45	D	VIR	24
340	5	Th.	6 58	E	4 12	A	9 14	25	22 27	6½	7	1 19	D	1 15	C	VIR	25
341	6	Fr.	6 59	E	4 12	A	9 13	25	22 34	7¼	7¾	2 19	E	1 46	C	VIR	26
342	7	Sa.	7 00	E	4 12	A	9 12	24	22 41	8	8½	3 22	E	2 21	B	VIR	27
343	8	**F**	7 01	E	4 12	A	9 11	24	22 47	8¾	9½	4 26	E	3 00	B	LIB	28
344	9	M.	7 02	E	4 12	A	9 10	23	22 53	9½	10¼	5 32	E	3 46	B	LIB	29
345	10	Tu.	7 03	E	4 12	A	9 09	23	22 58	10¼	11	6 36	E	4 39	B	OPH	0
346	11	W.	7 04	E	4 12	A	9 08	22	23 03	11¼	11¾	7 37	E	5 39	B	SAG	1
347	12	Th.	7 04	E	4 12	A	9 08	22	23 07	—	12	8 34	E	6 45	B	SAG	2
348	13	Fr.	7 05	E	4 12	A	9 07	21	23 11	12½	12¾	9 24	E	7 54	C	SAG	3
349	14	Sa.	7 06	E	4 12	A	9 06	21	23 15	1½	1¾	10 08	E	9 05	C	AQU	4
350	15	**F**	7 07	E	4 12	A	9 05	21	23 18	2¼	2½	10 47	D	10 15	D	CAP	5
351	16	M.	7 07	E	4 12	A	9 05	20	23 20	3¼	3½	11 23	D	11 P.M. 24	D	AQU	6
352	17	Tu.	7 08	E	4 13	A	9 05	20	23 22	4¼	4¾	11 A.M. 57	D	— —	–	PSC	7
353	18	W.	7 09	E	4 14	A	9 05	19	23 24	5¼	5¾	12 P.M. 30	C	12 A.M. 31	D	PSC	8
354	19	Th.	7 09	E	4 14	A	9 05	19	23 25	6¼	6¾	1 04	C	1 38	E	PSC	9
355	20	Fr.	7 10	E	4 14	A	9 04	18	23 25	7¼	7¾	1 40	B	2 42	E	CET	10
356	21	Sa.	7 10	E	4 14	A	9 04	18	23 25	8¼	8¾	2 18	B	3 45	E	ARI	11
357	22	**F**	7 11	E	4 15	A	9 04	17	23 25	9	9¾	3 00	B	4 46	E	TAU	12
358	23	M.	7 11	E	4 16	A	9 05	17	23 25	9¾	10½	3 46	B	5 43	E	TAU	13
359	24	Tu.	7 12	E	4 17	A	9 05	16	23 23	10½	11¼	4 35	B	6 36	E	AUR	14
360	25	W.	7 12	E	4 17	A	9 05	16	23 22	11¼	11¾	5 28	B	7 23	E	GEM	15
361	26	Th.	7 12	E	4 18	A	9 06	15	23 19	—	12	6 23	B	8 06	E	GEM	16
362	27	Fr.	7 13	E	4 19	A	9 06	15	23 17	12½	12½	7 18	C	8 44	E	CAN	17
363	28	Sa.	7 13	E	4 19	A	9 06	14	23 14	1¼	1¼	8 15	C	9 18	D	CAN	18
364	29	**F**	7 13	E	4 20	A	9 07	14	23 10	2	2	9 11	C	9 49	D	LEO	19
365	30	M.	7 13	E	4 21	A	9 08	13	23 06	2½	2¾	10 08	D	10 19	D	SEX	20
366	31	Tu.	7 13	E	4 22	A	9 09	13	23s.02	3¼	3½	11 P.M. 06	D	10 A.M. 47	C	LEO	21

DECEMBER hath 31 days. 1996

Hark, how all the welkin rings,
'Glory to the King of kings';
Peace on earth, and mercy mild,
God and sinners reconciled.
– *Charles Wesley*

D. M.	D. W.	Dates, Feasts, Fasts, Aspects, Tide Heights	*Weather* ↓
1	F	**1st S. in Advent** • ☾ at apo. • Tides {8.9 9.3 •	*Rain*
2	M.	Bill Valverde caught a 279-pound alligator gar in Texas, 1951 • {8.8 9.0 •	*changing*
3	Tu.	☌ ♂ ☾ • Illinois became 21st state, 1818 • Tides {8.8 8.8 •	*to*
4	W.	☾ on Eq. • ♄ stat. • *Diligence is the mother of good luck.* •	*snow,*
5	Th.	☾ at ☊ • Phi Beta Kappa, first U.S. scholastic fraternity, organized, 1776 •	*then*
6	Fr.	**St. Nicholas** • **First day of Chanukah** • {9.6 8.9 •	*melting*
7	Sa.	**St. Ambrose** • Pearl Harbor attacked, 1941 • Microwave oven patented, 1945 •	*in*
8	F	**2nd S. in Advent** • ☌ ♀ ☾ •	*sunglow.*
9	M.	Christmas Seals first sold to help fight tuberculosis, 1907 • Tides {10.9 9.8 •	*Our*
10	Tu.	New ● • First Nobel Prizes awarded, 1901 • {11.3 10.1 •	*chestnuts*
11	W.	☾ runs low • Indiana became 19th state, 1816 • Tides {11.7 10.3 •	*are*
12	Th.	☌ ☿ ☾ • ☌ ♃ ☾ • ☾ at perig. •	*roasting —*
13	Fr.	**St. Lucy** • ☌ ♆ ☾ • ☌ ♅ ☾ • Tides {10.4 11.7 •	*more*
14	Sa.	George Washington died, 1799 • Alabama became 22nd state, 1819 •	*like*
15	F	**3rd S. in Advent** • ☿ Gr. Elong. (20° E.) •	*April*
16	M.	Boston Tea Party, 1773 • Halcyon Days • Tides {10.4 10.6 •	*Fool*
17	Tu.	☾ on Eq. • ☾ at ☋ • ☌ ♄ ☾ • Tides {10.3 10.1 •	*than*
18	W.	Ember Day • First giant panda imported to San Francisco zoo, 1936 • {10.3 9.7 •	*Yule.*
19	Th.	Ben Franklin began publishing *Poor Richard's Almanack*, 1732 • Tides {10.4 9.5 •	*Wintry*
20	Fr.	Ember Day • Louisiana Purchase, 1803 • Beware the Pogonip. •	*blast,*
21	Sa.	**St. Thomas** • **Winter Solstice** • Ember Day • Tides {10.6 9.4 •	*snow*
22	F	**4th S. in Advent** • U.S. Golf Assoc. founded, 1894 •	*at*
23	M.	☿ stat. • *It is in living wisely and fully that one's soul grows.* • {10.7 9.4 •	*last!*
24	Tu.	☾ rides high • **Full Long Nights** ○ • Kit Carson born, 1809 •	*Count*
25	W.	**Christmas Day** • *Christmas in snow, Easter in mud.* •	*down*
26	Th.	**St. Stephen** • Boxing Day (Canada) • Tides {— 10.5 •	*minutes*
27	Fr.	**St. John** • Carrie Nation attacked her first saloon, Wichita, Kansas, 1900 •	*from*
28	Sa.	**Holy Innocents** • Iowa became 29th state, 1846 • {9.3 10.1 •	*eleven:*
29	F	**1st S. af. C.** • ☾ at apo. • Tides {9.2 9.8 •	*Here's a*
30	M.	-42° F, New York City, 1917 • Tides {9.1 9.4 •	*cheer for*
31	Tu.	*Be at war with your vices, at peace with your neighbors, and let every new year find you a better man.* (Franklin)	*'97!*

Farmer's Calendar

Children like to eat snow, of course, but the rest of us, as we get older, generally grow away from the stuff. We shouldn't, perhaps. We eat a lot of worse things, and snow on the palate has its own subtle character, as I have discovered in a brief and self-directed course of snow connoisseurship — a snow tasting, you could say.

I find fresh, dry, powdery snow is for me entirely without taste, but in heavier, wetter snow, and in snow that has lain for a while, I detect a more or less fleeting flavor, a tartness. It's a little like the taste of steel, of a nail, say, but that isn't it exactly. The fact is that with snow as with any other material, each thing tastes like itself and nothing tastes like anything else, which must be why wine tasting, for example, is such a racket. You are left, not with useful, repeatable distinctions, but with vague associations. Or with not-so-vague associations. For me, snow's faint metallic flavor is the taste of the forbidden.

When I was little, my mother didn't like me to eat snow. It was dirty, she said. Well, it was. I grew up in a big city where everybody, at the time, burned soft coal for heat. Black soot covered everything all winter. The snow was gray. My mother, naturally, didn't want her only child eating anything like that. I ate it anyway, and I thought the peculiar snow taste was the wicked taste of coal. Now for years I have lived in the country, where the snow is comparatively clean. And yet it tastes the same. No sense endures in memory with the liveliness of taste; I'm quite sure of my recollection. I can hear her: "Don't eat that. For John's sake. Come on!"

1997 JANUARY, THE FIRST MONTH

Now is when comet Hale-Bopp may be starting to look spectacular in the predawn sky (see the feature on page 52). If you rise that early, peer low in the southeast to the right of the comet. From the 11th to the 13th, Venus and much less brilliant Mercury will hover next to each other as the only bright "stars" in that horizon-hugging part of the sky. If you sleep through the dawn or your only unobstructed window faces west, then observe Saturn beginning an hour after January sunsets. This is its final month of prominence until the autumn. Earth is at perihelion on the 1st.

☾	Last Quarter	1st day	20th hour	45th min.
●	New Moon	8th day	23rd hour	26th min.
☽	First Quarter	15th day	15th hour	2nd min.
○	Full Moon	23rd day	10th hour	11th min.
☾	Last Quarter	31st day	14th hour	40th min.

For an explanation of this page, see "How to Use This Almanac," page 34; for values of Key Letters, see Time Correction Tables, page 200.

Day of Year	Day of Month	Day of Week	☉ Rises h. m.	Key	☉ Sets h. m.	Key	Length of Days h. m.	Sun Fast m.	Declination of Sun ° '	Full Sea Boston A.M.	Full Sea Boston P.M.	☽ Rises h. m.	Key	☽ Sets h. m.	Key	☽ Place	☽ Age
1	1	W.	7 14	E	4 23	A	9 09	12	22s.57	4	4½	— —	–	11 AM 16	C	VIR	22
2	2	Th.	7 14	E	4 23	A	9 09	12	22 51	5	5¼	12 AM 04	D	11 AM 45	C	VIR	23
3	3	Fr.	7 14	E	4 24	A	9 10	11	22 45	5¾	6¼	1 04	E	12 PM 17	B	VIR	24
4	4	Sa.	7 14	E	4 25	A	9 11	11	22 39	6½	7	2 06	E	12 53	B	LIB	25
5	5	**E**	7 14	E	4 26	A	9 12	10	22 33	7½	8	3 10	E	1 35	B	LIB	26
6	6	M.	7 13	E	4 27	A	9 14	10	22 25	8¼	9	4 14	E	2 23	B	SCO	27
7	7	Tu.	7 13	E	4 28	A	9 15	9	22 18	9¼	9¾	5 18	E	3 19	B	OPH	28
8	8	W.	7 13	E	4 29	A	9 16	9	22 09	10	10½	6 17	E	4 22	B	SAG	0
9	9	Th.	7 13	E	4 30	A	9 17	9	22 01	10¾	11½	7 12	E	5 32	C	SAG	1
10	10	Fr.	7 13	E	4 31	A	9 18	8	21 52	11¾	—	8 01	E	6 44	C	CAP	2
11	11	Sa.	7 12	E	4 33	A	9 21	8	21 42	12¼	12½	8 44	D	7 58	D	AQU	3
12	12	**E**	7 12	E	4 34	A	9 22	7	21 32	1¼	1½	9 23	D	9 10	D	AQU	4
13	13	M.	7 12	E	4 35	A	9 23	7	21 22	2	2¼	9 59	D	10 21	D	PSC	5
14	14	Tu.	7 11	E	4 36	A	9 25	7	21 12	3	3¼	10 33	C	11 PM 29	D	PSC	6
15	15	W.	7 11	E	4 37	A	9 26	6	21 01	4	4¼	11 07	C	— —	–	PSC	7
16	16	Th.	7 10	E	4 38	A	9 28	6	20 49	5	5¼	11 AM 43	B	12 AM 35	E	PSC	8
17	17	Fr.	7 10	E	4 39	A	9 29	6	20 37	6	6½	12 PM 20	B	1 39	E	ARI	9
18	18	Sa.	7 09	E	4 41	A	9 32	5	20 25	7	7½	1 00	B	2 40	E	TAU	10
19	19	**E**	7 09	E	4 42	A	9 33	5	20 12	7¾	8½	1 44	B	3 37	E	TAU	11
20	20	M.	7 08	E	4 43	A	9 35	5	19 59	8¾	9½	2 31	B	4 31	E	TAU	12
21	21	Tu.	7 07	E	4 44	A	9 37	4	19 46	9½	10¼	3 22	B	5 20	E	GEM	13
22	22	W.	7 07	E	4 46	A	9 39	4	19 33	10¼	10¾	4 16	B	6 04	E	GEM	14
23	23	Th.	7 06	D	4 47	A	9 41	4	19 19	11	11½	5 11	B	6 44	E	CAN	15
24	24	Fr.	7 05	D	4 48	A	9 43	4	19 04	11½	—	6 07	C	7 19	E	CAN	16
25	25	Sa.	7 04	D	4 49	A	9 45	3	18 49	12¼	12¼	7 03	C	7 52	D	LEO	17
26	26	**E**	7 03	D	4 51	A	9 48	3	18 34	12¾	1	8 00	D	8 22	D	LEO	18
27	27	M.	7 03	D	4 52	A	9 49	3	18 18	1½	1½	8 57	D	8 51	D	LEO	19
28	28	Tu.	7 02	D	4 53	A	9 51	3	18 02	2	2¼	9 54	D	9 19	C	VIR	20
29	29	W.	7 01	D	4 55	A	9 54	3	17 46	2¾	3	10 53	D	9 48	C	VIR	21
30	30	Th.	7 00	D	4 56	A	9 56	2	17 30	3½	3¾	11 PM 52	D	10 18	C	VIR	22
31	31	Fr.	6 59	D	4 57	A	9 58	2	17s.13	4¼	4½	— —	–	10 AM 51	B	VIR	23

JANUARY hath 31 days. 1997

The coldness seemed more nigh, the coldness deepened
As a sound deepens into silences;
It was of earth and came not by the air;
The earth was cooling and drew down the sky.
– *Gordon Bottomley*

D. M.	D. W.	Dates, Feasts, Fasts, Aspects, Tide Heights	*Weather* ↓
1	W.	New Year's Day • **Circumcision** • ☾ at ☊ • ⊕ at perih.	
2	Th.	*The most creative ideas come from beginners — not experts.* • Tides {9.0 / 8.6 •	*Good*
3	Fr.	Chester C. Stone patented waxed-paper drinking straws, 1888 • {9.2 / 8.5 •	*weather*
4	Sa.	St. Elizabeth Seton • Louis Braille born, 1809 • T. S. Eliot died, 1965 •	*for*
5	E	**2nd S. af. Ch.** • Twelfth Night •	*cyberspacin'*
6	M.	**Epiphany** • Human growth hormone synthesized U. of Cal., 1971 • {10.4 / 9.3 •	*or*
7	Tu.	☌ ♀ ☾ • Fannie Farmer published her first cookbook, 1896 •	*hibernation.*
8	W.	☾ runs low • New ● • Elvis Presley born, 1935 • {11.5 / 10.2 •	*It's a*
9	Th.	First manned free-balloon flight in America, 1793 • Concorde jet first tested, 1969	*game*
10	Fr.	☾ at perig. • Temperature dropped 47° in 15 minutes, Rapid City, S.D., 1911 •	*of*
11	Sa.	Alexander Hamilton born, 1755 • Tides {10.8 / 12.1 •	*inches —*
12	E	**1st S. af. Ep.** • ☌ ☿ ♀ • ☿ stat. •	*even an*
13	M.	St. Hilary • ☾ on Eq. • ☾ at ☋ • Plough Monday •	*Eskimo*
14	Tu.	☌ ♄ ☾ • Propitious day for birth of women. • {10.8 / 10.7 •	*flinches.*
15	W.	First NFL Pro Bowl game played, 1939 • 2" snow, Los Angeles, 1932 •	*Blizzard*
16	Th.	*When we are planning for posterity, we ought to remember that virtue is not hereditary.* •	*alert!*
17	Fr.	☌ ♆ ☉ • Benjamin Franklin born, 1706 • Tides {10.2 / 9.1 •	*It*
18	Sa.	Sale of sliced bread stopped until end of World War II, 1943 • {10.1 / 8.9 •	*wouldn't*
19	E	**2nd S. af. Ep.** • ☌ ♃ ☉ • Robert E. Lee born, 1807	*hurt*
20	M.	Martin Luther King Jr.'s Birthday • St. Fabian • {10.1 / 8.9 •	*to*
21	Tu.	St. Agnes • ☾ rides high • Stonewall Jackson born, 1824 •	*take off*
22	W.	St. Vincent • *Time and words can't be recalled, even if it was only yesterday.* •	*your*
23	Th.	Full Wolf ○ • John Hancock born, 1737 • Tides {10.3 / 9.2 •	*shirt —*
24	Fr.	☿ Gr. Elong. (25° W.) • ☌ ♅ ☉ • {10.3 / — •	*it's dandy.*
25	Sa.	Conversion of Paul • ☾ at apo. • Ava Gardner died, 1990 •	*But*
26	E	**Septuagesima** • Wayne Gretzky born, 1961 • {9.4 / 10.0	*smart*
27	M.	National Geographic Society founded, Washington, D.C., 1888 • Tides {9.4 / 9.8 •	*fellas*
28	Tu.	St. Thomas Aquinas • ☾ on Eq. • ☾ at ☊ • ☌ ♂ ☾	
29	W.	Baseball Hall of Fame established, Cooperstown, New York, 1936 • Tides {9.3 / 9.2 •	*keep*
30	Th.	Franklin Delano Roosevelt born, 1882 • {9.3 / 8.9 •	*umbrellas*
31	Fr.	First U.S. satellite, *Explorer I*, launched, 1958 • Tides {9.3 / 8.6 •	*handy.*

Farmer's Calendar

After the turn of the year, when winter has come to stay and the short, cold days and the long, cold nights offer little to choose between them, the house itself undergoes a kind of hibernation. It curls up on itself and tucks its nose deep into its chest like an old bear. It embraces its heat, and it waits.

As with animal hibernation, the hibernation of an old house in winter involves changes more profound than sleep. The entire organism contracts, slows down. The life processes of the house — its metabolism, so to speak — which in summer have filled the place from cellar to attic, now pull back. The spare bedroom gets closed up, then the back pantry, then the parlor. For the next couple of months the remoter outposts of the house are the abode of the hurrying mice and the still, dull cold. You can't heat the whole place, so you don't try. Rather than work vainly to make more heat, you make less house. You reduce the house to its essence: a warm place.

That place is apt to be the kitchen, where the woodstove and the cooking create a warm heart for the house. Just as the bodily life of a wintering woodchuck shrinks down to its heartbeat, so the spirit of a house in winter retreats to the kitchen. It's a confined life, certainly, but it's not without its consolations. The demands of the indoor winter life, if they are more urgent than the demands of other seasons, are also fewer: Keep warm and wait. A life temporarily pared down to its animal necessities has even a kind of ease, a subtle luxury. Or so you may be able to persuade yourself as you sit clamped to the stove, your exterior well cooked, your interior chilled — an animated Baked Alaska.

February finds Earth facing directly outward from our galaxy's core, toward the next spiral arm—the Orion Spur. This region of furious star formation gives moonless nights of winter the most star-spangled vistas of the year. Amid the glitter, Orion's famous belt points down and leftward to the brightest star in the heavens. This is Sirius, the Dog Star, whose kennel-club association began when the ancient Sumerians collectively hallucinated a mongrel in this part of the sky. Believing that hot weather occurred when the dazzling Dog Star and Sun rose together to combine their heat, the Egyptians gave us the expression "Dog Days." Nowadays the Dog Star sometimes generates UFO rather than canine sightings; it's not unusual for its light to twinkle furiously, breaking into a beautiful but otherworldly procession of colors.

●	New Moon	7th day	10th hour	6th min.
☽	First Quarter	14th day	3rd hour	57th min.
○	Full Moon	22nd day	5th hour	27th min.

For an explanation of this page, see "How to Use This Almanac," page 34; for values of Key Letters, see Time Correction Tables, page 200.

Day of Year	Day of Month	Day of Week	☉ Rises h. m.	Key	☉ Sets h. m.	Key	Length of Days h. m.	Sun Fast m.	Declination of Sun ° '	Full Sea Boston A.M.	Full Sea Boston P.M.	☽ Rises h. m.	Key	☽ Sets h. m.	Key	Place	☽ Age
32	1	Sa.	6 58	D	4 58	A	10 00	2	16 s.56	5	5½	12ᴹ53	E	11ᴹ29	B	LIB	24
33	2	**E**	6 57	D	5 00	A	10 03	2	16 39	6	6½	1 55	E	12ᴾᴹ12	B	LIB	25
34	3	M.	6 56	D	5 01	A	10 05	2	16 21	6¾	7½	2 57	E	1 02	B	OPH	26
35	4	Tu.	6 54	D	5 02	A	10 08	2	16 03	7¾	8½	3 58	E	2 00	B	SAG	27
36	5	W.	6 53	D	5 04	A	10 11	2	15 45	8¾	9¼	4 54	E	3 05	B	SAG	28
37	6	Th.	6 52	D	5 05	A	10 13	2	15 26	9¾	10¼	5 47	E	4 16	C	SAG	29
38	7	Fr.	6 51	D	5 06	A	10 15	1	15 08	10½	11	6 33	E	5 31	C	AQU	0
39	8	Sa.	6 50	D	5 08	B	10 18	1	14 48	11½	—	7 16	D	6 46	D	CAP	1
40	9	**E**	6 49	D	5 09	B	10 20	1	14 29	12	12¼	7 54	D	8 00	D	AQU	2
41	10	M.	6 47	D	5 10	B	10 23	1	14 10	12¾	1¼	8 31	D	9 12	D	PSC	3
42	11	Tu.	6 46	D	5 12	B	10 26	1	13 50	1¾	2	9 07	C	10 21	E	PSC	4
43	12	W.	6 45	D	5 13	B	10 28	1	13 30	2½	3	9 43	C	11ᴾᴹ28	E	PSC	5
44	13	Th.	6 43	D	5 14	B	10 31	1	13 10	3½	4	10 20	B	— — —		ARI	6
45	14	Fr.	6 42	D	5 15	B	10 33	1	12 49	4½	5	11 00	B	12ᴹ32	E	TAU	7
46	15	Sa.	6 41	D	5 17	B	10 36	1	12 29	5½	6	11ᴹ43	B	1 31	E	TAU	8
47	16	**E**	6 39	D	5 18	B	10 39	1	12 08	6½	7	12ᴾᴹ29	B	2 27	E	TAU	9
48	17	M.	6 38	D	5 19	B	10 41	2	11 47	7½	8¼	1 19	B	3 17	E	ORI	10
49	18	Tu.	6 36	D	5 21	B	10 45	2	11 26	8½	9	2 11	B	4 03	E	GEM	11
50	19	W.	6 35	D	5 22	B	10 47	2	11 05	9¼	9¾	3 05	B	4 44	E	GEM	12
51	20	Th.	6 33	D	5 23	B	10 50	2	10 43	10	10½	4 01	C	5 20	E	CAN	13
52	21	Fr.	6 32	D	5 24	B	10 52	2	10 21	10¾	11	4 57	C	5 54	D	LEO	14
53	22	Sa.	6 30	D	5 26	B	10 56	2	9 59	11¼	11¾	5 54	C	6 25	D	LEO	15
54	23	**E**	6 29	D	5 27	B	10 58	2	9 37	—	12	6 51	D	6 54	D	LEO	16
55	24	M.	6 27	D	5 28	B	11 01	2	9 15	12¼	12½	7 48	D	7 23	D	VIR	17
56	25	Tu.	6 26	D	5 29	B	11 03	2	8 53	12¾	1	8 46	D	7 51	C	VIR	18
57	26	W.	6 24	D	5 31	B	11 07	3	8 30	1½	1¾	9 45	E	8 21	C	VIR	19
58	27	Th.	6 23	D	5 32	B	11 09	3	8 08	2	2½	10 44	E	8 53	B	VIR	20
59	28	Fr.	6 21	D	5 33	B	11 12	3	7 s.45	2¾	3¼	11ᴹ45	E	9ᴹ28	B	LIB	21

FEBRUARY hath 28 days. 1997

"See us cuddle and hug," say the Pleiads,
"All six in a ring: it keeps us warm:
We huddle together like birds in a storm:
It's bitter weather tonight."
– *Robert Graves*

D. M.	D. W.	Dates, Feasts, Fasts, Aspects, Tide Heights	*Weather* ↓
1	Sa.	St. Brigid • ☌♀♆ • Tides {9.3 8.5 •	*Groundhogs*
2	E	Sexagesima • Candlemas • Groundhog Day •	*sit out*
3	M.	James A. Michener born, 1907 • Norman Rockwell born, 1894 • {9.9 8.8 •	*the*
4	Tu.	☾ runs low • Auspicious day for marriage and repair of ships. •	*media*
5	W.	St. Agatha • ☌♀♃ • ☌☿☾ •	*swarm. It's*
6	Th.	☌♆☾ • ♂ stat. • Babe Ruth born, 1895 • Tides {11.5 10.4 •	*not*
7	Fr.	☌♀♅ • New ● • ☌☿♆ • ☾ at perig. •	*fit out*
8	Sa.	*Knowledge is madness if good sense does not direct it.* • {12.2 — •	*for men*
9	E	Quinquagesima • U.S. Weather Bureau established, 1870 • {11.3 12.1	*or*
10	M.	☾ on Eq. • ☾ at ☋ • ☌♄☾ • {11.5 11.8	*marmots.*
11	Tu.	Shrove Tuesday • Nelson Mandela released from prison, 1990 •	*Smitten?*
12	W.	Ash Wednesday • ☌☿♃ • ☌☿♅ •	
13	Th.	Boston Latin School, first public school in America, opened, 1635 • Tides {10.8 9.9 •	*Buy*
14	Fr.	St. Valentine • **Sts. Cyril & Methodius** • Tides {10.4 9.2 •	*your*
15	Sa.	*There is no remedy for love but to love more.* • Charles Tiffany born, 1812 •	*love*
16	E	1st S. in Lent • ☌♃♅ • Tides {9.7 8.5 •	*some*
17	M.	Presidents Day • ☾ rides high • Winter's back breaks. •	*mittens.*
18	Tu.	Planet Pluto discovered, 1930 • Tides {9.6 8.7 •	*Mushier*
19	W.	Ember Day • *Hatred is like acid — it destroys the vessel that holds it.* • {9.8 8.9 •	*and*
20	Th.	President Lincoln's 11-year-old son, William, died at the White House, 1862 •	*slushier;*
21	Fr.	☾ at apo. • Ember Day • Malcolm X killed, 1965 • Tides {10.0 9.3 •	*watch*
22	Sa.	**Full Snow** ○ • George Washington born, 1732 • Ember Day •	*out*
23	E	2nd S. in Lent • W. E. B. Du Bois born, 1868 • {— 10.1	*for a*
24	M.	St. Matthias • ☾ on Eq. • ☾ at ☊ • ☌♂☾	*gusher!*
25	Tu.	Oregon became first state to tax gasoline, 1919 • Tides {9.7 9.8 •	*Drier —*
26	W.	"Buffalo Bill" Cody born, 1846 • Levi Strauss born, 1829 • {9.7 9.6 •	*build up*
27	Th.	*We overlook so much happiness because it costs nothing.* • Tides {9.7 9.3 •	*your*
28	Fr.	Vincente Minnelli born, 1913 • Last episode *M*A*S*H* aired on TV, 1983 •	*fire.*

Don't go around saying the world owes you a living; the world owes you nothing; it was here first.
– Mark Twain

Farmer's Calendar

Consider the half-smart man who took his savings out to Las Vegas with the plan of increasing them at the craps table. He had a system based, as he thought, on Bernoulli's theorem, sometimes called the "law of averages," a principle of statistics that says, very roughly, that the more often you play, the more often you win. Our hero took this to mean that if he doubled his bet each time he *lost,* he would necessarily come out ahead when he began to win, which from the theorem he was confident he would do.

In a day or so, of course, he was broke. As he was getting ready to make his penniless way back East, he was set straight by a taxi driver.

"I still can't believe it," the gambler moaned. "How could I have gone on losing? It's against Bernoulli's theorem!"

"Mister," the taxi driver said, "the dice ain't as smart as you. They don't know Bernoulli."

If I understand Bernoulli's theorem correctly, it is falsely interpreted when brought to support a gambling system like the one above. Nevertheless, a similar fallacy has led astray brighter people than our hero, and not only in Las Vegas. For misunderstood probability is at the heart of many of our assumptions about the weather. We believe that some law of averages operates to even out winter weather over the years. If we had a hard winter last year, we think, surely the winter to come will be easier. A string of two or three bitter winters will almost certainly be followed by a mild one. Or so we fondly believe. It isn't so. This winter doesn't remember last winter. The dice don't know Bernoulli — and neither does the snow.

The first total solar eclipse in two years occurs on the 8th. The bad news is total-
ity will be visible only in Siberia (on the 9th). Otherwise, stay home and experience
Mars — closest to Earth on the 17th. It's been 26 months since Mars has been so
bright. It is out all night and highest in the south at midnight. On the 23rd, Mars is
near the full Moon as it goes into eclipse. This striking lunar event reaches maximum
just before midnight, EST, and will be visible throughout North America except
Alaska and northwestern Canada. Vernal equinox is at 8:55 A.M., EST, on the 20th.

☾	Last Quarter	2nd day	4th hour	37th min.
●	New Moon	8th day	20th hour	15th min.
☽	First Quarter	15th day	19th hour	6th min.
○	Full Moon	23rd day	23rd hour	45th min.
☾	Last Quarter	31st day	14th hour	38th min.

For an explanation of this page, see "How to Use This Almanac," page 34; for values of
Key Letters, see Time Correction Tables, page 200.

Day of Year	Day of Month	Day of Week	☉ Rises h. m.	Key	☉ Sets h. m.	Key	Length of Days h. m.	Sun Fast m.	Declination of Sun ° '	Full Sea Boston A.M.	Full Sea Boston P.M.	☽ Rises h. m.	Key	☽ Sets h. m.	Key	☽ Place	☽ Age
60	1	Sa.	6 19	D	5 34	B	11 15	3	7 s.22	3½	4	— —	–	10♎08	B	LIB	22
61	2	**E**	6 18	D	5 35	B	11 17	3	6 59	4½	5	12♏45	E	10 53	B	OPH	23
62	3	M.	6 16	D	5 37	B	11 21	4	6 36	5¼	6	1 44	E	11♏46	B	OPH	24
63	4	Tu.	6 15	D	5 38	B	11 23	4	6 13	6¼	7	2 40	E	12♏45	B	SAG	25
64	5	W.	6 13	D	5 39	B	11 26	4	5 50	7¼	8	3 32	E	1 51	B	SAG	26
65	6	Th.	6 11	D	5 40	B	11 29	4	5 27	8¼	9	4 21	E	3 02	C	CAP	27
66	7	Fr.	6 10	D	5 41	B	11 31	4	5 03	9¼	10	5 05	D	4 16	D	CAP	28
67	8	Sa.	6 08	D	5 43	B	11 35	5	4 40	10¼	10¾	5 45	D	5 31	D	AQU	0
68	9	**E**	6 06	D	5 44	B	11 38	5	4 16	11	11½	6 23	D	6 45	D	PSC	1
69	10	M.	6 05	D	5 45	B	11 40	5	3 53	—	12	7 00	C	7 58	D	PSC	2
70	11	Tu.	6 03	D	5 46	B	11 43	5	3 30	12½	12¾	7 37	C	9 09	E	PSC	3
71	12	W.	6 01	C	5 47	B	11 46	6	3 06	1¼	1¾	8 16	B	10 16	E	CET	4
72	13	Th.	5 59	C	5 49	B	11 50	6	2 43	2	2½	8 56	B	11♏20	E	ARI	5
73	14	Fr.	5 58	C	5 50	B	11 52	6	2 19	3	3½	9 39	B	— —	–	TAU	6
74	15	Sa.	5 56	C	5 51	B	11 55	7	1 55	3¾	4½	10 25	B	12♏18	E	TAU	7
75	16	**E**	5 54	C	5 52	B	11 58	7	1 31	4¾	5½	11♏14	B	1 12	E	ORI	8
76	17	M.	5 53	C	5 53	B	12 00	7	1 07	5¾	6½	12♏06	B	2 00	E	GEM	9
77	18	Tu.	5 51	C	5 54	B	12 03	7	0 44	7	7½	1 00	B	2 42	E	GEM	10
78	19	W.	5 49	C	5 55	B	12 06	8	0 s.20	7¾	8½	1 55	B	3 21	E	CAN	11
79	20	Th.	5 47	C	5 57	C	12 10	8	0 N.02	8¾	9¼	2 51	C	3 55	D	CAN	12
80	21	Fr.	5 46	C	5 58	C	12 12	8	0 27	9½	10	3 47	C	4 27	D	LEO	13
81	22	Sa.	5 44	C	5 59	C	12 15	9	0 50	10¼	10½	4 44	D	4 57	D	SEX	14
82	23	**E**	5 42	C	6 00	C	12 18	9	1 14	10¾	11¼	5 41	D	5 26	D	LEO	15
83	24	M.	5 40	C	6 01	C	12 21	9	1 38	11½	11¾	6 40	D	5 54	C	VIR	16
84	25	Tu.	5 39	C	6 02	C	12 23	9	2 01	—	12	7 39	D	6 24	C	VIR	17
85	26	W.	5 37	C	6 03	C	12 26	10	2 25	12¼	12¾	8 38	E	6 55	C	VIR	18
86	27	Th.	5 35	C	6 05	C	12 30	10	2 48	1	1¼	9 39	E	7 29	B	LIB	19
87	28	Fr.	5 33	C	6 06	C	12 33	10	3 11	1½	2	10 38	E	8 08	B	LIB	20
88	29	Sa.	5 32	C	6 07	C	12 35	11	3 34	2¼	2¾	11♏37	E	8 51	B	OPH	21
89	30	**E**	5 30	C	6 08	C	12 38	11	3 58	3	3¾	— —	–	9 40	B	OPH	22
90	31	M.	5 28	C	6 09	C	12 41	11	4 N.21	4	4½	12♏33	E	10♏35	B	SAG	23

MARCH hath 31 days. 1997

It is the first mild day of March:
Each minute sweeter than before;
The redbreast sings from the tall larch
That stands beside our door.
– William Wordsworth

D. M.	D. W.	Dates, Feasts, Fasts, Aspects, Tide Heights	*Weather* ↓
1	Sa.	**St. David** • *Upon St. David's Day Put oats and barley in the clay.* • {9.6 / 8.8	*Town*
2	**E**	**3rd S. in Lent** • Dr. Seuss born, 1904 • {9.6 / 8.7 •	*meeting*
3	M.	Jackie Joyner-Kersee born, 1962 • Alexander Graham Bell born, 1847	*debaters*
4	Tu.	☾ runs low • Town Meeting Day, Vermont • Tides {10.0 / 9.0 •	*better*
5	W.	☌♆☾ • The "Boston Massacre," 1770 • {10.4 / 9.5 •	*wear*
6	Th.	☌♅☾ • ☌♃☾ • Alan Greenspan born, 1926 •	*waders.*
7	Fr.	**St. Perpetua** • Luther Burbank born, 1849 • Tides {11.4 / 10.8 •	*Beware*
8	Sa.	☾ at perig. • **New** ● • Eclipse ☉ •	*the ice*
9	**E**	**4th S. in Lent** • ☾ on Eq. • ☾ at ☋ • {12.0 / 11.7 •	*of*
10	M.	**Pure Monday** • ♇ stat. • ☌♄☾ • { — / 11.9 •	*March.*
11	Tu.	☿ in sup. ☌ • Dow Jones average passed 1,000 mark, 1976 •	*Lots of*
12	W.	**St. Gregory** • Girl Scouts of U.S.A. founded, 1912 • {11.7 / 11.1 •	*flurries;*
13	Th.	*Laziness is nothing more than the habit of resting before you get tired.* • {11.4 / 10.4 •	*wear*
14	Fr.	Eli Whitney patented cotton gin, 1794 • Albert Einstein born, 1879 • {10.8 / 9.7 •	*your*
15	Sa.	Beware the Ides of March • Buzzards return to Hinckley, Ohio • {10.3 / 9.1 •	*furries.*
16	**E**	**5th S. in Lent** • **Sunday of Orthodoxy** • ☾ rides high •	
17	M.	**St. Patrick** • ♂ at ☊ • Nat "King" Cole born, 1919 •	*Snow*
18	Tu.	Grover Cleveland born, 1837 • *Good example is half a sermon.* • {9.2 / 8.5 •	*drifting,*
19	W.	**St. Joseph** • Swallows return to San Juan Capistrano • {9.2 / 8.7 •	*clouds*
20	Th.	☾ at apo. • **Vernal Equinox** • ♂ closest approach • {9.4 / 9.0 •	*rifting;*
21	Fr.	Sorosis, first club for professional women, organized, 1868 • Tides {9.6 / 9.3 •	*warm*
22	Sa.	Andrew Lloyd Webber born, 1948 • Marcel Marceau born, 1923 •	*deluge*
23	**E**	**Palm Sunday** • ☾ on Eq. • **Full Worm** ○ • Eclipse ☾	
24	M.	*Exxon Valdez* ran aground in Prince William Sound, Alaska, 1989 • {10.0 / 10.0 •	*before*
25	Tu.	Arturo Toscanini born, 1867 • Poll tax declared unconstitutional, 1966 •	*they're*
26	W.	Robert Frost born, 1874 • Tennessee Williams born, 1911 • {10.1 / 9.8 •	*lifting.*
27	Th.	*No matter how thin you slice it, there are always two sides.* • Tides {10.2 / 9.7 •	*Dry?*
28	Fr.	**Good Friday** • Edmund S. Muskie born, 1914 •	*Here's*
29	Sa.	Cy Young born, 1867 • Knights of Columbus chartered, 1882 • Tides {10.1 / 9.3 •	*mud*
30	**E**	**Easter** • ☌♄☉ • U.S. purchased Alaska, 1867 •	*in your*
31	M.	☾ runs low • Daylight Saving Time first went into effect in U.S., 1918 • {10.0 / 9.0 •	*eye!*

Farmer's Calendar

March 2. A filthy day, perfectly filthy. Clammy mists obscure the woods, and fogs weigh on the hillsides. Gray, gray, gray everywhere, but not an honest gray. Rather the soiled gray of rotten snow, the color of an unclean sheep: March arriving not like a lamb but like a shabby old mutton. For some reason the wind has come around to the southwest, and it drives a raw, cold rain straight against the side of the house. The rain gets in at the windows. It drips on the sills.

There's nothing to do with a day like this but stand morosely at the spattered window and watch it happen, like a train wreck. The rain, near freezing, has iced over the roads and paths. Outdoors you can't say what's more nearly impossible, driving or walking. Altogether it's the kind of day for which houses were invented, and yet there's no satisfaction in being safe indoors. It's not cold enough for the warmth of the house to be comforting; there's no snow to shelter from. A day whose only purpose is oppression.

Cheer up: Next week is Town Meeting. An encouraging notion on a day like this, a notion to perk you up if you reflect on how intelligently political life fits into — shall we say — real life. Town Meeting Day, historically, is said to come in early March because in the farming communities where it was founded, this was a relatively idle season. Isn't it at least as likely that Town Meeting was timed as an antidote to dirty, useless days exactly like this one, the accumulation of which at this time of year has driven everybody so nearly nuts that the business of democratic self-government, normally a drag, seems like a party?

1997 APRIL, THE FOURTH MONTH

Early April boasts perfect moonless conditions for comet Hale-Bopp, now at its best during the first hour after nightfall in the western sky. While you're looking that way, try to locate Mercury to the comet's left. Many astronomers admit to never having seen that broiling innermost world, but it is not difficult during April's first two weeks. This is Mercury's best evening apparition of the year; an unobstructed western view is the only real requirement. Some 45 minutes after sunset, look low in the deepening twilight. Any "star" seen in that direction means that you have indeed found the solar system's most elusive planet. Daylight Saving Time begins at 2:00 A.M. on the 6th.

● New Moon	7th day	6th hour	2nd min.
☽ First Quarter	14th day	12th hour	0 min.
○ Full Moon	22nd day	15th hour	33rd min.
☾ Last Quarter	29th day	21st hour	37th min.

ADD 1 hour for Daylight Saving Time after 2 A.M., April 6th.

For an explanation of this page, see "How to Use This Almanac," page 34; for values of Key Letters, see Time Correction Tables, page 200.

Day of Year	Day of Month	Day of Week	☉ Rises h. m.	Key	☉ Sets h. m.	Key	Length of Days h. m.	Sun Fast m.	Declination of Sun ° '	Full Sea Boston A.M.	P.M.	☽ Rises h. m.	Key	☽ Sets h. m.	Key	Place	☽ Age
91	1	Tu.	5 27	B	6 10	C	12 43	12	4N.44	5	5½	1♪25	E	11♪37	B	SAG	24
92	2	W.	5 25	B	6 11	C	12 46	12	5 07	6	6¾	2 13	E	12♪43	C	CAP	25
93	3	Th.	5 23	B	6 12	C	12 49	12	5 30	7	7¾	2 57	E	1 53	C	AQU	26
94	4	Fr.	5 21	B	6 14	C	12 53	12	5 53	8	8¾	3 38	D	3 06	C	AQU	27
95	5	Sa.	5 20	B	6 15	D	12 55	13	6 16	9	9½	4 16	D	4 19	D	AQU	28
96	6	**E**	5 18	B	6 16	D	12 58	13	6 39	10	10½	4 53	D	5 32	D	PSC	29
97	7	M.	5 16	B	6 17	D	13 01	13	7 01	10¾	11¼	5 29	C	6 44	E	PSC	0
98	8	Tu.	5 15	B	6 18	D	13 03	14	7 24	11¾	—	6 07	C	7 54	E	PSC	1
99	9	W.	5 13	B	6 19	D	13 06	14	7 46	12	12½	6 47	B	9 01	E	ARI	2
100	10	Th.	5 11	B	6 20	D	13 09	14	8 08	12¾	1¼	7 30	B	10 04	E	TAU	3
101	11	Fr.	5 10	B	6 21	D	13 11	14	8 30	1½	2¼	8 16	B	11 02	E	TAU	4
102	12	Sa.	5 08	B	6 23	D	13 15	15	8 52	2½	3	9 05	B	11♪53	E	TAU	5
103	13	**E**	5 06	B	6 24	D	13 18	15	9 14	3¼	4	9 57	B	— —	—	GEM	6
104	14	M.	5 05	B	6 25	D	13 20	15	9 35	4¼	5	10 51	B	12♪39	E	GEM	7
105	15	Tu.	5 03	B	6 26	D	13 23	15	9 57	5¼	6	11♪46	C	1 19	E	CAN	8
106	16	W.	5 02	B	6 27	D	13 25	16	10 18	6¼	7	12♪42	C	1 55	E	CAN	9
107	17	Th.	5 00	B	6 28	D	13 28	16	10 39	7¼	7¾	1 39	C	2 28	D	LEO	10
108	18	Fr.	4 58	B	6 29	D	13 31	16	11 00	8	8½	2 35	D	2 58	D	LEO	11
109	19	Sa.	4 57	B	6 30	D	13 33	16	11 21	9	9¼	3 33	D	3 28	D	LEO	12
110	20	**E**	4 55	B	6 32	D	13 37	17	11 41	9¾	10	4 31	D	3 56	D	VIR	13
111	21	M.	4 54	B	6 33	D	13 39	17	12 02	10¼	10½	5 30	D	4 25	C	VIR	14
112	22	Tu.	4 52	B	6 34	D	13 42	17	12 22	11	11¼	6 30	E	4 56	C	VIR	15
113	23	W.	4 51	B	6 35	D	13 44	17	12 42	11¾	11¾	7 31	E	5 30	B	LIB	16
114	24	Th.	4 49	B	6 36	D	13 47	17	13 02	—	12¼	8 32	E	6 07	B	LIB	17
115	25	Fr.	4 48	B	6 37	D	13 49	18	13 21	12½	1	9 32	E	6 49	B	SCO	18
116	26	Sa.	4 46	B	6 38	D	13 52	18	13 41	1	1¾	10 30	E	7 36	B	OPH	19
117	27	**E**	4 45	B	6 39	D	13 54	18	14 00	1¾	2½	11♪23	E	8 30	B	SAG	20
118	28	M.	4 43	B	6 41	D	13 58	18	14 18	2¾	3¼	— —		9 30	B	SAG	21
119	29	Tu.	4 42	B	6 42	D	14 00	18	14 37	3½	4¼	12♪12	E	10 34	B	SAG	22
120	30	W.	4 41	B	6 43	D	14 02	18	14N.55	4½	5¼	12♪56	E	11♪41	C	AQU	23

APRIL hath 30 days. 1997

This is the weather the cuckoo likes
And so do I;
When showers betumble the chestnut spikes,
And nestlings fly.
– *Thomas Hardy*

D. M.	D. W.	Dates, Feasts, Fasts, Aspects, Tide Heights	*Weather* ↓
1	Tu.	All Fools • U.S. invasion of Okinawa began, 1945 • Tides {10.0 / 9.1	*Fool's*
2	W.	☌ ♆ ☾ • ♀ in sup. ☌ • ☌ ♅ ☾ •	*gold—*
3	Th.	☌ ♃ ☾ • George Washington received honorary degree from Harvard, 1776 •	*then*
4	Fr.	*Ben Hur* won 11 Academy Awards, 1960 • Tides {10.7 / 10.5 •	*mighty*
5	Sa.	☾ at ☋ • ☾ at perig. • ☿ Gr. Elong. (19° E.) • {11.1 / 11.1	*cold!*
6	E	**1st S. af. Easter** • ☾ on Eq. • **Daylight Saving Time begins, 2 A.M.**	
7	M.	**Annunciation** • **New ●** • Billie Holiday born, 1915 • {11.5 / 11.9	*It's*
8	Tu.	☌ ☿ ☾ • 85° F, New York City, 1929 • {11.5 / — •	*terra firma*
9	W.	*If you keep doing what you've always done, you'll keep getting what you've always gotten.* •	*now,*
10	Th.	First human cannonball act performed in London, 1877 • Tides {11.7 / 10.7 •	*hurray!*
11	Fr.	*Apollo 13* launched, 1970 • Luther Burbank died, 1926 • {11.3 / 10.2	*Robins*
12	Sa.	Salk vaccine for polio announced safe and effective, 1955 • Tides {10.8 / 9.6 •	*share*
13	E	**2nd S. af. Easter** • ☾ runs high • {10.2 / 9.1 •	*a worm*
14	M.	Noah Webster obtained copyright for first edition of his dictionary, 1828 • {9.6 / 8.7 •	*a day.*
15	Tu.	☿ stat. • *The income tax has made liars out of more Americans than golf.* •	*Rainbows*
16	W.	Kareem Abdul-Jabbar born, 1947 • Tides {9.0 / 8.6 •	*shimmer—*
17	Th.	☾ at apo. • John Pierpont Morgan born, 1837 • {9.0 / 8.8 •	*dimmer*
18	Fr.	82° F at Logan Airport in Boston, 1964 • "Midnight Ride" of Paul Revere, 1775 •	*and*
19	Sa.	☾ at ☊ • ☌ ♂ ☾ • Tides {9.3 / 9.5 •	*grimmer.*
20	E	**3rd S. af. Easter** • ☾ on Eq. • {9.5 / 9.8 •	*Now*
21	M.	**St. Anselm** • Baron von Richthofen, the "Red Baron," shot down and killed over France, 1918 •	*we*
22	Tu.	**First day of Passover** • **Full Pink ○** • {9.8 / 10.3 •	*simmer.*
23	W.	**St. George** • Shirley Temple Black born, 1928 • Tides {9.8 / 10.5 •	*Soon*
24	Th.	Robert B. Thomas born, 1766 • Spain declared war on U.S., 1898 •	*you'll*
25	Fr.	**St. Mark** • ☿ in inf. ☌ • Ella Fitzgerald born, 1918 • {10.6 / 9.8	*need*
26	Sa.	*Even if you're on the right track, you'll get run over if you just sit there.* • {10.7 / 9.7 •	*your*
27	E	**4th S. af. Easter** • **Orthodox Easter** • ☾ runs low •	
28	M.	Maryland became seventh state, 1788 • James Monroe born, 1758 • {10.5 / 9.5 •	*garden*
29	Tu.	**St. Catherine** • ♂ stat. • ☌ ♆ ☾ • ☌ ♅ ☾ •	
30	W.	☌ ♃ ☾ • Louisiana Purchase, 1803 • {10.2 / 9.6 •	*trimmer!*

A great many people think they are thinking when they are merely rearranging their prejudices. – William James

Farmer's Calendar

New work gloves this spring. The old ones have utterly had the course. With me, a pair of heavy leather gloves is good for three years. Decline is evident after about year one. First to go is either the fore or the second finger of the right hand, where a hole appears, grows. The right thumb wears through, then the left. The curved seam that joins the right thumb to the palm splits. Finally, in no predictable order, the other fingers on both hands give out, either at the stitching or through the leather. By the end of year three, the condition of the gloves is such that wearing them would be no hindrance to my playing the flute, say (if I could play the flute). At that point, it's time to face the end.

The life of a pair of work gloves gives us a version of our own mortality in miniature. Only the other day, it seems, they gleamed on the shelf at the hardware store: bright, supple, the color of a fox, their new leather strong and richly napped. In their youth they owned a pleasant, utilitarian smell like the interior of a classic roadster. Now their smell is less welcome, a matter of sweat, oil, and dirt. Their look is the same: Their color is that of a road-killed woodchuck in the rain. They're stiff, greasy, bald, gapped, and busted. Removed, the worn-out gloves hold the curl of the hand, clenched in rigor mortis. Work hard all your life, and what do you get?

It seems a pity to throw them in the trash. It seems ungrateful, like shooting the hired man. There needs to be an Old Soldiers' Home for used-up work gloves, a sunny place where they can sit on the porch all day and chew tobacco and beat their toothless gums — a cowhide Valhalla.

While Mars and comet Hale-Bopp fade and the bright winter stars crumble into the western twilight and vanish, we can turn our attention to everybody's favorite star — the Sun. The 11-year cycle of sunspots should be by now in its upswing period and with it the increased likelihood of displays of the Northern Lights. Dark, unpolluted rural skies are a "must" for properly seeing the aurora, which appears almost monthly over the northern third of the U.S. Meanwhile, the Sun itself becomes surprisingly powerful in May; sunlight is now more intense than it is in August!

● New Moon	6th day	15th hour	46th min.
☽ First Quarter	14th day	5th hour	55th min.
○ Full Moon	22nd day	4th hour	13th min.
☾ Last Quarter	29th day	2nd hour	51st min.

ADD 1 hour for Daylight Saving Time.

For an explanation of this page, see "How to Use This Almanac," page 34; for values of Key Letters, see Time Correction Tables, page 200.

Day of Year	Day of Month	Day of Week	☉ Rises h. m.	Key	☉ Sets h. m.	Key	Length of Days h. m.	Sun Fast m.	Declination of Sun ° '	Full Sea Boston A.M.	P.M.	☽ Rises h. m.	Key	☽ Sets h. m.	Key	☽ Place	☽ Age
121	1	Th.	4 39	B	6 44	D	14 05	18	15N.13	5½	6¼	1ᴬ36	D	12ᴹ50	D	CAP	24
122	2	Fr.	4 38	B	6 45	D	14 07	19	15 31	6¾	7¼	2 14	D	2 01	D	AQU	25
123	3	Sa.	4 37	B	6 46	D	14 09	19	15 49	7¾	8¼	2 49	D	3 12	D	PSC	26
124	4	**E**	4 35	A	6 47	D	14 12	19	16 07	8¾	9¼	3 25	C	4 22	E	PSC	27
125	5	M.	4 34	A	6 48	D	14 14	19	16 24	9¾	10	4 01	C	5 33	E	PSC	28
126	6	Tu.	4 33	A	6 49	D	14 16	19	16 41	10½	10¾	4 39	B	6 41	E	ARI	0
127	7	W.	4 32	A	6 51	D	14 19	19	16 57	11½	11¾	5 20	B	7 47	E	ARI	1
128	8	Th.	4 30	A	6 52	D	14 22	19	17 13	—	12¼	6 05	B	8 48	E	TAU	2
129	9	Fr.	4 29	A	6 53	D	14 24	19	17 29	12½	1	6 53	B	9 43	E	TAU	3
130	10	Sa.	4 28	A	6 54	D	14 26	19	17 45	1¼	1¾	7 45	B	10 33	E	ORI	4
131	11	**E**	4 27	A	6 55	D	14 28	19	18 00	2	2¾	8 39	B	11 16	E	GEM	5
132	12	M.	4 26	A	6 56	D	14 30	19	18 15	2¾	3½	9 35	B	11ᴹ54	E	GEM	6
133	13	Tu.	4 25	A	6 57	D	14 32	18	18 30	3¾	4¼	10 31	C	— —	–	CAN	7
134	14	W.	4 24	A	6 58	D	14 34	18	18 44	4½	5¼	11ᴬ28	C	12ᴸ29	D	LEO	8
135	15	Th.	4 23	A	6 59	E	14 36	19	18 58	5½	6¼	12ᴹ25	C	1 00	D	LEO	9
136	16	Fr.	4 22	A	7 00	E	14 38	19	19 12	6½	7	1 22	D	1 29	D	LEO	10
137	17	Sa.	4 21	A	7 01	E	14 40	19	19 26	7¼	7¾	2 19	D	1 58	C	VIR	11
138	18	**E**	4 20	A	7 02	E	14 42	19	19 40	8¼	8½	3 18	D	2 26	C	VIR	12
139	19	M.	4 19	A	7 03	E	14 44	19	19 52	9	9¼	4 18	E	2 56	C	VIR	13
140	20	Tu.	4 18	A	7 04	E	14 46	19	20 05	9¾	10	5 19	E	3 28	C	VIR	14
141	21	W.	4 17	A	7 05	E	14 48	19	20 17	10½	10¾	6 21	E	4 04	B	LIB	15
142	22	Th.	4 16	A	7 06	E	14 50	19	20 29	11¼	11¼	7 23	E	4 44	B	LIB	16
143	23	Fr.	4 16	A	7 07	E	14 51	19	20 40	—	12	8 23	E	5 31	B	OPH	17
144	24	Sa.	4 15	A	7 08	E	14 53	19	20 51	12	12¾	9 19	E	6 23	B	SAG	18
145	25	**E**	4 14	A	7 09	E	14 55	19	21 02	12¾	1½	10 11	E	7 22	B	SAG	19
146	26	M.	4 14	A	7 10	E	14 56	19	21 13	1½	2¼	10 57	E	8 26	B	SAG	20
147	27	Tu.	4 13	A	7 10	E	14 57	19	21 23	2½	3	11ᴹ38	E	9 33	C	AQU	21
148	28	W.	4 12	A	7 11	E	14 59	18	21 32	3¼	4	— —	–	10 41	C	CAP	22
149	29	Th.	4 11	A	7 12	E	15 01	18	21 41	4¼	5	12ᴬ16	D	11ᴬ51	C	AQU	23
150	30	Fr.	4 11	A	7 13	E	15 02	18	21 50	5¼	6	12 52	D	1ᴹ00	D	PSC	24
151	31	Sa.	4 10	A	7 14	E	15 04	18	21N.59	6½	7	1ᴬ26	C	2ᴹ09	D	PSC	25

May come up with fiddle-bows,
May come up with blossom,
May come up with the same again,
The same again but different.
– *Louis MacNeice*

Farmer's Calendar

What we know of nature and how we know it are matters of imagination and circumstance as much as choice. One student may travel the country observing shorebirds, say. Another student may stay home. I stay home. The understanding that appeals to my imagination has always been minute rather than extended. I like the idea of knowing every shoot, sparrow, and green stick in a very small patch; let somebody else be the frequent flyer.

Still, it's not easy. Gaining a complete idea of the creatures large and small that share your little corner is no mere matter of looking. Even in a tame, temperate neighborhood like mine, thousands of species are about, many of them small, shy, nocturnal, and otherwise elusive. Then, too, the observer in this case is often at fault. I find nearsightedness, sloth, lack of system, and the occasional necessity of doing other things get seriously in the way of even the limited expertise that is all I aspire to. Left alone, I'd never get on. Fortunately, I have help.

My assistants are five hardworking cats whose knowledge of the local fauna is profound, exact, and entirely practical. They go where I cannot go, see what I cannot see, wait when I become impatient. Many species I would hardly have known were here without the help of these cats: the flying squirrel, meadow vole, jumping mouse, shrew. As collectors, they are without equal. There is, however, one problem. Cats don't operate on the catch-and-release line. Therefore their collecting is subject to a kind of Uncertainty Principle. For any creature on our home ground, if the cats have found it, it isn't on our home ground anymore.

D.M.	D.W.	Dates, Feasts, Fasts, Aspects, Tide Heights	*Weather* ↓
1	Th.	Sts. Philip & James • ♆ stat. • Tides {10.2 9.9 •	*Till*
2	Fr.	St. Athanasius • Riots broke out at Alcatraz prison, 1946 • Tides {10.3 10.3 •	*your*
3	Sa.	☾ on Eq. • ☾ at ☍ • ☾ perig. • at Invention of the Cross	*gardens,*
4	E	Rogation ☙. • ♂♄☾ • Tides {10.7 11.3 •	*then*
5	M.	♂♀☾ • 12" snow, Denver, Colorado, 1917 • {10.8 11.6 •	*seed' em.*
6	Tu.	New ● • Babe Ruth hit his first major-league home run, 1915 • {10.9 11.8 •	*Buy*
7	W.	☿ stat. • Passenger liner Lusitania sunk by German submarine, 1915 • {10.8 11.8 •	*your*
8	Th.	Ascension • Julian of Norwich • Harry S. Truman born, 1884 •	*Mom*
9	Fr.	St. Gregory of Nazianzus • Tides {11.5 10.3 •	*galoshes —*
10	Sa.	☾ rides high • Golden spike driven to connect transcontinental railroad, 1869 •	*she'll*
11	E	1st ☙. af. Asc. • Three • {10.6 9.5 •	*need' em.*
12	M.	Farley Mowat born, 1921 • Yogi Berra born, 1925 • Chilly • {10.1 9.1 •	*Rainy*
13	Tu.	☉ stat. • Texas farmer killed in hailstorm, 1930 • Saints •	*spell,*
14	W.	Forgive your enemies, but never forget their names. • Tides {9.2 8.8 •	*and then*
15	Th.	☾ at apo. • Max Anderson completed first nonstop balloon flight across U.S., 1980 •	*it's*
16	Fr.	♂♂☾ • Liberace born, 1919 • Studs Terkel born, 1912 • {8.9 9.0 •	*hot;*
17	Sa.	☾ on Eq. • ☾ at ☍ • Tides {8.9 9.3 •	*predictable*
18	E	Whit ☙. • Pentecost • TVA established, 1933 •	*this*
19	M.	St. Dunstan • Victoria Day (Canada) • Tides {9.2 10.0 •	*month*
20	Tu.	Amelia Earhart became first woman to fly solo across the Atlantic, 1932 • Tides {9.4 10.3 •	*is*
21	W.	Ember Day • Be generous with praise but cautious with promises. • {9.5 10.6 •	*not.*
22	Th.	Full ○ • ☿ Gr. Elong. (25° W.) • Mary Cassatt born, 1844 •	*In the*
23	Fr.	Ember Day • New York Public Library incorporated, 1895 • {— 9.8 •	*wind is*
24	Sa.	☾ runs low • Ember Day • Duke Ellington died, 1974 •	*summer's*
25	E	Trinity • ♇ at ☍ • Tides {11.1 10.0 •	*solace —*
26	M.	St. Augustine of Canterbury • Memorial Day • ♂♆☾ •	
27	Tu.	♂☉☾ • Isadora Duncan born, 1878 • Tides {11.0 10.0 •	*Listen!*
28	W.	♂♃☾ • The best tranquilizer is a clear conscience. • {10.7 10.0 •	*You*
29	Th.	Corpus Christi • ☾ at perig. • Patrick Henry born, 1736 • {10.5 10.2 •	*can*
30	Fr.	☾ on Eq. • ☾ at ☍ • Benny Goodman born, 1909 •	*hear it*
31	Sa.	Visit. of Mary • ♂♄☾ • Tides {10.1 10.6 •	*call us.*

1997 JUNE, THE SIXTH MONTH

Nightfall now finds us facing out of our Milky Way and toward the emptiness of intergalactic space. The sky boasts three brilliant stars (Arcturus overhead, Capella in the northwest, and Vega in the northeast), but most of the firmament appears strangely vacant. Mars, still moderately bright, marks a particularly interesting piece of blank celestial real estate halfway up the southern sky. This is the "realm of the galaxies" — the Virgo cluster, of which our own galaxy is just an outlying member. Facing this way we are looking downtown toward the center of our own galactic neighborhood. Summer solstice arrives at 3:20 A.M., EST, on the 21st.

●	New Moon	5th day	2nd hour	3rd min.
☽	First Quarter	12th day	23rd hour	51st min.
○	Full Moon	20th day	14th hour	9th min.
☾	Last Quarter	27th day	7th hour	42nd min.

ADD 1 hour for Daylight Saving Time.

For an explanation of this page, see "How to Use This Almanac," page 34; for values of Key Letters, see Time Correction Tables, page 200.

Day of Year	Day of Month	Day of Week	☉ Rises h. m.	Key	☉ Sets h. m.	Key	Length of Days h. m.	Sun Fast m.	Declination of Sun ° '	Full Sea Boston A.M.	Full Sea Boston P.M.	☽ Rises h. m.	Key	☽ Sets h. m.	Key	☽ Place	☽ Age
152	1	E	4 10	A	7 15	E	15 05	18	22N.07	7½	8	2 A.M. 00	C	3 P.M. 18	D	PSC	26
153	2	M.	4 09	A	7 15	E	15 06	18	22 14	8½	8¾	2 36	C	4 25	E	CET	27
154	3	Tu.	4 09	A	7 16	E	15 07	18	22 22	9½	9¾	3 15	B	5 31	E	ARI	28
155	4	W.	4 09	A	7 17	E	15 08	17	22 29	10½	10½	3 57	B	6 34	E	TAU	29
156	5	Th.	4 08	A	7 17	E	15 09	17	22 35	11¼	11¼	4 43	B	7 32	E	TAU	0
157	6	Fr.	4 08	A	7 18	E	15 10	17	22 42	—	12	5 33	B	8 24	E	TAU	1
158	7	Sa.	4 08	A	7 19	E	15 11	17	22 48	12	12¾	6 27	B	9 11	E	GEM	2
159	8	E	4 07	A	7 19	E	15 12	17	22 53	12¾	1½	7 23	B	9 52	E	GEM	3
160	9	M.	4 07	A	7 20	E	15 13	16	22 58	1½	2¼	8 19	C	10 28	D	CAN	4
161	10	Tu.	4 07	A	7 20	E	15 13	16	23 02	2¼	3	9 16	C	11 01	D	CAN	5
162	11	W.	4 07	A	7 21	E	15 14	16	23 06	3	3¾	10 13	C	11 31	D	LEO	6
163	12	Th.	4 07	A	7 22	E	15 15	16	23 10	4	4½	11 A.M. 10	D	11 P.M. 59	C	SEX	7
164	13	Fr.	4 07	A	7 22	E	15 15	16	23 14	4¾	5½	12 P.M. 07	D	— —	–	LEO	8
165	14	Sa.	4 07	A	7 22	E	15 15	15	23 17	5¾	6¼	1 05	D	12 A.M. 28	C	VIR	9
166	15	E	4 07	A	7 23	E	15 16	15	23 19	6½	7	2 04	D	12 56	C	VIR	10
167	16	M.	4 07	A	7 23	E	15 16	15	23 21	7½	7¾	3 04	E	1 27	B	VIR	11
168	17	Tu.	4 07	A	7 24	E	15 17	15	23 23	8¼	8½	4 06	E	2 01	B	LIB	12
169	18	W.	4 07	A	7 24	E	15 17	15	23 24	9¼	9¼	5 08	E	2 38	B	LIB	13
170	19	Th.	4 07	A	7 24	E	15 17	14	23 25	10	10	6 10	E	3 22	B	OPH	14
171	20	Fr.	4 07	A	7 24	E	15 17	14	23 25	10¾	10¾	7 09	E	4 12	B	OPH	15
172	21	Sa.	4 08	A	7 25	E	15 17	14	23 25	11½	11¾	8 04	E	5 09	B	SAG	16
173	22	E	4 08	A	7 25	E	15 17	14	23 25	—	12¼	8 54	E	6 13	B	SAG	17
174	23	M.	4 08	A	7 25	E	15 17	14	23 25	12½	1	9 38	E	7 21	B	CAP	18
175	24	Tu.	4 08	A	7 25	E	15 17	13	23 23	1¼	2	10 18	D	8 31	C	AQU	19
176	25	W.	4 09	A	7 25	E	15 16	13	23 22	2¼	2¾	10 55	D	9 41	D	AQU	20
177	26	Th.	4 09	A	7 25	E	15 16	13	23 20	3	3¾	11 P.M. 30	D	10 A.M. 52	D	AQU	21
178	27	Fr.	4 09	A	7 25	E	15 16	13	23 17	4	4¾	— —	–	12 P.M. 01	D	PSC	22
179	28	Sa.	4 10	A	7 25	E	15 15	12	23 14	5	5¾	12 A.M. 04	C	1 09	E	PSC	23
180	29	E	4 10	A	7 25	E	15 15	12	23 11	6¼	6¾	12 39	C	2 16	E	PSC	24
181	30	M.	4 11	A	7 25	E	15 14	12	23N.08	7¼	7½	1 A.M. 15	B	3 P.M. 21	E	ARI	25

JUNE hath 30 days. 1997

Wake up, Golden Head! Wake up, Brownie!
Cat-bird wants you in the garden soon.
You and I, butterflies, bobolinks, and clover,
We've a lot to do on the first of June.
– Charles C. D. Roberts

D. M.	D. W.	Dates, Feasts, Fasts, Aspects, Tide Heights	*Weather* ↓
1	E	2nd S. af. P. • Brigham Young born, 1801 •	*Splishes*
2	M.	*The two hardest things to handle in life are failure and success.* • {10.1 / 11.2 •	*splashes*
3	Tu.	☌ ☿ ☾ • Jefferson Davis born, 1808 • {10.1 / 11.4 •	*lightning*
4	W.	Sierra Club organized in San Francisco, 1892 • Battle of Midway began, 1942 •	*flashes.*
5	Th.	St. Boniface • Orthodox Ascension • New ● • {10.1 / 11.3 •	
6	Fr.	☾ rides high • ☌ ♀ ☾ • D-Day, 1944 • {— / 10.0 •	*Powers*
7	Sa.	*The $64,000 Question* made TV debut, 1955 • Jessica Tandy born, 1909 • {11.1 / 9.8 •	*of*
8	E	3rd S. af. P. • Frank Lloyd Wright born, 1867 •	*showers,*
9	M.	Cole Porter born, 1892 • *Marrying for money is the hardest way to get it.* • {10.5 / 9.4 •	*then*
10	Tu.	♃ stat. • Alcoholics Anonymous founded, 1935 • {10.1 / 9.2 •	*turning*
11	W.	St. Barnabas • Shavuot • Jacques Cousteau born, 1910 •	*cool—*
12	Th.	☾ at apo. • *Anne Frank: The Diary of a Young Girl* published, 1952 • {9.3 / 9.0 •	*Kids*
13	Fr.	☾ on Eq. • ☾ at ☊ • ☌ ♂ ☾ • {9.0 / 9.1 •	*can't*
14	Sa.	St. Basil • First U.S. breach of promise suit, 1623 • Tides {8.8 / 9.2 •	*wait*
15	E	4th S. af. P. • Orthodox Pentecost • {8.7 / 9.4 •	*to*
16	M.	*Life is like a blind date. Sometimes you just have to have a little faith.* • Tides {8.7 / 9.7 •	*get*
17	Tu.	Five men arrested at Democratic Party Headquarters, Watergate complex, Washington, D.C., 1972 •	*out*
18	W.	U.S. declared war on Great Britain, 1812 • Paul McCartney born, 1942 • {9.1 / 10.5 •	*of*
19	Th.	First Father's Day observed, Spokane, Washington, 1910 • Tides {9.4 / 10.9 •	*school.*
20	Fr.	Full Rose ○ • Oil began flowing through the trans-Alaska pipeline, 1977 • {9.7 / 11.2 •	*A*
21	Sa.	☾ runs low • Summer Solstice • Martha Washington born, 1731 •	*damp*
22	E	5th S. af. P. • Orthodox All Saints • ☌ ♆ ☾ •	
23	M.	☌ ♅ ☾ • Midsummer Eve • Tides {11.6 / 10.4 •	*farewell*
24	Tu.	Nativ. John the Baptist • ☾ at perig. • ☌ ♃ ☾ •	*to*
25	W.	☿ in sup. ☌ • Prayer in public schools ruled unconstitutional, 1962 • {11.3 / 10.6	*alma*
26	Th.	☾ at ☋ • World's tallest building, the CN Tower, opened, Toronto, 1976	*mater—*
27	Fr.	☾ on Eq. • H. Ross Perot born, 1930 • Tides {10.6 / 10.6 •	*Glory be!*
28	Sa.	St. Irenaeus • ☌ ♄ ☾ • First color TV broadcast, 1951 • {10.2 / 10.6	*It's*
29	E	6th S. af. P. • William James Mayo born, 1861 •	*getting*
30	M.	Sts. Peter & Paul • G.M. unveiled the Corvette, 1953 • {9.6 / 10.8	*hotter!*

Two essential elements for a happy marriage: Separate checking accounts and separate bathrooms.

Farmer's Calendar

Most years, it is sometime in June that the mosquitoes arrive to finish up whatever blood has been left us by the blackflies, whose high season comes a few weeks earlier. The mosquito is altogether grander and more formidable than the fly. Whereas the fly is little more than a black speck that somehow bites, the mosquito is a creature whose menace is evident in its form: a syringe with wings.

Still, the mosquitoes hereabouts are neither particularly large nor particularly aggressive. It's farther north that the mosquito comes into its own, becoming practically a mythical beast — and not for nothing. I well remember a summer along Muscongus Bay, Maine, when mosquitoes the size of barn swallows tormented the day. Maine mosquitoes are too big and too tough to slap. We ended up having to shoot them down with a .22 rifle. That worked all right, but it became an expensive solution.

In these parts mosquitoes come and go. Some years there will be few or none. Fortunately, we needn't be without them, even in an off year. Benjamin Franklin, in *Poor Richard's Almanack* for 1748, gives a recipe for mosquitoes. "In a scarce summer," Ben writes, "any citizen may provide Musketoes sufficient for his own family, by leaving tubs of rain-water uncover'd in his yard; for in such water they lay their eggs, which when hatch'd, . . . put forth legs and wings, leave the water, and fly into your windows." Make of that what you like. Ben worked in Philadelphia, but he was a Boston man by birth and schooling, and he has the anarchic, deadpan Yankee wit that looks you blandly in the face and dares you to doubt.

1997 JULY, THE SEVENTH MONTH

While waiting for the fireworks to start, you may notice a dazzling "star" in the twilight, just left of where the Sun set. This is the return of the Evening Star, Venus, unseen since spring of 1996. Emerging from the Sun's glare, the Evening Star is still a bit faint but will grow brighter and higher between now and Christmas. Naked-eye observers will enjoy a visual feast as this nearest planet dominates the western twilight for the rest of the year. After 10 P.M. look for brilliant Jupiter in the east. Mars remains in Virgo in the southern sky. Earth is at aphelion on the 4th.

●	New Moon	4th day	13th hour	40th min.
☽	First Quarter	12th day	16th hour	44th min.
○	Full Moon	19th day	22nd hour	20th min.
☾	Last Quarter	26th day	13th hour	28th min.

ADD 1 hour for Daylight Saving Time.

For an explanation of this page, see "How to Use This Almanac," page 34; for values of Key Letters, see Time Correction Tables, page 200.

Day of Year	Day of Month	Day of Week	☼ Rises h. m.	Key	☼ Sets h. m.	Key	Length of Days h. m.	Sun Fast m.	Declination of Sun ° '	Full Sea Boston A.M.	Full Sea Boston P.M.	☽ Rises h. m.	Key	☽ Sets h. m.	Key	☽ Place	☽ Age
182	1	Tu.	4 11	A	7 25	E	15 14	12	23N.04	8¼	8½	1 A.M. 55	B	4 P.M. 24	E	TAU	26
183	2	W.	4 12	A	7 25	E	15 13	12	22 59	9¼	9½	2 39	B	5 23	E	TAU	27
184	3	Th.	4 12	A	7 24	E	15 12	11	22 54	10	10¼	3 26	B	6 17	E	TAU	28
185	4	Fr.	4 13	A	7 24	E	15 11	11	22 49	10¾	11	4 18	B	7 06	E	GEM	0
186	5	Sa.	4 13	A	7 24	E	15 11	11	22 43	11½	11¾	5 12	B	7 49	E	GEM	1
187	6	**E**	4 14	A	7 24	E	15 10	11	22 37	—	12¼	6 08	B	8 27	E	CAN	2
188	7	M.	4 15	A	7 23	E	15 08	11	22 31	12½	1	7 06	C	9 02	D	CAN	3
189	8	Tu.	4 15	A	7 23	E	15 08	11	22 25	1	1¾	8 03	C	9 33	D	LEO	4
190	9	W.	4 16	A	7 22	E	15 06	10	22 17	1¾	2½	9 00	C	10 02	D	LEO	5
191	10	Th.	4 17	A	7 22	E	15 05	10	22 10	2½	3	9 56	D	10 30	D	LEO	6
192	11	Fr.	4 18	A	7 21	E	15 03	10	22 01	3¼	3¾	10 53	D	10 58	C	VIR	7
193	12	Sa.	4 18	A	7 21	E	15 03	10	21 53	4¼	4¾	11 A.M. 51	D	11 27	C	VIR	8
194	13	**E**	4 19	A	7 20	E	15 01	10	21 44	5	5½	12 P.M. 49	E	11 P.M. 59	B	VIR	9
195	14	M.	4 20	A	7 20	E	15 00	10	21 35	5¾	6¼	1 49	E	— —	–	LIB	10
196	15	Tu.	4 21	A	7 19	E	14 58	10	21 25	6¾	7	2 51	E	12 A.M. 34	B	LIB	11
197	16	W.	4 21	A	7 18	E	14 57	10	21 16	7¾	8	3 52	E	1 14	B	SCO	12
198	17	Th.	4 22	A	7 18	E	14 56	10	21 06	8½	8¾	4 53	E	2 00	B	OPH	13
199	18	Fr.	4 23	A	7 17	E	14 54	9	20 55	9½	9½	5 51	E	2 53	B	SAG	14
200	19	Sa.	4 24	A	7 16	E	14 52	9	20 45	10¼	10½	6 44	E	3 54	B	SAG	15
201	20	**E**	4 25	A	7 15	E	14 50	9	20 33	11	11¼	7 32	E	5 01	B	SAG	16
202	21	M.	4 26	A	7 15	E	14 49	9	20 22	—	12	8 15	E	6 12	C	AQU	17
203	22	Tu.	4 27	A	7 14	E	14 47	9	20 10	12¼	12¾	8 55	D	7 25	D	AQU	18
204	23	W.	4 28	A	7 13	E	14 45	9	19 57	1	1½	9 31	D	8 38	D	AQU	19
205	24	Th.	4 29	A	7 12	E	14 43	9	19 44	2	2½	10 06	D	9 50	D	PSC	20
206	25	Fr.	4 30	A	7 11	E	14 41	9	19 31	2¾	3¼	10 41	C	11 A.M. 00	D	PSC	21
207	26	Sa.	4 31	A	7 10	D	14 39	9	19 18	3¾	4¼	11 18	C	12 P.M. 08	E	PSC	22
208	27	**E**	4 32	A	7 09	D	14 37	9	19 05	4¾	5¼	11 P.M. 56	B	1 14	E	ARI	23
209	28	M.	4 33	A	7 08	D	14 35	9	18 51	5¾	6¼	— —	–	2 17	E	TAU	24
210	29	Tu.	4 34	A	7 07	D	14 33	9	18 37	7	7¼	12 A.M. 38	B	3 17	E	TAU	25
211	30	W.	4 35	A	7 06	D	14 31	9	18 23	8	8¼	1 24	B	4 12	E	TAU	26
212	31	Th.	4 36	A	7 05	D	14 29	9	18N.08	9	9¼	2 A.M. 13	B	5 P.M. 02	E	ORI	27

JULY hath 31 days. 1997

This is the garden: colors come and go,
frail azures fluttering from the night's outer wing,
strong silent greens serenely lingering,
absolute lights like baths of golden snow.
– e. e. cummings

D. M.	D. W.	Dates, Feasts, Fasts, Aspects, Tide Heights	Weather ↓
1	Tu.	Canada Day • Estee Lauder born, 1908 • Tides {9.5 10.9 •	*Showers*
2	W.	President James A. Garfield shot, 1881 (He died from his injuries September 19.) • {9.5 10.9 •	*can't*
3	Th.	Dog Days begin. • George Washington took command of Continental Army, 1775 •	*spoil*
4	Fr.	Independence Day • ☾ rides high • ⊕ at aphelion • New ● •	
5	Sa.	Henry Cabot Lodge Jr. born, 1902 • Tides {9.6 10.7 •	*a nation's*
6	E	7th S. af. P. • ☌ ♀ ☾ • Tides {— 9.5 •	*pride.*
7	M.	French and English designated as the official languages of Canada, 1969 • Tides {10.6 9.5 •	*Be*
8	Tu.	Elisabeth Kubler-Ross born, 1926 • The Liberty Bell cracked, 1835 •	*careful*
9	W.	☾ at apo. • John D. Rockefeller born, 1839 • Tides {10.1 9.4 •	*when*
10	Th.	☾ at ☊ • If it rains today, it will rain for seven weeks. • {9.7 9.3 •	*you*
11	Fr.	☾ on Eq. • ☌ ♂ ☾ • John Quincy Adams born, 1767 •	*tan*
12	Sa.	*If you give a pig and a boy everything they want, you'll get a good pig and a bad boy.* • {9.0 9.2 •	*your*
13	E	8th S. af. P. • "Live Aid" famine relief concerts held, 1985 •	*hide;*
14	M.	Bastille Day • Gerald R. Ford born, 1913 • Tides {8.6 9.5 •	*grease*
15	Tu.	St. Swithin • The FDA approved the use of aspartame ("Nutrasweet"), 1981 • {8.6 9.7 •	*it*
16	W.	Congress established the District of Columbia, 1790 • Earthquake, 7.7 magnitude, Philippines, 1990	*up*
17	Th.	James Cagney born, 1899 • Cornscateous air is everywhere. • Tides {9.0 10.6 •	*or*
18	Fr.	☾ runs low • Hume Cronyn born, 1911 • Riots in Harlem, 1964 •	*you'll*
19	Sa.	Full Buck ○ • First Special Olympics held, Chicago, 1968 • Tides {9.8 11.5 •	*get*
20	E	9th S. af. P. • ☌ ♆ ☾ • ☌ ♅ ☾ •	*fried.*
21	M.	♆ at ☍ • ☌ ♃ ☾ • ☾ at perig. • {— 10.7 •	*This*
22	Tu.	St. Mary Magdalene • Rose Kennedy born, 1890 • {11.9 11.0	*month's*
23	W.	☾ at ☋ • Don Drysdale born, 1936 • {11.9 11.1 •	*weather's*
24	Th.	☾ on Eq. • *As the days begin to shorten, So the heat begins to scorch 'em.* •	*Jekyll*
25	Fr.	St. James • ☌ ♄ ☾ • First airplane crossing of English Channel, 1909 •	*and*
26	Sa.	St. Ann • Carl Jung born, 1875 • Tides {10.5 10.9 •	*Hyde —*
27	E	10th S. af. P. • U.S. Dept. of State established, 1789 •	*hottish,*
28	M.	Beatrix Potter born, 1866 • First singing telegram delivered, 1933 •	*coolish,*
29	Tu.	Sts. Mary & Martha • ♅ at ☍ • Tides {9.3 10.4 •	*it*
30	W.	Casey Stengel born, 1891 • Emily Brontë born, 1818 • Tides {9.1 10.4 •	*can't*
31	Th.	☾ rides high • U.S. Patent Office issued first patent, 1790 • {9.2 10.4 •	*decide!*

Farmer's Calendar

It's curious how extremes of temperature at opposite ends of the thermometer seem to converge in the effects they produce on people and their doings. A couple of summers back, a spell of hot weather visited my section. Very hot weather. All over the state, temperatures reached 100° F. Everybody knows summer doesn't do that in Vermont; indeed, those 100-plus-or-minus readings were 50-year highs in many towns.

What did people do? They reacted with a kind of stunned silence. They lay low. In the furnace of the afternoon, the streets of the nearest good-size town to me were nearly empty of people. Anybody who had to go out moved slowly, sluggishly. Even cars seemed to roll reluctantly along the streets. People reacted to 100 much as they would react to 25 below zero. They shut down, slowed, stopped, disappeared.

It wasn't only people who responded to the heat by making themselves scarce. In the woods, the birds were silent. Horses, cattle, and sheep abandoned their pastures to wait in the shade at the edges. The dogs were nowhere to be seen. Even the cats were useless. The sun came down with a flat, brassy glare, like a torch, making light and shade painful in their contrast. On most bright, hot days the flower beds at this house are full of butterflies. Now one or two flitted listlessly across the yard, then crashed. The flowers themselves seemed to close their petals against the worst of the heat or else to flop wearily on their stems. As in the deepest cold, nature seemed to take the heat with a shocked, speechless surprise, as though the weather had with no warning reached out and slapped it in the face.

1997 AUGUST, THE EIGHTH MONTH

A month of sky treasures! From the 2nd through the 4th see Mars graze the blue star Spica in the south. On the 5th watch Venus, Mercury, and a slender crescent Moon gather low in the twilight a half hour after sunset. August 9th is Jupiter's opposition when the giant planet stands closest to Earth. The night of the 11th-12th offers this year's best meteor shower. The Moon will set before midnight, so viewing will not be a problem when the Perseid meteors become more numerous. Peaking before dawn, Perseids are fast meteors that commonly display glowing trails.

●	New Moon	3rd day	3rd hour	14th min.
☽	First Quarter	11th day	7th hour	42nd min.
○	Full Moon	18th day	5th hour	55th min.
☾	Last Quarter	24th day	21st hour	23rd min.

ADD 1 hour for Daylight Saving Time.

For an explanation of this page, see "How to Use This Almanac," page 34; for values of Key Letters, see Time Correction Tables, page 200.

Day of Year	Day of Month	Day of Week	☉ Rises h. m.	Key	☉ Sets h. m.	Key	Length of Days h. m.	Sun Fast m.	Declination of Sun ° '	Full Sea Boston A.M.	Full Sea Boston P.M.	☽ Rises h. m.	Key	☽ Sets h. m.	Key	☽ Place	☽ Age
213	1	Fr.	4 37	A	7 04	D	14 27	9	17 N.52	9¾	10	3 A.M. 06	B	5 P.M. 47	E	GEM	28
214	2	Sa.	4 38	A	7 02	D	14 24	9	17 37	10½	10¾	4 01	B	6 27	E	CAN	29
215	3	E	4 39	A	7 01	D	14 22	9	17 21	11¼	11¼	4 57	C	7 02	E	CAN	0
216	4	M.	4 40	A	7 00	D	14 20	10	17 05	—	12	5 54	C	7 35	D	LEO	1
217	5	Tu.	4 41	A	6 59	D	14 18	10	16 49	12	12½	6 51	C	8 05	D	LEO	2
218	6	W.	4 42	A	6 57	D	14 15	10	16 32	12¾	1¼	7 48	D	8 33	D	LEO	3
219	7	Th.	4 43	A	6 56	D	14 13	10	16 15	1¼	1¾	8 45	D	9 01	C	VIR	4
220	8	Fr.	4 44	A	6 55	D	14 11	10	15 58	2	2½	9 41	D	9 29	C	VIR	5
221	9	Sa.	4 45	A	6 54	D	14 09	10	15 41	2¾	3¼	10 39	D	9 59	C	VIR	6
222	10	E	4 46	A	6 52	D	14 06	10	15 24	3½	4	11 A.M. 37	E	10 32	B	VIR	7
223	11	M.	4 47	A	6 51	D	14 04	10	15 06	4¼	4¾	12 P.M. 36	E	11 09	B	LIB	8
224	12	Tu.	4 48	A	6 49	D	14 01	11	14 48	5¼	5½	1 36	E	11 P.M. 51	B	LIB	9
225	13	W.	4 49	A	6 48	D	13 59	11	14 30	6¼	6½	2 36	E	— —	–	OPH	10
226	14	Th.	4 50	A	6 47	D	13 57	11	14 11	7	7¼	3 34	E	12 A.M. 39	B	OPH	11
227	15	Fr.	4 51	B	6 45	D	13 54	11	13 53	8	8¼	4 29	E	1 35	B	SAG	12
228	16	Sa.	4 52	B	6 44	D	13 52	11	13 34	9	9¼	5 20	E	2 38	B	SAG	13
229	17	E	4 54	B	6 42	D	13 48	11	13 14	9¾	10	6 06	E	3 48	B	CAP	14
230	18	M.	4 55	B	6 41	D	13 46	12	12 55	10¾	11	6 48	D	5 01	C	CAP	15
231	19	Tu.	4 56	B	6 39	D	13 43	12	12 35	11½	11¾	7 27	D	6 15	D	AQU	16
232	20	W.	4 57	B	6 38	D	13 41	12	12 15	—	12¼	8 04	C	7 30	D	PSC	17
233	21	Th.	4 58	B	6 36	D	13 38	12	11 55	12¾	1¼	8 41	C	8 43	D	CET	18
234	22	Fr.	4 59	B	6 34	D	13 35	13	11 35	1½	2	9 18	C	9 55	D	PSC	19
235	23	Sa.	5 00	B	6 33	D	13 33	13	11 15	2½	3	9 56	B	11 A.M. 04	E	CET	20
236	24	E	5 01	B	6 31	D	13 30	13	10 55	3½	4	10 38	B	12 P.M. 09	E	ARI	21
237	25	M.	5 02	B	6 30	D	13 28	13	10 34	4½	5	11 P.M. 23	B	1 11	E	TAU	22
238	26	Tu.	5 03	B	6 28	D	13 25	14	10 14	5½	6	— —	–	2 08	E	TAU	23
239	27	W.	5 04	B	6 26	D	13 22	14	9 53	6¾	7	12 A.M. 11	B	2 59	E	ORI	24
240	28	Th.	5 05	B	6 25	D	13 20	14	9 31	7¾	8	1 02	B	3 46	E	GEM	25
241	29	Fr.	5 06	B	6 23	D	13 17	15	9 10	8½	8¾	1 56	B	4 27	E	GEM	26
242	30	Sa.	5 07	B	6 21	D	13 14	15	8 48	9½	9¾	2 52	B	5 04	D	CAN	27
243	31	E	5 08	B	6 20	D	13 12	15	8 N.27	10¼	10¼	3 A.M. 48	C	5 P.M. 37	D	LEO	28

AUGUST hath 31 days. 1997

Sing a song of Summer,
The world is nearly still,
The mill-pond has gone to sleep,
And so has the mill.
— *Cosmo Monkhouse*

Farmer's Calendar

Every year I remember to do so, I plant a row of sunflowers in my vegetable patch; and every year I forget, I miss them. The sunflower seems to me to be one of the flowers that even a small and casual garden should by no means be without. I understand there are 70 species of sunflower (genus *Helianthus*), perennials and annuals, wild and cultivated, some grown for crops, most for fun. Some of these, the perennial species in particular, are demure and well-mannered flowers, flowers of good taste. They do not interest me. I like the big, loud annuals that produce flowers the size of dinner plates, having raggedy, butter-yellow petals and fat, bulging centers. Beside their reticent cousins, these flowers come on like an excited and overfriendly retriever. They are essential in the garden because of their high spirits and because of a symbolic, representative quality that they have. The sunflower is all flowers, the epitome. If you give a little kid a box of crayons and ask him to draw a flower, a sunflower is what you'll get.

For all its exuberance and fun, there is something touching about the sunflower as well, something to do with its famous turning after the Sun. You can see its heavy flowerhead bend on its stalk to follow the Sun through its daily arc. That faithful, mechanical movement has a sadness. The poet Blake noticed it: "Ah, sunflower! weary of time," he wrote. Perhaps its faint sorrow is another aspect of the sunflower's role in the garden: It marks the passing summer. Especially at this time of year, the Sun it watches is going away unmistakably farther each day, and where it's going the rooted sunflower can't follow.

D.M.	D.W.	Dates, Feasts, Fasts, Aspects, Tide Heights	Weather ↓
1	Fr.	**Lammas Day** • Francis Scott Key born, 1779 • Tides {9.2 / 10.5} •	*In*
2	Sa.	♄ stat. • First street mailboxes installed, Boston and New York, 1858 • {9.3 / 10.5} •	*for*
3	E	**11th S. af. P.** • New ● • ☿ Gr. Elong. (27° E.) •	*a*
4	M.	*Behold the guarantee — the bold print giveth and the fine print taketh away.* • {— / 9.5} •	*soaking*
5	Tu.	♂♀♌ • First traffic light installed, Cleveland, 1914 • Tides {10.4 / 9.6} •	*and*
6	W.	**Transfiguration** • ♌ at ☊ • ♂♀♌ •	*we're*
7	Th.	**Name of Jesus** • ♌ on Eq. • Garrison Keillor born, 1942 • {10.0 / 9.6} •	*not*
8	Fr.	**St. Dominic** • 105° F, Denver, Colorado, 1878 • Tides {9.7 / 9.5} •	*joking.*
9	Sa.	♃ at ☍ • ♂♂♌ • Tides {9.4 / 9.5} •	*Gadzooks!*
10	E	**12th S. af. P.** • Herbert Hoover born, 1874 • {9.1 / 9.4} •	*Look*
11	M.	**St. Clare** • Dog Days end. • Andrew Carnegie died, 1919 • {8.8 / 9.4} •	*at*
12	Tu.	Baseball strike began, 1994 • *Ambition is the grand enemy of all peace.* • {8.6 / 9.5} •	*those*
13	W.	The border was sealed and construction begun on the Berlin Wall, 1961 •	*cukes!!*
14	Th.	FDA banned cyclamates, 1970 • Social Security Act passed, 1935 • {8.8 / 10.2} •	*Great*
15	Fr.	**Assumption** • ♌ runs low • Julia Child born, 1912 • Tides {9.2 / 10.7} •	*for*
16	Sa.	♇ stat. • ♂ ♅ ♌ • ☿ stat. • Tides {9.7 / 11.2} •	*hikes*
17	E	**13th S. af. P.** • ♂ ☌ ☾ • ♂ ♃ ☾ • Cat Nights begin. •	*and*
18	M.	**Full Sturgeon** ○ • First issue *Saturday Evening Post* published, 1821 •	*and*
19	Tu.	♌ at ☍ • ♌ perig. • Tides {11.3 / 12.1} •	*mountain*
20	W.	♌ on Eq. • Jim Reeves born, 1923 • Tides {11.6} •	*bikes.*
21	Th.	♂♄☾ • Christopher Robin Milne born, 1920 •	*Golfers*
22	Fr.	Mormon (Tabernacle) Choir gave first public performance, 1847 • {11.6 / 11.6} •	*put*
23	Sa.	*Freedom exists only where people take care of the government.* • {11.0 / 11.3} •	*away*
24	E	**14th S. af. P.** • Sabin polio vaccine approved, 1960 • {10.4 / 10.9} •	*their*
25	M.	U.S. and French troops liberated Paris, 1944 • Tides {9.8 / 10.5} •	*putters*
26	Tu.	Lee De Forest, "Father of Radio," born, 1873 • Albert Sabin born, 1906 • {9.3 / 10.2} •	*when*
27	W.	♌ high • Mother Teresa born, 1910 • {9.0 / 10.0} •	*lightning*
28	Th.	**St. Augustine of Hippo** • March on Washington, 1963 •	*flickers*
29	Fr.	2.5" snow atop Mount Washington in New Hampshire, 1965 • Tides {9.0 / 10.0} •	*and*
30	Sa.	*The only true happiness comes from squandering ourselves for a purpose.* • {9.2 / 10.1} •	*thunder*
31	E	**15th S. af. P.** • ☿ in inf. ♂ • {9.4 / 10.2} •	*mutters.*

1997   SEPTEMBER, The Ninth Month

Jupiter stands low in the southeast at nightfall and is out all night long. This is the best time to observe the mysterious planet, now just a few weeks past opposition. Appearing at magnitude -2.5 (some ten times brighter than anything else in the midnight sky), its steady white dazzle dominates the southern heavens. Meanwhile, after midmonth, early risers can observe Mercury 45 minutes before sunrise, very low in the east, making its best morning appearance of the year. The autumnal equinox occurs at 6:56 P.M., EST, on the 22nd.

● New Moon	1st day	18th hour	52nd min.
☽ First Quarter	9th day	20th hour	31st min.
○ Full Moon	16th day	13th hour	50th min.
☾ Last Quarter	23rd day	8th hour	35th min.

ADD 1 hour for Daylight Saving Time.

For an explanation of this page, see "How to Use This Almanac," page 34; for values of Key Letters, see Time Correction Tables, page 200.

Day of Year	Day of Month	Day of Week	☉ Rises h. m.	Key	☉ Sets h. m.	Key	Length of Days h. m.	Sun Fast m.	Declination of Sun °	Full Sea Boston A.M.	P.M.	☽ Rises h. m.	Key	☽ Sets h. m.	Key	Place	Age
244	1	M.	5 09	B	6 18	D	13 09	15	8 N.05	10¾	11	4 ♏45	C	6 ♏07	D	LEO	0
245	2	Tu.	5 10	B	6 16	D	13 06	16	7 43	11½	11½	5 42	C	6 36	D	LEO	1
246	3	W.	5 12	B	6 15	D	13 03	16	7 21	—	12	6 38	D	7 04	C	VIR	2
247	4	Th.	5 13	B	6 13	D	13 00	16	6 59	12¼	12½	7 35	D	7 33	C	VIR	3
248	5	Fr.	5 14	B	6 11	D	12 57	17	6 36	1	1¼	8 32	D	8 02	C	VIR	4
249	6	Sa.	5 15	B	6 09	D	12 54	17	6 14	1½	1¾	9 29	E	8 33	C	VIR	5
250	7	E	5 16	B	6 08	D	12 52	17	5 52	2¼	2½	10 27	E	9 08	B	LIB	6
251	8	M.	5 17	B	6 06	D	12 49	18	5 29	3	3¼	11 ♏26	E	9 47	B	LIB	7
252	9	Tu.	5 18	B	6 04	C	12 46	18	5 06	3¾	4	12 ♏24	E	10 31	B	OPH	8
253	10	W.	5 19	B	6 02	C	12 43	18	4 44	4¾	5	1 21	E	11 ♏22	B	OPH	9
254	11	Th.	5 20	B	6 01	C	12 41	19	4 21	5½	6	2 16	E	— —	—	SAG	10
255	12	Fr.	5 21	B	5 59	C	12 38	19	3 58	6½	7	3 07	E	12 ♏20	B	SAG	11
256	13	Sa.	5 22	B	5 57	C	12 35	20	3 35	7½	7¾	3 55	E	1 24	C	CAP	12
257	14	E	5 23	B	5 55	C	12 32	20	3 12	8½	8¾	4 38	E	2 34	C	AQU	13
258	15	M.	5 24	B	5 54	C	12 30	20	2 49	9½	9¾	5 19	D	3 47	D	AQU	14
259	16	Tu.	5 25	B	5 52	C	12 27	21	2 26	10¼	10¾	5 57	D	5 02	D	AQU	15
260	17	W.	5 26	B	5 50	C	12 24	21	2 02	11	11½	6 34	C	6 17	D	PSC	16
261	18	Th.	5 27	B	5 48	C	12 21	21	1 39	—	12	7 12	C	7 32	E	PSC	17
262	19	Fr.	5 28	B	5 47	C	12 19	22	1 16	12½	12¾	7 52	B	8 45	E	PSC	18
263	20	Sa.	5 29	C	5 45	C	12 16	22	0 53	1¼	1½	8 33	B	9 54	E	ARI	19
264	21	E	5 31	C	5 43	C	12 12	22	0 30	2¼	2½	9 18	B	11 ♏00	E	TAU	20
265	22	M.	5 32	C	5 41	C	12 09	23	0 N.06	3	3½	10 06	B	12 ♏00	E	TAU	21
266	23	Tu.	5 33	C	5 40	C	12 07	23	0 s.16	4	4½	10 57	B	12 55	E	TAU	22
267	24	W.	5 34	C	5 38	C	12 04	23	0 40	5¼	5½	11 ♏51	B	1 44	E	GEM	23
268	25	Th.	5 35	C	5 36	C	12 01	24	1 03	6¼	6½	— —	—	2 27	E	GEM	24
269	26	Fr.	5 36	C	5 34	C	11 58	24	1 27	7¼	7½	12 ♏46	B	3 05	E	CAN	25
270	27	Sa.	5 37	C	5 32	C	11 55	24	1 50	8¼	8½	1 42	C	3 39	D	CAN	26
271	28	E	5 38	C	5 31	B	11 53	25	2 13	9	9¼	2 39	C	4 10	D	LEO	27
272	29	M.	5 39	C	5 29	B	11 50	25	2 36	9¾	10	3 36	C	4 39	D	LEO	28
273	30	Tu.	5 40	C	5 27	B	11 47	25	3 s.00	10¼	10½	4 ♏32	D	5 ♏08	D	LEO	29

SEPTEMBER hath 30 days. 1997

Now the beautiful business of summer is over,
Earth wraps herself in a bright, leaf-patterned shawl.
The hives cement the prodigal juice of the clover
And spendthrift gold is hoarded in bin and stall.
– Jean S. Untermeyer

D. M.	D. W.	Dates, Feasts, Fasts, Aspects, Tide Heights	*Weather* ↓
1	M.	**Labor Day** • New ● • Eclipse ⊙ • {9.6 10.2 •	*Apples*
2	Tu.	☾ at ☊ • ☾ at apo. • 126° F, Mecca, California, 1950 • {9.7 10.2 •	*are*
3	W.	☾ on Eq. • Frederick Douglass began his escape to freedom, 1838 • {— 9.8 •	*red*
4	Th.	George Eastman patented his Kodak No. 1 camera, 1888 • Tides {10.1 9.9 •	*and*
5	Fr.	☌♀☾ • Jesse James born, 1847 • {9.9 9.8 •	*schoolbuses*
6	Sa.	*What you can't get out of get into wholeheartedly.* • Tides {9.7 9.8 •	*yellow;*
7	E	**16th S. af. P.** • ☌♂☾ • {9.4 9.7 •	*autumn*
8	M.	Kennedy Center for the Performing Arts opened, Washington, D.C., 1971 • {9.1 9.6 •	*wine*
9	Tu.	☿ stat. • The designation "United States" became official, 1776 • {8.8 9.6 •	*is*
10	W.	Snow in Johannesburg, South Africa; first in 17 years, 1981 • Tides {8.7 9.7 •	*dry*
11	Th.	☾ runs low • *Better a friendly refusal than an unwilling promise.* • {8.7 9.9 •	*and*
12	Fr.	☌♆☾ • H. L. Mencken born, 1880 • Tides {9.0 10.3 •	*mellow.*
13	Sa.	☌♅☾ • ☌♃☾ • Roald Dahl born, 1916 • {9.5 10.7 •	*From*
14	E	**17th S. af. P.** • Margaret Sanger born, 1879 •	*Eastport,*
15	M.	**Holy Cross** • Gaylord Perry born, 1938 • Tides {10.8 11.7 •	*Maine,*
16	Tu.	☾ at perig. • **Full Harvest** ○ • ☾ at ☋ • ☿ Gr. Elong. (18° W.) •	
17	W.	☾ on Eq. • Ember Day • Camp David accord signed between Egypt and Israel, 1978 •	*to*
18	Th.	Occn. ♄ by ☾ • Greta Garbo born, 1905 • Tides {— 12.1 •	*old*
19	Fr.	Ember Day • Storm from the south today means a mild winter. •	*Nantucket,*
20	Sa.	Ember Day • Jelly Roll Morton born, 1885 • Electric range patented, 1859 •	*rain*
21	E	**18th S. af. P.** • H. G. Wells born, 1866 • Tides {10.8 11.3 •	*is*
22	M.	**St. Matthew** • **Autumnal Equinox** • St. Matthew brings on the cold dew.	*coming*
23	Tu.	Lewis and Clark returned from their expedition, 1806 • Tides {9.6 10.2 •	*down*
24	W.	☾ rides high • -9° F, Yellowstone Park, caused great crop destruction, 1926 • {9.1 9.8 •	*in*
25	Th.	*Fly the pleasure that will bite tomorrow.* • Barbara Walters born, 1931 •	*buckets.*
26	Fr.	George Gershwin born, 1898 • T. S. Eliot born, 1888 • Tides {8.9 9.6 •	*Stick*
27	Sa.	*Be not the first by whom the new are tried, Nor yet the last to lay the old aside.* •	*around*
28	E	**19th S. af. P.** • Al Capp born, 1909 • Tides {9.3 9.8 •	*for*
29	M.	**St. Michael** • ☾ at ☊ • ☾ at apo. • {9.6 9.9	*summer's*
30	Tu.	**St. Jerome** • Heavy snow U.S.-Quebec border, 1835 • {9.8 10.0	*encore.*

Consider that people are like tea bags. They don't know their own strength until they get into hot water. – Dan McKinnon

Farmer's Calendar

"We need the rain," we like to tell each other, and perhaps we do; but a point is reached past which I begin to ask myself, Who is *we?*

It's at this time of year, about the fall equinox, when strings of soaking days are common, that the benefit of rainy weather is most confidently asserted. We need the rain. Sure we do. July and August are dry. Farmers and gardeners need the rain. They need a day of rain, two days. Do they need four? Five? They do not. And in truth, as far as I can tell, farmers and gardeners never get the weather they like for more than two days. Soon enough they'll begin to complain of unworkable ground, damp, rot, as eloquently as the week before they complained of drought. They need the rain. But enough is enough.

Who else needs the rain? Not I. I dislike the stuff. I would rather deal with a foot of snow than with a spell of rain that would hardly fill a half cup. Rain as material, so to speak, seems to me entirely unsatisfactory. What can you do with it? You can't shovel it, sweep it, or otherwise move it out of your way. You can't watch your dogs try to mine it. You can't make it into snowballs to throw playfully at your loved ones. All you can do is watch it come down and prepare to remove to high ground. And as I am already on high ground, I lack, with respect to rain, even a convincing cause of anxiety.

But, as Saint Matthew observed of the rain, it falleth on the just and the unjust, and it quitteth not until it's damn good and ready. Therefore we may as well agree we need the rain, as an expression not of science, not of gratitude, but of resignation.

1997   OCTOBER, The Tenth Month

Saturn reaches opposition on the 9th. Its rings now tilted majestically, the surreal planet is better placed than it has been in 12 years. Rising at sunset and in the south around midnight, it is the only bright star (but not superbright, like Jupiter) in that section of the heavens. At least 30x is needed to view the rings, putting that awesome sight out of binocular range. Meanwhile, evening twilight continues to feature Venus. Daylight Saving Time ends at 2:00 A.M. on the 26th.

● New Moon	1st day	11th hour	51st min.
☽ First Quarter	9th day	7th hour	22nd min.
○ Full Moon	15th day	22nd hour	46th min.
☾ Last Quarter	22nd day	23rd hour	48th min.
● New Moon	31st day	5th hour	1st min.

ADD 1 hour for Daylight Saving Time until 2 A.M., October 26th.

For an explanation of this page, see "How to Use This Almanac," page 34; for values of Key Letters, see Time Correction Tables, page 200.

Day of Year	Day of Month	Day of Week	☉ Rises h. m.	Key	☉ Sets h. m.	Key	Length of Days h. m.	Sun Fast m.	Declination of Sun ° '	Full Sea Boston A.M.	Full Sea Boston P.M.	☽ Rises h. m.	Key	☽ Sets h. m.	Key	☽ Place	☽ Age
274	1	W.	5 41	C	5 25	B	11 44	26	3 s.23	10¾	11¼	5♒29	D	5♏36	C	VIR	0
275	2	Th.	5 42	C	5 24	B	11 42	26	3 46	11½	11¾	6 26	D	6 05	C	VIR	1
276	3	Fr.	5 44	C	5 22	B	11 38	26	4 09	—	12	7 24	E	6 36	B	VIR	2
277	4	Sa.	5 45	C	5 20	B	11 35	27	4 33	12½	12¾	8 22	E	7 09	B	LIB	3
278	5	**E**	5 46	C	5 19	B	11 33	27	4 56	1	1¼	9 20	E	7 46	B	LIB	4
279	6	M.	5 47	C	5 17	B	11 30	27	5 19	1¾	2	10 18	E	8 28	B	SCO	5
280	7	Tu.	5 48	C	5 15	B	11 27	28	5 42	2½	2¾	11♒15	E	9 16	B	OPH	6
281	8	W.	5 49	C	5 14	B	11 25	28	6 05	3¼	3½	12♒09	E	10 09	B	SAG	7
282	9	Th.	5 50	C	5 12	B	11 22	28	6 27	4¼	4½	1 00	E	11♏09	B	SAG	8
283	10	Fr.	5 51	C	5 10	B	11 19	28	6 50	5¼	5½	1 47	E	— —	—	SAG	9
284	11	Sa.	5 53	C	5 09	B	11 16	29	7 13	6¼	6½	2 30	E	12♏14	C	AQU	10
285	12	**E**	5 54	C	5 07	B	11 13	29	7 35	7¼	7½	3 11	D	1 24	C	CAP	11
286	13	M.	5 55	C	5 05	B	11 10	29	7 58	8	8½	3 49	D	2 36	C	AQU	12
287	14	Tu.	5 56	D	5 04	B	11 08	29	8 20	9	9½	4 26	D	3 49	D	PSC	13
288	15	W.	5 57	D	5 02	B	11 05	30	8 42	9¾	10¼	5 03	C	5 04	D	CET	14
289	16	Th.	5 58	D	5 00	B	11 02	30	9 04	10¾	11¼	5 42	C	6 18	E	PSC	15
290	17	Fr.	5 59	D	4 59	B	11 00	30	9 26	11½	—	6 24	B	7 31	E	ARI	16
291	18	Sa.	6 01	D	4 57	B	10 56	30	9 48	12	12¼	7 08	B	8 41	E	TAU	17
292	19	**E**	6 02	D	4 56	B	10 54	31	10 09	1	1¼	7 56	B	9 46	E	TAU	18
293	20	M.	6 03	D	4 54	B	10 51	31	10 31	1¾	2	8 48	B	10 45	E	TAU	19
294	21	Tu.	6 04	D	4 53	B	10 49	31	10 52	2¾	3	9 42	B	11♏38	E	GEM	20
295	22	W.	6 05	D	4 51	B	10 46	31	11 13	3¾	4	10 38	B	12♏24	E	GEM	21
296	23	Th.	6 07	D	4 50	B	10 43	31	11 34	4¾	5	11♏35	B	1 05	C	CAN	22
297	24	Fr.	6 08	D	4 48	B	10 40	31	11 55	5¾	6	— —	—	1 40	C	CAN	23
298	25	Sa.	6 09	D	4 47	B	10 38	31	12 16	6¾	7	12♏32	C	2 13	D	LEO	24
299	26	**E**	6 10	D	4 45	B	10 35	32	12 37	7½	7¾	1 28	C	2 42	D	LEO	25
300	27	M.	6 11	D	4 44	B	10 33	32	12 57	8¼	8¾	2 25	C	3 11	D	LEO	26
301	28	Tu.	6 13	D	4 43	B	10 30	32	13 17	9	9½	3 22	D	3 39	C	VIR	27
302	29	W.	6 14	D	4 41	B	10 27	32	13 37	9¾	10	4 19	D	4 07	C	VIR	28
303	30	Th.	6 15	D	4 40	B	10 25	32	13 57	10¼	10¾	5 17	D	4 37	C	VIR	29
304	31	Fr.	6 16	D	4 39	B	10 23	32	14 s.16	11	11¼	6♏15	E	5♏10	B	VIR	0

OCTOBER hath 31 days. 1997

The trees are in their autumn beauty,
The woodland paths are dry,
Under the October twilight the water
Mirrors a still sky.
– *William Butler Yeats*

D. M.	D. W.	Dates, Feasts, Fasts, Aspects, Tide Heights	*Weather* ↓
1	W.	St. Remigius • ☾ on Eq. • New ● • Jimmy Carter born, 1924 •	*It*
2	Th.	Rosh Hashanah • *The Twilight Zone* made TV debut, 1959 •	*doesn't*
3	Fr.	First magnetic videotape recording was produced by Bing Crosby Enterprises, 1952 • {— / 10.2}	*seem*
4	Sa.	St. Francis of Assisi • Rutherford B. Hayes born, 1822 • {9.8 / 10.1}	*like*
5	E	20th S. af. P. • ☌ ♀ ☾ • Tides {9.6 / 10.1} •	*fall*
6	M.	☌ ♂ ☾ • Anwar Sadat assassinated, 1981 • Tides {9.4 / 10.0}	*at all —*
7	Tu.	*What you dislike in another take care to correct in yourself.* • Desmond Tutu born, 1931 •	*in*
8	W.	☾ runs low • ♃ stat. • ♆ stat. • {9.0 / 9.8} •	*summary,*
9	Th.	♄ at ☍ • Benjamin Banneker, "first black man of science," died, 1806 • {8.9 / 9.8} •	*it's*
10	Fr.	☌ ♆ ☾ • ☌ ♅ ☾ • Tides {9.0 / 10.0} •	*summery.*
11	Sa.	Yom Kippur • ☌ ♃ ☾ • Eleanor Roosevelt born, 1884 • {9.4 / 10.3}	*Is*
12	E	21st S. af. P. • Luciano Pavarotti born, 1935 •	*this warm*
13	M.	Columbus Day • Thanksgiving Day (Canada) • ☾ at ☋ • ☿ in sup. ☌	
14	Tu.	☾ on Eq. • ♅ stat. • ☾ at perig. • {11.2 / 11.4} •	*October*
15	W.	☌ ♄ ☾ • Full Hunter's ○ • Tides {11.8 / 11.6} •	*born*
16	Th.	Succoth • *You can't get enough of what you really don't want.* • Tides {12.2 / 11.6} •	*of*
17	Fr.	St. Ignatius of Antioch • Arthur Miller born, 1915 • {12.3 / —} •	*CO_2*
18	Sa.	St. Luke • Saint Luke's little summer • Thomas Edison died, 1931 • {11.4 / 12.1} •	*and*
19	E	22nd S. af. P. • Tides {11.0 / 11.8} •	*methane?*
20	M.	U.S.-Canada border set at 49th parallel from Lake of the Woods to the Rockies, 1818 • {10.5 / 11.2} •	*Or*
21	Tu.	☾ rides high • Americans won all 5 Nobel prizes for 1976. • {9.9 / 10.6} •	*are*
22	W.	Complete Torah published in English for first time, 1952 • Annette Funicello born, 1942 •	*we*
23	Th.	Michael Crichton born, 1942 • Swallows depart San Juan Capistrano • {9.1 / 9.6}	*singed*
24	Fr.	*Advice is what we ask for when we already know the answer but wish we didn't.* • {8.9 / 9.3} •	*by*
25	Sa.	St. Crispin • 5" snow, Worcester, Mass., 1962 • {8.9 / 9.2} •	*birch's*
26	E	23rd S. af. P. • ☌ ♀ ♂ • **Daylight Saving Time ends, 2 A.M.** •	
27	M.	☾ at ☊ • ☾ at apo. • John Cleese born, 1939 • Tides {9.4 / 9.4} •	*tinge*
28	Tu.	Sts. Simon & Jude • ☾ on Eq. • Jonas Salk born, 1914 • {9.7 / 9.5} •	*and*
29	W.	New York Stock Exchange crashed, 1929 • Tides {10.0 / 9.6} •	*maple's*
30	Th.	*Some people are in such a hurry to get to the good life that they rush right past it.* • {10.2 / 9.7} •	*ruddy*
31	Fr.	All Hallows Eve • New ● • Tides {10.3 / 9.7} •	*flame?*

Farmer's Calendar

The summer birds are gone. The last robin, bluebird, swallow have surreptitiously decamped. In the spring, it seems, they arrive in big, noisy flights full of greeting, but when they turn south they go by ones and twos, they slip away, almost as if they were a little embarrassed to be leaving the rest of us up here to face the winter while they take it easy in the islands.

According to the migration maps, the robin favors Florida in winter, the tree swallow, Cuba and the Caribbean. It took a long time to figure that out. The annual disappearance of the common birds of passage remained a mystery longer than seems necessary. What happened to the birds in winter? Nobody knew. For most of history, the best scientists of their times believed birds hibernated like bats and groundhogs. Not until the last century was it known that the same species returned to the same winter ranges year after year.

I have always thought it strange that the solution to the mystery of migration, in its main outlines, should have taken centuries to find. After all, the robins, the warblers, and the rest aren't hiding out down there. They're easy to spot. And since the Renaissance, navigators and other travelers have frequented the tropics of both hemispheres where migratory birds winter. Those old, bold navigators weren't paying attention, I guess. If you are seeking a mountain made of silver, or a city made of gold, or a broad passage to the East, you learn to look far away. You miss the unremarkable creatures that fly about the eaves — though they are really there, and the mountains and cities are really not.

1997   NOVEMBER, The Eleventh Month

An extraordinary gathering of planets appears at nightfall. While their most dense concentration will occur early next month, now we can observe every planet in the solar system at once! Pluto requires a powerful telescope and good star chart, while Neptune and Uranus demand a telescope or binoculars. The rest stand brightly after sunset, stretched leftward along the solar system's plane (the zodiac) from southwest to southeast. At nightfall, Venus is brightest and lowest, Jupiter far to its left, while less brilliant Saturn rises in the southeast. On the 3rd the Moon, Mars, and Venus form a striking triangle in the southwest 45 minutes after sunset.

☽ First Quarter	7th day	16th hour	43rd min.
○ Full Moon	14th day	9th hour	12th min.
☾ Last Quarter	21st day	18th hour	58th min.
● New Moon	29th day	21st hour	14th min.

For an explanation of this page, see "How to Use This Almanac," page 34; for values of Key Letters, see Time Correction Tables, page 200.

Day of Year	Day of Month	Day of Week	☉ Rises h. m.	Key	☉ Sets h. m.	Key	Length of Days h. m.	Sun Fast m.	Declination of Sun °	Full Sea Boston A.M.	Full Sea Boston P.M.	☽ Rises h. m.	Key	☽ Sets h. m.	Key	Place	☽ Age
305	1	Sa.	6 18	D	4 37	B	10 19	32	14s.35	11½	—	7ᴍ14	E	5ᴾᴍ46	B	LIB	1
306	2	E	6 19	D	4 36	B	10 17	32	14 54	12	12¼	8 13	E	6 27	B	LIB	2
307	3	M.	6 20	D	4 35	B	10 15	32	15 13	12¾	12¾	9 11	E	7 13	B	OPH	3
308	4	Tu.	6 21	D	4 34	B	10 13	32	15 31	1¼	1½	10 06	E	8 04	B	SAG	4
309	5	W.	6 23	D	4 32	B	10 09	32	15 49	2¼	2¼	10 58	E	9 02	B	SAG	5
310	6	Th.	6 24	D	4 31	B	10 07	32	16 07	3	3¼	11ᴀ45	E	10 04	B	SAG	6
311	7	Fr.	6 25	D	4 30	B	10 05	32	16 25	3¾	4	12ᴾᴍ29	E	11ᴾᴍ10	C	CAP	7
312	8	Sa.	6 26	D	4 29	A	10 03	32	16 43	4¾	5	1 09	D	— —	—	CAP	8
313	9	E	6 28	D	4 28	A	10 00	32	17 00	5¾	6¼	1 46	D	12ᴀ18	C	AQU	9
314	10	M.	6 29	D	4 27	A	9 58	32	17 17	6¾	7¼	2 22	D	1 29	D	AQU	10
315	11	Tu.	6 30	D	4 26	A	9 56	32	17 33	7¾	8¼	2 57	D	2 40	D	PSC	11
316	12	W.	6 31	D	4 25	A	9 54	31	17 50	8¾	9¼	3 34	C	3 53	D	PSC	12
317	13	Th.	6 33	D	4 24	A	9 51	31	18 05	9½	10	4 13	B	5 05	E	CET	13
318	14	Fr.	6 34	D	4 23	A	9 49	31	18 21	10¼	11	4 56	B	6 17	E	ARI	14
319	15	Sa.	6 35	D	4 22	A	9 47	31	18 36	11¼	11¾	5 43	B	7 25	E	TAU	15
320	16	E	6 36	D	4 21	A	9 45	31	18 51	—	12	6 33	B	8 29	E	TAU	16
321	17	M.	6 38	D	4 20	A	9 42	31	19 06	12½	12¾	7 28	B	9 27	E	ORI	17
322	18	Tu.	6 39	D	4 20	A	9 41	31	19 20	1½	1½	8 25	B	10 17	E	GEM	18
323	19	W.	6 40	D	4 19	A	9 39	30	19 34	2¼	2½	9 23	B	11 01	E	GEM	19
324	20	Th.	6 41	D	4 18	A	9 37	30	19 48	3¼	3¼	10 21	B	11ᴀ40	D	CAN	20
325	21	Fr.	6 42	D	4 17	A	9 35	30	20 01	4	4¼	11ᴍ18	B	12ᴾᴍ14	D	LEO	21
326	22	Sa.	6 44	D	4 17	A	9 33	30	20 14	5	5¼	— —	—	12 44	D	LEO	22
327	23	E	6 45	D	4 16	A	9 31	29	20 26	6	6¼	12ᴀ15	D	1 13	D	LEO	23
328	24	M.	6 46	D	4 16	A	9 30	29	20 38	6¾	7¼	1 12	D	1 41	D	VIR	24
329	25	Tu.	6 47	D	4 15	A	9 28	29	20 50	7½	8	2 09	D	2 09	C	VIR	25
330	26	W.	6 48	D	4 15	A	9 27	28	21 01	8¼	8¾	3 06	D	2 38	C	VIR	26
331	27	Th.	6 49	E	4 14	A	9 25	28	21 12	9	9½	4 05	E	3 10	B	VIR	27
332	28	Fr.	6 51	E	4 14	A	9 23	28	21 23	9¾	10¼	5 04	E	3 44	B	LIB	28
333	29	Sa.	6 52	E	4 13	A	9 21	27	21 34	10½	11	6 04	E	4 23	B	LIB	0
334	30	E	6 53	E	4 13	A	9 20	27	21s.43	11	11½	7ᴍ04	E	5ᴍ08	B	OPH	1

No shade, no shine, no butterflies,
no bees
No fruit, no flowers, no leaves,
no birds — No-vember!
– Thomas Hood

Farmer's Calendar

The attack of the Asian ladybugs is no myth: You can read about it in *The New York Times*. The invader is *Harmonia axyridis*, a quarter-inch beetle, orange and covered with black speckles. In the northeastern states for the past few years, *H. axyridis* has begun turning up in people's houses around this time. It's looking for a warm place to hibernate. That is what everybody in this part of the country needs, and most householders wouldn't begrudge the ladybug its winter shelter — except that the little things arrive in large numbers. Now, *H. axyridis* is harmless. In fact, as a predator of insect pests, it's highly beneficial. Still, as the *Times* report observed, "If a woman wakes up in the morning and finds 20,000 ladybugs on her kitchen ceiling, she doesn't care that they eat aphids."

The Asian ladybug has traveled up here from the south, where it was introduced to control aphids and other harmful insects. It does that admirably, but it also swarms in alarming numbers and inconvenient places. The story of *H. axyridis*, therefore, would seem to be a classic of unintended consequences, another case in which importing exotic creatures for a good reason comes to a bad end. But wait a minute. Not all foreign transplants go wrong. I myself, I reflect, am no native of New England. I was imported from farther west. But I feel I have settled in pretty well, and if I don't exhibit conspicuously beneficial behavior (I don't eat aphids, for example), neither do I do much serious harm. Nor does *H. axyridis*, and it may be that is all that should be asked of either of us, especially as both the beetle and I are certainly here to stay.

D. M.	D. W.	Dates, Feasts, Fasts, Aspects, Tide Heights	Weather ↓
1	Sa.	**All Saints** • Famous "Dark Day" in New England, 1716 • Tides {10.4 / —} •	Cool
2	E	**24th ♒. af. ℣.** • James K. Polk born, 1795 • {9.6 / 10.5} •	and
3	M.	**All Souls** • Never try to wear a hat that has more character than you do. • {9.5 / 10.4} •	wet,
4	Tu.	♂♂☾ • ♂♀☾ • Election Day • {9.4 / 10.4} •	the
5	W.	☾ runs low • First U.S. cross-country airplane flight, 1911 • Tides {9.3 / 10.3} •	Sun
6	Th.	♀ Gr. Elong. (47° E.) • ♂♅☾ • Tides {9.2 / 10.1} •	with-
7	Fr.	♂☖☾ • ♂♃☾ • Joni Mitchell born, 1943 •	holds
8	Sa.	Take care that old age does not wrinkle your spirit even more than your face. • {9.4 / 10.0} •	its
9	E	**25th ♒. af. ℣.** • ☾ at ☊ •	blessing,
10	M.	**St. Leo the Great** • Richard Burton born, 1925 • Tides {10.3 / 10.4} •	and
11	Tu.	**St. Martin** • **Veterans Day** • ☾ on Eq. • Occn. ♄ by ☾ •	we
12	W.	☾ at perig. • If All Saints brings out winter, St. Martin brings out Indian Summer. •	all
13	Th.	Great Leonid meteor display, midnight to dawn, 1833 • Tides {11.8 / 11.0} •	get
14	Fr.	**Full Beaver** ○ • Mamie Eisenhower born, 1896 • Tides {12.1 / 11.0} •	colds.
15	Sa.	Keep a green tree in your heart and perhaps the singing bird will come. • {12.1 / 10.8} •	Awake
16	E	**26th ♒. af. ℣.** • W. C. Handy born, 1873 • {— / 11.9} •	to
17	M.	**St. Hugh of Lincoln** • ☾ rides high • Suez Canal opened, 1869 •	flakes.
18	Tu.	**St. Hilda** • CBS sold its record division to Sony, 1987 • Tides {10.1 / 11.0} •	In
19	W.	Ford Motor Co. discontinued the Edsel, 1959 • Roy Campanella born, 1921 •	the
20	Th.	Alistair Cooke born, 1908 • Robert F. Kennedy born, 1925 • {9.3 / 9.8} •	woods
21	Fr.	Mayflower Compact signed, 1620 • Stan Musial born, 1920 • {9.0 / 9.4} •	the
22	Sa.	U.S. ended 22-year ban on travel to mainland China, 1972 • Billie Jean King born, 1943 •	deer's
23	E	**27th ♒. af. ℣.** • ☾ at ☍ • ☾ at apo. •	a
24	M.	☾ on Eq. • If you add to the truth, you subtract from it. • Tides {9.1 / 8.9} •	wraith,
25	Tu.	Pope John XXIII born, 1881 • Joe DiMaggio born, 1914 • {9.3 / 8.9} •	as
26	W.	Charles M. Schulz born, 1922 • Sojourner Truth died, 1883 • Tides {9.6 / 9.1} •	we
27	Th.	**Thanksgiving** • ♇ in ♂ with ☉ • Tides {9.9 / 9.2} •	ponder
28	Fr.	☿ Gr. Elong. (22° E.) • Cocoanut Grove nightclub fire, 1942 • {10.2 / 9.4} •	Pilgrim
29	Sa.	New ● • C. S. Lewis born, 1898 • Tides {10.5 / 9.5} •	faith.
30	E	**1st ♒. in Advent** • Winston Churchill born, 1874 •	

*You've got to be very careful if you don't know where
you are going, because you might not get there.*   *– Yogi Berra*

1997 DECEMBER, THE TWELFTH MONTH

The year ends on a spectacular note as all the planets bunch into one side of the heavens, simultaneously visible. Mercury scrapes the low southwest horizon a half hour after sunset. Higher and leftward stands the closely spaced duo of dim Mars and dazzling Venus (awesome at magnitude -5). Then come naked-eye-invisible Uranus and Neptune; even farther leftward brilliant Jupiter hovers some 30 degrees above the southern horizon. And then, Saturn, the solitary bright "star" in the southeast. This is the century's final simultaneous display of all planets and a holiday feast for all who look heavenward. Winter begins on the 21st at 3:07 P.M., EST.

☽	First Quarter	7th day	1st hour	9th min.
○	Full Moon	13th day	21st hour	37th min.
☾	Last Quarter	21st day	16th hour	43rd min.
●	New Moon	29th day	11th hour	56th min.

For an explanation of this page, see "How to Use This Almanac," page 34; for values of Key Letters, see Time Correction Tables, page 200.

Day of Year	Day of Month	Day of Week	☉ Rises h. m.	Key	☉ Sets h. m.	Key	Length of Days h. m.	Sun Fast m.	Declination of Sun ° '	Full Sea Boston A.M.	Full Sea Boston P.M.	☽ Rises h. m.	Key	☽ Sets h. m.	Key	☽ Place	☽ Age
335	1	M.	6 54	E	4 13	A	9 19	27	21s.52	11¾	—	8 A.M. 01	E	5 P.M. 59	B	OPH	2
336	2	Tu.	6 55	E	4 12	A	9 17	26	22 01	12¼	12½	8 55	E	6 55	B	SAG	3
337	3	W.	6 56	E	4 12	A	9 16	26	22 10	1	1¼	9 45	E	7 57	B	SAG	4
338	4	Th.	6 57	E	4 12	A	9 15	26	22 17	1¾	2	10 30	E	9 02	C	CAP	5
339	5	Fr.	6 58	E	4 12	A	9 14	25	22 25	2¾	2¾	11 11	D	10 09	C	AQU	6
340	6	Sa.	6 59	E	4 12	A	9 13	25	22 32	3½	3¾	11 A.M. 48	D	11 P.M. 18	C	AQU	7
341	7	E	7 00	E	4 12	A	9 12	24	22 39	4½	4¾	12 P.M. 24	D	— —	–	AQU	8
342	8	M.	7 01	E	4 11	A	9 10	24	22 46	5½	5¾	12 58	D	12 A.M. 27	D	PSC	9
343	9	Tu.	7 02	E	4 11	A	9 09	23	22 52	6½	7	1 32	C	1 37	D	PSC	10
344	10	W.	7 03	E	4 12	A	9 09	23	22 57	7½	8	2 09	C	2 47	E	PSC	11
345	11	Th.	7 03	E	4 12	A	9 09	23	23 02	8¼	9	2 48	B	3 57	E	ARI	12
346	12	Fr.	7 04	E	4 12	A	9 08	22	23 06	9¼	9¾	3 32	B	5 05	E	TAU	13
347	13	Sa.	7 05	E	4 12	A	9 07	22	23 10	10	10¾	4 20	B	6 11	E	TAU	14
348	14	E	7 06	E	4 12	A	9 06	21	23 14	10¾	11½	5 13	B	7 12	E	TAU	15
349	15	M.	7 06	E	4 12	A	9 06	21	23 17	11¾	—	6 09	B	8 06	E	GEM	16
350	16	Tu.	7 07	E	4 13	A	9 06	20	23 20	12¼	12½	7 07	B	8 54	E	GEM	17
351	17	W.	7 08	E	4 13	A	9 05	20	23 22	1	1¼	8 06	B	9 36	E	CAN	18
352	18	Th.	7 08	E	4 13	A	9 05	19	23 23	1¾	2	9 05	C	10 13	E	CAN	19
353	19	Fr.	7 09	E	4 14	A	9 05	19	23 24	2¾	2¾	10 03	C	10 45	D	LEO	20
354	20	Sa.	7 10	E	4 14	A	9 04	18	23 25	3½	3¾	11 00	D	11 15	D	LEO	21
355	21	E	7 10	E	4 14	A	9 04	18	23 25	4¼	4½	11 P.M. 57	D	11 A.M. 43	D	LEO	22
356	22	M.	7 11	E	4 15	A	9 04	17	23 25	5	5½	— —	–	12 P.M. 11	C	VIR	23
357	23	Tu.	7 11	E	4 15	A	9 04	17	23 25	6	6¼	12 A.M. 54	D	12 39	C	VIR	24
358	24	W.	7 12	E	4 16	A	9 04	16	23 24	6¾	7¼	1 52	D	1 09	C	VIR	25
359	25	Th.	7 12	E	4 17	A	9 05	16	23 22	7½	8¼	2 50	E	1 42	B	LIB	26
360	26	Fr.	7 12	E	4 18	A	9 06	15	23 20	8½	9	3 50	E	2 18	B	LIB	27
361	27	Sa.	7 12	E	4 18	A	9 06	15	23 17	9¼	9¾	4 50	E	3 00	B	SCO	28
362	28	E	7 13	E	4 19	A	9 06	14	23 14	9¾	10½	5 49	E	3 49	B	OPH	29
363	29	M.	7 13	E	4 20	A	9 07	14	23 11	10½	11¼	6 46	E	4 44	B	SAG	0
364	30	Tu.	7 13	E	4 21	A	9 08	13	23 07	11¼	—	7 40	E	5 45	B	SAG	1
365	31	W.	7 13	E	4 21	A	9 08	13	23s.03	12	12	8 A.M. 28	E	6 P.M. 51	B	SAG	2

DECEMBER hath 31 days. 1997

All glory be to God on high,
And to the earth be peace;
Good-will henceforth from heaven to men
Begin, and never cease! – *Nahum Tate*

D. M.	D. W.	Dates, Feasts, Fasts, Aspects, Tide Heights	*Weather* ↓
1	M.	☌☿☾ • Boys Town founded near Omaha, Neb., 1917 • {10.8 —	*'Tis the*
2	Tu.	☾ runs low • Ford unveiled the Model A, 1927 • Tides {9.6 10.8 •	*season*
3	W.	☌♂☾ • ☌♀☾ • ☌♆☾ • {9.6 10.8 •	*for*
4	Th.	☌♅☾ • Last American hostage released, Lebanon, 1991 • {9.7 10.7 •	*rain*
5	Fr.	☌♃☾ • Walt Disney born, 1901 • Tides {9.7 10.5 •	*that's*
6	Sa.	St. Nicholas • Explosion destroyed Halifax, Nova Scotia, 1917 •	*freezin'.*
7	E	2nd S. in Advent • ☾ at ☋ • ☿ stat. • ☌♀♆	
8	M.	☾ on Eq. • James Thurber born, 1894 • Tides {10.2 9.9 •	*Hang*
9	Tu.	☌♄☾ • ☾ at perig. • 61° F, Boston 1 A.M., 1980 •	*mistletoe*
10	W.	*Opportunity is missed by most people because it is dressed in overalls and looks like work.* •	*as*
11	Th.	♀ Greatest Brilliancy • Snow, Phoenix, Arizona, 1985 • Tides {11.2 10.1 •	*you*
12	Fr.	Francis Chichester completed solo voyage, England to Australia, 1966 •	*whistle "O*
13	Sa.	St. Lucy • Full Cold ○ • {11.7 10.3 •	*Tannenbaum."*
14	E	3rd S. in Advent • Halcyon Days • {11.6 10.2 •	*Build a*
15	M.	☾ rides high • ☌♂♆ • Tides {11.5 — •	*snowman;*
16	Tu.	*Always put off till tomorrow what you shouldn't do at all.* • Tides {10.0 11.2 •	*watch*
17	W.	☿ in inf. ☌ • ♄ stat. • Ember Day • Tides {9.8 10.7 •	*him*
18	Th.	Ty Cobb born, 1886 • Antonio Stradivari died, 1737 • {9.6 10.3 •	*melt down*
19	Fr.	Ember Day • National Hockey League began first pro season, 1917 •	*as the*
20	Sa.	☾ at ☊ • Ember Day • Branch Rickey born, 1881 • {9.1 9.3 •	*rain*
21	E	4th S. in Advent • Winter Solstice • ☾ at apo. •	*begins*
22	M.	St. Thomas • ☾ on Eq. • ☌♀♂ • Tides {9.0 8.6 •	*to*
23	Tu.	Boogie-woogie music first performed at Carnegie Hall, 1938 • {9.0 8.5 •	*pelt down.*
24	W.	First day of Chanukah • Beware the Pogonip. • {9.2 8.5 •	*Gather*
25	Th.	Christmas Day • ♀ stat. • {9.4 8.6 •	*friends*
26	Fr.	St. Stephen • ☌♂♅ • Boxing Day (Canada) • {9.8 8.8 •	*and*
27	Sa.	St. John • ☿ stat. • ☌☿☾ • {10.1 9.0 •	*celebrate:*
28	E	1st S. af. C. • Woodrow Wilson born, 1856 •	*peace*
29	M.	Holy Innocents • ☾ runs low • New ● • {10.8 9.6 •	*and*
30	Tu.	*Begin the new year square with every man.* (Robert B. Thomas) • Tides {11.1 — •	*joy*
31	W.	☌♆☾ • ☌♀☾ • ☌♅☾ • {9.9 11.2 •	*in '98!*

Farmer's Calendar

It is a question for the ages whether people who live in cities envy country people as much as they say they do — or whether if they don't, they should. Peace is what they want, or so they say. But how peaceful do they think it is up here? And anyway, how much peace can a person stand?

Well, these are not questions we can settle in this space today, but let us admit one realm in which rural life seems plainly to have an advantage: the realm of the weather. Weather of all kinds, but especially winter weather, visits the city more harshly than it does less settled districts. Consider a moderately heavy snowstorm: In Vermont it's a struggle. In Boston it's a calamity. In part that's because of the inevitable obstacle put in the way of transportation by snow as it falls. But surely the worst of a snowstorm in the city comes from other reasons, reasons related to the rhythm or tempo of a storm in town compared to one in the country.

Up here, to oversimplify only a little, when a storm is over, it's over. When the snow stops falling, the ordeal is finished, and we can get on to other things. In the city when the snow stops falling, the ordeal has only begun. You have to plow out, clear off, and shovel, but you can't because there's no place to put the snow. You can't put it in the street, because the street must be clear for cars. You can't put it beside the street, because the sidewalk must be clear for people. In New York they solve the problem by piling the snow up at the street *corners* and climbing over it with ropes. You can see how a day or so of that leads to envy of those located some place — anyplace — else.

What AMERICAN TUNE Always Gets A STANDING OVATION?

- photo from the collection of Paul E. Bierley

THREE HINTS:

1) **It's 100 years old this year.**

2) **John Philip Sousa's band never gave a concert without playing it.**

3) **In 1987 President Ronald Reagan made it America's National March.**

BY VICTORIA DOUDERA

One hundred years ago, on May 14, 1897, a Philadelphia music critic attended a concert of the famous Sousa Band. The band's leader, John Philip Sousa, composer of such popular marches as "Liberty Bell," "El Capitan," and "Washington Post," was introducing a brand-new march. In the next day's paper the reviewer wrote: "Sousa's latest march, 'The Stars and Stripes Forever,' was given for the first time and the audience was not satisfied until they heard it *three* times. . . . The Sousa swing and vigor that have

made all his compositions of this character distinctive are very evident, and it will likely become as popular as its predecessors."

Another reviewer was not so restrained. He wrote, in the usually staid *Philadelphia Public Ledger,* " 'The Stars and Stripes Forever' was stirring enough to rouse the American eagle from his crag and set him to shriek exultantly, while he hurls his arrows at the aurora borealis."

From the first, the march provoked emotional responses in audiences, with listeners rising to their feet in respect when it was played. After its premiere, Sousa included it in every concert, even if the march was not on the printed program. Paul E. Bierley, author of *John Philip Sousa, American Phenomenon* (New York: Appleton, Century, Crofts, 1973), interviewed many former

Sousa band members and found that none could recall a concert in which "The Stars and Stripes Forever" was not played. Band members remembered repeating it several times on many occasions.

A century later, Americans still thrill to the sounds of Sousa's most popular march. For many of us, the familiar, rousing strains of the "Stars" (as Sousa referred to it) evoke memories of that most American of holidays, the Fourth of July. Harold C. Schonberg, music critic for *The New York Times,* said in 1978 that "The Stars and Stripes Forever" may be "the greatest piece of music ever written by an American composer."

John Philip Sousa (1854-1932) was born in Washington, D.C. He was a gifted classical violinist before becoming, in 1880, the conductor of the United States Marine Band,

Sousa (front row, center) and his band on tour in Hamburg, Germany, May 30, 1900.

★

> **T**he main melody . . .
> is the North. The South
> is symbolized by the lilting
> piccolo obbligato, and
> the bold West by the ripping
> trombone countermelody.

which he developed into one of the best military bands in the world. In 1892 he formed his own touring band. Wearing new white gloves for every performance, custom-made shoes, and a uniform sporting 35 yards of braid, Sousa and his wildly successful band entertained America for almost 40 years. Along the way he composed songs, operettas, and his famous marches, invented an instrument called the sousaphone, and penned a few books. His profession, he said, was "salesman of Americanism, globe-trotter, and musician."

The inspiration for "The Stars and Stripes Forever" came to Sousa in November 1896 while vacationing in Europe. Sousa was homesick. He thought wistfully of his days in Washington, D.C., as the leader of the Marine Band and often pictured the flag flying from its staff on the grounds of the White House. "To my imagination it seemed to be the biggest, grandest flag in the world, and I could not get back under it quick enough."

....

"The Stars and Stripes Forever," featuring a lilting piccolo part (inset) in the trio section, became Sousa's own favorite composition and most-performed piece.

The vacation ended suddenly in December when news of his manager's death reached Sousa. Sailing home, Sousa had an experience that he described in his autobiography, *Marching Along:*

"As the vessel steamed out of the harbor, I was pacing the deck, absorbed in thoughts of my manager's death and the many duties and decisions which awaited me in New York. Suddenly, I began to sense the rhythmic beat of a band playing within my brain. It kept on ceaselessly, playing, playing, playing. Throughout the whole tense voyage, that imaginary band continued to unfold the same themes, echoing and re-echoing the most distinct melody. I did not transfer a note of that music to paper while I was on the steamer, but when we reached shore, I set down the measures that my brain-band had been playing for me, and not a note of it has ever been changed. The composition is known the world over as 'The Stars and Stripes Forever' and is probably my most popular march."

Sousa's original piano score for the march is housed at the Library of Congress. He completed it on Christmas Day 1896, just two days after his ship docked in New York. A later score added band parts, in particular the brass and piccolo themes unique to the march. This band score, complete with penciled notations and changes, is among more than 120 Sousa manuscripts — an estimated 74 percent of his work — at the University of Illinois's John Philip Sousa Collection.

"A march stimulates every center of vitality, wakens the imagination, and spurs patriotic impulses which may have been dormant for years," said Sousa, who insisted that all good marches must appeal to the musical and unmusical alike. He quipped that *his* music could make a man with a wooden leg get up and march.

Sousa intended the three themes in the march to represent different parts of the United States. The main melody, full of contrasts, is the North. The South is symbolized by the lilting piccolo obbligato, and the bold West by the ripping trombone countermelody. When Sousa's band performed the march, his piccolo and brass sections would line up across the front of the stage for the march's finale, playing directly to the audience for a rousing finish.

(continued)

SING ALONG WITH THE "STARS"

■ Sousa himself wrote these words when he used his march as the finale to a patriotic pageant in 1898, just before the Spanish-American War. The first 12 lines are sung with the main melody; the last nine lines with the trio (that's the section with the fancy piccolo part).

Let martial note in triumph float
And liberty extend its mighty hand;
A flag appears 'mid thunderous
*   cheers,*
The banner of the Western land.
The emblem of the brave and true.
Its folds protect no tyrant crew;
The red and white and starry blue
Is freedom's shield and hope.
Other nations may deem their flags
*   the best*
And cheer them with fervid elation.
But the flag of the North and South
*   and West*
Is the flag of flags, the flag of
*   Freedom's nation.*

Hurrah for the flag of the free!
May it wave as our standard
*   forever,*
The gem of the land and the sea,
The banner of the right.
Let despots remember the day
When our fathers with mighty
*   endeavor*
Proclaimed as they marched to the
*   fray,*
That by their might and by their
*   right*
It waves forever.

– John Philip Sousa

Americans aren't the only ones who love "The Stars and Stripes Forever." When Arthur Fiedler directed the World Symphony Orchestra in 1972, he chose to end each concert with Sousa's famous march. The late maestro was initially criticized for choosing such a partisan piece, but Fiedler defended the march. "I put my foot down, explaining that 'The Stars and Stripes Forever' was great music and that it would stand on its own merits. As it turned out, it was a grand concluding number, bringing standing ovations at every concert."

The march is such a part of the American experience that over the years citizens have sought official national recognition for it. Early efforts failed because of disorganization, but a new generation of Sousa fans succeeded in November of 1987. The bill passed with ease in both the House and the Senate, and on December 11, 1987, Presi-

dent Ronald Reagan added his signature, making "The Stars and Stripes Forever" the United States of America's National March.

That Sousa himself loved the march was no secret. When asked by the musical magazine *Étude* in July of 1930 what musical composition he would choose to hear if he were told he had but 24 hours to live, Sousa answered, "The Stars and Stripes Forever." He said, "I would meet my Maker face to face with the inspiration that grows out of the melody and the patriotism that gives it being." Fittingly, "The Stars and Stripes Forever" was the last composition played under Sousa's baton, and a fragment of the march is inscribed on his tombstone.

Though a hundred years has passed since this most American of tunes was introduced, its melody continues to inspire us. May John Philip Sousa's famous "Stars" shine brightly forever.   □□

Keith Brion, conductor

– courtesy Eugene Cook

THE NEW SOUSA BAND

■ Care to step back in time and hear "The Stars and Stripes Forever" in the style Sousa and his band would have performed it? Thanks to conductor Keith Brion, you can do just that. Brion not only portrays the legendary band leader (down to the white hair, braided uniform, immaculate gloves, and conducting mannerisms), but he also sets the stage and arranges

the program as was done a century ago. Brion's *Sousa at the Symphony* concerts feature musicians of extraordinary quality (he has performed the concerts with most of America's major and regional orchestras), who "play to relive the

wonderful Sousa experience."

Keith Brion and his New Sousa Band have scheduled concerts commemorating the anniversary of "The Stars and Stripes Forever" around the country (and overseas) for the 1996-97 season. For more information and a performance schedule, contact Keith Brion, Conductor, New Sousa Band, 57 Mill Rock Road, Hamden, CT 06517.

Heartburn passes in a few hours.

A broken heart may ache for half a lifetime — particularly if you

listen to country music. But there are helpful things you might consider doing . . .

How to Mend a Broken

We must begin by saying that a broken heart cannot, in all honesty, be c o m p l e t e l y mended, only sutured. But we can assure you that once the stitches come out, you'll be left with a hideous scar that your friends (and future lovers) will admire with great sympathy. And though the scar itself won't make the agony you've suffered worthwhile, it will at least provide inspiration for some great and tragic tale. Yes, of course, you would have preferred a happy-ever-after ending, but you must remember that heart-rending operas and tear-jerking poems are not written about ponderously perfect marriages where only an occasional fingernail is broken.

No, as far as great literature is concerned, the wretched heart remains the traumatic body part of choice. If you are in the midst of some horrible affair, count yourself in good company. Dante took inspiration from his unre-quited devotion to Beatrice (a married Florence woman who died at 24) to write the *Divine Comedy*. The Italian poet and playwright Gabriel D'Annunzio wrote his

scandalously successful play *Flame of Life* after his youthful passion for the aging actress Eleonora Duse went unfulfilled. And then there was the poet John Milton, whose 16-year-old bride got bored after a month of marriage and went home to her family. His heartache turned him not simply to despair, but to the inkwell. Four years later he had the last word through his now-famous essays on divorce.

You, too, can use your sorry state of heartbreak for such literary pathos. Go ahead, make the guy who just dumped you a character in a novel, set him on the edge of a steep cliff, then with a slight push of the pen, knock the no-good into oblivion. Feel better?

If not, you can always sue. A few years ago a lawyer in Chicago filed a suit against his fiancée for breach of promise after she broke the engagement two days before the wedding. He demanded she pay back the $40,310.48 he had spent courting her (including $22 on a red pullover and $7.99 on a Patsy Cline cassette). His vengeful approach, however, was sidetracked by a statement in the court papers saying that he would still marry her if she changed her mind. For those tempted to try a similar strategy, we should note here that lawsuits may be effective for re-

Heart *by Christine Schultz*

coupling financial loss, but *not* for reigniting romance.

Bear in mind that real hearts don't come cheap these days. A heart valve alone will cost you close to $45,000, and the complete organ itself will put you $100,000 to $125,000 in the hole. (What's worse is that your ex-lover can fix *his* broken heart of steel for under $3 with a little Krazy Glue from the local hardware store.) So before you blow your whole life savings on a replacement, make sure you don't have just heartburn. You can tell the difference by the length of time the pain persists. Heartburn will pass in a few hours. A

– Photofest

ne Rhode Island gentleman ran a marathon to win back his *girlfriend. She wasn't interested. "I'd do it again," the rejected man told a reporter, "but not for her."*

broken heart will ache for half a lifetime.

It doesn't even seem to matter if the relationship itself was short-lived. In fact, as La Bruyère said in 1688, "Sudden love takes the longest time to be cured." Romeo and Juliet were the classic case. In Shakespeare's original version the lovers knew each other for only four fleeting days. Still, their heartbreak was eternal: "For never was a story of more woe/ Than this of Juliet and Romeo." Death was easier to face than life lived alone.

Often suicide is the first resort of the broken-hearted. (We wouldn't recommend it ourselves.) To help avoid self-imposed death, *don't* listen to country music. Really. Country music only makes things worse. Jim Gundlach, a sociologist from Auburn University in Alabama, found that greater airplay of country music corresponded with higher rates of suicide in 49 metropolitan areas. "You tend to have single men lined up at the country-music bar drinking their beer as the music wails about being alone," say Gundlach.

Lover's leaps are to be avoided, as well. Though they exist in every region of the country and make good stories, they don't solve a thing. We'd suggest chocolate instead. Chocolate, you see, contains phenylethylamine (PEA) — the exact same chemical that the brain releases during the early stages of infatuation. Sure, chocolate has more calories than Chuck's kisses, but what the heck, chocolate won't walk out on you in the morning the way Chuck did. *(Oh Henry!)*

The other useful drug recently tried on lovesick patients by psychiatrists Michael Liebowitz and Donald Klein is a monoamine oxidase (MAO) inhibitor. MAO inhibitors seem to boost the level of PEA in romance junkies, making it unnecessary for them to search out that high from an ill-fated love affair.

"To everyone's astonishment," writes Helen Fisher in *Anatomy of Love,* "within weeks of receiving MAO inhibitors, one perpetually lovesick man began to choose his partners more carefully, even starting to live comfortably without a mate." Who knows, it could work for you.

People will go to any lengths to outdistance a broken heart. One Rhode Island gentleman ran a marathon to win back the girlfriend who'd recently rejected him, but when he arrived exhausted at her house 26 miles and four hours later, she wasn't even there. A relative came out to say she really wasn't interested. "I'd do it again," the rejected man told a reporter, "but not for her."

If you let it, the heart will eventually mend itself by twisting around to take

care of you again. When death stole the wife of the Pre-Raphaelite painter Gabriel Rossetti, he was so heartbroken that he laid his love poems in her hands and had them buried with her body. But seven years later a change of heart made him dig her coffin up, dust off his poems,

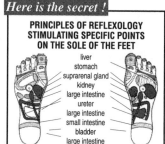
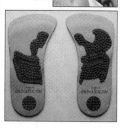

n average, the heart beats 2.8 billion times per life. It does so with the expert efficiency of a perfect pump.

and get them published. Though that may seem unromantic, it may have helped heal his heart when his poems earned him more fame than his artwork ever did.

Death, on the other hand, can just as easily twist a heart in ways you wouldn't have guessed. Though Joe DiMaggio had been divorced from Marilyn Monroe for eight years, her suicide in 1962 tore sobs from him at the funeral. For the next  two decades he sent roses to her grave site three times a week.

And then there was the tale of Lady Jane Franklin, whose husband, arctic explorer Sir John Franklin, was lost in 1847 on a voyage to find the Northwest Passage. Forty different expeditions searched the Arctic for 13 years for a clue to the fate of Franklin and his men. Finally Lady Franklin set out herself at age 78 to search for his ship. A glove from his hand, a note from his journal, or any such remembrance would have been enough to ease her saddened heart. Despite all her courage and searching, however,  Lady Jane did not find her lost love. She died in London five years after her voyage, leaving behind a bust of her husband that bore the inscription, ". . . after long waiting and sending many in search of him, [Lady Jane] herself departed to seek and to find him in the realms of the light."

As poignant as the historical tale of Lady Jane is the modern-day account of Chester Szuber, a retired owner of a Christmas tree farm. For two decades Chester Szuber had battled heart disease. Then, in August of 1994, his 22-year-old daughter, Patti, died in a car accident, and he was faced with the devastating decision of whether to accept her heart as a transplant for his own. It was a decision no father should have to make, but Chester Szuber did. He realized the transplant would have been Patti's final wish and decided to go ahead with it. The operation went well, and Mr. Szuber survived in better health than he'd ever been. He thinks of Patti with every beat of his heart.

On average, the heart beats 2.8 billion times per life. It does so with the expert efficiency of a perfect  pump. It performs so well, in fact, that you will often fail to notice it at all. From time to time, your heart will remind you how essential it is by doing what it should not. It will leap from your chest and stop up your throat; it will worm its way onto your sleeve and fling itself upon the floor. Though highly distressful, this is to be expected. You will endure the suffering in hopes that one day some kind person will notice those little pieces at your feet, pick them up from the ground, and hold them together in his or her hands. If that kind person proceeds to follow you around wherever you go, pay attention. It will happen only once in a blue swooning moon. It is the best remedy there is for a broken heart. We call it love. □ □

The Book of Love (Random House, 1996) by Christine Schultz will be available in September 1996.

No Matter What The Weather, As Long As We're Together...

THE BIG RIVER HARP AND INSTRUCTIONAL PACKAGE

Learn how to play the harmonica quickly and easily with the Big River instructional package. The package includes Hohner's German-made Big River Harp and case, a 60-minute audio cassette and instructional booklet. All you need to get started. **Order today!**

$19⁹⁵

Four Months on the Trail to "The Right Place"

In the evenings there would be no card playing. No checkers or dominoes. No dancing or fiddling. A bugle at 8:30 P.M. signaled all to retire to their wagons to pray. Campfires were to be extinguished by 9 P.M. and the bugle sounded again at 5 A.M. It was the most disciplined westward migration in American history...
by Dayton Duncan

One hundred and fifty years ago, on New Year's Eve 1846, Wilford Woodruff sat down with his journal to take stock of the year just ending and to contemplate the prospects for 1847. He had much to report.

Woodruff was a Mormon, a high-ranking member of the new Church of Jesus Christ of Latter-day Saints. His people had already been driven from New York, Ohio, Missouri, and finally Nauvoo, Illinois, where their founder and prophet Joseph Smith had

been murdered by a mob. They believed, among other things, that Jesus Christ had preached in America after the Resurrection and would return to it once a new, true church — theirs — was established to prepare the way.

Now they also believed that the only way for that church to survive was for the Mormons to get as far away as possible from the persecutions of the nonbelievers they called Gentiles. So they were headed west, beyond the Continental Divide and existing boundary of the United States.

Woodruff, age 39, well educated, once prosperous, and utterly devout, had paid a heavy price for his beliefs in 1846. The evacuation from Nauvoo had forced him to abandon his house and property. On the west bank of the Missouri River, where they had thrown together a collection of rough huts called Winter Quarters, hundreds began perishing from disease and exposure. Woodruff's 16-month-old son, Joseph, died from a respiratory infection. Then his wife, Phebe, went into premature labor and delivered another son, who died two days later.

There were other trials. A tree Woodruff was chopping down pinned him against a standing oak and broke his left arm, his breastbone, and three ribs. In accordance with Smith's teachings — and over the initial protests of Phebe — Woodruff had entered plural

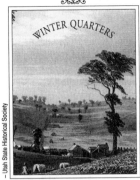

They left markers every ten miles, sometimes with messages in boxes attached to 12-foot poles, telling where the nearest good water or best campsite could be found.

marriage by taking on three more wives that year. (Polygamy was a secret Mormon practice at first, not publicly announced until 1852.) In Winter Quarters two of them, ages 17 and 18, began consorting with younger men. Woodruff arranged for the boys to be whipped, then divorced the girls and sent them back to their parents.

But like most of the other 8,000 Mormons huddled at Winter Quarters, and an equal number shivering in camps spread out across Iowa, Woodruff believed that God was testing the Latter-day Saints, just as He had once tested the Hebrews of old, when they passed from bondage in Egypt to the Promised Land. The year 1847, he predicted in his journal, would reward the faithful.

The exodus began in earnest in the spring of 1847. At its head was a man the Mormons considered their own Moses — Brigham Young. A sturdy farmer and carpenter and Joseph Smith's successor as Mormon president and prophet, Young, a Vermonter, was as practical as he was pious. "Prayer is good," he once said, "but when baked potatoes and pudding and milk are needed, prayer will not supply their place." Young and his advisers had considered a number of places for their new Zion, including California, Oregon, and Texas. But after reading the reports of the explorer John C. Frémont, Young had fastened on the Great Basin in the vast interior of the West, shielded from the United States by the Wasatch Mountains. Though technically part of Mexico, it was so remote and harsh that only a few Indian tribes and virtually no white people lived there — the most likely spot, Young decided, where the Mormons could both prosper and be left alone.

On April 16, he set out with his "Pioneer band" to find the best location and prepare for the rest of the Mormons. Young had originally called for 144 men, 12 for each of the Twelve Tribes of Israel, but his brother insisted on taking along his asthmatic wife and two children. Brigham and his second in command, Heber Kimball, each then decided to bring along one of their wives as well.

Three of the Pioneers were slaves.

In his long tenure as head of the church, Young would have only one divine revelation, and it came now: It outlined in precise detail how the Mormons should organize themselves for

Brigham Young, the Mormons' Moses, led them to their remote Utopia.

their trip west. Young directed all Mormons (Pioneers and followers) to divide into companies of hundreds, fifties, and tens, with captains for each — a pyramid of authority that converged on him and enforced his decisions down to the most minute detail. (Wilford Woodruff was captain of a company of ten, he proudly noted in his diary.) Camp rules called for a bugle call at 5 A.M. and everyone ready to roll at 7, with food already cooked for a short noon meal. At night the wagons were circled, the left back wheel of each one interlocked with the right front wheel of the next. Fires were built outside the circle, horses corralled inside. A bugle at 8:30 P.M. signaled all to retire to their wagons and pray, with everyone in bed and the fires out by 9. On Sabbaths, they would rest. The rules had been inspired by God, Young told his followers, but anyone who violated them would answer first to him. "I will do the scolding to this camp," he told them, "no other man shall."

It was the most organized and disciplined westward migration in American history. During nearly four months on the trail, the Pioneers would lose more days to the Sabbath than to any overland obstacle, and no one would die. It was singular in another respect: While most emigrants on the overland trails focused entirely on getting themselves to their destination, the Mormon Pioneers were equally concerned with improving the trail for those who would follow them to Zion. They left markers every ten miles (measured by a device they rigged to a wagon wheel), sometimes with messages in boxes attached to 12-foot poles, telling where the nearest good water or best campsite could be found.

Across what is now Nebraska, they followed the Platte River: broad and shallow, yet fast running and often lined with quicksand, "the most singular river I ever beheld," Woodruff wrote. They kept to the north shore, even though the other side promised an easier path (Oregon and California emigrants had been traveling along the south bank for six years by this time). They were going west to get away from other Americans, so the Mormons decided to stay as separate as possible en route as well.

On May 1 they experienced the thrill that had entranced every newcomer to the West since Coronado: A herd of buffalo crossed their path. Woodruff was among the small group Young permitted to give chase, and his diary goes on for pages recounting

This 1866 group followed the trail marked by the 1847 Mormon Pioneers.

FORT LARAMIE

. . . few wagon trains had

ever attempted the route,

and for good reason. It was a

tangle of canyons, steep and

rocky slopes, and twisted,

willow-choked streams.

the exciting details. The hunters killed 12 buffalo, he reported, and during the wild ride galloped across "one of the largest prairie dog towns nearly ever seen" — ten miles long, two miles wide, and full of burrows.

At the end of May, as they neared what is now Wyoming, Young called the Pioneers together and gave them a blistering tongue-lashing. In the last week, he said, some of them had ignored his rules. They had stayed up after hours, kept fires going, danced and fiddled late into the night, played cards and checkers and dominoes, and fallen into quarrels. "Do you suppose," he said, "that we are going to [find] a home for the Saints, a resting place, a place of peace where we can build up the Kingdom and bid the nations welcome, with a low, mean, dirty, trifling, covetous, wicked spirit dwelling in our bosoms?"

Chastened, the men all publicly reaffirmed their faith in God and allegiance to Young. Woodruff even suggested that anyone with cards, dominoes, or checkers burn them on the spot. As the Pioneers moved on, one wrote, "It seemed as though the cloud had burst, and we had emerged into a new element, a new atmosphere, a new society, and a new world."

They were almost out of the Plains, halfway to their goal, but the hardest half was still ahead.

At the Fort Laramie trading post in early June, the rugged terrain on the north side of the river forced them to cross the North Platte. Now they would be traveling the same route as some of the Gentiles they considered mortal enemies. On June 5 a wagon train bound for Oregon passed them on the trail; then another the next morning, including people some of the Mormons recognized from their troubles in Missouri.

It was rough country. The Pioneers slowed down to

Wyoming

CONTINENTAL DIVIDE

North Platte River

SOUTH PASS

JUNE 27

JUNE 16

JUNE 1

Fort Laramie

GREAT SALT LAKE

JULY 8

Fort Bridger

Salt Lake City

ECHO CANYON

JULY 22-24

JULY 12

Uinta Mountains

Utah

Colorado

Despite the suffering in Winter Quarters and on the trail in 1847, elder Wilford Woodruff kept the faith. He later became head of the Mormon church.

move rocks out of the way, dig out better descents to small streams, and generally smooth the way for the Saints farther back. Young sent a smaller group ahead with a leather boat to prepare for the final river crossing near what is now Casper, Wyoming. When the main party arrived, they found the small boat already in use — ferrying Gentiles across the swollen river for $1.50 a load, payable in flour or cash.

Woodruff compared the windfall to the "Children of Israel fed with manna in the wilderness" and declared it a miracle. Brigham Young discerned a greater opportunity. He put his own carpentry skills to work building a big, solid raft capable of carrying loaded wagons. Once the Pioneers had crossed on it, he left ten men behind at what became known as the Mormon Ferry. In the years that followed,

This 1867 photograph shows the precipitous descent into Echo Canyon, where 20 years earlier Brigham Young nearly died of fever.

– Utah State Historical Society

THE EMIGRANT TRAIL

– Yankee Archives

"We gazed with wonder

and admiration,"

Woodruff told his journal.

". . . We contemplated

that [in] not many years

the House of God would

stand upon the top of the

mountains. . . ."

An artist's rendering of Brigham Young's first view of Salt Lake Valley.

– Utah State Historical Society

Saints crossed free, Gentiles paid the going rate, and the Mormon church made money.

On June 27, they crossed the Continental Divide at South Pass. Strawberries were in bloom, yet snowdrifts hugged the roadside, a true sign they had indeed entered a new world. They were outside the boundaries of the United States at last, and although it was the third anniversary of Joseph Smith's martyrdom and a Sunday, the Pioneers traveled anyway, anxious to put as many miles as they could between themselves and the bitter memory.

On the parched, alkali slopes west of South Pass, they turned from the main trail and headed southwest toward the Wasatch Mountains and the Great Basin. A mountain man named Moses Harris gave them a discouraging report about prospects for starting a settlement there. Jim Bridger, another mountain man, was less pessimistic, but said he doubted that corn could be grown in the Salt Lake Valley because of early frosts.

Then a fellow Saint unexpectedly showed up. At Young's behest in 1846, Sam Brannan had sailed with several hundred Mormons from the East Coast to California, where he had started a small colony. Now he had crossed the deserts to bring them news of California's wonderful climate and soil, to tell them that John Sutter would welcome all the Saints to the fertile Sacramento valley.

Brigham Young was unmoved. He wanted a place where the Mormons could be solitary and safe. For such a purpose, the Great Basin sounded better than sunny California. They pushed on.

Nearing the northern edge of the Uinta range, they encountered streams that caught Woodruff's eye. On July 8, he unpacked a fly rod he had purchased in England during a missionary assignment, attached an artificial fly

"If I told you that I can end a lifetime of foot pain instantly, you probably wouldn't believe me..."

"Half a million other men and women didn't either... until they tried this revolutionary European discovery that positively killed their foot pain dead!

"Don't live with foot pain a moment longer! If you're ready to recapture the vitality and energy that healthy feet provide, I'll give you 60 days to try the remarkable foot support system I discovered in Europe. You will immediately experience relief and freedom from foot ailments. I GUARANTEE IT!

"How can I make such an unprecedented guarantee? Because I personally lived in constant, agonizing foot pain for years before my exciting discovery. What started out as simple aching from corns and calluses grew into full-blown, incapacitating misery only a few other foot pain sufferers could understand.

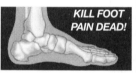

"Believe me, I tried all the so-called remedies I could get my hands on (and feet into), but none of them really worked. It wasn't until my wife and I took a trip to Europe that I discovered a remarkable invention called Flexible Featherspring® Foot Supports. Invented in Germany, these custom-formed foot supports absorb shock as they cradle your feet as if on a cushion of air.

Harvey Rothschild,
Founder of Featherspring Int'l.

"Imagine my complete surprise as I slipped a pair of custom-formed Feathersprings into my shoes for the first time and began the road to no more pain. The tremendous pain and pressure I used to feel every time I took a step was gone! I could scarcely believe how great a relief I felt even after walking several hours. And after just a few days of use, my pain disappeared totally - *and has never returned.*

"Whatever your problem— corns, calluses, bunions, pain in the balls of your feet, toe cramps, fallen arches, burning nerve endings, painful ankles, back aches, or just generally sore, aching feet and legs – *my Feathersprings are guaranteed to end your foot pain or you don't pay a penny.*

"But don't just take my word for it: Experience for yourself the immediate relief and renewed energy that Feathersprings provide. Send for your FREE kit today on our no risk, 60-day trial offer!"

to its line, and lightly flicked it onto the waters. "I watched it as it floated upon the water," he wrote, "with as much intense interest as Franklin did his kite, when he tried to draw lightning from the skies." And he was equally rewarded with a strike at the end of the line. He caught 12 cutthroat trout that day — more fish, and bigger ones, he confided to his diary, than any of the Pioneers using grasshoppers and bait, "proof positive to me that the artificial fly is far the best thing now known to fish trout with." (Woodruff so loved fly-fishing that years later, when Mormons were being jailed for polygamy, he reportedly disguised himself in a woman's dress to go fishing. In fact, it would be Woodruff himself, as head of the Mormon church, who would end the practice of polygamy in 1890 and open the door to statehood for Utah.)

The last 100 miles proved to be the hardest of the 1,073 miles the Pioneers traveled. Other than the ill-fated Donner party, few wagon trains had ever attempted the route, and for good reason. It was a tangle of canyons, steep and rocky slopes, and twisted, willow-choked streams. Some days they made only a few miles. Many of them contracted Colorado tick fever, with its excruciating headaches, severe pain in the joints and spine, high fevers, and occasional delirium.

On July 12, as they neared Echo Canyon, Brigham Young himself came down with the fever, making him, in his own words, "almost mad with pain." An advance group led by Orson Pratt pressed on to find a way through to the Basin and break a trail. The main party followed, while a smaller contingent lagged behind with the ailing prophet, who at one point was reported "nigh unto death." Young sent messages ahead, giving detailed instructions and urging his men to hurry because "the time for planting is fully come."

Finally, on July 22, the scouts and main party caught their first view of the Salt Lake Valley and descended into it, making a camp next to a small stream, near the center of what is now Salt Lake City. Two days later Wilford Woodruff, carrying a weak but recuperating Brigham Young in his wagon bed, came down Emigration Canyon and pulled around at an overlook so the patriarch could see the vista below them.

"We gazed with wonder and admiration," Woodruff told his journal. ". . . We contemplated that [in] not many years the House of God would stand upon the top of the mountains while the valleys would be converted into orchard, vineyard, gardens, and fields by the inhabitants of Zion, and the standard be unfurled for the nations to gather thereto."

(Not everyone was as enchanted by the view. "We have traveled fifteen hundred miles over prairies, desert, and mountains," wrote Lorenzo Young's wife, Harriet, "but, feeble as I am, I would rather go a thousand miles farther than stay in such a place as this.")

Thirty-three years later, Woodruff would remember Young as saying, "It is enough. This is the right place, drive on." None of the journals from that day — including Woodruff's and Young's — record such a phrase.

Overlooking the fact that most of the Pioneers had already been in the valley for two days, July 24 is celebrated as the second most important day in the Mormon calendar (behind April 6, the day Joseph Smith organized the church). It was on that day that Wilford Woodruff's new year's prediction came true, and he brought his church's Moses down into the valley of the Promised Land.

Organized as always, the Pioneers had already plowed five acres of ground, dammed a stream for irrigating, and commenced planting crops. After supper, Woodruff took a half bushel himself and "planted my potatoes, hoping with the blessings of God at least to save the seed for another year." ☐ ☐

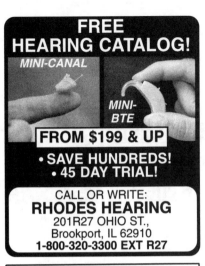

ADVERTISEMENT

Horse Liniment Eases Arthritis Pain

LOUISVILLE, KY -- An ingredient derived from hot peppers that decreases inflammation in racehorse's legs, has now been approved by government researchers for human use. The ingredient has been formulated into a product called ARTH-Rx®. ARTH-Rx comes in a strength designed for humans. Researchers are excited and say the formula can relieve arthritis pain for millions.

Developed by the Phillips Gulf Corporation, ARTH-Rx is a breakthrough in the treatment of painful disorders ranging from minor aches and pains to more serious conditions such as arthritis, bursitis, rheumatism, tendonitis, backache and more.

Although the mechanism by which ARTH-Rx works to relieve pain is not totally clear, scientists suggest that pain is relieved because ARTH-Rx intercepts the messenger substance that sends pain signals to the brain, thereby eliminating pain in the affected area..

ARTH-Rx is available in a convenient roll-on applicator at pharmacies and no prescription is required. According to a spokesperson for the company, due to the overwhelming demand for ARTH-Rx, supplies are sometimes limited. ARTH-Rx can also be ordered by sending $19.98 plus $3 shipping and handling to Phillips Gulf Corporation, 8767 115th Avenue North, Dept OFA, Largo, FL 34643 or for even faster service VISA/Mastercard is accepted by calling 1-800-729-8446. © 1996 PGC

"How A <u>Desperate</u> 53 Year Old Pennsylvania Housewife <u>Finally</u> Discovers The Secret to Safe, Gentle <u>Arthritis</u> <u>Pain Relief</u>"

Marcella Hardinger suffered from terrible arthritis pain for years. Recently, she stumbled onto a "relief secret" that has given her a new lease on life. Read her amazing story and discover it for yourself.

My name is Marcella Hardinger. I'm 53 years old. 5 foot 3 inches tall. My hair is silver-white. Naturally curly. I have blue-green eyes. Dark complexion. I'm also 47 pounds too heavy.

I live on a rural route a quarter of a mile north of the Mason Dixon Line — 25 miles south of Bedford, Pennsylvania.

I went to Fort Hill High in Cumberland, Maryland. I married my husband, Wilbur, in February 1961 and have lived in this house for 28 years.

I have four boys: Marty (my eldest), Scott, Ed and Steve.

I only wish I had known years ago what I am about to share with you now. To think of the pain — *the endless torture* — I could have avoided.

Arthritis Clobbers Me At Age 30

Let's go back in time. I'm 30 years old. Arthritis attacks my right foot. Then it spreads to my upper back. At first I *don't* realize it's arthritis. Why? Because a creek runs through the back of my property. The water is cold as ice. I swim in it. I think the cold water causes my pain, so I immediately stop swimming. The result?

Continuing Ache.

In fact, the pain in my upper back becomes *almost unbearable.* I *cannot* even turn over in bed. Peaceful sleep? Out of the question. Completely. Then I

have a *brainwave.* I think, "It must be the mattress!" So what do I do? I promptly buy a new one at L. Bernstein Furniture Company.

And the outcome? *No help.*

Out of *desperation* I finally see a doctor. He takes an X-ray and diagnoses me with *osteoarthritis.* He asks if arthritis runs in my family. I tell him my father, Marshall Adams, and his sister, Lorena Thompson, are both *crippled* by it.

Things go downhill fast. In 1985 I'm diagnosed with *rheumatoid arthritis* in both knees, both hips and my lower back!

To make matters worse, the middle finger in my right hand and the one next to it lock in a downward curve. The doctor calls it "trigger finger." They *won't straighten. I can't write.* Can you imagine not writing?!? The mental anguish is almost too much for me.

And . . . just as I think that nothing else can possibly go wrong . . .

My Arthritis Actually Rips the Cartilage In My Right Knee!

My doctor drains the fluid with a needle and gives me a shot of cortisone. It *doesn't* help, though. He says he can operate, but the arthritis may tear my cartilage *again.*

I decline.

Now I'm alarmed. Really scared. I picture myself *crippled* — like my father and aunt. I'm desperate —

don't know where to turn.

My pain is *brutal.* I try many strong "chemical" medications in search of relief. Sometimes *15 pills a day.* But over a long period they can produce many undesirable side-effects. Ulcers, chest pain, internal bleeding and stomach disorders. So I stop.

Dressing in the morning requires *Herculean strength.* I *cannot* even walk the length of the mall. Standing in one spot washing the dishes is *unbearable.* I have 3 flights of stairs in my home. I *cannot* walk up a single one — *all because of the pain!*

Anyway, recently I decide to try an *all natural* homeopathic remedy called Arthritis-Ease™. I'm extremely skeptical, but because I'm so *desperate* I figure, "What can I lose?"

The conclusion? Within several weeks, I notice a *real* difference. Something is *definitely working.* My pain is easing. Feet. Knees. Hips. Upper and lower back. Neck. Everywhere. *Blessed relief.*

I have less inflammation. Less bloating. Less swelling. More mobility. More agility. Do you know what this spells?

L-E-S-S P-A-I-N!

My body seems to dance with joy. And for good reason. I *couldn't* bend or scrub the floors before — from agony. Now I take a walk. Wash the dishes. Brush my teeth. Get dressed. Open a jar of canned fruit. Apply my makeup. Work in my garden. Best of all . . .

I stride up all 3 flights of stairs — virtually pain free! So what's the bottom line? Arthritis-Ease™ works for me. I believe in it. 100%. And most importantly . . .

It Can Work for You, Too!

Imagine doing things. Little things: tying your shoe laces. Shaving. Walking. Exercising. Bending. Stretching. Writing. Knitting. Holding a cup. Mowing the lawn. Now imagine doing them *without* squirming. Without *yelping.*

The company that distributes these amazing capsules has not paid me any money to write this letter.

The fact is, I'm so excited I did some homework on it. Turns out that homeopathic medicine is a science that has flourished in Europe for *two centuries.* It is based on the premise that humans — like animals and plants — have the ability to *self heal.*

Good health depends on a state of balance. When your equilibrium is disturbed, illness results. Samuel Hahnemann, who founded homeopathy 200 years ago, discovered that *minute* doses of substances known to produce certain symptoms can actually *combat a disease* producing the same symptoms. It's mind boggling.

It works in a quiet, special way — stimulating your *own* healing process. Many *traditional drugs* seek to suppress or eliminate symptoms, while homeopathy actually uses them to restore your health.

This "alternative medicine" brings about natural relief . . .

Without Side-Effects!

Arthritis-Ease™ is a *safe* and

gentle approach to arthritis pain. No harsh ingredients. No dangerous chemicals. No aspirin. No yeast. No eggs. No dairy products. No salt. No artificial colors or flavors. No sucrose sugar. No caffeine. And certainly no threat to your digestive system. Simply put: it *won't* tear up your stomach lining, or any part of your body. Just *safe, dependable* relief.

Arthritis-Ease™ is a 100% *natural* blend of the *highest quality* homeopathic ingredients in an herbal base.

Plus, it comes in capsules. Easy-to-swallow. There's a 30, 60 or 90 day supply. I *strongly* suggest that you start with at least a two month supply, as results vary.

Arthritis-Ease™ is *not* sold in stores. You can only acquire it direct, by mail.

No Risk Three Month Unconditional Trial Period

You get a 90-day unconditional money-back guarantee. If you're not satisfied for any reason, or no reason, simply return the *empty* container(s) for a full refund of the purchase price.

Still skeptical? As an extra safeguard you can even post date your check for 40 days ahead if you like. This way it's 100% non-cashable. You have plenty of time to put Arthritis-Ease™ to the test and prove things for yourself — while they *don't* even have your money.

If you're not satisfied, return the empty containers and you'll get your *original* check back — uncashed!

Early Bird FREE Gift

That's not all. Send for Arthritis-Ease™ within 11 days and you'll receive a valuable bonus report, **"Homeopathy: The Non-Harmful Healing Alternative to Harsh Drugs"** *FREE!* This awesome guide gives you helpful facts about treating

ailments with safe, gentle medicine — and the *truth* about using "normal" drugs.

It's a $15.00 value. But yours *free,* to keep forever no matter what, just for ordering *immediately.*

Why are they making this completely and totally risk-free for you? Simple: they *know* you will have less swelling. Less inflammation. Less stiffness. *Less pain.*

You *must* get blessed relief — guaranteed — or *they* will be left holding the short end of the stick.

They ship their capsules promptly. And ordering is a snap. Fill out the handy coupon. Mail it with your payment. In a hurry? Have your credit card ready. Call toll-free . . .

1-800-749-3937 Ext. 3

(9:00 am to 5:30 pm Pacific Time, weekdays only)

I urge you to try at least a 60 day supply, at no risk to you. And I mean *none* whatever.

Sincerely,

Marcella Hardinger

Marcella Hardinger

P.S. Order within 11 days and you'll receive a valuable $15.00 bonus report, *"Homeopathy: The Non-Harmful Healing Alternative to Harsh Drugs." FREE!* It's yours to keep forever, no matter what.

P.P.S. Give it a chance to work for you. A *real* chance. **I strongly recommend at least a two month supply.** However, a three month supply is your best bargain as you save $17.94. Your satisfaction is guaranteed, unconditionally, for 90 days. Remember, you can even post date your check for 40 days. Your arthritis pain must ease, or you get your money back.

If this desperate 53 year old Pennsylvania housewife can get safe, gentle arthritis pain relief... *you can, too.*

(Over Please)

I have used "Arthritis-Ease" for a couple of months. I have severe osteo arthritis and have had surgery to replace two hips. I'm in my sixties & with the hips replaced I do not have the mobility I had as a young woman. I do have arthritis in other parts of my body also. What I have discovered in taking Arthritis-Ease™ has been that my arthritis pain has been eased, and it also gives me a reason for getting up & a wellness feeling.

Elizabeth Billings, AZ

LYNN SCHWARTZ
Registered Nurse

I just had to write to you. I am a fifty one year old Registered Nurse and have been in Florida for the past 20 years. I have suffered from arthritis for the past 6 years and have been taking prescription drugs — Feldine 20mgs every day along with Axid 150 mgs twice a day.

On June 13, I started taking Arthritis-Ease™ along with my prescription drugs. I continued this regimen for 3 weeks. On July 4, I cut back my Rx medications to three days a week.

On July 18, I stopped taking Rx medications. I can't thank you enough for providing such a simple and inexpensive alternative to Rx drugs. I am feeling better physically. Moreover emotionally things are wonderful. Not taking drugs that are most probably harming other organs in my system has made a great impact in my life.

Lynn Schwartz, Registered Nurse
(Note: Consult your physician before changing any medications.)

Thank you for sending Arthritis-Ease™. I've had arthritis in both knees for about 6 years, but since last Christmas it is worse than ever.

I've been taking Anacin and Tylenol for the pain. I don't like Aspirin. Since taking your product I have received blessed relief in my knees.

Sincerely,
Carrie West, IL

I've had arthritis for many years, and when I would sit too long, I could hardly move. When I got up it hurt to move. The short time that I've been on Arthritis-Ease™ I have noticed a big difference. I've started walking again due to the pain relief. I do about a mile and a half, in 35 minutes. I'm glad I found Arthritis-Ease™, and I would recommend it to other sufferers.

Sincerely,
Shirley Mohrman, AZ

When I first received Arthritis-Ease we were out of town, so it was about 3 weeks later before I started using it. After 1 week to 10 days later I became aware that that blasted pain that so much a part of my every-day life was definitely lessened. Then I had knee surgery (arthritis-related) and had to curtail the product. Now I'm back on it (for about a week) and already feeling better again. Being realistic, I know it won't remove the spurs on my hips and knees, but less pain makes living definitely worth-while.

Marion Bullock, AZ

Today I'm half way through my 2nd bottle of Arthritis-Ease. My hands are much better-swelling is down, and my movement is improved. We are in the middle of a major snow storm which usually made me worse.

Bill Stark, CO

I find Arthritis-Ease™ very, very helpful. I have put aside the prescription tablets I had been taking for pain for quite some time. I recommend "Arthritis Ease™ " highly.
Mary Mason, CA

Important: Consult your physician before making any changes in your medication. This offer and product are not intended as a substitute for medical advice. Results vary from individual to individual and you may receive greater or lesser relief than those whose stories are enclosed.

PREDICT THE FUTURE ACCURATELY EVERY TIME

OR

WHO'S KIDDING WHOM?

To ascertain the state of the art in predicting the future, we asked writers and researchers from around the country to send us the latest theories on predicting everything from earthquakes to weather disasters to presidential elections to the stock market. Here are the results . . .

Earthquakes

When in Doubt, Apply the Chaos Theory

■ A new theory about earthquake mechanics emerged late in 1995 when two researchers, a geophysicist from the United States and a seismologist from Chile, proposed that explosive quakes along known fault lines can be predicted according to the position of the two colliding tectonic plates. When the plates are pushing against  each other from opposite directions, increased friction makes large earthquakes more likely. When one plate dives beneath another and both are moving in the same direction, there is less friction and less likelihood of a cataclysmic quake. Although this theory may not be a predictor of whether a given location will have an earthquake tomorrow, it may be useful in identifying high-risk areas. According to this model, one such area considered likely to produce a powerful earthquake is the northern California-Oregon-Washington basin known to seismologists as Cascadia.

However, many leading seismologists have concluded that earthquakes are inherently unpredictable,

. . . many leading seismologists have concluded that earthquakes

a classic example of a chaotic system. Those who support the chaos theory point out that the Earth's crust is always shifting, especially along fault lines, and small earthquakes occur all the time. For example, in California more than 25,000 small earthquakes a year are detected. For reasons not well understood, occasionally a small earthquake will set off a slightly larger one, and the effect will mushroom into a large quake. Dr. Thomas Heaton, a seismologist at the U.S. Geological Survey in Pasadena, California, hypothesizes that a large earthquake may simply be "a small one that ran away." He thinks we may never be able to predict which of the small quakes will explode into a large one.

P.S. from the Editors: Never say never, Dr. Heaton. Consider this little story from the Almanac archives:

At noon on August 16, 1959, every bird around Lake Hebgen, 12 miles west of Yellowstone National Park, began to leave the area. By nightfall, not a single bird was to be found on or around the lake — an event so singular that it aroused national as well as local scientific interest.

At midnight the first shocks of Yellowstone's huge 1959 earthquake began just west of the park.

Dr. John Aldrich of the U.S. Department of the Interior searched for evidence of similar bird evacuations in that area during previous years, but failed to find any. The only thing science really acknowledges here is that birds *are* acutely sensitive to atmospheric pressure, but the connection of that to an imminent earthquake is still mysterious.

Hurricanes
Just Ask Dr. Gray of Colorado

■ The leading forecaster of Atlantic hurricanes is Dr. William Gray of Colorado State University, who successfully predicted the active 1995 season. He and his colleagues consider five main factors in their forecasts:

1. The strength or weakness of the El Niño-Southern Oscillation, which measures sea sur-

Volcanoes
Perhaps Mountains Sing Before They Erupt

■ Figuring out when a known volcano will erupt next is a science in its infancy. Volcanologists study the eruptive history of an area and monitor it with sensitive equipment but still have trouble predicting (accurately) the

timing, size, or nature of any eruption. Time and again veteran scientists have been caught by surprise, sometimes with fatal results, while studying a volcano thought to be quiet.

As it turns out, volcanic mountains aren't quiet at all. Scientists recently put sensitive recording devices on the slopes of Mount Semeru, an active volcano and the highest mountain on the Indonesian island of Java. The researchers hoped that underground movement of gases and magma would send distinct vibrations toward the surface, and they expected to find irregular sounds much like the rumbling of a hungry stomach. To their surprise, they recorded a single, deep, constant sound, like one note from a pipe organ. The tone, or song, of the mountain was measured at below 8 hertz, inaudible to human ears (our low threshold is 20 hertz). What the scientists do not yet know is the meaning of this lonely note sounding from the heart of a volcano.

are inherently unpredictable, a classic example of a chaotic system.

face temperatures in the eastern equatorial Pacific. A moderate or strong El Niño enhances westerly winds over the Caribbean Basin and inhibits hurricane activity. (El Niño subsided in 1994, so the current cooler temperatures may allow for more hurricane activity.)

2. The strength of variable winds that circle the globe in the stratosphere near the equator, called the Quasi-Biennial Oscillation (QBO). When the prevailing QBO winds blow from the west, hurricanes in the Atlantic basin nearly double.

3. Rainfall in the West African Sahel region and the Gulf of Guinea, with higher amounts of rainfall in Africa associated with greater storminess in the Atlantic basin.

4. Temperature and pressure gradients in West Africa from February to May, which predict Atlantic hurricane activity later in the year.

5. Caribbean Basin sea-level pressure readings and measurements of winds at 40,000 feet during June and July of a hurricane season.

Gray's forecast for the 1996 season (which may be updated after the Almanac goes to press) calls for 11 named storms, seven of which will become hurricanes. The average season sees ten storms, six of them hurricanes. A forecast for 1997 was not available. During the next decade or two, as global wind and storm patterns shift, Gray and his team predict a dramatic increase in the number of Atlantic hurricanes making landfall.

What Will Happen Next?

Astrology Has the Answers — If You Believe

■ "We live in an oscillating universe, where cycles repeat and interact with each other," says David Solte of San Diego. For nearly 20 years, Solte has been analyzing historic and current events in relation to planetary cycles.

Solte began wondering about political astrology in the 1970s and was puzzled that the "birth sign" of the United States would be Cancer (a relatively shy and nurturing sign), based on the July 4, 1776, "birthday" of the country. It was not until he recast the country's chart using the date of the approval of the Articles of Confederation on November 15, 1777, that he felt he had found the real national horoscope. Using the Scorpio perspective, Solte says he found evidence for the nation's super-

---

During the next decade or two, Gray and his team predict a dramatic

---

Predicting Weather by the Moon

(Or Is It the Elves?)

■ Is there such a thing as "Moon weather"? Country wisdom says that the full Moon brings frosts in spring and fall and periods of extreme cold in winter. But researchers are finding that there is a striking correlation between the full Moon and cloudiness, rainfall, and thunderstorms. Astronomer Bob Berman, reporting in *Discover* magazine, wrote that the full Moon

raises temperatures in the lower four miles of the Earth's atmosphere by a few hundredths of a degree, a subtle change to be sure, but not negligible. Some scientists think that the full Moon's gravity is strong enough to distort the Earth's magnetic field, which in turn could trigger thunderstorms.

Which brings us to the subject of elves. These are not Santa's merry workers. To geophysicists, elves are extremely bright flashes of lightning at the very edge of space, high above garden-variety lightning storms. Researchers theorize that elves and their kin, called

---

power ambitions, military might, and love of guns; for our history of Yankee ingenuity and tradition of volunteerism; for status as the world's superconsumer; and for our tendency to continually reinvent ourselves.

Solte believes that the planetary cycle most important in shaping American history is the 14-year Jupiter-Uranus cycle. Every seven years, the two planets are at either opposition or conjunction. Both aspects coincide with major "discovery events" from Columbus's discovery of the New World to Neil Armstrong's landing on the Moon. "No other culture in history is as obsessed with discovery as we are," says Solte.

Of immediate import, according to Solte, is a Jupiter-Uranus conjunction in Aquarius, which will be in operation during the 1996 election season

and into 1997. Solte calls this "the most powerful planetary configuration in U.S. history," indicating a "revolution in government, a revolution from the grassroots, an era of the common man . . . and a transformation of the American economy." He adds that "Election Day 1996 is one of the most stressed-out election-day charts I've ever seen." (Let's all take a couple of deep breaths when we wake up on November 5, and not too much coffee, OK?)

What does Solte see for the future? Quoting Thomas Jefferson, Solte says, "We may consider each generation a distinct nation." To Solte this means a transition from the

Age of Gemini, which began in 1964 (according to the astrologically "progressed" chart) and was characterized by experimentation, polarization, and division, to the Age of Cancer, which began in 1995 and will usher in a 30-year "era of nurturing and inner healing." Solte predicts these trends will shape American culture in the coming decades:

■ Emphasis on home, family, community, and the environment, with innovations at state and local levels.

■ Working from the home as the predominant lifestyle, thanks to computer technology.

■ Social tribalism, gated communities, and other evidence of isolationism.

■ Women rising to new heights of prominence and power.

■ The return of neighborhood schools and an increase in home schooling.

■ Political success for candidates who support these things.

– Peg Boyles

(continued on next page)

increase in the number of major Atlantic hurricanes making landfall.

jets and sprites, introduce large amounts of nitrogen oxides into the stratosphere and just might affect global weather, ozone depletion, and storm formation. Elves materialize in the ionosphere right after large bolts of lightning hit the ground and can appear as fiery disks (UFOs, anyone?).

Finally, there is, of course, *The Old Farmer's Almanac* method of predicting the weather, a method newly improved and expanded upon from the basic theory used, with moderate to good success, for the past 205 years. Simply put, the Almanac theory correlates

complex activity on the Sun with fluctuating weather here on Earth. **(Elves and sprites? We'll have to look into that idea for next year! – Ed.)**

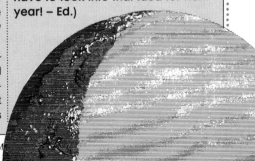

Presidential Elections...

Can You Prove the Answer Is in the Moon? (A Contest for *Old Farmer's Almanac* Readers)

■ The chart at right, prepared using data on the Moon's age from past editions of this Almanac, begins on November 7, 1848, when presidential elections were first conducted on a uniform election day.

Lines in italics indicate presidents who took office due to the death or resignation of the elected president; in those instances the Moon's age is given for the date that the vice president took the oath of office.

We will give a prize of $100 for the best analysis of the data, either proving or disproving the notion that the Moon can influence the outcome of presidential elections. Deadline is February 28, 1997. Please send your analysis to: Elections, *The Old Farmer's Almanac*, Main Street, Dublin, NH 03444. Thank you!

Approximate Correlation Between Moon Age and Moon Phase:

0 1 2 3 4 5 6 7 **8** 9 10 11 12 13 14 15
New Moon   **First Quarter**

➡ **W A X I N G** ➡

16 17 18 19 20 21 22 **23** 24 25 26 27 28 29
Full Moon   **Last Quarter**

➡ **W A N I N G** ➡

Outcomes of Presidential Elections Through All the Lunations of Voting Day

DATE	MOON AGE	PRESIDENT	PARTY
Nov. 7, 1848	12	Zachary Taylor	W*
July 10, 1850	*1*	*Millard Fillmore*	*W*
Nov. 2, 1852	20	Franklin Pierce	D
Nov. 4, 1856	7	James Buchanan	D
Nov. 6, 1860	23	Abraham Lincoln	R
Nov. 8, 1864	9	Abraham Lincoln	R
Apr. 15, 1865	*19*	*Andrew Johnson*	*R*
Nov. 3, 1868	19	Ulysses S. Grant	R
Nov. 5, 1872	4	Ulysses S. Grant	R
Nov. 7, 1876	21	Rutherford B. Hayes	R
Nov. 2, 1880	New	James A. Garfield	R
Sept. 20, 1881	*27*	*Chester A. Arthur*	*R*
Nov. 4, 1884	17	Grover Cleveland	D
Nov. 6, 1888	3	Benjamin Harrison	R
Nov. 8, 1892	19	Grover Cleveland	D
Nov. 3, 1896	28	William McKinley	R
Nov. 6, 1900	Full	William McKinley	R
Sept. 14, 1901	*2*	*Theodore Roosevelt*	*R*
Nov. 8, 1904	1	Theodore Roosevelt	R
Nov. 3, 1908	9	William H. Taft	R
Nov. 5, 1912	26	Woodrow Wilson	D
Nov. 7, 1916	12	Woodrow Wilson	D
Nov. 2, 1920	22	Warren G. Harding	R
Nov. 4, 1924	7	Calvin Coolidge	R
Nov. 6, 1928	24	Herbert Hoover	R
Nov. 8, 1932	10	Franklin D. Roosevelt	D
Nov. 3, 1936	19	Franklin D. Roosevelt	D
Nov. 5, 1940	6	Franklin D. Roosevelt	D
Nov. 7, 1944	21	Franklin D. Roosevelt	D
Apr. 12, 1945	*New*	*Harry S. Truman*	*D*
Nov. 2, 1948	1	Harry S. Truman	D
Nov. 4, 1952	16	Dwight D. Eisenhower	R
Nov. 6, 1956	4	Dwight D. Eisenhower	R
Nov. 8, 1960	19	John F. Kennedy	D
Nov. 22, 1963	*7*	*Lyndon B. Johnson*	*D*
Nov. 3, 1964	29	Lyndon B. Johnson	D
Nov. 5, 1968	15	Richard M. Nixon	R
Nov. 7, 1972	1	Richard M. Nixon	R
Aug. 9, 1974	*21*	*Gerald R. Ford*	*R*
Nov. 2, 1976	10	Jimmy Carter	D
Nov. 4, 1980	27	Ronald Reagan	R
Nov. 6, 1984	13	Ronald Reagan	R
Nov. 8, 1988	29	George Bush	R
Nov. 3, 1992	9	Bill Clinton	D

* Whig

(continued on page 114)

DISCOVER AMERICA'S #1 "OFF-LAWN" MOWER!

Send for your FREE CATALOG on the amazing TROY-BILT® Sickle Bar Mower!

If you own an acre or more of property, the TROY-BILT® Sickle Bar Mower is the perfect "OFF-LAWN" Mower for cutting tall grass and weeds of any height — practically anywhere you can walk!

Now with power steering for greater maneuverability!

Comfortable, vibration-absorbing handlebars!

Powered wheels just roll over rugged terrain!

3 Models up to 5HP, 42" cut!

Mow Anything...Anywhere!
- **Clear overgrown areas** with far less effort.
- **Amazingly fast...** clears an acre in just 1 hour!
- **Cut your tallest weeds** — thorny brambles, sumac, goldenrod — even brush and saplings up to 1" thick.
- **Blaze trails** for walking, riding, skiing or snowmobiling!
- **Enjoy your property more** by making it useful & attractive!

BEFORE

Easily mow 2,800 square feet of tall weeds in less than 5 minutes with this amazing "Off-Lawn" Mower!

AFTER

For a FREE CATALOG, Call
1-800-908-2266 Dept. 5108
or send coupon today!

⬡ TROY-BILT®
America's Backyard Legend

NEW!

…and Other Natural Disasters

If You Can Understand Catastrophe Options, You're a Genius (or a Fool)

■ Emanating from unlikely origins on the volatile trading floor of the Chicago Board of Trade comes a glimmer of hope for softening the economic blow of high winds, flooding, earthquakes, volcanoes, tidal waves, even asteroid collisions — and even for predicting their occurrence. It's a financial device called catastrophe options contracts. "Cat options," as they are called, are emerging as a way for individuals, insurers, and entire nations to weather the tremendous costs of events such as 1992's Hurricane Andrew (estimated $20 billion in losses) by spreading the costs around.

And because so much money is at risk, "cat option investors" are scouring the universe for every available scientific indicator of an upcoming disaster. If you're concerned about the potential for disaster in your area, consider tossing out the Ouija board and reading the financial columns instead.

Catastrophe futures work in the way familiar crop futures work: Hedgers (those who are attached to the status quo, such as insurance companies) shift their risk to speculators (who are willing to bet on a change in the status quo in pursuit of profit). Those who want to dabble in this relatively new way to make (or lose) a pile of money buy cat options through Property Claims Services (PCS), a recognized property-casualty insurance authority for calculating property damage estimates through nine indices for trading at the Chicago Board of Trade. There are five regional indices for the United States, three indices specific to the states of Florida, Texas, and California, and a national index. Each index is based on estimated upcoming quarterly "loss periods" calculated by the insurance industry. If losses for the quarter are less than the price of the index at the time of sale, the speculator earns a profit.

Russ Ray, professor of finance at the University of Louisville's College of Business and Public Administration, described the potential of catastrophe futures in a recent issue of *The Futurist:* "Once they become

(continued on p. 116)

more common, catastrophe futures may become an invaluable tool for predicting natural catastrophes. . . . This is because futures are nothing more than predicted prices, and people become very good predictors when their own money is on the line."

However, here's one caveat for anyone anxious to jump on the bandwagon: **Do not try this at home! Call your broker!** And don't be too surprised if he or she has never heard of cat options. Meanwhile, you can check out the PCS options' quotes weekly in *Business Insurance* magazine, or visit the Internet home page of the Chicago Board of Trade at http://www.cbot.com.

Where else can you make money by betting on how bad the weather's going to be? — *David Lord*

Booms and Busts

Just Use the K Wave Hypothesis. It Works. (Some of the time.)

■ The K wave, as postulated by Russian economist Nikolai Kondratieff in the 1920s, is a recurring 50- to 60-year cycle of boom and bust in capitalist economies. Kondratieff, studying data from the rise of the Western industrial economy in the 1790s, concluded that prices and production rise and fall cyclically and inevitably, due to the nature of capitalism.

David Knox Barker, a modern investment analyst, has taken the K wave hypothesis further by suggesting that the boom-and-bust cycle has origins not only in the laws of the marketplace but also in human psychology and the physical laws of the universe itself. In his book *The K Wave: Profiting from the Cyclical Booms and Busts in the Global Economy* (Irwin Professional Publishing, 1995), Barker says that post-World War II prosperity crested around 1981. He sees us as being in a global depression that will last until about 2007, when recovery will begin, with another downturn from 2030 to 2054.

Barker's belief in his expanded K wave theory is bolstered by a study at the Massachusetts Institute of Technology, using a computer model of 45- to 60-year peaks of high prices and industrial productivity that closely match Kondratieff's findings. Barker also believes that something much more basic is at work: As memory of an economic depression fades, people (and businesses) become more arrogant and greedy, take on too much debt, produce more than the market will bear, and *voilà*, a new economic depression comes along as a rude awakening. □ □

U s e Insects as Thermometers —
THEY'RE FREE!

by E r i c a L . G l a s e n e r

Did you know that you can tell how hot it is by listening to insects? Insects are very sensitive to temperature changes, and the reaction of some species to heat and cold is a good indication of temperature, wrote J. Henryette Hallenbeck in a 1931 edition of *Boys' Life*.

The grasshopper is loudest at 95° F and is unable to chirp when the temperature falls below 62° F. He cannot fly at a temperature below 45° F, and at 36° or 37° F he is unable to jump. Whenever you hear a grasshopper, you know the temperature is at least 62° F.

Crickets are still more accurate. Two species of crickets — the common house cricket and the white tree cricket — are excellent thermometers. To calculate the temperature from the house cricket's tune,

count the number of chirps he makes in 14 seconds, to that add 40, and you will have the temperature — that is, the temperature at the location of the cricket.

The number of chirps in the song of the white tree cricket and its relation to the temperature have been reduced to a similar mathematical formula, which Hallenbeck attributed to a Professor Dolbear of Massachusetts (although a Dr. Robert Ede found this formula one degree too high). The white tree cricket chirps four times per minute for every degree of temperature above 40° F.

The white tree cricket is a more useful thermometer than the house cricket because, while each proclaims the temperature of the air around him, the former is out in the open while the latter usually is in some warm nook in the house where the temperature may be quite different from that outdoors.

The katydid's night call is most emphatic above 80° F — "Katee did it!" And his cadence drops by ap-

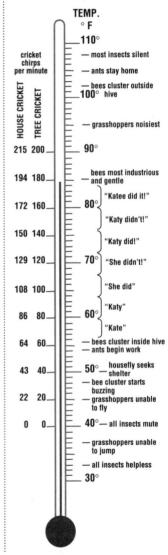

TEMP.
° F

cricket chirps per minute

HOUSE CRICKET	TREE CRICKET		
		110°	
			— most insects silent
			— ants stay home
			— bees cluster outside
		100°	hive
215	200		— grasshoppers noisiest
		90°	
194	180		bees most industrious — and gentle
172	160	**80°**	"Katee did it!"
			"Katy didn't!"
150	140		"Katy did!"
129	120	**70°**	"She didn't!"
108	100		"She did"
86	80	**60°**	"Katy"
			"Kate"
64	60		— bees cluster inside hive — ants begin work
43	40	**50°**	housefly seeks — shelter
			— bee cluster starts buzzing
22	20		— grasshoppers unable to fly
0	0	**40°**	—all insects mute
			— grasshoppers unable to jump
			— all insects helpless
		30°	

proximately four-degree intervals to "Katy didn't!" to "Katy did!" to "She didn't," "She did," and "Katy." Below 60° F, the cry is a feeble "Kate." The first call ("Katee did it!") rarely is heard, for in the katydid season (late summer) the temperature usually is below 80° F by sunset. The last two ("Katy" and "Kate") are also seldom heard, for most people are in bed asleep before the little fellow gets down to his last notes.

Honeybees cluster outside their hive when the temperature reaches 102° F and cluster compactly inside their hive when the temperature falls to 57° F. At 48° F the clustered bees begin buzzing to generate heat. The best working temperature for bees is 85° F; at this degree they are also very gentle, but at temperatures below 70° F they are very irritable and will attack people without provocation.

Ants do not emerge from their subterranean dens until the temperature has risen to 55° F, and they return home when it reaches 105° F. It is said that there are species of ants in Arizona, however, that remain active at temperatures above 105° F.

At 40° F all insects are silent, and at 33° or 34° F our insect thermometer ceases to register because all the insects are helpless.

This article was adapted from "Curious But True: An Insect's Thermometer," from the June 1931 edition of *Boys' Life*. The *Old Farmer's Almanac* was unable to locate J. Henryette Hallenbeck but welcomes her comments.

More

AMAZING STUFF

About Bugs

Insect World Records

What started as a classroom assignment to improve entomology students' research and writing skills developed into a fascinating stop on the Internet. Published electronically by the University of Florida in Gainesville, the *Book of Insect Records* was the brainchild of Professor Thomas J. Walker and his Insect Ecology students. Here are a few highlights:

■ **Fastest Fliers.** At speeds of over 60 miles per hour, the dragonfly (*Austrophlebia costalis*) might be considered the Carl Lewis of the insect world — except when it comes to chasing women. The gold medal in that event goes to the male horsefly (*Hybomitra hinei wrighti*), which travels at over 90 miles per hour when pursuing the object of his affection.

■ **Longest Migration:** In the fall of 1988, the desert locust (*Schistocerca gregaria*) from northern Africa traveled over 2,800 miles to the Caribbean islands and parts of South America.

■ **Most Spectacular Mating:** In the world of honeybees (*Apis mellifera*), a swarm of males called drone comets chase the queen, hovering around her until it is their turn to mate. Once a drone mates with the queen, he loses part of his phallus and dies. The queen usually mates with an average of seven to ten different males. Reports cite queens taking on as many as 17 different mates.

■ **Least Picky Eater:** Gardeners will find no solace in learning that North America's fall web worm (*Hyphantria cunea*) made it into the record book for having the widest host range — over 600 different species of plants throughout the world, more than the gypsy moth or the Japanese beetle.

■ **Most Hardy:** The African midge (*Polypedilum vanderplanki*) is a two-time winner. As the most tolerant of cold, it can survive when submersed in liquid helium (-270° C), and its larvae are most tolerant of desiccation. What's surprising is that this hardy record holder hails from the tropical climate of West Africa.

■ **Most Resistant to Pesticides:** One champion that's hard to cheer about, especially for farmers, is the green peach aphid (*Myzus persicae*). Known to resist 71 synthetic chemical insecticides and to carry viruses that attack potatoes and other crops, this aphid can cause tremendous economic loss.

If you would like to contribute to this effort, contact Thomas J. Walker, Editor, *Book of Insect Records*, Department of Entomology & Nematology, University of Florida, Gainesville, FL 32611-0620. Fax 904-392-0190; tjw@gnv.ifas.ufl.edu for E-mail. Send contributions of insect superlatives to http://gnv.ifas.ufl.edu/~tjw/recbk.htm. ☐☐

GENERAL WEATHER FORECAST
1 9 9 6 - 1 9 9 7

(For details see regional forecasts beginning on page 122.)

NOVEMBER THROUGH MARCH will start relatively mild from New England south to the Carolinas and westward to the eastern Great Lakes, but the latter half of the winter will be cold. Temperatures in Florida will be below normal. From Texas to Georgia and northward to the Canadian border, the winter will, on average, be milder than usual, especially in December. February temperatures from Kansas and Missouri northward to the Dakotas will be unusually mild, but March will be quite chilly. Temperatures in the West will be near or slightly above normal. **Precipitation** will be above normal from New England to the mid-Atlantic, in Florida, from New York through the Great Lakes, in the central and northern Great Plains, in the Rockies, and in the Pacific Northwest. Much of the area from the Carolinas to the Tennessee and Ohio River valleys to the Gulf states will be drier than normal. Precipitation will also be below normal in the Southwest. **Snowfall** is expected to be above normal in much of the eastern and central parts of the country. From New England westward into the northern Great Plains, snowfall will be fairly heavy. Snowfall will be about normal near the coast from New York City southward, but above normal from the interior of the Atlantic States all the way west to Kansas and Nebraska, except near normal in the Ohio Valley. Snowfall in the Rocky Mountains and Northwest will generally be below normal, but above-normal amounts are expected in the California mountains.

APRIL THROUGH JUNE will be relatively cool in much of the country, with above-normal temperatures from Texas and Oklahoma eastward to the Atlantic and in the Rockies and Pacific Northwest. Especially cool temperatures will occur in April in the northern Great Plains and in May from the mid-Atlantic to the Tennessee Valley. The Southeast will have a warm June. Precipitation will be above normal in New England, in Florida, from New York through the Great Lakes and Ohio Valley, in a swath from Texas to South Dakota, in the desert Southwest, and in much of the Rocky Mountain region. Rainfall will be below normal along much of the Atlantic and Pacific coasts.

JULY AND AUGUST will be hotter than normal from Maryland through Florida, in most of the Southeast and Gulf states, in Texas and Oklahoma, and in the northern Great Plains. Relatively cool temperatures will prevail in the Northeast, the Great Lakes, the central Great Plains, and on the Pacific coast. Temperatures will be near normal elsewhere. Summer rainfall will be below normal from New England to Florida, near normal in the West, and above normal elsewhere.

SEPTEMBER AND OCTOBER will be unusually warm across most of the country, but cooler than normal from the Rockies to the Pacific. Rainfall will be above normal in Florida, the Great Lakes, southeast New England, northern Great Plains, and Pacific Northwest. It will be relatively dry in the central Great Plains, Texas, and the Southwest.

– Beth Krommes

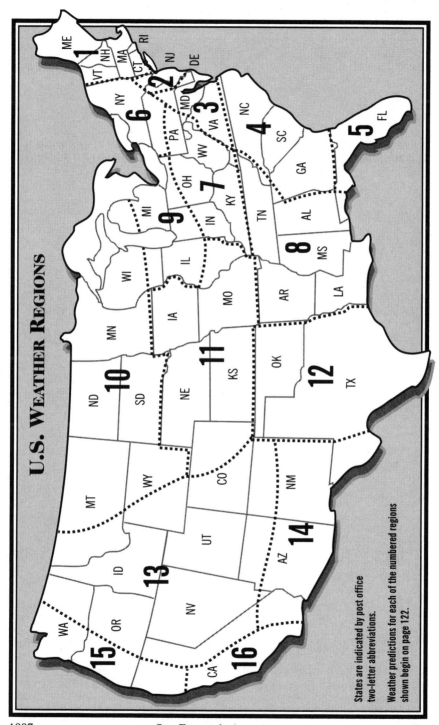

U.S. WEATHER REGIONS

States are indicated by post office two-letter abbreviations.

Weather predictions for each of the numbered regions shown begin on page 122.

SUMMARY: *Temperatures during the period from November through March are expected to average near normal in the east and below normal in the west despite a warm November and a big January thaw. Most of New England will have above-normal snowfall, with the bulk of the snow after the new year begins. November will start and end with heavy rain, with mostly dry, warm weather in between. The week before Christmas will be cold enough to keep any white on the ground. Particularly stormy weeks in January may occur after New Year's Day and during midmonth, followed by a January thaw. February and early March will generally be snowy and cold, with a few heavy snowstorms.*

April and May will be highly variable, with alternating warmth and unseasonable chilliness. April showers will lead to May rainstorms, with heavy rain about once a week.

Temperatures in the period from June through August will average 2 to 3 degrees below normal, with slightly below normal rainfall. The best chances for heat waves are in mid- to late June, mid-July, and early August. A final hot spell in late August will be followed by cooler weather to start September. One or two hurricanes may hit New England in September, with the the most likely times being early in the month and again around midmonth. October will be warm and dry.

NOV. 1996: Temp. 52° (7° above avg.); precip. 4.5" (1.5" above avg.). 1-3 Warm, heavy rain. 4-8 Sunny, mild. 9-11 Cold, rainy; snow north. 12-20 Mostly dry, seasonable. 21-25 Sunny, warm. 26-30 Heavy rain, warm, then cooler.

DEC. 1996: Temp. 35° (2° above avg.; 4° above north); precip. 4" (0.5" above avg.; 2" above north). 1-6 Rain, snow north. 7-8 Warmer. 9-11 Rainy, warm. 12-15 Mild, showers. 16-19 Mild, rain southeast. 20-23 Cold, flurries. 24-25 Milder. 26-27 Cold; snow north, rain south. 28-31 Cold, flurries north.

JAN. 1997: Temp. 27° (3° below avg.; avg. north); precip. 2.5" (0.5" below avg.; 0.5" above southeast). 1-3 Milder, dry. 4-6 Very cold. 7-10 Snowy, cold. 11-12 Bitter cold. 13-16 Blizzard. 17-22 Cold, snow showers. 23-25 January thaw. 26-27 Cold snap. 28-31 Mild, then snow.

FEB. 1997: Temp. 27° (3° below avg.; 1° below north); precip. 2.5" (0.5" below avg.); 1-5 Bitter cold, light snow. 6-8 Snow, mild. 9-11 Cold, dry. 12-15 Cold, snow. 16-17 Very cold. 18-19 Milder. 20-22 Rain, then snow north. 23-26 Mild, rain. 27-28 Cool, dry.

MAR. 1997: Temp. 35° (3.5° below avg.; 5° below north); precip. 4" (0.5" above avg.). 1-3 Rain south, snow north. 4-6 Warm, dry. 7-10 Rain, snow; cold. 11-14 Showers south, flurries north. 15-16 Cold, dry. 17-18 Snow, heavy east. 19-22 Chilly. 23-24 Rain, warm. 25-27 Cool. 28-31 Rain southeast, snow north.

APR. 1997: Temp. 47° (1.5° below avg.; avg. northeast); precip. 3.5" (avg.). 1-4 Warm then cold, snow north. 5-9 Mainly dry. 10-12 Mild, showers. 13-18 Seasonable, rain north. 19-22 Stormy. 23-26 Warm, dry. 27-30 Showers, seasonable.

MAY 1997: Temp. 59° (2° above avg. north; 1° below south); precip. 4" (0.5" above avg.; 3" above southeast). 1-2 Rain, chilly. 3-5 Sunny, warm. 6-8 Rain, cool. 9-11 Dry, chilly. 12-14 Rainstorm. 15-18 Sunny, seasonable. 19-20 Windy, heavy coastal rain. 21-24 Sunny. 25-26 Heavy rain. 27-31 Seasonable.

JUNE 1997: Temp. 66° (2° below avg.); precip. 3" (0.5" below avg. north; 0.5" above south). 1-5 Warm, thunderstorms. 6-11 Showers, then cool. 12-16 Cool, mainly dry. 17-20 Showers, cool. 21-26 Sunny, hot. 27-30 Showers, seasonable.

JULY 1997: Temp. 72° (1° below avg.; 3° below north); precip. 3.5" (avg.). 1-4 Cool, showers. 5-8 Sunny, comfortable. 9-14 Some showers. 15-17 Hot, humid. 18-20 Thunderstorms then cool, less humid. 21-24 Sunny, warm. 25-27 Rainy, cool. 28-31 Warmer.

AUG. 1997: Temp. 69° (3° below avg.; 6° below northwest); precip. 2.5" (1" below avg.). 1-4 Hot, few thunderstorms. 5-6 Less humid. 7-8 Showers north, rain south. 9-12 Seasonable, showers. 13-14 Damp, rainy. 15-19 Cool. 20-22 Hot then cooler, thunderstorms. 23-26 Comfortable. 27-29 Hot, thunderstorms. 30-31 Dry, cool.

SEPT. 1997: Temp. 66° (2° above avg.; 4° above north); precip. 4" (1" above avg.; 4" above southeast). 1-2 Sunny, cool. 3-4 Rain. 5-8 Seasonable. 9-11 Showers, warm. 12-14 Cool. 15-16 Rain, coastal flooding. 17-19 Cool north with showers, dry south. 20-23 Cool, rainy. 24-30 Warm.

OCT. 1997: Temp. 61° (6° above avg.; 8° above avg. south); precip. 2.5" (1" below avg.). 1-4 Sunny, warm. 5-8 Warm, showers. 9-11 Cool, rain. 12-15 Warmer, showers. 16-19 Sunny, warm. 20-28 Mainly dry, warm spells. 29-31 Warm, showers.

Caribou

Burlington

Boston

Hartford

Andy Griffith

Sings For You In His
"Precious Memories"
Songs Of Faith Treasury

I've always liked to sing. Don Knotts (Barney Fife) and I used to sing on the old "Andy Griffith Show"...often hymns. I even sang on that lawyer show, "Matlock". But never like this...with some of the finest singers and musicians in the world.

"These Are The Songs I've Known All My Life... I Hope You'll Let Me Share Them With You!"

The first solo I ever sang in church was "Sweet Hour Of Prayer". I was fifteen years old. My family was proud and now I'm proud. I get a chance to sing again for you and your family. There are 33 beautiful old-time hymns on this album. They are Precious Memories...with hope and inspiration for today and tomorrow.   *-ANDY GRIFFITH-*

Read the wonderful list of titles below. These are the enduring songs of faith that have brought hope and inspiration to generations. Every cherished favorite sung in the sincere, heart-touching style that has made Andy Griffith one of America's most beloved stars. We guarantee you and your family will play and enjoy this album more than any other. Don't miss out! Order yours today.

★ ★ ★ ★ ★ ★ ★ 33 BEAUTIFUL SONGS OF FAITH ★ ★ ★ ★ ★ ★ ★

Sweet Hour Of Prayer • Will The Circle Be Unbroken • Precious Memories • The Old Rugged Cross • In The Garden • Softly And Tenderly • When They Ring The Golden Bells • In The Sweet By And By • Shall We Gather At The River • What A Friend We Have In Jesus • When The Saints Go Marching In • How Great Thou Art • Sweet Prospect • I Am Bound For The Promised Land • Amazing Grace • I Love To Tell The Story • Wayfaring Stranger • Near The Cross • Precious Lord, Take My Hand • Just A Closer Walk With Thee • Whispering Hope • When We All Get To Heaven • We'll Understand It By And By • When the Roll Is Called Up Yonder ... AND MANY MORE!

The Beautiful Music Co., Dept. GF-93, 320 Main St., Northport, N.Y. 11768

Please rush my "Precious Memories" on your unconditional money-back guarantee.

- ☐ I enclose $12.98. Send 2 Cassettes.
- ☐ I enclose $12.98. Send 2 Records.
- ☐ I enclose $16.98. Send 1 Compact Disc.

You Save! FREE Shipping & Handling!

Or Charge My: ☐ Visa ☐ MasterCard
          ☐ American Express ☐ Discover

Name _____

Address _____

City _____

Card No. _____

Exp. Date _____   State _____ Zip _____

2 GREATER NEW YORK-NEW JERSEY
FORECAST

SUMMARY: *The period from November through March will bring several major storms, with snow in the interior and rain along the coast. Snowfall will generally be above normal, heaviest in the higher elevations. Look for major snowstorms in mid-December, early and mid-January, the last week of February, and the first week of March. Temperatures will average near to below normal, with the coldest temperatures in January surrounding a major thaw. Several unseasonably warm spells may occur in November and December; cold spells will occur into April.*

April and May will be cool and cloudy, with some warm spells. Although the amount of rainfall may be below normal, many days will be dampened by gusty showers as heavy rain passes near the coast.

Temperatures in the period from June through August will average 1 to 2 degrees below normal, with near-normal rainfall. Look for the first heat wave in mid- to late June, with sweltering heat and humidity in mid-July and early and late August. The final heat wave may be concluded by severe thunderstorms. September and October will be several degrees warmer than normal, with above-normal rainfall in September, but mainly dry weather in October. A hurricane may brush the eastern part of the region in mid-September. October will be relatively mild, suggesting little of the winter that will inevitably follow.

NOV. 1996: Temp. 51.5° (4° above avg.); precip. 4.5" (1" above avg.). 1-3 Windy, heavy rain. 4-8 Sunny, mild. 9-11 Cold rain, snow inland. 12-18 Sunny, cool. 19-24 Dry, mild. 25-30 Rainy, turning colder.

DEC. 1996: Temp. 38.5° (2° above avg.); precip. 4" (0.5" above avg.). 1-5 Seasonable, showers. 6-8 Dry, milder. 9-11 Heavy rain. 12-15 Mild, showers. 16-18 Heavy rain and snow. 19-23 Sunny, cold. 24-27 Milder, showers. 28-31 Sunny, cold.

JAN. 1997: Temp. 28° (3° below avg.); precip. 2.5" (0.5" below avg.). 1-2 Snow west, rain east. 3-6 Dry, cold. 7-10 Snow north, rain south and east. 11-13 Sunny, cold. 14-16 Rain, then snow. 17-18 Windy, cold. 19-20 Snow, then rain. 21-25 January thaw. 26-28 Cold. 29-31 Milder, showers.

FEB. 1997: Temp. 31° (2° below avg.); precip. 2.5" (0.5" below avg.). 1-5 Sunny, cold. 6-8 Snow north. 9-12 Cold, dry. 13-14 Mild. 15-17 Thunderstorm, then bitter cold. 18-20 Warm. 21-23 Rain, snow northwest. 24-28 Seasonable, flurries north.

MAR. 1997: Temp. 41.5° (avg.); precip. 4" (1" above avg.). 1-3 Showers. 4-7 Colder, snow inland, rain coast. 8-10 Sunny, cold. 11-14 Milder. 15-18 Rain, snow inland. 19-22 Dry, cool. 23-25 Rainy. 26-31 Showers, cool.

APR. 1997: Temp. 51° (avg.); precip. 2.5" (1" below avg.). 1-3 Sunny, cool. 4-5 Rain, snow north. 6-9 Sunny, cool. 10-12 Warm, showers. 13-18 Showers north, dry and warm south. 19-21 Heavy rain. 22-25 Warmer. 26-30 Showers.

MAY 1997: Temp. 60° (2° below avg.); precip. 2.5" (1" below avg.). 1-2 Heavy rain north, showers south. 3-5 Sunny. 6-8 Warm south, then rain. 9-11 Cool, dry. 12-14 Damp, cool. 15-20 Cool, dry. 21-25 Showers, cool. 26-31 Sunny, seasonable.

JUNE 1997: Temp. 70° (1° below avg.); precip. 3.5" (avg.). 1-5 Sunny, warm. 6-8 Showers. 9-14 Cool, dry. 15-19 Hot, humid, afternoon thunderstorms. 20-22 Cool. 23-30 Dry, hot.

JULY 1997: Temp. 75.5° (1° below avg.); precip. 2" (2" below avg.). 1-3 Cool, dry. 4-12 Muggy, thunderstorms. 13-16 Sunny, seasonable. 17-18 Heat wave. 19-24 Warm, showers. 25-31 Sunny, warm and humid.

AUG. 1997: Temp. 73° (2° below avg.); precip. 5" (1" above avg.). 1-5 Sunny, hot and humid. 6-8 Heavy rain. 9-12 Seasonable. 13-14 Severe thunderstorms. 15-18 Sunny. 19-22 Hot, then thunderstorms, cooler. 23-26 Showery. 27-31 Seasonable, showers north.

SEPT. 1997: Temp. 70° (2° above avg.); precip. 3.5" (0.5" above avg.; 2" above east). 1-2 Sunny, cool. 3-4 Rain north. 5-11 Mostly sunny, warmer. 12-13 Seasonable. 14-15 Rain northeast. 16-18 Sunny, cool. 19-25 Unsettled, showers. 26-30 Sunny, mild.

OCT. 1997: Temp. 63° (5° above avg.); precip. 1" (2" below avg.). 1-6 Sunny, warm. 7-9 Very warm, thunderstorms. 10-12 Cool. 13-17 Sunny, warm. 18-26 Cooler, few showers. 27-31 Warm, then showers.

New York

Philadelphia

Atlantic City

3 MIDDLE ATLANTIC COAST
F O R E C A S T

SUMMARY: *The period from November through March will be colder and snowier than normal. It will be a winter of storms and rumors of storms, but with more gentle thaws we should avoid a repeat of last January's flooding. November and December will feature mild spells with temperatures averaging above normal, but by the time March marches out, average temperatures for the entire season will have fallen below normal. The best chance for snow in December is midmonth, but watch for three snowstorms in January. Most storms in February will just miss the region, but heavy rain and possibly snow should hit toward month's end.*

April and May will bring hints of summer, but frequent cool spells in May will delay any early trips to the beach.

Temperatures in the period from June to August will average near normal, but with spells of low humidity, some of the nights will be cool enough for you to turn off the fans. Watch for heat waves in mid-June, mid-July, and early and late August. Rainfall during the summer will be below normal, but with enough thunderstorms and rainy spells to avoid a serious drought. Severe thunderstorms and even a tornado may move through in mid- to late August.

September and October will be unusually warm and dry, with several record high temperatures possible. But don't be lulled into thinking winter might not come; it's still ahead.

NOV. 1996: Temp. 52° (4° above north; 1° above south); precip. 3" (avg.; 2" above southwest). 1-2 Rain. 3-7 Sunny, warmer. 8-9 Colder. 10-11 Cold rain. 12-18 Sunshine, cool. 19-24 Dry, mild. 25-30 Rain, then cooler.

DEC. 1996: Temp. 42.5° (3° above avg.); precip. 3" (avg.; 2" above south). 1-6 Sunny, cold. 7-14 Mild, occasional rain. 15-18 Heavy rain and snow. 19-23 Sunny, very cold. 24-26 Milder, showers. 27-31 Sunny, cold.

JAN. 1997: Temp. 33.5° (1° below avg.); precip. 2.5" (avg.). 1-2 Showers. 3-12 Cool, dry. 13-15 Rain, then snow. 16-17 Sunny, cold. 18-20 Heavy snow, then rain. 21-25 Warmer, showers. 26-28 Rain, then snow, colder. 29-31 Unseasonably warm.

FEB. 1997: Temp. 34.5° (3° below avg.); precip. 2.5" (avg.). 1-5 Sunny, cold. 6-7 Milder. 8-13 Cold, dry. 14-17 Warm, then very cold. 18-20 Sunny, warm. 21-23 Dry, seasonable. 24-26 Heavy rain. 27-28 Dry, cool.

MAR. 1997: Temp. 44° (3° below avg.); precip. 3" (avg.). 1-3 Sunny, cool. 4-7 Stormy, heavy rain. 8-10 Sunny, cold. 11-14 Warm days, cold nights. 15-18 Cloudy, damp. 19-24 Milder, then showers. 25-28 Sunny, seasonable. 29-31 Warm, showers.

APR. 1997: Temp. 56.5° (avg.; 2° above southwest). 1-3 Warm days, cool nights. 4-6 Warm, thunderstorms, then cooler. 7-9 Cool, drizzle. 10-12 Warm, thunderstorms. 13-18 Sunny, pleasant. 19-21 Periods of rain. 22-26 Sunny. 27-30 Showers.

MAY 1997: Temp. 61.5° (5° below avg.); precip. 3.5" (0.5" below avg.). 1-3 Warm, then cloudy and cool. 4-6 Sunny, warmer. 7-10 Thunderstorms, then cool. 11-13 Showers. 14-16 Sunny, cool. 17-25 Periods of rain. 26-31 Sunny, seasonable.

JUNE 1997: Temp. 75.5° (avg.; 2° above south); precip. 3.5" (avg.). 1-7 Sunshine, warm. 8-10 Cooler. 11-15 Warm, showers. 16-19 Hot, humid, afternoon thunderstorms. 20-22 Cloudy, cool. 23-25 Pleasant. 26-30 Hot, hazy.

JULY 1997: Temp. 80° (avg.; 2° above south); precip. 2" (2" below avg.). 1-4 Sunny, comfortable. 5-7 Hot and humid, thunderstorms. 8-16 Seasonable. 17-18 Heat wave. 19-25 Warm, showers. 26-31 Sunny, warm and humid.

AUG. 1997: Temp. 77.5° (1° below avg.); precip. 3.5" (0.5" below avg.). 1-4 Heat wave. 5-9 Humid, thunderstorms. 10-12 Less humid. 13-17 Thunderstorms, then sunny and comfortable. 18-20 Hot. 21-24 Severe thunderstorms. 25-27 Sunny, cooler. 28-31 Hot, humid.

SEPT. 1997: Temp. 76° (5° above avg.); precip. 1.5" (2" below avg.). 1-6 Sunny, pleasant. 7-12 Heat wave. 13-15 Unsettled, thunderstorms. 16-18 Sunny, cool. 19-23 Sunny, hot. 24-30 Showers, then sunny, seasonable.

OCT. 1997: Temp. 71° (7° above avg.); precip. 2" (1" below avg.). 1-4 Sunny, hot. 5-10 Hot, occasional thunder. 11-13 Much cooler. 14-18 Sunny, warm. 19-20 Rain, then cool. 21-25 Sunny, cooler. 26-31 Warm, then showers.

Baltimore

Washington

Richmond

Roanoke

PSORIASIS?

By Tom Randles

If you suffer from *Psoriasis* like I do, you should know about a wonderful new cream that's guaranteed to work better than anything you have ever used before!

I have suffered with *Psoriasis* for more than 20 years and found very little relief with other products. Then I discovered the gentle, therapeutic rub-on **Burdock Folate Lotion**™. Before I knew it my *Psoriasis* disappeared. All my scaly, itchy skin disappeared; in its place was new natural skin—soft and normal looking. The redness and irritation was GONE and I never felt or looked better.

I swear by it and highly recommend it to anyone with *Psoriasis, eczema, contact allergies* or other *skin disorders.*

It works very fast, almost overnight, and provides long lasting, soothing relief. Stop suffering! Order *Burdock Folate Lotion*™ right now. *It's guaranteed to work for you or you will get every penny of your money back.* **Send $16.95 plus $3.00 S&H to:**

Total Research, Inc., Dept. PC-FRM
PO Box 667, Taylor, MI 48180

'Lady's Nails Grow So Long And Hard, Husband Uses Them As A Screw Driver!'

If your nails are weak, chip or break off easily, grow at a snails pace, look dull and unhealthy or are even plagued by ugly fungus, a wonderful new nail treatment called **Nail Gro**™ could be the answer to your prayers.

In just a few weeks you can have the most gorgeous looking nails you could ever imagine—the results are guaranteed! **Nail Gro**™ repairs damaged and weak nails. Its revolutionary approach transforms lifeless nails into *brilliant gems*. It nourishes your nails with a combination of vitamins and nutrients including horsetail, and repairs unhealthy bacteria ridden nails. The end result is so breathtaking you probably won't let your husband use them as a screw driver!

Any ugly fungus or bacteria that your finger or toe nails may be harboring disappear. Your nails glow with a healthy sheen. And your won't believe how hard, long and strong they become. You can throw away your fake nails because you can have your own perfect looking nails with *Nail Gro*™. Order today. *Results are guaranteed.* You will be 100% satisfied or your money back—no questions asked!

Simply send $15.95 plus $3.00 S&H to:
Total Research, Dept. GRO-FRM
Box 667, Taylor, MI 48180

Mother's Thin Hair Problem

By John Peters

My mother's hair was extremely thin. She was terribly embarrassed by it. You could look right through the hair and see large spots of exposed scalp; and she had split ends. She tried everything available but nothing worked. Today, my mother's hair looks thick and gorgeous; she looks younger, and you would never know she had a problem.

She credits her new hair look to **Neutrolox**™ hair thickening cream. I told my mother about this great product. I also have a severe hair thinning problem and was at my wits end until I discovered **Neutrolox**™.

The product is so effective that we both are getting compliments on the appearance of our hair for the first time in years. We honestly believe in **Neutrolox**™. We know you will too! It's great for men and women and can be used on color-treated or processed hair. Try **Neutrolox**™, if you don't agree I'll send every penny of your money back—no one can beat a 100% no-risk money-back guarantee. **To order send $11.95 for a small or SAVE money by sending $15.95 for a medium, or the most savings come with the large for $24.95.** *Please add $1.00 S&H for each order. Send to:*

Neutrolox, Dept. FRM-N1
Box 366, Taylor, MI 48180

WRINKLES?

By James Brothers

My dear mother's face was covered with wrinkles, she had severe prune lips, crows feet and dark age spots that were getting worse. *Tears would come to her eyes when she spoke of the old days when her face glowed with perfection.* She was so embarrassed by her appearance, she had nearly given up hope when we discovered a cream, **NEW FACE WRINKLE AND AGE SPOT**™ and the **New Face Plan**™.

In just a few weeks, we could see a remarkable transformation in the appearance of her skin. **My mother's wrinkles began disappearing, her facial muscles tightened up and she no longer had severe drooping jowls. The age spots had faded; and she looked like a million dollars without those horrible deep-seated prune lips.**

Today mother looks years younger. She is getting honest compliments for the first time in years on how great she looks. She swears by the cream and the plan and recommends it to everyone. It's 100% guaranteed to work for you or your money back. **To order NEW FACE**™ send $16.95 plus $3.00 S&H to:

**Total Research, Inc., Dept NF1-FRM,
Box 667, Taylor, MI 48180**

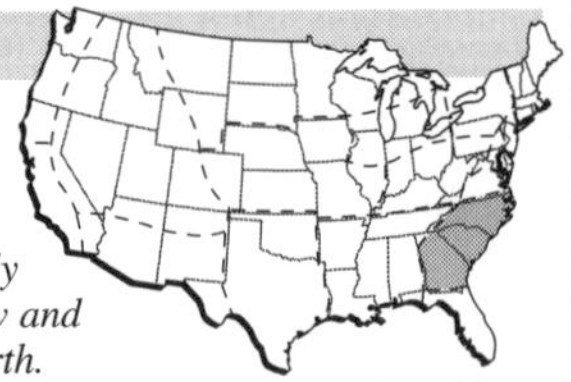

SUMMARY: *The period from November through March is expected to average near normal in temperature and precipitation. But don't let that fool you, because there will be several cold spells and snow and ice storms. Late December and early January will be particularly cold and stormy with heavy snow and ice in the Piedmont, perhaps all the way to the coast in the north.*

Suddenly, as quickly as it began, winter will end. April will be warmer than normal, and there may even be some record high temperatures around midmonth. May will be cooler than normal, which could give some locations a cooler May than April.

Summer will arrive with a vengeance. The period from June through August is expected to average 4 degrees above normal. Look for heat waves in mid-June, the first half of July, and in much of August. The combination of heat and below-normal rainfall may lead to a drought. Rumbles of thunder in the western mountains may bring relief there.

A few heavy thunderstorms in September and October will bring temporary relief from the heat and any drought, but temperatures will average well above normal, with below-normal rainfall. Look for record heat in early October. Chilly nights late in the month will leave no doubt that summer is over.

NOV. 1996: Temp. 54° (2° above avg.); precip. 1" (2" below avg.; 0.5" above north). 1-4 Sunny, cool. 5-7 Pleasant. 8-9 Rainy. 10-15 Sunny, cold nights. 16-23 Dry, turning milder. 24-28 Showers, mild. 29-30 Cool.

DEC. 1996: Temp. 42.5° (1° above avg. north; 1° below south); precip. 7.5" (4" above avg.). 1-3 Dry, chilly. 4-7 Cool. 8-10 Heavy rain. 11-12 Seasonable. 13-18 Heavy rain, snow in the higher elevations. 19-23 Cold. 24-29 Periods of rain, ice west. 30-31 Dry.

JAN. 1997: Temp. 39° (avg.; 2° above west); precip. 1.5" (2.5" below avg.). 1-3 Rainy, ice west. 4-13 Mostly dry, cold. 14-15 Showers. 16-17 Cold. 18-20 Snow north, rain south. 21-26 Milder, few showers. 27-31 Cold, then milder.

FEB. 1997: Temp. 40.5° (2° below avg.; avg. south); precip. 3" (avg.; 2" below west). 1-6 Sunny, seasonable. 7-11 Mostly dry, colder. 12-15 Milder, then showers. 16-19 Rather mild. 20-28 Cloudy, some rain.

MAR. 1997: Temp. 51° (2° below avg. northeast; 1° above south); precip. 4" (1" above avg. north; 0.5" below south). 1-3 Sunny, mild. 4-7 Rain, colder. 8-12 Sunny, chilly. 13-16 Dry, warmer. 17-18 Heavy rain. 19-22 Sunny, chilly. 23-25 Rain. 26-29 Damp north, warm south. 30-31 Rain.

APR. 1997: Temp. 64.5° (5° above avg.; 1° above northeast); precip. 2.5" (1" below avg.). 1-4 Showers. 5-8 Sunny, seasonable. 9-12 Warm. 13-17 Showers, cooler. 18-21 Warmer, thunder-

storms. 22-30 Mainly dry, warm.

MAY 1997: Temp. 63.5° (4° below avg.; 1° below south); precip. 3" (0.5" below avg.; 0.5" above south). 1-7 Thunderstorms, warm. 8-14 Cool, dry. 15-19 Rain, chilly. 20-24 Milder, showers. 25-31 Sunny, cool.

JUNE 1997: Temp. 79.5° (4° above avg.; 7° above south); precip. 1.5" (2" below avg.; avg. north). 1-7 Very warm, showers. 8-10 Cooler. 11-20 Hot, some sun, afternoon thunderstorms. 21-25 Warm, dry. 26-30 Heat wave.

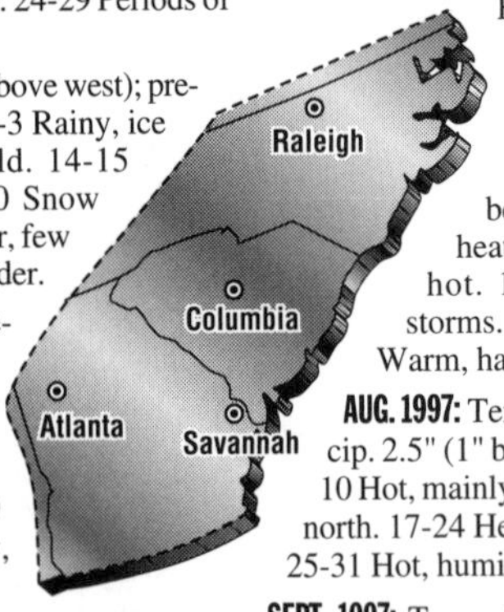

JULY 1997: Temp. 83° (4° above avg.); precip. 2.5" (2" below avg.). 1-12 Oppressive heat and humidity. 13-16 Not as hot. 17-21 Hazy sun, thunderstorms. 22-26 Hot, showers. 27-31 Warm, hazy sun.

AUG. 1997: Temp. 79° (3° above avg.); precip. 2.5" (1" below avg.; 1" above west). 1-10 Hot, mainly dry. 11-16 Hot south, cooler north. 17-24 Heat wave, occasional thunder. 25-31 Hot, humid, hazy sun.

SEPT. 1997: Temp. 78° (6° above avg.); precip. 3.5" (avg.). 1-2 Downpours. 3-7 Sunny, warm. 8-14 Sunny, very hot. 15-17 Warm. 18-20 Thunderstorms. 21-25 Hot, humid. 26-30 Warm days, cooler nights.

OCT. 1997: Temp. 72° (6° above avg.); precip. 2" (1.5" below avg.). 1-9 Sunshine, record heat. 10-13 Thunderstorms, then much cooler. 14-17 Sunny, warm. 18-20 Heavy thunderstorms. 21-27 Sunny, chilly nights. 28-31 Sunny.

Map labels: Raleigh, Columbia, Atlanta, Savannah

5 FLORIDA

FORECAST

SUMMARY: *The period from November through March is expected to be colder than normal, with two to three threats of freezes well into central Florida. The best chances for a freeze in the citrus regions are just before Christmas, mid-January, and the first part of February. Rainfall will be above normal in November and December, especially in the central part of the state. January through March is expected to be somewhat drier than normal, with above-normal sunshine. Snow and ice may occur unusually far south in early to mid-February.*

April and May will be warmer than normal, though near normal in the south. Rainfall will be above normal, especially in the south, where Tropical Storm Ana, in late May, could threaten the Keys before the official start of hurricane season on June 1.

Summer will be very warm, with temperatures from June through August ranging from 1 degree above average in the south to 3 degrees above average in the north. Frequent showers in early June will make overall precipitation above normal in the south. Otherwise, rainfall from June through August will be somewhat below normal. Expect heavy widespread thunderstorm activity in late June and mid-July. The rest of the season, thunderstorm activity will be near or a little below normal.

September and October will be much warmer than normal in the north, a little above normal elsewhere. Rainfall will be near normal in September, then above normal in October, with the greatest threat of a hurricane in the first half of October.

NOV. 1996: Temp. 67° (1° below avg.); precip. 2.5" (0.5" below avg.; 2" above central). 1-2 Showers. 3-5 Cool. 6-8 Pleasant. 9-11 Heavy rain. 12-13 Sunny. 14-20 Cool north, showers south. 21-26 Sunny, warm. 27-30 Thunderstorms, some heavy.

DEC. 1996: Temp. 62° (1° below avg. north; 1° above south); precip. 7" (4" above avg.; 0.5" above south). 1-7 Sunny, cool. 8-12 Showers, mild. 13-17 Dry south, showers north. 18-23 Sunny, chilly; freeze north. 24-29 Rain, locally heavy. 30-31 Chilly.

JAN. 1997: Temp. 57° (3° below avg.); precip. 2.5" (1" below avg.). 1-4 Showers, mild. 5-10 Sunny, mild. 11-13 Sunny, cold nights. 14-20 Mild, showers. 21-25 Sunny, warm. 26-31 Showers north, warm south.

FEB. 1997: Temp. 61° (2° above avg. north; 2° below south); precip. 2" (1" below avg.). 1-6 Mostly dry, seasonable. 7-9 Sunny, cold. 10-12 Cold rain, snow north. 13-17 Cool, dry. 18-23 Sunny, warmer. 24-28 Showers, mild.

MAR. 1997: Temp. 67° (avg. north; 2° above south); precip. 1.5" (2" below avg.; avg. south). 1-3 Seasonable. 4-5 Heavy thunderstorms. 6-8 Cool, dry. 9-13 Heavy rain south, chilly north. 14-18 Warmer. 19-22 Sunny, cool. 23-25 Heavy thunderstorms. 26-31 Sunny, warm.

APR. 1997: Temp. 74° (3° above avg.; 1° below south); precip. 3.5" (2" below avg. north; 2" above south). 1-6 Sunny, warm. 7-14 Rain south, mostly dry north. 15-20 Sunny, warm. 21-23 Few showers. 24-30 Showers, especially south.

MAY 1997: Temp. 77° (avg.); precip. 6" (1" above avg. north; 4" above south). 1-9 Warm, locally heavy thunderstorms. 10-15 Pleasant. 16-18 Heavy rain south, showers north. 19-23 Warm, showers south. 24-29 Dry north, showers south. 30-31 Tropical storm south.

JUNE 1997: Temp. 85° (4° above avg.; avg. south); precip. 7.5" (1" below avg. north; 4" above south). 1-8 Frequent showers, especially south. 9-12 Sunny, warm. 13-15 Hot, humid. 16-18 Few showers. 19-30 Some sun, locally heavy thunderstorms.

JULY 1997: Temp. 86° (3° above avg. north; 0.5° above south); precip. 5" (avg.). 1-7 Hot north, showers south. 8-14 Locally heavy thunderstorms. 15-19 Dry north, thunderstorms south. 20-26 Hot north, showers south. 27-31 Showers, warm.

AUG. 1997: Temp. 82° (avg.); precip. 4" (3" below avg.; avg. central). 1-6 Sunshine, few showers. 7-14 Mostly dry, thunderstorms central. 15-20 Sunny, hot. 21-24 Hot, thunderstorms. 25-31 Seasonable.

SEPT. 1997: Temp. 82° (1° above avg.; 4° above north); precip. 6" (avg.). 1-6 Hot, locally heavy thunderstorms. 7-13 Sunshine, few showers. 14-19 Hot, thunderstorms. 20-25 Seasonable, thunderstorms. 26-30 Frequent showers.

OCT. 1997: Temp. 75.5° (0.5° above avg.; 3° above north); precip. 5" (2" above avg.). 1-6 Warm, frequent showers. 7-9 Sunny, warm. 10-13 Heavy thunderstorms. 14-18 Warm, showers. 19-26 Sunny, cool. 27-31 Sunny.

Jacksonville

Orlando

Tampa

Miami

SUMMARY: *The period from November through March will bring frequent swings in temperature. Overall, temperatures should average above normal, but the heart of the winter will be below normal, with above-average snowfall. Heavy lake snows in mid-November will be a harbinger of things to come, with big snowstorms in mid-December, early and mid-January, early February, and early March. Although most of the relatively mild temperatures in the winter season will occur early, a January thaw will bring some relief from the cold waves that serve as its bookends.*

Chilly weather will continue well into spring, with April and May averaging 2 degrees below normal. A big snowstorm may serve as nature's April Fools joke, but snow melts quickly in April. Overall, spring rain will be near normal, with the heaviest rain in the west.

The summer, overall, will be near average in temperature. A brief June heat wave will note the start of summer, with the most severe heat and humidity in mid-July and early August. Late August and early September will be a different story, with heavy rain and cool temperatures. The remainder of the early autumn will feature well above normal temperatures, with long sunny intervals. Late September and October, in particular, are expected to be especially mild, with temperatures averaging 6 degrees above normal. Heavy rains in mid-September and mid- and late October will separate the sunny, pleasant spells. Oh well, at least it's not snow.

NOV. 1996: Temp. 44° (4° above avg.; avg. west); precip. 4.5" (1" above avg.; 0.5" below southeast). 1-3 Rain, heavy east. 4-7 Sunny, mild. 8-12 Windy, cold, heavy lake snows. 13-18 Sprinkles, cool. 19-24 Sunny, mild. 25-30 Periods of rain, turning colder.

DEC. 1996: Temp. 32.5° (6° above avg.; 1° above northeast); precip. 2.5" (0.5" below avg.). 1-3 Dry, cold. 4-8 Showers and flurries. 9-11 Rain, snow north. 12-14 Rain. 15-18 Mild, showers. 19-23 Very cold, lake snows. 24-25 Sunny, milder. 26-31 Cold, flurries.

JAN. 1997: Temp. 20.5° (avg.); precip. 3" (0.5" above avg.). 1-3 Windy, cold. 4-5 Snow. 6-10 Cold, snowstorm. 11-18 Cold, lake snows. 19-21 Cold, snow. 22-25 January thaw. 26-28 Cold. 29-31 Milder, rain and snow.

FEB. 1997: Temp. 22.5° (1° below avg.); precip. 3" (1" above avg.; avg. east). 1-2 Rain and snow. 3-8 Cold, snow. 9-11 Cold, dry. 12-14 Snow showers. 15-18 Sunshine, cold. 19-21 Stormy, rain and snow. 22-24 Sunny, mild. 25-28 Colder, flurries.

MAR. 1997: Temp. 32° (2° below avg.); precip. 4" (1" above avg.). 1-3 Rain, snow west. 4-5 Mild. 6-10 Colder, rain changing to snow. 11-16 Sunny, cool. 17-20 Colder, some snow. 21-24 Mild, showers. 25-27 Cold, snow west. 28-31 Mild, showers.

APR. 1997: Temp. 45.5° (0.5° below avg.); precip. 3" (0.5" above avg.; 3" above west). 1-3 Heavy rain to snow. 4-8 Chilly, showers and flurries. 9-12 Milder, some rain. 13-17 Cool,

showers. 18-21 Damp, mild. 22-27 Warm, showers. 28-30 Seasonable.

MAY 1997: Temp. 54.5° (3° below avg.); precip. 4" (avg.). 1-3 Rainy, cool. 4-6 Sunny, mild. 7-10 Rain, then cooler. 11-16 Rainy, cool. 17-20 Sunny, mild. 21-23 Sunny, cool. 24-26 Rain east. 27-31 Sunny, seasonable.

JUNE 1997: Temp. 68° (1° above avg.); precip. 3" (1" below avg.). 1-4 Sunny, dry. 5-10 Breezy, showers. 11-19 Warmer, showers. 20-23 Cool, dry. 24-25 Sunny, hot. 26-30 Cooler, showers.

JULY 1997: Temp. 73° (1° above avg.); precip. 1.5" (2" below avg.; avg. west). 1-6 Cool, sprinkles. 7-12 Showers, cool. 13-16 Sunny, pleasant. 17-18 Hot, thunderstorms. 19-22 Sunny, cool. 23-31 Warm, showers.

AUG. 1997: Temp. 68° (2° below avg.); precip. 3.5" (avg.). 1-4 Hot, humid, thunderstorms. 5-6 Sunny. 7-9 Heavy rain. 10-12 Seasonable. 13-17 Showers, cool. 18-23 Warm, few showers. 24-27 Sunny, warm. 28-31 Thunderstorms, cooler.

SEPT. 1997: Temp. 61° (avg.); precip. 4" (avg. west; 2" above east). 1-5 Heavy rain. 6-8 Sunny, warm. 9-11 Showers, warm. 12-16 Cloudy, cool. 17-20 Rainy, chilly. 21-26 Cloudy, seasonable. 27-30 Warm, mainly dry.

OCT. 1997: Temp. 56° (6° above avg.); precip. 2" (1" below avg.; 2" above west). 1-3 Sunny, nice. 4-10 Heavy rain, then cooler. 11-13 Sunny, cold. 14-17 Rainy episodes. 18-23 Warm east, rain west. 24-28 Seasonable. 29-31 Rain.

Syracuse

Rochester

Scranton

Buffalo

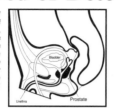

SUMMARY: *The period from November through March is expected to average near normal in temperature and precipitation, with above-normal snowfall, especially in the east. Temperatures through early January should be above average, but the latter half of the winter will be colder than normal. Watch for cold spells before Christmas, around New Year, in mid-January, and in mid-February. Cold, snowy weather may arrive around Thanksgiving, but Christmas could be milder than usual. A few heavy snowstorms will hit the east in January, but snowfall will be lighter elsewhere in the region. The trend may reverse in February, with the heaviest snow in the west. In March, look for two or three storms that start with rain but end with heavy snow.*

April showers will be more frequent than normal. May will have cooler than normal temperatures. The summer will feature near-normal temperatures, but well above normal rainfall. The first heat wave will occur just after the official start of summer, with additional heat waves in mid-July and early August. The first half of June will bring several rainy periods. Heavy thunderstorms in mid-July and late August may be locally severe, with the possibility of widespread severe weather. Some of the hottest weather of the season may occur in early to mid-September. Rainfall will be below normal in September, just above in October, with two heavy rainstorms. Cold Canadian air in late October will feel even colder than it is, in contrast to the mild temperatures preceding it.

NOV. 1996: Temp. 46° (avg.); precip. 2.5" (0.5" below avg.). 1-3 Showers, cool. 4-7 Sunny, mild. 8-11 Colder, snow showers. 12-16 Sunny, seasonable. 17-23 Sunny, mild. 24-27 Rain and snow, colder. 28-30 Flurries.

DEC. 1996: Temp. 37° (3° above avg.); precip. 2" (1" below avg.). 1-5 Snow showers. 6-10 Periods of rain. 11-14 Mild, showers. 15-18 Cold, rain and snow. 19-23 Very cold. 24-26 Milder, showers. 27-31 Flurries, cold.

JAN. 1997: Temp. 30° (1° above avg.); precip. 2" (0.5" below avg.). 1-4 Cold. 5-6 Sunny, seasonable. 7-13 Cold, snow east. 14-17 Cold, flurries. 18-21 Snow east, cold. 22-24 Milder, showers. 25-27 Colder. 28-31 Milder, rain and snow.

FEB. 1997: Temp. 34° (3° above avg. west; 1° below east); precip. 3.5" (1" above avg.; 0.5" below east). 1-2 Sunny, cold. 3-12 Cold, flurries east. 13-14 Milder. 15-17 Cold. 18-21 Milder, rain. 22-28 Mild, showers.

MAR. 1997: Temp. 39° (5° above avg.); precip. 5" (1" above avg.). 1-6 Chilly, rain and snow. 7-12 Sunny, cold. 13-16 Seasonable. 17-19 Colder, rain to snow. 20-22 Milder. 23-25 Rain to snow. 26-28 Milder. 29-31 Rain, colder.

APR. 1997: Temp. 54.5° (0.5° above avg.); precip. 5.5" (2" above avg.; avg. east). 1-3 Heavy rain to snow. 4-8 Windy, cold. 9-12 Warmer, showers. 13-15 Cooler, rain. 16-20 Milder, showers. 21-25 Sunny, warm. 26-30 Rain.

MAY 1997: Temp. 60° (4° below avg.); precip. 3.5" (1" below avg.). 1 Rain. 2-4 Seasonable.

5-7 Showers. 8-9 Cold rain. 10-15 Chilly, sprinkles. 16-22 Sunny, seasonable. 23-26 Cool. 27-31 Showers, cool.

JUNE 1997: Temp. 73° (1° above avg.); precip. 5.5" (2" above avg.). 1-2 Rain. 3-4 Warm. 5-8 Heavy showers. 9-11 Cool, damp. 12-19 Thunderstorms, very warm. 20-22 Rainy, cool. 23-25 Sunny, hot. 26-30 Showers, seasonable.

JULY 1997: Temp. 76° (1° above avg. west; 1° below east); precip. 6" (2" above avg.; 1" below east). 1-3 Sunny, cool. 4-8 Warmer, mostly dry. 9-11 Thunderstorms. 12-15 Sunny, cool. 16-17 Sunny, hot. 18-20 Thunderstorms, then cool. 21-25 Very warm, thunderstorms west. 26-31 Sunny, warm.

AUG. 1997: Temp. 75° (avg.); precip. 7.5" (4" above avg.; 1" above east). 1-9 Humid, thunderstorms. 10-11 Sunny. 12-15 Showers, cool. 16-20 Warmer, thunderstorms. 21-25 Sunny, seasonable. 26-31 Thunderstorms, then cooler.

SEPT. 1997: Temp. 73° (5° above avg.); precip. 1" (2" below avg.). 1-3 Very warm, showers. 4-8 Sunny, seasonable. 9-11 Hot and humid. 12-17 Dry and cooler. 18-25 Showers, unsettled. 26-30 Sunny, seasonable.

OCT. 1997: Temp. 63° (7° above avg.); precip. 4" (1" above avg.). 1-3 Sunny, warm. 4-9 Cloudy, heavy rain. 10-13 Sunny, cooler. 14-17 Showers, warm. 18-21 Heavy rain. 22-26 Sunny, cold. 27-31 Showers.

Pittsburgh
Indianapolis
Cincinnati
Charleston
Louisville

SUMMARY: *Temperatures in the coming year might suggest "global warming" across the South, as nine or ten months are expected to have above-normal temperatures. But other parts of the country will have below-normal temperatures. Winter temperatures in the south are expected to average about 2 degrees above normal, but it certainly will not be mild all of the time. The coldest weather will occur in mid-December, early January, and mid-February. Warm winter temperatures are most likely near Christmas and in mid-January. New Year may be a different story, with the possibility of snow and ice all the way to the Gulf coast.*

April and May will feature well above normal temperatures, but also above-normal rainfall. Early May, in particular, will bring heavy downpours.

June through August will be even hotter than normal. July may be one of the hottest months on record, especially in the first half. Although the extreme heat may not be as persistent in August, records may again be set at midmonth. Summer precipitation will largely consist of hit-and-miss thunderstorms, which will bring brief, cooling downpours. The best chances for more widespread thunderstorms are in late July and early August.

September will start with oppressive heat, followed by lower humidity and more comfortable nights. The fall will be very warm. Rainfall will be below normal in most places, although heavy thunderstorms may bring above-normal rain to the west.

NOV. 1996: Temp. 52.5° (2° above avg. northwest; 2° below southeast); precip. 5.5" (1" above avg.; avg. east). 1-4 Sunny, cool. 5-7 Sunny, pleasant. 8-13 Showers, chilly. 14-21 Mild days, cold nights. 22-26 Showers, some heavy. 27-30 Cool, sprinkles.

DEC. 1996: Temp. 44.5° (1° above avg.); precip. 4.5" (2" below avg. north; 1" above south). 1-4 Cool, showers. 5-10 Warm, heavy rain. 11-17 Colder, showers. 18-23 Sunny, cold. 24-26 Milder, showers. 27-29 Sunny, cold. 30-31 Rain, possible snow and ice.

JAN. 1997: Temp. 41.5° (5° above avg. southwest; 2° below northeast); precip. 5.5" (2" above avg.). 1-3 Rain. 4-5 Sunny, chilly. 6-13 Sunny, milder. 14-16 Rain, snow north. 17-19 Heavy rain. 20-22 Cloudy, cold. 23-25 Warm, heavy rain. 26-31 Cold, then milder.

FEB. 1997: Temp. 45° (1° above avg.; 3° above southeast); precip. 4" (1" above avg. west; 1" below east). 1-3 Cloudy, rain. 4-9 Sunny, mild. 10-12 Sunny, cold. 13-15 Sunny, milder. 16-20 Showers, mild. 21-28 Seasonable, showers.

MAR. 1997: Temp. 51° (2° below avg.; avg. south); precip. 6.5" (1" above avg.). 1-3 Mild, showers. 4-10 Showers, chilly. 11-16 Sunny, warmer. 17-21 Thunderstorms, then cooler. 22-31 Warm, spring showers.

APR. 1997: Temp. 67° (4° above avg.; avg. southwest); precip. 6.5" (1" above avg.). 1-4 Showers, cooler. 5-11 Sunny, warmer. 12-20 Frequent showers. 21-25 Sunny, warm. 26-30 Warm, humid, showers.

MAY 1997: Temp. 70° (6° below avg. northeast; 2° below southwest); precip. 5.5" (2" above avg. west; 1" below east). 1-7 Humid, downpours. 8-10 Cool, dry. 11-17 Cool, frequent showers. 18-20 Sunny, cool. 21-26 Showers, still cool. 27-31 Warmer, few thunderstorms.

JUNE 1997: Temp. 79° (avg.; 4° above southeast); precip. 3" (0.5" below avg.; 1" above west). 1-6 Showers, very warm. 7-10 Thunderstorms, cooler. 11-17 Sunny, hot. 18-26 Hot, humid, thunderstorms. 27-30 Hazy, hot, humid.

JULY 1997: Temp. 85° (2° above avg.; 5° above southeast); precip. 3.5" (2" below avg. northeast; 2" above southwest). 1-11 Heat wave. 12-14 Sunny, hot. 15-19 Hot and humid. 20-22 Very hot, thunderstorms. 23-26 Hot and humid, thunderstorms. 27-31 Hazy, hot, few thunderstorms.

AUG. 1997: Temp. 81.5° (0.5° above avg.); precip. 3.5" (avg.). 1-6 Very warm, thunderstorms. 7-9 Sunny, hot. 10-13 Hot, locally heavy thunderstorms. 14-22 Blazing sunshine, very hot. 23-26 Heavy thunderstorms. 27-31 Hazy, hot and humid.

SEPT. 1997: Temp. 79° (5° above avg.); precip. 3" (0.5" below avg.; 2" below southeast). 1-3 Very hot. 4-9 Hot, less humid. 10-13 Thunderstorms. 14-16 Sunny, cooler. 17-20 Sunny, hot. 21-25 Humid, thunderstorms. 26-30 Sunny, warm.

OCT. 1997: Temp. 70° (7° above avg.); precip. 1" (2" below avg.; 2" above west). 1-8 Sunny, hot, humid. 9-13 Thunderstorms, then cooler. 14-18 Warm, few showers. 19-25 Sunny, cooler. 26-31 Sunny, warm.

Nashville

Little Rock

Montgomery

Mobile

Shreveport

New Orleans

SUMMARY: *Technically it would be correct to say that both temperatures and precipitation in the period from November through March will be near normal. But that would be misleading, because while the average may be near normal, wild fluctuations will make most days anything but. Record cold may occur in mid- to late December, in mid-January, and in mid-February. But record warmth may occur in the first part of December and just before mid-February. Very cold temperatures after a mid-December snowstorm will be enough to ensure a white Christmas for most of the region. Other major snowstorms may occur in early March and early April.*

The spring will be a chilly one, with temperatures in April and May 2 to 4 degrees below average. Snow flurries may occur all the way into mid-May, at least in the north.

June through August will bring near-normal temperatures and rainfall. Heat waves are most likely to occur in the latter half of June, in mid- to late July, and toward the middle of September. The autumn will be unusually warm, with September and October averaging 5 to 6 degrees above normal. September will be rather dry, but heavy rains in October may lead to widespread flooding.

NOV. 1996: Temp. 40.5° (1° below avg.); precip. 2" (1" below avg.; 1" above north). 1-2 Showers. 3-7 Sunny, mild. 8-12 Colder, rain/snow showers. 13-16 Sunny, seasonable. 17-23 Sunny, warm. 24-26 Rain changing to snow, colder. 27-30 Cold, flurries.

DEC. 1996: Temp. 31° (3° above avg.; 6° above east); precip. 2" (1" below avg.). 1-4 Snow showers. 5-10 Milder, rainy. 11-13 Mild, rainy. 14-17 Sunny, cool. 18-22 Snow, then very cold. 23-26 Milder, rain/snow showers. 27-31 Flurries, cold.

JAN. 1997: Temp. 21° (2° below avg.; 1° above west); precip. 1" (0.5" below avg.). 1-4 Flurries, cold. 5-7 Sunny, mild. 8-12 Colder, flurries. 13-21 Very cold, few flurries. 22-25 Milder, rain to snow. 26-27 Very cold. 28-31 Rain south, snow north.

FEB. 1997: Temp. 32° (5° above avg.; 1° above east); precip. 2.5" (1" above avg.). 1-5 Cold, flurries. 6-7 Milder. 8-11 Snow showers. 12-14 Milder. 15-16 Very cold. 17-20 Snow, then rain. 21-23 Sunny, mild. 24-28 Mild, showers.

MAR. 1997: Temp. 34° (4° below avg.); precip. 5" (2" above avg.). 1-5 Heavy wet snow. 6-10 Cold, flurries. 11-13 Sunny, cold. 14-19 Cold, snow showers. 20-23 Rainy, milder. 24-27 Colder, flurries. 28-31 Heavy rain, colder.

APR. 1997: Temp. 50° (avg.; 2° below north); precip. 4" (1" above west; avg. east). 1-3 Heavy wet snow. 4-8 Cold, few flurries. 9-11 Warmer, showers. 12-14 Cold, rain. 15-18 Sunny, warmer. 19-23 Showers, mild. 24-30 Heavy rain.

MAY 1997: Temp. 56° (4° below avg.; avg. north-west); precip. 3.5" (avg.). 1-3 Cool. 4-7 Showers, mild. 8-15 Chilly, showers, flurries north. 16-20 Sunny, warmer. 21-25 Cloudy, cool. 26-31 Sunshine, mild.

JUNE 1997: Temp. 72.5° (2° above avg.); precip. 4.5" (0.5" above avg.). 1-2 Heavy rain. 3-5 Showers, warm. 6-8 Chilly, rain. 9-14 Sunny and warmer. 15-21 Hot, mostly dry. 22-25 Hot, thunderstorms. 26-28 Cloudy and cooler. 29-30 Hot.

JULY 1997: Temp. 75° (avg.); precip. 4" (avg.). 1-3 Sunny and cool. 4-6 Thunderstorms, warm. 7-9 Cool. 10-11 Heavy thunderstorms. 12-15 Sunny, seasonable. 16-17 Sunny and hot. 18-20 Thunderstorms, then cooler. 21-25 Hot, thunderstorms west. 26-31 Sunny and warm.

AUG. 1997: Temp. 72.5° (1° below avg.); precip. 5.5" (2" above avg.; avg. east). 1-8 Warm, humid, few thunderstorms. 9-11 Sunny, comfortable. 12-14 Showers, humid. 15-17 Cool. 18-23 Seasonable, thunderstorms. 24-27 Sunny, warm. 28-31 Heavy thunderstorms.

SEPT. 1997: Temp. 70° (4° above avg.); precip. 2.5" (1" below avg.). 1-7 Sunny, warm. 8-10 Hot and humid. 11-16 Showers, then cooler. 17-21 Unsettled, showers. 22-24 Sunny, warm. 25-26 Thunderstorms. 27-30 Sunny, warm.

OCT. 1997: Temp. 58° (7° above avg.); precip. 5.5" (3" above avg.). 1-2 Sunny, warm. 3-9 Heavy rain, warm. 10-12 Sunny, cooler. 13-20 Heavy rain, flooding likely. 21-25 Sunny, cold. 26-31 Milder, then showers.

Honey, Garlic and Vinegar Better Than Prescription Drugs?

(SPECIAL) We know that ancient civilizations relied on their healing power for a wide variety of ailments. In fact, honey was so prized by the Romans for its medicinal properties that it was used instead of gold to pay taxes. Egyptian doctors believed garlic was the ultimate cure-all. And vinegar has been used for everything from arthritis to obesity for over 7000 years.

Today doctors and researchers hail the healing abilities of honey, garlic and vinegar as much more than folklore. Hundreds of scientific studies have been conducted on this dream team of healers. The results are conclusive on their amazing power to prevent and cure many common health problems.

These studies prove that this trio from nature's pharmacy can help **reduce blood pressure, lower cholesterol, improve circulation, lower blood sugar levels and help fight cancer.** Scientific evidence also indicates that they can be of medicinal value in the treatment of: **arthritis, athlete's foot, bronchitis, burns, colds and flu, cold sores, constipation, cramps, diarrhea, eczema, earaches, fatigue, fungus, heart problems, muscle aches, prostatitis, psoriasis, rheumatism, ringworm, sinus congestion, sore throat, urinary infections, virus and yeast infections and more.**

A new Doctor's book called *Honey, Garlic & Vinegar Home Remedies* is now available to the general public. It shows you exactly how to make hundreds of remedies using honey, garlic and vinegar separately and in unique combinations. Each preparation is carefully described along with the health condition for which it is formulated .

Learn how to prepare ointments, tonics, lotions, poultices, syrups and compresses in your own kitchen. Whip up a batch to treat:

- **ARTHRITIS:** Doctor reports that this remedy helps relieve the pain with no side effects
- **AGE SPOTS:** Watch them fade with this mixture
- **CORNS & CALLOUSES:** Get rid of them fast with this natural method
- **HANGOVER:** Feel like your old self in no time
- **HEADACHE:** Enjoy fast relief without drugs
- **HEMORRHOIDS:** Don't suffer another day without this proven recipe
- **LEG CRAMPS:** Try this simple way to quick relief
- **MUSCLE ACHES:** Just mix up a batch of this and rub it on
- **STINGS & BITES:** Medical journals recommend this remedy to reduce pain and swelling fast
- **STOMACH PROBLEMS:** This remedy calms upset stomach and is noted in medical journals for ulcers
- **TOOTHACHE:** This remedy gives instant relief until you can get to the dentist
- **WEIGHT LOSS:** Secret remedy speeds fat burn and flushes stubborn fat from hiding places

Discover all these health tips and more. You'll find: ***Dozens of easy-to-make beauty preparations for hair and skin, including a wrinkle smoother that really works. *Hundreds of delicious recipes using these health-giving super foods. *Over 100 money-saving cleaning compounds to keep your home, car and clothing sparkling.**

Right now, as part of a special introductory offer, you can receive a special press run of the Doctor's book *Honey, Garlic & Vinegar Home Remedies* for only $8.95 plus $1.00 postage and handling. Your satisfaction is 100% guaranteed. You must be completely satisfied, or simply return it in 90 days for a full refund — no questions asked.

HERE'S HOW TO ORDER: Simply print your name and address and the word "Remedies" on a piece of paper and mail it along with a check or money order for only $9.95 to: THE LEADER CO., INC., Publishing Division, Dept. HG272, P.O. Box 8347, Canton, Ohio 44711. (Make checks payable to The Leader Co., Inc.) VISA or MasterCard send card number and expiration date. Act now. Orders are filled on a first-come, first-served basis. ©1996 The Leader Co., Inc.

NORTHERN GREAT PLAINS-GREAT LAKES

F O R E C A S T

SUMMARY: *The period from November through March is expected to average 1 to 2 degrees warmer than normal, with above-normal precipitation and snowfall. A blizzard may occur around Thanksgiving, then December will be relatively mild with many sunny days. January should bring closer to normal temperatures, with above-normal precipitation. The coldest weather of the season is likely to occur in mid-January. February will feature well above normal temperatures, with record highs possible in the latter half of the month. Temperatures in March will be almost as much below normal as they were above in February. Look for the heaviest snowstorm of the season in the middle of the month.*

April and early May will continue to be relatively cold, with snow possible into early May. The latter half of May will warm up quite a bit, with heavy rain to end the month.

Temperature and precipitation will average near normal in the summer. June rains will be heaviest in the central part of the region, and the first heat wave of the season is expected in the latter half of June. The most severe heat of the summer will start in the west and progress across the remainder of the region in mid-July.

September will be a month of contrasts, with very warm temperatures in the east and cool temperatures in the west. The month will be rainy. October is expected to bring above-normal temperatures, but snow early and late in the month will remind us that winter is just around the corner.

NOV. 1996: Temp. 32° (1° below avg.); precip. 2" (0.5" above avg.; 0.5" below west). 1-8 Sunny, mild. 9-12 Snow west, dry east. 13-16 Sunny, cold. 17-21 Sunny, mild. 22-27 Colder, heavy snow east and central. 28-30 Cold, flurries.

DEC. 1996: Temp. 24° (6° above avg.; avg. west); precip. 0.5" (0.5" below avg.; 2" above west). 1-3 Sunny, cold. 4-10 Snow, rain east. 11-15 Sunny, cold. 16-21 Flurries. 22-24 Sunny, mild. 25-27 Snow, then colder. 28-31 Mild, dry.

JAN. 1997: Temp. 11° (1° below avg.); precip. 1.5" (0.5" above avg.). 1-4 Flurries, mild. 5-12 Sunny, mild. 13-17 Cold, snow showers east. 18-24 Flurries, very cold. 25-28 Milder. 29-31 Flurries.

FEB. 1997: Temp. 24° (6° above avg.; 11° above central); precip. 1.2" (0.5" above avg.; 2" above east). 1-3 Sunny, cold. 4-13 Sunny, mild. 14-16 Cold, flurries. 17-22 Sunny, unseasonably mild. 23-28 Mild, rain and snow.

MAR. 1997: Temp. 27° (4° below avg.; 8° below central); precip. 3" (1" above avg.). 1-3 Sunny, mild. 4-8 Sunny, very cold. 9-13 Mild and dry. 14-18 Heavy snow. 19-22 Seasonable, rain/snow showers. 23-26 Cool. 27-31 Rain, then snow, colder.

APR. 1997: Temp. 40.5° (6° below avg.); precip. 2.5" (avg.; 1" above central). 1-6 Cold, snow showers. 7-10 Sunny, milder. 11-15 Mild east, chilly west. 16-19 Warmer, showers east. 20-22 Sunny, cool. 23-26 Showers, then cold. 27-30 Warmer, showers.

MAY 1997: Temp. 58.5° (avg.); precip. 3" (0.5" below avg.). 1-6 Cold rain, snow north. 7-12 Sunny, cool. 13-18 Sunny, warmer. 19-23 Showers, cool. 24-27 Warmer, thunderstorms. 28-31 Heavy rain.

JUNE 1997: Temp. 67° (1° below avg.); precip. 3.5" (0.5" below avg.; 2" above central). 1-5 Damp, heavy rain central. 6-8 Sunny, cool. 9-14 Sunny east, heavy rain central. 15-19 Hot, then thunderstorms. 20-24 Showers west, heavy thunderstorms east. 25-30 Hot and humid.

JULY 1997: Temp. 74.5° (1° above avg.; 4° above north); precip. 3.5" (avg.). 1-3 Hot, thunderstorms. 4-6 Cooler, showers. 7-10 Thunderstorms, hot west. 11-16 Heat wave west, showers east. 17-23 Thunderstorms, hot. 24-31 Warm, mainly dry.

AUG. 1997: Temp. 69.5° (1° below avg.); precip. 4.5" (1" above avg.). 1-4 Rainy, cooler. 5-10 Sunny, warm. 11-13 Warm, showers. 14-17 Sunny, seasonable. 18-21 Hot, thunderstorms, then cooler. 22-26 Warm, thunderstorms. 27-31 Warm west, showers east.

SEPT. 1997: Temp. 60.5° (6° above avg. east; 6° below west); precip. 4.5" (2" above avg.). 1-6 Hot east, showers west. 7-10 Warm, showers. 11-13 Cool, mainly dry. 14-20 Cold west, warm and damp east. 21-30 Mainly sunny, warm.

OCT. 1997: Temp. 52° (3° above avg.); precip. 1" (1" below avg.). 1-4 Occasional rain. 5-10 Sprinkles, snow north. 11-15 Sunny, milder. 16-17 Rain. 18-24 Sunny, cool. 25-27 Sunny, mild. 28-31 Colder, rain and snow.

Bismarck

Minneapolis

Rapid City

11 CENTRAL GREAT PLAINS
FORECAST

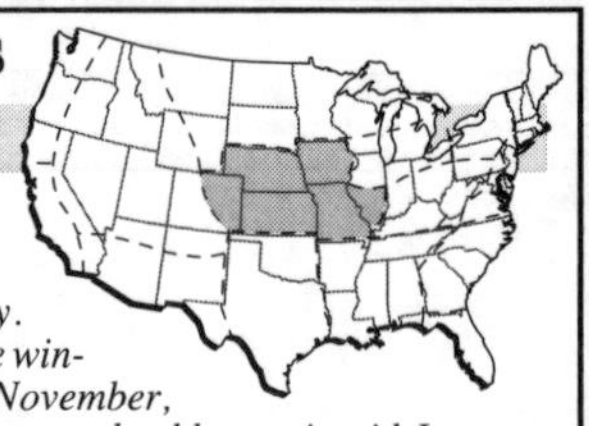

SUMMARY: *Temperatures during the period from November through March are expected to average a bit above normal, especially in the central part of the region in February. Precipitation will be above normal, except in Kansas, where the winter should be relatively dry. Snowiest periods will be in late November, early and late December, and late February. The coldest temperatures should occur in mid-January, with a cold outbreak also likely around Christmas.*

April and May will be slightly cooler and damper than usual. Heavy rain is likely in late April and early May. Both storms hold the potential to bring heavy snow to the north and west, especially in the higher elevations.

Temperatures in the summer will average near normal. Hot weather is expected in the latter half of June. After a slight cool-down in early July, expect record heat in the middle of the month. Precipitation will be near normal in June and July, but frequent heavy thunderstorms in August will bring localized flooding, especially during the first half of the month.

September will be a month of contrasts, with below-normal temperatures in the west and well above normal temperatures in the east. Record high temperatures may occur in the east during the first week of September. In contrast, snow may fall in the west the following week. October should be relatively mild, with temperatures 5 degrees above average and the heaviest rain in the southeast.

NOV. 1996: Temp. 38° (1° below avg.); precip. 2.5" (2" above avg. north; 1" below south). 1-6 Sunny, mild. 7-11 Sunny east, snow west. 12-16 Sunny, cool. 17-21 Sunny, mild. 22-27 Rain east, heavy snow north and west. 28-30 Sunny, cool.

DEC. 1996: Temp. 26° (2° above avg.; 6° above north); precip. 1" (0.5" below avg.). 1-4 Sunny, mild. 5-10 Heavy snow, rain east. 11-15 Sunny, cold. 16-19 Sunny, mild. 20-21 Flurries, colder. 22-24 Sunny, mild. 25-27 Colder, snow. 28-31 Mild, dry.

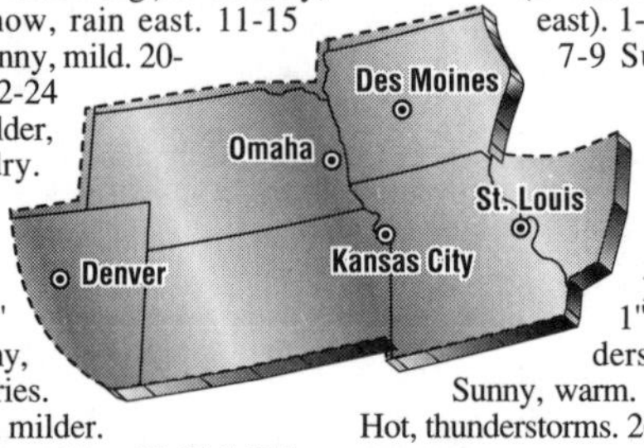

JAN. 1997: Temp. 18° (1° below avg.; 3° above central); precip. 1" (0.5" below avg.; 1" above west). 1-12 Sunny, mild. 13-19 Cold, flurries. 20-23 Very cold, then milder. 24-28 Rain/snow, then colder. 29-31 Milder.

FEB. 1997: Temp. 26° (2° above avg.; 10° above central); precip. 2" (1" above avg.). 1-4 Sunny, cold. 5-13 Sunny, milder. 14-16 Sunny, colder. 17-21 Milder, rain east. 22-26 Heavy snow west, rain central. 27-28 Sunny, mild.

MAR. 1997: Temp. 34° (3° below avg.; avg. west); precip. 3" (1" above avg.; 3" above east; 1" below central). 1-4 Mild, showers. 5-8 Snow showers. 9-12 Sunny, cold. 13-14 Sunny, mild. 15-19 Rain and snow, then cold. 20-23 Milder, rain east. 24-27 Sunny, cool. 28-31 Heavy rain east, flurries west.

APR. 1997: Temp. 48° (3° below avg.; 1° above southeast); precip. 4" (2" above avg. east; 1" below west). 1-4 Colder, snow showers. 5-8 Sunny, milder. 9-14 Cold west, warm and wet east. 15-17 Sunny, mild. 18-22 Showers, cool. 23-26 Heavy rain, snow north. 27-30 Warmer, showers.

MAY 1997: Temp. 62° (1° above avg. north; 2° below south); precip. 3" (0.5" below avg.). 1-3 Showers. 4-7 Rain, snow north and west. 8-11 Cool, rain east. 12-18 Sunny, warmer. 19-25 Showers. 26-31 Showers, heavy rain east.

JUNE 1997: Temp. 73° (1° above avg.); precip. 6" (2" above avg.; 0.5" below northeast). 1-2 Sunny. 3-6 Heavy rain. 7-9 Sunny, cool. 10-17 Hot, thunderstorms central. 18-21 Warm, thunderstorms. 22-30 Sunny, hot and humid.

JULY 1997: Temp. 76° (avg.); precip. 2" (2" below avg.; 1" above central). 1-8 Thunderstorms, seasonable. 9-14 Sunny, warm. 15-18 Record heat. 19-25 Hot, thunderstorms. 26-31 Cooler, few showers.

AUG. 1997: Temp. 75° (1° below avg.); precip. 8" (4" above avg.). 1-3 Sunny, hot. 4-7 Humid, heavy thunderstorms. 8-12 Cooler, local downpours. 13-14 Sunny. 15-18 Heavy thunderstorms, hot south. 19-22 Thunderstorms, hot east. 23-26 Warm, thunderstorms. 27-31 Very warm, thunderstorms east.

SEPT. 1997: Temp. 67° (3° below avg. west; 7° above east); precip. 4.5" (1" above avg.). 1-8 Warm west, heat wave east. 9-14 Cool rain west, warm east. 15-20 Sunny, warm. 21-24 Cool west, thunderstorms and hot east. 25-30 Sunny, warm.

OCT. 1997: Temp. 59° (5° above avg.); precip. 2.5" (1" above avg. south; 1" below north). 1-4 Warm, few showers. 5-11 Heavy rain south, sprinkles north. 12-17 Cool west, heavy rain east. 18-23 Sunny, cool. 24-28 Showers, mild. 29-31 Rainy, colder.

Map labels: Des Moines · Omaha · St. Louis · Denver · Kansas City

SUMMARY: *Temperatures during the period from November through March are expected to average a degree or two above normal, despite some very cold weather in late January. The warmest temperatures, compared to normal, are expected in the northwest. Temperatures in the southeast may actually be a bit below normal for the winter as a whole. Precipitation will be somewhat lighter than normal, although severe ice and snow storms are likely in the northern and central parts of the region. Snow may come just in time for a white Christmas in central areas. Then mid-January will bring a couple of snow and ice threats across the northern and central parts of the region. The highlight (or low point) of the winter will be a Blue Norther in late January, followed by a deep freeze that may reach all the way into the hill country. The final snow and ice threat of the season is expected in early to mid-March, followed by much warmer weather.*

April and May will bring near-normal temperatures. April showers will be relatively infrequent, but several heavy rains in May will more than make up for the lack of rain in April.

Temperatures in the period from June through August won't stray far from normal, except in the west, where August should be very hot. Rainfall will be near normal, with showers and thunderstorms popping up in the usual places at the usual times. The early autumn will bring above-normal temperatures in the east, with near or slightly below normal temperatures in the west. Watch for the threat of a tropical storm along the Gulf in October.

NOV. 1996: Temp. 57.5° (0.5° above avg.; 2° above south); precip. 0.5" (2" below avg.). 1-3 Sunny, cool. 4-6 Showers south. 7-11 Cool, showers. 12-21 Sunny, warm days, cold nights. 22-25 Showers, heavy north. 26-30 Sunny, seasonable.

DEC. 1996: Temp. 51° (3° above avg.; 1° below south); precip. 1.5" (0.5" below avg.; 1" above south). 1-4 Sunny, pleasant. 5-8 Mild, few showers. 9-13 Sunny, clouds south, mild. 14-17 Rain east, cold west. 18-22 Sunny, seasonable. 23-27 Turning colder, rain south, snow central. 28-31 Sunny, then rain.

JAN. 1997: Temp. 46° (1° above avg.); precip. 1" (1" below avg.). 1-7 Sprinkles south, sunny elsewhere. 8-12 Sunny, mild. 13-16 Rain, snow and ice north. 17-22 Warm south, ice to rain north. 23-24 Warm. 25-27 Blue Norther, deep freeze. 28-31 Milder, showers.

FEB. 1997: Temp. 50° (1° above avg.); precip. 2" (avg.). 1-5 Warm, occasional rain. 6-9 Sunny, warm. 10-18 Sunny, seasonable. 19-23 Mild, showers. 24-28 Sunny, mild.

MAR. 1997: Temp. 57° (1° below avg.; 2° above west); precip. 2" (1" below avg.). 1-3 Sunny, warm. 4-6 Sunny, cold. 7-11 Rain south, snow and ice north. 12-16 Sunny, warm. 17-24 Cooler, few showers. 25-28 Warm, thunderstorms north. 29-31 Seasonable.

APR. 1997: Temp. 67° (avg.); precip. 3.5" (0.5" below avg.; 2" below southeast). 1-10 Mostly dry, cool, then warmer. 11-19 Showers and thunderstorms. 20-25 Sunny and warm.

26-30 Seasonable with thunderstorms.

MAY 1997: Temp. 72° (2° below avg.; 1° above southeast); precip. 7" (2" above avg.). 1-7 Seasonable, downpours east. 8-13 Cool, showers east. 14-16 Cool, heavy rain. 17-22 Mostly dry, cool. 23-31 Warmer, heavy thunderstorms north.

JUNE 1997: Temp. 82° (avg.; 1° below west); precip. 3.5" (avg.; 1" above east). 1-7 Cool west, thunderstorms east. 8-15 Sunny, hot. 16-26 Hot, humid, few thunderstorms. 27-30 Thunderstorms south.

JULY 1997: Temp. 87° (1° above avg.); precip. 2.5" (avg.). 1-7 Mainly dry, rather hot. 8-17 Heat wave. 18-21 Few thunderstorms. 22-31 Heat wave.

AUG. 1997: Temp. 86.5° (1° above avg.; 4° above west); precip. 2.5" (avg.). 1-6 Humid, thunderstorms. 7-10 Sunny, hot. 11-21 Hot, few thunderstorms. 22-26 Humid, heavy downpours. 27-31 Very warm, showers south.

SEPT. 1997: Temp. 85° (5° above avg.; 1° below northwest); precip. 1.5" (2" below avg.). 1-3 Showers east. 4-9 Sunny, very warm. 10-17 Showers, cooler west. 18-22 Sunny, very warm. 23-30 Thunderstorms, cooler north.

OCT. 1997: Temp. 70° (4° above avg. east; 1° below west); precip. 3.5" (1" above avg. north; avg. south). 1-5 Heavy thunderstorms south and east. 6-7 Sunny. 8-11 Possible tropical storm. 12-14 Sunny, hot. 15-19 Few showers. 20-25 Sunny, seasonable. 26-31 Showers, cool.

(Map labels: Amarillo, Oklahoma City, Dallas, Houston, San Antonio)

SUMMARY: *The period from November through March is expected to be colder and wetter than normal in the north and east but warmer than normal with near-normal precipitation in the southwest. Sunny, mild periods will alternate with cold, stormy weather in November and early December. The latter half of December and early January will be mainly dry. Storminess will pick up again by mid-January, and the month may end with very heavy rain and snowfall. Relatively mild weather will alternate with cold in February and March. The best chances for snowstorms are in the mid- to late portions of each month.*

Precipitation in April and May should be above normal, except below normal in the northwest. Temperatures will be above normal except a bit below in the south.

June will be warmer and wetter than normal in the north but cool and dry elsewhere. July and August will bring near-normal temperatures and precipitation, except in the northwest, where it should be wetter than normal. Summer heat waves are most likely in mid- to late June, in mid-July, and in early and mid-August. The best chances for widespread rain events are in late June, late July, and early and late August.

September and October will bring typical weather for early autumn. For the most part, the weather will be quite pleasant, with hit-and-miss thunderstorms in mid- and late September and in mid-October. Sharply colder air will arrive in the last week of October, reminding us that no matter what we do, winter is on the way.

NOV. 1996: Temp. 43° (2° above avg.; 2° below east); precip. 1" (0.5" above avg. northwest; 0.5" below southeast). 1-5 Sunny, mild. 6-10 Showers, snow mountains. 11-19 Mild, showers north. 20-24 Colder, heavy snow south. 25-30 Cold, then milder.

DEC. 1996: Temp. 30° (avg.; 3° below north); precip. 2.5" (1" above avg.). 1-3 Sunny, mild. 4-7 Cold, showers, snow mountains. 8-14 Cold, sprinkles and flurries, locally heavy snow mountains. 15-22 Sunny, mild. 23-31 Colder, flurries.

JAN. 1997: Temp. 28° (avg.); precip. 1.5" (avg.). 1-5 Sunny, seasonable. 6-11 Rain and snow, showers north. 12-15 Sunny, cold. 16-18 Snow and rain. 19-22 Seasonable, mainly dry. 23-27 Rain, snow mountains. 28-31 Heavy snow and rain.

FEB. 1997: Temp. 35° (1° above avg.); precip. 1.2" (0.5" above avg. north; 0.5" below south). 1-5 Sunny, mild. 6-14 Sunny, cold. 15-19 Rain, snow mountains. 20-23 Rain to snow, colder. 24-28 Sunny, cold, then mild.

MAR. 1997: Temp. 41° (3° below avg. north; 1° above south); precip. 3" (1" above avg.; 0.5" below northwest). 1-5 Sunny, cold. 6-11 Sunny, mild. 12-16 Stormy, heavy rain and snow. 17-20 Sunny, cold. 21-29 Showers, heavy snow mountains. 30-31 Cloudy.

APR. 1997: Temp. 50° (avg.); precip. 2.5" (0.5" above avg.; 1" below northwest). 1-4 Rain to snow. 5-10 Sunny south, showers north. 11-16 Sunny, turning milder. 17-19 Showers, snow mountains.

20-23 Sunny, cool. 24-30 Milder, sprinkles.

MAY 1997: Temp. 72° (3° above avg.; 1° below south); precip. 3" (1" above avg.; 0.5" below northwest). 1-5 Rain, snow mountains. 6-12 Sunny, turning warmer. 13-16 Showers. 17-23 Sunny, hot. 24-31 Cooler, thunderstorms central.

JUNE 1997: Temp. 67° (2° below avg.; 4° above north); precip. 2" (1" above avg.; 0.5" below northwest). 1-7 Showers north, sunny south. 8-14 Showers, cool. 15-20 Cool, showers, dry south. 21-27 Sunny, hot. 28-30 Rain, cool.

JULY 1997: Temp. 78° (avg.; 1° above central); precip. 0.8" (avg.; 2" above northeast). 1-6 Sunny, seasonable. 7-19 Hot, mountain thunderstorms. 20-26 Cooler, thunderstorms. 27-31 Seasonable, sprinkles.

AUG. 1997: Temp. 76° (avg.); precip. 1" (avg.). 1-6 Sunny, hot. 7-10 Thunderstorms, cooler. 11-17 Seasonable, mountain thunderstorms. 18-23 Sunny, becoming hot. 24-27 Thunderstorms. 28-31 Sunny, seasonable.

SEPT. 1997: Temp. 71° (avg.); precip. 1.5" (avg.). 1-5 Sunny, warm. 6-12 Seasonable, few thunderstorms. 13-18 Sunny, thunderstorms south. 19-25 Showers north, sunny south. 26-30 Seasonable, few showers.

OCT. 1997: Temp. 52° (avg.); precip. 1.5" (avg.). 1-5 Sunny, mild. 6-12 Seasonable, showers. 13-17 Sunny, warm, showers central. 18-23 Sunny, warm. 24-31 Cold, showers, snow mountains.

SOUTHWEST DESERT
FORECAST

SUMMARY: *The period from November through March is expected to be slightly cooler and drier than normal in the north, and warmer and wetter than normal in the south and west. After showers and warm temperatures to start November, it will turn cooler, with sunny days and very cold nights toward the end of the month. December will feature many sunny days with chilly nights and three periods of unsettled weather. The weather will be cool, but quite pleasant in the first half of January; heavy thunderstorms, with snow in the north, will move through in the latter half of the month. February will warm up, with showers mainly in the middle of the month. March should be relatively cool and damp.*

The spring months will be damp with temperatures a bit cooler than normal. The first hot weather of the season is expected to occur in mid-April. May and June will be relatively cool and damp. Watch for locally heavy thunderstorms in late May and late June.

July and August will bring near-normal temperatures and rainfall. The hottest temperatures are expected in the second week of July, the end of July, and in the first week of August.

September and October will be drier than normal, with most days bright and sunny. A few days of showers are most likely in early September, mid-September, late September, and early October. Temperatures in the autumn will gradually cool down, with the first cold nights of the season occurring in late October.

NOV. 1996: Temp. 62° (avg.; 2° above west); precip. 0.3" (0.5" below avg.). 1-3 Showers. 4-8 Sunny, warm. 9-13 Sunny, cooler. 14-20 Sunny, very mild. 21-24 Chilly, showers. 25-30 Sunny, cold nights.

DEC. 1996: Temp. 53.5° (0.5° below avg.); precip. 1" (avg.). 1-5 Sunny, mild. 6-9 Showers, cool. 10-13 Sunny, cool. 14-16 Showers, snow north and east. 17-23 Sunny, mild days, cold nights. 24-27 Colder, showers, snow north. 28-31 Sunny, cool.

JAN. 1997: Temp. 53° (0.5° above avg.; 1° below north); precip. 0.7" (0.5" above avg.; 1" below north). 1-12 Sunny, comfortable days, cold nights. 13-19 Showers, snow north. 20-22 Sunny, cool. 23-25 Thunderstorms. 26-31 Sunny, warm.

FEB. 1997: Temp. 59° (1° above avg.); precip. 1.2" (0.5" above avg.). 1-9 Sunny, mild. 10-19 Rather warm, few showers. 20-24 Sunny, cold. 25-28 Sunny, warmer.

MAR. 1997: Temp. 61° (1° below avg.; 3° above south); precip. 1.5" (0.5" above avg.). 1-3 Sunny, warm. 4-6 Clouds, cooler. 7-9 Showers, cool. 10-13 Sunny, warm. 14-19 Some sun, cool. 20-24 Clouds, sprinkles. 25-29 Chilly, thunderstorms. 30-31 Sunny.

APR. 1997: Temp. 71° (1° above avg.); precip. 0.4" (avg.). 1-5 Sunny, cool. 6-11 Sunny, warmer. 12-15 Sunny, hot. 16-19 Showers north and east. 20-24 Sunny, hot. 25-30 Cooler, showers.

MAY 1997: Temp. 78° (1° below avg.); precip. 0.7" (0.5" above avg.). 1-6 Showers, cool. 7-13 Sunny, seasonable. 14-16 Cloudy, cool. 17-20 Sunny, hot. 21-25 Thunderstorms, local downpours. 26-31 Seasonable, showers east.

JUNE 1997: Temp. 86° (2° below avg.); precip. 0.5" (0.5" above avg.). 1-3 Sunny, cool. 4-8 Sunny, seasonable. 9-16 Sunny, cool. 17-20 Cloudy, few showers. 21-27 Sunny, hot. 28-30 Thunderstorms.

JULY 1997: Temp. 94° (avg.); precip. 0.8" (avg.). 1-3 Sunny, warm. 4-7 Seasonable, few thunderstorms. 8-11 Sunny, hot. 12-16 Warm, thunderstorms. 17-24 Warm, showers. 25-28 Cool, thunderstorms. 29-31 Sunny, hot.

AUG. 1997: Temp. 92° (avg.); precip. 1" (avg.). 1-6 Thunderstorms, hot. 7-9 Rainy, cooler. 10-15 Warm, thunderstorms. 16-19 Sunny, showers east. 20-22 Sunny, hot. 23-27 Warm, local downpours. 28-31 Sunny, warm.

SEPT. 1997: Temp. 85° (avg.); precip. 0.5" (0.5" below avg.). 1-2 Sunny, hot. 3-6 Hot, local downpours. 7-12 Sunny, warm. 13-16 Showers. 17-24 Sunny, hot. 25-30 Cooler, showers.

OCT. 1997: Temp. 74.5° (avg.); precip. 0.5" (0.5" below avg.). 1-4 Sunny, warm. 5-7 Showers. 8-11 Warm, few showers. 12-20 Sunny, warm. 21-26 Sunny, warm days, cool nights. 27-31 Sunny, chilly.

Phoenix
Tucson
Albuquerque
El Paso

SUMMARY: *The period from November through March is expected to be wetter and slightly warmer than normal, with above-normal snowfall in the mountains. It will rain most days in November and December near the coast, but there may be a few bright and sunny days in mid-November. Snow is expected to be limited to the mountains through early January, but a couple of more widespread snowstorms may occur in the latter half of the month. January will be a very wet month, but probably not with flooding as severe as last year. Showers and sprinkles will predominate in February, but some sunshine is likely in the first half of the month. March will dry out, although a major snowstorm may occur around midmonth.*

The spring will be cool but relatively dry. April will start cold, but warm up by midmonth. The best chances for substantial rainfall are in the second week of April and again at month's end. May will be cool through most of the region, but warmer than usual in central sections. The warmest weather will occur just after midmonth.

June through August will be relatively cool, with slightly above normal rainfall. The best chance for a heat wave is in early to mid-July. September and October will be cooler and wetter than normal in the south, but near normal elsewhere. Very warm weather is most likely to occur in late September.

NOV. 1996: Temp. 48° (2° above avg.; 4° above central); precip. 7" (2" above avg.). 1-5 Rain north. 6-8 Cold. 9-11 Rain. 12-13 Sunny, mild. 14-19 Cloudy, rain. 20-26 Heavy rain, snow mountains. 27-30 Mild, rain north.

DEC. 1996: Temp. 41° (1° below avg. north; 3° above south); precip. 6.5" (0.5" above avg.). 1-7 Mild, rain. 8-13 Rain, heavy north and central. 14-16 Light rain. 17-20 Sprinkles north, dry south. 21-24 Heavy rain. 25-26 Cloudy, chilly. 27-31 Light rain, snow mountains.

JAN. 1997: Temp. 40° (avg.); precip. 8" (3" above avg.). 1-5 Light rain. 6-8 Heavy rain, snow mountains. 9-13 Rain, showers south. 14-17 Mainly dry, chilly north. 18-22 Heavy rain, snow north. 23-25 Cold, flurries north. 26-27 Heavy rain and snow. 28-31 Flurries north, heavy rain south.

FEB. 1997: Temp. 44° (avg.; 2° below north); precip. 4" (1" above avg. north; 1" below south). 1-4 Showers. 5-12 Seasonable, some sun. 13-17 Heavy rain, snow mountains. 18-25 Rain, seasonable. 26-28 Cloudy, few sprinkles.

MAR. 1997: Temp. 46° (1° below avg.); precip. 1" (2" below avg.). 1-4 Seasonable, showers north. 5-9 Sunny, cold nights. 10-15 Snow, rain south. 16-20 Showers north. 21-27 Sunny north, rain south. 28-31 Showers, flurries north.

APR. 1997: Temp. 50° (1° below avg.; 4° below north); precip. 2" (0.5" below avg.). 1-4 Sunny, cold. 5-12 Periods of rain. 13-15 Warm. 16-18

Showers. 19-24 Sprinkles north, dry south. 25-28 Cloudy, seasonable. 29-30 Rain.

MAY 1997: Temp. 56.5° (0.5° below avg.; 1° above central); precip. 1.5" (0.5" below avg.). 1-8 Cloudy, sprinkles north. 9-12 Sunny, mild. 13-16 Showers north. 17-23 Sunny, warm. 24-31 Showers, cool.

JUNE 1997: Temp. 63° (avg.); precip. 1.5" (0.5" below avg. north; 1" above south). 1-4 Showers, cool. 5-7 Sunny, mild. 8-12 Cloudy, rain. 13-18 Seasonable, few showers. 19-24 Cool, showers. 25-28 Sunny, seasonable. 29-30 Showers.

JULY 1997: Temp. 66° (2° below avg.); precip. 1.5" (2" above avg. north; avg. south). 1-5 Rain north, dry south. 6-10 Sunny, hot. 11-15 Showers, cool. 16-22 Mostly dry, cool. 23-25 Showers. 26-31 Sunny, cool.

AUG. 1997: Temp. 66.5° (2° below avg.); precip. 1" (avg.). 1-5 Sunny, mild. 6-8 Showers north. 9-15 Mostly dry, cool. 16-23 Cloudy, cool, occasional rain. 24-31 Cool, showers.

SEPT. 1997: Temp. 62° (1° below avg.); precip. 1.5" (avg.; 1" above south). 1-4 Mild, showers. 5-9 Cloudy, cool. 10-16 Milder, sprinkles. 17-22 Cool, showers. 23-27 Cloudy, seasonable. 28-30 Sunny, warm.

OCT. 1997: Temp. 54.5° (1° above avg. north; 1° below south); precip. 1" (avg.; 0.5" above central). 1-9 Cloudy, cool. 10-16 Occasional rain, cool. 17-22 Sunny, mild. 23-27 Rain, snow mountains. 28-31 Some sun, cold.

Seattle

Portland

Eugene

Eureka

CALIFORNIA
F O R E C A S T

SUMMARY: *The period from November through March is expected to be warmer and drier than normal overall, with near-normal snowfall in the mountains. The last two months of 1996 will see above-normal temperatures, but below-normal precipitation throughout the region. In January, temperatures will be a bit below normal in the south, but continue relatively mild elsewhere. Two or three major storms in the last week or two of the month will bring heavy rain and strong, damaging winds. Snow flurries in the first half of February could fall unusually far south and west, but the month as a whole is expected to be relatively dry, with above-normal temperatures in the south. A major freeze in the central valley seems unlikely, although several frosts will occur in February and March. March will be very wet across the north, but dry weather may predominate across the south. A storm toward the end of the month may be especially severe, with flooding rains, very heavy snow in the mountains, and winds gusting to 80 miles per hour near the northern coast.*

April is expected to be rather mild, with unseasonably hot temperatures in the interior during the latter half of the month. However, the end of April and early May will be rather cool, and these cooler temperatures will predominate in May. Rainfall during April and May will be below normal.

Summer will be cooler than normal along the coast, with near- to below-normal temperatures in the interior. The best chances for heat waves are in late June, mid-July and early to mid-August. September will start hot, but the autumn will be cooler and drier than normal. Late October will be particularly cold.

NOV. 1996: Temp. 56° (1° above avg.); precip. 2.5" (0.5" below avg.; avg. east). 1-3 Sunny, warm. 4-9 Sprinkles, cool. 10-15 Sunny, mild. 16-19 Showers, seasonable. 20-30 Breezy, showers north.

DEC. 1996: Temp. 51.5° (2° above avg.); precip. 2" (1" below avg.). 1-6 Sunny, seasonable. 7-11 Showers. 12-20 Sunny, warm. 21-25 Cooler, showers north, flurries mountains. 26-31 Sunny, mild days, cold nights.

JAN. 1997: Temp. 51° (2° above avg.; 1° below south); precip. 4.5" (avg.). 1-6 Sunny and mild. 7-13 Seasonable with showers north. 14-16 Cooler, some showers. 17-19 Sunny. 20-31 Stormy, rain, locally heavy, snow mountains.

FEB. 1997: Temp. 50° (2° below avg.; 3° above south); precip. 1" (2" below avg.). 1-11 Warm south, sprinkles and flurries north. 12-15 Cloudy, cool. 16-21 Cold, rain, snow mountains. 22-28 Sunny, turning warmer.

MAR. 1997: Temp. 51° (2° below avg.); precip. 5" (2" above avg.; 1" below south). 1-7 Sunny, warm. 8-15 Cool, showers north. 16-19 Sunny, seasonable. 20-26 Windy, heavy rain, snow mountains. 27-31 Few showers.

APR. 1997: Temp. 56.5° (1° above avg.); precip. 1" (0.5" below avg.). 1-4 Mild, showers. 5-7 Sunny, warm. 8-11 Mild, showers north. 12-22 Sunny, hot. 23-30 Sunny, hot, then cooler.

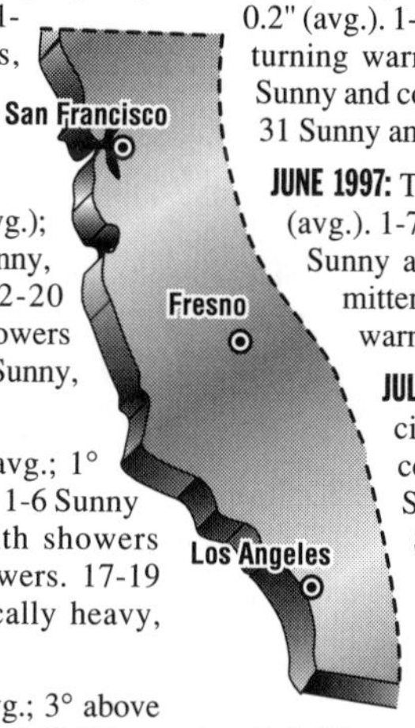

MAY 1997: Temp. 56° (2° below avg.); precip. 0.2" (avg.). 1-3 Cool, showers. 4-12 Sunny, turning warmer. 13-14 Showers. 15-19 Sunny and cool. 20-26 Hot and sunny. 27-31 Sunny and cooler.

JUNE 1997: Temp. 61.5° (avg.); precip. 0" (avg.). 1-7 Sunny and seasonable. 8-11 Sunny and hot. 12-16 Warm, intermittent sprinkles. 17-23 Sunny and warm. 24-30 Sunny, hot inland.

JULY 1997: Temp. 63° (avg.); precip. 0" (avg.). 1-5 Sunny and cool. 6-9 Hot and sunny. 10-14 Sunny and warm. 15-22 Sunny, hot inland. 23-28 Sunny, seasonable. 29-31 Intermittent sprinkles.

AUG. 1997: Temp. 61.5° (2° below avg.); precip. 0" (avg.). 1-7 Sunny, hot inland. 8-11 Sprinkles, cooler. 12-16 Sunny, hot inland. 17-24 Sunny, cool. 25-31 Sunny, hot inland.

SEPT. 1997: Temp. 61.5° (3° below avg.); precip. 0" (0.2" above avg.; avg. north). 1-6 Hot and sunny. 7-13 Sunny and cool. 14-17 Intermittent sprinkles north. 18-25 Sunny and cool. 26-30 Hot and sunny.

OCT. 1997: Temp. 57° (4° below avg.; avg. east); precip. 1" (avg.; 1" below central). 1-7 Turning cooler. 8-16 Seasonable, few sprinkles. 17-20 Sunny, hot inland. 21-24 Seasonable, showers north. 25-31 Sunny, cold.

(Map labels: San Francisco, Fresno, Los Angeles)

She Is The *Only*[†] Psychic To Have Been Granted An Audience *With The Pope*

"Why Is Maria Duval Offering You Her Help For Free?" *

...to "see" the changes awaiting you in your future, and to make your dearest wishes come true, *fast.* (absolutely FREE offer) *

- The most famous people in the world line up at her door — and are delighted to pay her as much as $700 per visit.
- Thousands have transformed their lives for the better with her help.
- Why is Maria Duval now offering this help *absolutely for free* to anyone who mails in the *original* Free Help Coupon below before midnight, Friday next week?

Major study financed by the National Parapsychology Center

What is your most cherished — and pressing — wish at this moment?

Is it to be luckier and to win a large amount of money unexpectedly? Is it to resolve some tough financial situation or pay off a debt? Is it to find a new or better job? Is it to discover the person who really loves you? Is it to improve a marital or domestic situation gone bad? Or does it involve the answer to some other key question about your future?

1. Whatever your most pressing wish, Maria Duval personally pledges to help you achieve it *fast*—if you respond quickly, *and for free*—as part of this research study.

But that's not all...
Maria Duval also pledges:
2. To answer the question that disturbs you most about your future, *for free*;
3. To send you a *personal* detailed study of at least 15 pages, providing astonishing predictions on *your* future, *for free*;
4. To send you your personal lucky numbers (for the lottery and other games of chance), *for free*;
5. Maria Duval also offers you her precious personal and authentic lucky talisman, to attract good luck and to protect you, *for free*.

What changes will occur in your future?

Let Maria Duval be your personal psychic. All her predictions come true.

She can *really* help you fulfill your desires. Whether your concerns involve your financial situation, overcoming bad luck, a job problem, your love life — or any other subject that is important to you and pertains to your future.

Now let Maria Duval personally put her psychic powers and her clairvoyance to work for you. She can truly help you change your life for the better as she has already done thousands of times before for others.

How to explain Maria Duval's unlimited powers?

Although her powers seem to defy comprehension or explanation, experts tend to believe that her direct descent from a long line of famous psychics, could, over the generations, have enhanced her extrasensory abilities. This could be the key to Maria Duval's passage into a place in space-time that eludes the rest of us. This is how they believe she can see into the future.

And this is how Maria Duval has been helping so many people in the past obtain luck, money, love, self-confidence and success.

Juicy Fruit gum, bleach, banana peels, strings of Christmas tree lights — sometimes the craziest-sounding things can solve the most perplexing gardening problems.

UNCOMMON ANSWERS TO COMMON GARDENING QUESTIONS

by Georgia Orcutt

– Nancy Didion

Q How can I keep woodchucks out of my garden?

A ■ **Feed them Juicy Fruit gum.** Buy several jumbo packs, unwrap each stick, and lay the sticks down all along the row where woodchucks have started to snack — or where you don't want them to. They will eat the gum and go away.

Vermont Public Radio commentator Ruth Page says she first heard this hint from a listener. "A woodchuck was going after my broccoli, and I decided to try it. My granddaughter and I unwrapped all the gum and put it down on the soil. We felt pretty silly. But the next day the gum was all gone — and the woodchuck never came back."

Note: One widely published garden guru begged us not to repeat this hint, citing it as sheer rubbish. Who knows if the gum really had anything to do with the woodchuck's disappearance? Try it yourself and see.

Q How can I keep deer out of my garden?

A ■ **String blinking outdoor Christmas** tree lights around the perimeter and keep them on from dusk to dawn. While deer will leap high fences, learn to ignore smelly hotel soap, and overlook bags of human hair (all commonly offered solutions), they don't like blinking lights. Perhaps a strobe light would work as well?

What's the best way to prevent moles from tunneling in the lawn?	■ **Give them a good dose of castor oil.** Moles are carnivores that make themselves at home in lawns rich in grubs and insects. When their food is seasoned with castor oil, they will go elsewhere for meals. (Wouldn't you?) Mix up a spray of 3 parts castor oil to 1 part dish detergent; use 4 tablespoons of this concoction in a gallon of water, and soak the tunnels and the entrances. Or invest in Mole-Med, a commercially available repellent with castor oil as its active ingredient. Check out your soil for the presence of pests; if you have a lot of moles, you probably have an oversupply of grubs and bugs.
How can I get rid of slugs?	■ **First, trap the slugs.** Go out to the garden in the late afternoon and lay boards or pieces of cardboard on the bare soil around your plantings. In the morning turn the boards over and scrape the hiding slugs into a large yogurt or cottage cheese container. Cover and place in your freezer for three hours. When they're frozen stiff, dump them on your compost pile. 
How can I get rid of red spider mites on hanging plants?	■ **Douse them with cold water.** Mites hate cold baths and will head for the hills if you spray them with water that is between 32° and 40° F. If you find an infested plant, attack with ice water. Keep a spray bottle in the refrigerator and mist once or twice a day until the mites are all gone. 
What can I do with an over-abundance of zucchini?	■ **Cut it into little pieces and toss it on the compost pile.** Don't feel one ounce of guilt. It is a fine soil amendment and will teach you the wisdom of returning nutrients to the garden — and of planting no more than four hills next year. Or maybe two.
What's the best way to keep sweet corn fresh?	■ **Soak it in bleach.** Well, not just bleach. University of Maryland professor Don Schlimme suggests picking the ears early in the day, husking them, and chilling them in ice-cold water (32° to 40° F). For every gallon of water add a teaspoon of bleach and a teaspoon of white vinegar. Soak the ears for 30 minutes, drain, and immediately pack in resealable plastic bags, about four ears per bag, and refrigerate. The corn will remain fresh for two to three weeks, depending on how cold your refrigerator runs. 
What's an unusual way to control weeds in the garden?	■ **Attack them with a flame gun.** While this may sound too ballistic for your backyard Eden, carefully applied heat will make short work of emerging weeds. Before planting in the spring, encourage weeds to grow by laying sheets of clear plastic over the soil to warm it and bring out those weeds. When they're up several inches, blast them — or if you prefer, pull them out or cut them down with a hoe — and then put your seeds in the ground. *(continued)* 

Q What's the best fertilizer for roses?

 A ■ **Mushy bananas.** Bury one old brown banana at the base of each of your rose bushes or apply the peels only, laying them flat on the soil. Repeat every few weeks as the peels decompose. Banana peels act as a time-release fertilizer rich in calcium, magnesium, sulfur, and phosphates — all things roses love.

 Q What's the best fertilizer for a flower garden?

 A ■ **Don't overlook urine,** a fine source of organic nitrogen, rich in urea metabolized from used protein. Use it for annuals and perennials alike. Fill your watering can with half urine, half water, and go quietly about your rounds, daily or several times a week, starting after the last frost has passed. When neighbors marvel about your garden, you can decide whether or not to share your secret.

 Q Is there a law that says you must mow your lawn?

 A ■ **There might be, but you can get around it.** In some communities, people who create natural landscapes or encourage lawn grass to reach its fullest height find themselves defending their gardens in a court of law. If you embrace the philosophy of fruitarians and believe that plants feel pain when they are cut, you may persuade a judge that your lawn can go unshorn for religious reasons. Local weed laws may be cited by your neighbors, but some natural-lawn advocates have found constitutional grounds for battle: If you think of your natural lawn as a way to proclaim your concern for the environment, it becomes an act of symbolic speech, which is protected as oral speech under the First Amendment.

Q Is there any way to camouflage a chain-link fence?

 A ■ **Pretend you are building a wattle hedge** in the English countryside. First, paint the fence a nice dull earth tone — a sort of grayish brown. Every time you prune a tree or clip a woody stem, weave it into the chain link. The branches will dry and weather, hiding the metal and softening the lines of the fence for years to come.

FROSTS AND GROWING SEASONS

Courtesy of National Climatic Center

Dates given are normal averages for a light freeze (32° F); local weather and topography may cause considerable variations. The possibility of frost occurring after the spring dates and before the fall dates is 50 percent. The classification of freeze temperatures is usually based on their effect on plants, with the following commonly accepted categories: **Light freeze:** 29° F to 32° F — tender plants killed, with little destructive effect on other vegetation. **Moderate freeze:** 25° F to 28° F — widely destructive effect on most vegetation, with heavy damage to fruit blossoms and tender and semihardy plants. **Severe freeze:** 24° F and colder — heavy damage to most plants.

CITY	Growing Season (Days)	Last Frost Spring	First Frost Fall	CITY	Growing Season (Days)	Last Frost Spring	First Frost Fall
Mobile, AL	272	Feb. 27	Nov. 26	North Platte, NE	136	May 11	Sept. 24
Juneau, AK	133	May 16	Sept. 26	Las Vegas, NV	259	Mar. 7	Nov. 21
Phoenix, AZ	308	Feb. 5	Dec. 15	Concord, NH	121	May 23	Sept. 22
Tucson, AZ	273	Feb. 28	Nov. 29	Newark, NJ	219	Apr. 4	Nov. 10
Pine Bluff, AR	234	Mar. 19	Nov. 8	Carlsbad, NM	223	Mar. 29	Nov. 7
Eureka, CA	324	Jan. 30	Dec. 15	Los Alamos, NM	157	May 8	Oct. 13
Sacramento, CA	289	Feb. 14	Dec. 1	Albany, NY	144	May 7	Sept. 29
San Francisco, CA	*	*	*	Syracuse, NY	170	Apr. 28	Oct. 16
Denver, CO	157	May 3	Oct. 8	Fayetteville, NC	212	Apr. 2	Oct. 31
Hartford, CT	167	Apr. 25	Oct. 10	Bismarck, ND	129	May 14	Sept. 20
Wilmington, DE	198	Apr. 13	Oct. 29	Akron, OH	168	May 3	Oct. 18
Miami, FL	*	*	*	Cincinnati, OH	195	Apr. 14	Oct. 27
Tampa, FL	338	Jan. 28	Jan. 3	Lawton, OK	217	Apr. 1	Nov. 5
Athens, GA	224	Mar. 28	Nov. 8	Tulsa, OK	218	Mar. 30	Nov. 4
Savannah, GA	250	Mar. 10	Nov. 15	Pendleton, OR	188	Apr. 15	Oct. 21
Boise, ID	153	May 8	Oct. 9	Portland, OR	217	Apr. 3	Nov. 7
Chicago, IL	187	Apr. 22	Oct. 26	Carlisle, PA	182	Apr. 20	Oct. 20
Springfield, IL	185	Apr. 17	Oct. 19	Williamsport, PA	168	Apr. 29	Oct. 15
Indianapolis, IN	180	Apr. 22	Oct. 20	Kingston, RI	144	May 8	Sept. 30
South Bend, IN	169	May 1	Oct. 18	Charleston, SC	253	Mar. 11	Nov. 20
Atlantic, IA	141	May 9	Sept. 28	Columbia, SC	211	Apr. 4	Nov. 2
Cedar Rapids, IA	161	Apr. 29	Oct. 7	Rapid City, SD	145	May 7	Sept. 29
Topeka, KS	175	Apr. 21	Oct. 14	Memphis, TN	228	Mar. 23	Nov. 7
Lexington, KY	190	Apr. 17	Oct. 25	Nashville, TN	207	Apr. 5	Oct. 29
Monroe, LA	242	Mar. 9	Nov. 7	Amarillo, TX	197	Apr. 14	Oct. 29
New Orleans, LA	288	Feb. 20	Dec. 5	Denton, TX	231	Mar. 25	Nov. 12
Portland, ME	143	May 10	Sept. 30	San Antonio, TX	265	Mar. 3	Nov. 24
Baltimore, MD	231	Mar. 26	Nov. 13	Cedar City, UT	134	May 20	Oct. 2
Worcester, MA	172	Apr. 27	Oct. 17	Spanish Fork, UT	156	May 8	Oct. 12
Lansing, MI	140	May 13	Sept. 30	Burlington, VT	142	May 11	Oct. 1
Marquette, MI	159	May 12	Oct. 19	Norfolk, VA	239	Mar. 23	Nov. 17
Duluth, MN	122	May 22	Sept. 21	Richmond, VA	198	Apr. 10	Oct. 26
Willmar, MN	152	May 4	Oct. 4	Seattle, WA	232	Mar. 24	Nov. 11
Columbus, MS	215	Mar. 27	Oct. 29	Spokane, WA	153	May 4	Oct. 5
Vicksburg, MS	250	Mar. 13	Nov. 18	Parkersburg, WV	175	Apr. 25	Oct. 18
Jefferson City, MO	173	Apr. 26	Oct. 16	Green Bay, WI	143	May 12	Oct. 2
Fort Peck, MT	146	May 5	Sept. 28	Janesville, WI	164	Apr. 28	Oct. 10
Helena, MT	122	May 18	Sept. 18	Casper, WY	123	May 22	Sept. 22
Blair, NE	165	Apr. 27	Oct. 10	*Frosts do not occur every year.			

OUTDOOR PLANTING TABLE
1 9 9 7

The best time to plant flowers and vegetables that bear crops above the
ground is during the *light* of the
Moon; that is, between the day the
Moon is new to the day it is full.
Flowering bulbs and vegetables
that bear crops below ground
should be planted during the *dark*
of the Moon; that is, from the day

after it is full to the day before it is new
again. The dates given here are based on
the safe periods for planting in areas
that receive frost and the Moon's
phases for 1997. Consult page 155
for dates of frosts and length of
growing season. See calendar pages
54-80 for the exact days of the new
and full Moons.

☞ **Above-Ground Crops Marked (*)**   ☞ **E means Early**   ☞ **L means Late**

	Planting Dates	Moon Favorable	Planting Dates	Moon Favorable	Planting Dates	Moon Favorable
*Barley	5/15-6/21	5/15-22, 6/5-20	3/15-4/7	3/15-23, 4/7	2/15-3/7	2/15-22
*Beans (E)	5/7-6/21	5/7-22, 6/5-20	4/15-30	4/15-22	3/15-4/7	3/15-23, 4/7
(L)	6/15-7/15	6/15-20, 7/4-15	7/1-21	7/4-19	8/7-31	8/7-18
Beets (E)	5/1-15	5/1-5	3/15-4/3	3/24-4/3	2/7-28	2/23-28
(L)	7/15-8/15	7/20-8/2	8/15-31	8/19-31	9/1-30	9/17-30
*Broccoli (E)	5/15-31	5/15-22	3/7-31	3/8-23	2/15-3/15	2/15-22, 3/8-15
Plants (L)	6/15-7/7	6/15-20, 7/4-7	8/1-20	8/3-18	9/7-30	9/7-16
*Brussels Sprouts	5/15-31	5/15-22	3/7-4/15	3/8-23, 4/7-15	2/11-3/20	2/11-22, 3/8-20
*Cabbage Plants	5/15-31	5/15-22	3/7-4/15	3/8-23, 4/7-15	2/11-3/20	2/11-22, 3/8-20
Carrots (E)	5/15-31	5/23-31	3/7-31	3/24-31	2/15-3/7	2/23-3/7
(L)	6/15-7/21	6/21-7/3, 7/20-21	7/7-31	7/20-31	8/1-9/7	8/19-31
*Cauliflower (E)	5/15-31	5/15-22	3/15-4/7	3/15-23, 4/7	2/15-3/7	2/15-22
Plants (L)	6/15-7/21	6/15-20, 7/4-19	7/1-8/7	7/4-19, 8/3-7	8/7-31	8/7-18
*Celery Plants (E)	5/15-6/30	5/15-22, 6/5-20	3/7-31	3/8-23	2/15-28	2/15-22
(L)	7/15-8/15	7/15-19, 8/3-15	8/15-9/7	8/15-18, 9/1-7	9/15-30	9/15-16
*Collards (E)	5/15-31	5/15-22	3/7-4/7	3/8-23, 4/7	2/11-3/20	2/11-22, 3/8-20
(L)	7/1-8/7	7/4-19, 8/3-7	8/15-31	8/15-18	9/7-30	9/7-16
*Corn, Sweet (E)	5/10-6/15	5/10-22, 6/5-15	4/1-15	4/7-15	3/15-31	3/15-23
(L)	6/15-30	6/15-20	7/7-21	7/7-19	8/7-31	8/7-18
*Cucumber	5/7-6/20	5/7-22, 6/5-20	4/7-5/15	4/7-22, 5/6-15	3/7-4/15	3/8-23, 4/7-15
*Eggplant Plants	6/1-30	6/5-20	4/7-5/15	4/7-22, 5/6-15	3/7-4/15	3/8-23, 4/7-15
*Endive (E)	5/15-31	5/15-22	4/7-5/15	4/7-22, 5/6-15	2/15-3/20	2/15-22, 3/8-20
(L)	6/7-30	6/7-20	7/15-8/15	7/15-19, 8/3-15	8/15-9/7	8/15-18, 9/1-7
*Flowers (All)	5/7-6/21	5/7-22, 6/5-20	4/15-30	4/15-22	3/15-4/7	3/15-23, 4/7
*Kale (E)	5/15-31	5/15-22	3/7-4/7	3/8-23, 4/7	2/11-3/20	2/11-22, 3/8-20

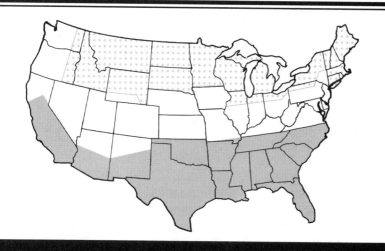

	Planting Dates	Moon Favorable	Planting Dates	Moon Favorable	Planting Dates	Moon Favorable
*Kale (L)	7/1-8/7	7/4-19, 8/3-7	8/15-31	8/15-18	9/7-30	9/7-16
Leek Plants	5/15-31	5/23-31	3/7-4/7	3/24-4/6	2/15-4/15	2/23-3/7, 3/24-4/6
*Lettuce	5/15-6/30	5/15-22, 6/5-20	3/1-31	3/8-23	2/15-3/7	2/15-22
*Muskmelon	5/15-6/30	5/15-22, 6/5-20	4/15-5/7	4/15-22, 5/6-7	3/15-4/7	3/15-23, 4/7
Onion Sets	5/15-6/7	5/23-6/4	3/1-31	3/1-7, 3/24-31	2/1-28	2/1-6, 2/23-28
*Parsley	5/15-31	5/15-22	3/1-31	3/8-23	2/20-3/15	2/20-22, 3/8-15
Parsnips	4/1-30	4/23-30	3/7-31	3/7, 3/24-31	1/15-2/4	1/24-2/4
*Peas (E)	4/15-5/7	4/15-22, 5/6-7	3/7-31	3/8-23	1/15-2/7	1/15-23, 2/7
(L)	7/15-31	7/15-19	8/7-31	8/7-18	9/15-30	9/15-16
*Pepper Plants	5/15-6/30	5/15-22, 6/5-20	4/1-30	4/7-22	3/1-20	3/8-20
Potato	5/1-31	5/1-2, 5/23-31	4/1-30	4/1-6, 4/23-30	2/10-28	2/23-28
*Pumpkin	5/15-31	5/15-22	4/23-5/15	5/6-15	3/7-20	3/8-20
Radish (E)	4/15-30	4/23-30	3/7-31	3/7, 3/24-31	1/21-3/1	1/24-2/6, 2/23-3/1
(L)	8/15-31	8/19-31	9/7-30	9/17-30	10/1-21	10/16-21
*Spinach (E)	5/15-31	5/15-22	3/15-4/20	3/15-23, 4/7-20	2/7-3/15	2/7-22, 3/8-15
(L)	7/15-9/7	7/15-19, 8/3-18	8/1-9/15	8/3-18, 9/1-15	10/1-21	10/1-15
*Squash	5/15-6/15	5/15-22, 6/5-15	4/15-30	4/15-22	3/15-4/15	3/15-23, 4/7-15
Sweet Potatoes	5/15-6/15	5/23-6/4	4/21-30	4/23-30	3/23-4/6	3/24-4/6
*Swiss Chard	5/1-31	5/6-22	3/15-4/15	3/15-23, 4/7-15	2/7-3/15	2/7-22, 3/8-15
*Tomato Plants	5/15-31	5/15-22	4/7-30	4/7-22	3/7-20	3/8-20
Turnips (E)	4/7-30	4/23-30	3/15-31	3/24-31	1/20-2/15	1/24-2/6
(L)	7/1-8/15	7/1-3, 7/20-8/2	8/1-20	8/1-2, 8/19-20	9/1-10/15	9/17-30
*Watermelon	5/15-6/30	5/15-22, 6/5-20	4/15-5/7	4/15-22, 5/6-7	3/15-4/7	3/15-23, 4/7
*Wheat, Winter	8/11-9/15	8/11-18, 9/1-15	9/15-10/20	9/15-16, 10/1-15	10/15-12/7	10/31-11/14, 11/29-12/7
Spring	4/7-30	4/7-22	3/1-20	3/8-20	2/15-28	2/15-22

LOSING WEIGHT:
"Amazing Skin Patch Melts Away Body Fat"

Results of a study conducted for the United Research Center by G. Fleming

- **Clinically tested in the United States**
- **Recommended by doctors and pharmacists**
- **Hundreds of thousands of boxes sold in a few months in European pharmacies (simply by word-of-mouth!).**

Is the once-a-day *Svelt PATCH* really revolutionary? And does it really give the promised results?

Following a survey, the United Research Center is so convinced of the efficiency of this new weight-loss plan that now, for the first time, it is making an at-home, risk-free trial offer of the famous *Svelt PATCH* Weight-Loss Plan to anyone wishing to lose weight and stay slim — with *no* obligation to buy. Read how you can take advantage of this special offer.

The new *Svelt PATCH* Weight-Loss Plan is now available in the United States without prescription.

Below you will discover:

• How the dual-action *Svelt PATCH* Weight-Loss Plan works.

• How it makes you lose weight—*really* lose weight. Effectively. By eating up to 5 times daily. With no medication. No strenuous exercise.

• Why it guarantees such long-lasting results.

• How, for the first time in the United States you can receive your *genuine Svelt PATCH* Weight-Loss Plan, with the same Svelt PATCHES as those sold in European pharmacies, for a 90-day at-home risk-free trial offer—with *no* obligation to buy.

A fter having surpassed the effectiveness of *all* methods for quitting smoking, Anti-Tobacco Patches created a world-wide revolution.

Now the new *Svelt PATCH* Weight-Loss Plan is also enjoying phenomenal success in Europe. Within the next few years, this plan is likely to take the lead over all other weight-loss programs.

Finally available in the United States, you can now obtain an at-home risk-free trial of this plan—with no obligation to buy. That way, you can see the spectacular results of the *Svelt PATCH* Weight-Loss

Plan *for yourself.* Here is how it works:

The weight-loss plan of the 21st century is now available.

Yes. The *Svelt PATCH* Weight-Loss Plan can finally help you lose weight. *Really* lose weight. Quickly. Easily. Eating up to 5 meals a day. With no medication. Without any strenuous exercise. This Plan guarantees long-lasting results. With a *maximum* loss of water and fat. And a *minimum* loss of muscle.

The results have been proven. Thousands of times.

How many pounds do you want to lose? 15 pounds, 25 pounds, 35 pounds? More than 45 pounds? The new *Svelt PATCH* Weight-Loss Plan can really help you lose weight.

Doctor Marvin Kaplan observed weight losses of as much as: 16 pounds the first week • 25 pounds in 2 weeks • 33 pounds in 3 weeks • 41 pounds in 1 month • 71 pounds in 2 months.

Weight-loss patches have been scientifically tested in the USA and are used in European hospitals and clinics.

In the United States, Dr. Marvin Kaplan recently tested the weight-loss patch on 100 individuals. *All* participants had already tried *many* other weight-loss schemes over the prior years, without success. Twenty-five percent of them were thus doubtful about how well the weight-loss patch would work. But here are the results:

• The measured effectiveness of the weight-loss patch was 100%: absolutely *all* participants lost weight.

• Fifty-six percent of the participants lost *at least* 20 pounds in 2 months (between 20 and 71 pounds in only 2 months).

• *Average* weight losses in women was 4.9 pounds the first week, 12.8 pounds the first month, and 21.9 pounds in 2 months.

• *Average* weight loss in men was 4.7 pounds the first week, 15.7 pounds the first month, and 25.1 pounds in 2 months.

How does the *Svelt PATCH* Weight-Loss Plan work?

The *Svelt PATCH* Weight-Loss Plan includes:

1. A weight-loss plan which begins by explaining in detail:

• How to let your body burn up 77% *more* calories than it absorbs — easily and eating up to 5 meals a day.

• How to easily *speed up* your body's metabolism.

• How to *maximize* losses of water and fat

• How to *minimize* muscle loss — and even increase muscle mass to get your body back in shape.

2. Stick-on *Svelt PATCHES.*

Just put one stick-on PATCH anywhere on your body. Replace it with another stick-on *Svelt PATCH* after 24 hours.

Svelt PATCHES contain concentrated fucus. In contrast with most weight-loss products — which only work for a few hours following their consumption — *Svelt PATCH* fucus is absorbed by your body, through the skin, *the entire* day and while

"The Svelt-PATCH speeds Up The Body's Metabolism And Burns Up Fat"

By Thomas Anglim — Extract of the article published in the Globe , August 16, 1994 - p.27 (7 million readers)

Forget calorie counting, working out and gulping down yucky food supplements — it's now possible to peel off those unwanted pounds simply by wearing a tiny pink skin patch.

And because you wear it day and night, you can lose weight even while you sleep.

"We tested 100 overweight men and women for 60 days, whithout having them change their normal lifestyle in any way," says a company spokesman.

"Every one of these people had spent many years trying — unsuccessfully — a wide range of diets and weight control gimmicks."

"Most of the people in our trial came out more than 20 pounds lighter.

"The secret to the Svelt Patch' success is a kelplike seaweed called fucus, which is found along the Atlantic coast. It's loaded with iodine, which speeds up the body's metabolism and then burns up unwanted fat and cholesterol."

"Fucus is registered as a food additive and a weight - control product by the United States Food and Drugs Administration. And that, for me, is as good as the Bible".

---

you sleep — up to 24 hours per day.

What is fucus?

Fucus is a type of natural algae containing very high levels of certain ingredients. Biologist Duchesne Dupont was the first to discover fucus's ability to absorb fat and to trigger the "combustion" of fat. Fucus is now recommended by many physicians to those who want to lose weight.

Fucus is very rich in iodine. It also contains an extraordinary amount—15%—of certain minerals *essential* to your body. These minerals are often lacking in our daily diets.

How fucus helps your body

⬛ Controls your appetite .

⬛ **Stimulates your metabolism:** iodine, niacin, riboflavin, potassium, magnesium and vitamin C stimulate cellular oxygenation, facilitates the assimilation of glucides, and helps your body transform food into energy (and not fat) by triggering the metabolism of fat.

⬛ **Control and balance in producing hormones** through the very large quantity of iodine which ensures *proper functioning of the thyroid* (essential to weight loss).

⬛ **Acts on the muscular system:** thiamine, silicon and potassium, sodium and calcium help *nourish* muscles and *prevent* muscle loss when losing body weight.

⬛ **Eliminates active toxins** with iron.

⬛ **Maintains weight loss** with indispensable cyanocobalamin

⬛ **Helps fight water retention** with potassium.

⬛ **Cuts fatigue** with vitamin C.

⬛ **Reduces cholesterol** with niacin.

A study published in England in November 1991 showed that people wanting to lose weight did so *200% as quickly* with fucus than those who tried to lose weight without fucus, with both groups eating the same quantities of food.

Are there any drawbacks to the *Svelt PATCH* Weight-Loss Plan? '

Although the *Svelt PATCH* Weight-Loss

> Here is exactly how the entirely new *Svelt PATCH* double-action Weight-Loss Plan can help you lose a total of 15, 25, 35, 45 and even more than 55 pounds in record time.

Plan permits truly fast, effective results, it is completely natural. It poses no risk if you are in good health. In fact, it lets your body work *better*.

The Plan lets you lose weight quickly and efficiently—and obtain long-lasting results:

• By eating up to 5 times a day • Without any medication • Without strenuous exercise

Here is how the *Svelt PATCH* Weight-Loss Plan will change *your* life

Through the *Svelt PATCH* Weight-Loss Plan, you'll be losing weight 24 hours per day. Even while you sleep. Day after day, you'll see the results on the scale. Week after week your body will be transformed—and your figure will become slimmer and more attractive. You will be able to lose your excess weight efficiently and quickly, and experience long-lasting results. Do you know what this really means?

• You will be able to wear the fashionable clothing you like, and you'll feel good about it.

• You will have greater self-confidence, and a personal image that pleases you. You will feel more at ease.

• You will appear younger and in better health. You will be in better shape, more

Please, turn over —>

vital, and more active.
- Your love life will be more interesting.
- Your entire life will improve. Your spouse, your family, and your friends will find you more attractive.

For the first time, a risk-free home trial — with *no* obligation to buy

Just fill out the coupon below and mail it today to the exclusive distributor—the United Research Center—at the address indicated below. You will soon receive the *Svelt PATCH* Weight-Loss Plan at your home. Just follow the *Svelt PATCH* Weight-Loss Plan as indicated.

If, *for any reason whatsoever*, you're not 100% satisfied with the results of the *Svelt PATCH* Weight-Loss Plan, simply send the Weight-Loss Plan back to us within 90 days, and we will give you a *100% refund*. Yes. A ONE HUNDRED PERCENT REFUND. And we'll do so without asking you any questions. A cheque in your name for this full refund will promptly be sent to you.

This is a written, formal guarantee, enabling you to try the new *Svelt PATCH* Weight-Loss Plan without any obligation on your part.

Only read this if you have decided NOT to benefit from this risk-free trial offer

Perhaps you believe you're a special, difficult, or desperate case. Or perhaps you're still somewhat skeptical. That's perfectly reasonable.

If so, *at least* take a trial. Just out of pure curiosity. Show the *Svelt PATCH* Weight-Loss Plan to your physician. Ask his or her opinion. If, for any reason, you are not totally satisfied *with the results*, just return your Svelt PATCH Weight-Loss Plan. You will be *reimbursed in full*. This trial will have cost you nothing. Not one penny.

As you can see, there's *no* obligation on your part. We are prepared to make this kind of unique offer, only because we are convinced that you, like thousands before you, will be pleased as you never have been previously by the results from your *Svelt PATCH* Weight-Loss Plan.

You will soon receive your *Svelt PATCH* Weight-Loss Plan at home. And you will see yourself lose weight quickly, every single week. You will see the results really work. You will see your body transformed—and enjoy long-lasting results. You will be

proud of your new appearance and your new, totally revitalized life.

Act now. Don't wait until later. That way you might forget—and later regret having missed this special introductory offer enabling you to take a home trial—with no obligation to buy. Fill out the coupon below right now and mail it today.

You will soon see *for yourself* how quick and effective *Svelt PATCH* Weight-Loss Plan results really are. You will be very pleased with your decision. We guarantee this formally—and in writing.

Free: If you mail your coupon before 5 p.m. Friday of next week, we will include, in addition to your shipment, *a free magnificent surprise gift.*

Doctors: If you are a doctor and would like to receive the *Svelt PATCH* Weight-Loss Plan, just enclose your business card along with your letterhead and the coupon below.

Each *Svelt PATCH* Weight-Loss Plan is accompanied with copies of numerous scientific studies on fucus and on the Svelt Patch.

GARDENING BY THE MOON'S SIGN

It is important to note that *the actual placements of the planets through the signs of the zodiac are not the same in astronomy and astrology.* The *astrological* placement of the Moon, by sign, is given in the chart below. (The *astronomical* placement is given in the Left-Hand Calendar Pages 54-80.)

For planting, the most fertile signs are the three water signs: Cancer, Scorpio, and Pisces. Taurus, Virgo, and Capricorn would be good second choices for sowing.

Weeding and plowing are best done when the Moon occupies the signs of Aries, Gemini, Leo, Sagittarius, or Aquarius. In-sect pests can also be handled at those times. Transplanting and grafting are best done under a Cancer, Scorpio, or Pisces Moon. Pruning is best done under an Aries, Leo, or Sagittarius Moon, with growth encouraged during the waxing stage (between new and full Moon) and discouraged during waning (day after full to the day before new Moon). (The dates of the Moon's phases can be found on pages 54-80.) Clean out the garden shed when the Moon occupies Virgo so that the work will flow smoothly. Fences or permanent beds can be built or mended when Capricorn predominates. Avoid indecision when under the Libra Moon.

MOON'S PLACE IN THE ASTROLOGICAL ZODIAC

	NOV. 96	DEC. 96	JAN. 97	FEB. 97	MAR. 97	APR. 97	MAY 97	JUNE 97	JULY 97	AUG. 97	SEPT. 97	OCT. 97	NOV. 97	DEC. 97
1	CAN	LEO	LIB	SCO	SAG	CAP	PSC	ARI	GEM	CAN	VIR	LIB	SCO	CAP
2	LEO	VIR	LIB	SAG	SAG	AQU	PSC	TAU	GEM	LEO	VIR	LIB	SAG	CAP
3	LEO	VIR	SCO	SAG	SAG	AQU	ARI	TAU	GEM	LEO	VIR	SCO	SAG	CAP
4	LEO	VIR	SCO	CAP	CAP	PSC	ARI	GEM	CAN	LEO	LIB	SCO	CAP	AQU
5	VIR	LIB	SCO	CAP	CAP	PSC	ARI	GEM	CAN	VIR	LIB	SCO	CAP	AQU
6	VIR	LIB	SAG	AQU	AQU	ARI	TAU	CAN	LEO	VIR	SCO	SAG	CAP	PSC
7	LIB	SCO	SAG	AQU	AQU	ARI	TAU	CAN	LEO	LIB	SCO	SAG	AQU	PSC
8	LIB	SCO	CAP	PSC	PSC	TAU	GEM	CAN	VIR	LIB	SCO	CAP	AQU	ARI
9	LIB	SAG	CAP	PSC	PSC	TAU	GEM	LEO	VIR	LIB	SAG	CAP	PSC	ARI
10	SCO	SAG	AQU	ARI	ARI	GEM	CAN	LEO	VIR	SCO	SAG	AQU	PSC	TAU
11	SCO	CAP	AQU	ARI	ARI	GEM	CAN	VIR	LIB	SCO	CAP	AQU	ARI	TAU
12	SAG	CAP	PSC	TAU	TAU	GEM	LEO	VIR	LIB	SAG	CAP	PSC	ARI	GEM
13	SAG	AQU	PSC	TAU	TAU	CAN	LEO	VIR	LIB	SAG	AQU	PSC	TAU	GEM
14	CAP	AQU	ARI	TAU	GEM	CAN	LEO	LIB	SCO	SAG	AQU	PSC	TAU	GEM
15	CAP	PSC	ARI	GEM	GEM	LEO	VIR	LIB	SCO	CAP	PSC	ARI	GEM	CAN
16	AQU	PSC	TAU	GEM	CAN	LEO	VIR	SCO	SAG	CAP	PSC	ARI	GEM	CAN
17	AQU	PSC	TAU	CAN	CAN	VIR	LIB	SCO	SAG	AQU	ARI	TAU	CAN	LEO
18	PSC	ARI	GEM	CAN	CAN	VIR	LIB	SCO	CAP	AQU	ARI	TAU	CAN	LEO
19	PSC	ARI	GEM	LEO	LEO	VIR	LIB	SAG	CAP	PSC	TAU	GEM	LEO	VIR
20	ARI	TAU	GEM	LEO	LEO	LIB	SCO	SAG	AQU	PSC	TAU	GEM	LEO	VIR
21	ARI	TAU	CAN	LEO	VIR	LIB	SCO	CAP	AQU	ARI	GEM	CAN	LEO	VIR
22	ARI	GEM	CAN	VIR	VIR	SCO	SAG	CAP	PSC	ARI	GEM	CAN	VIR	LIB
23	TAU	GEM	LEO	VIR	VIR	SCO	SAG	AQU	PSC	TAU	CAN	LEO	VIR	LIB
24	TAU	GEM	LEO	LIB	LIB	SCO	CAP	AQU	ARI	TAU	CAN	LEO	LIB	SCO
25	GEM	CAN	LEO	LIB	LIB	SAG	CAP	PSC	ARI	GEM	CAN	LEO	LIB	SCO
26	GEM	CAN	VIR	LIB	SCO	SAG	AQU	PSC	TAU	GEM	LEO	VIR	LIB	SCO
27	CAN	LEO	VIR	SCO	SCO	CAP	AQU	ARI	TAU	CAN	LEO	VIR	SCO	SAG
28	CAN	LEO	LIB	SCO	SCO	CAP	AQU	ARI	TAU	CAN	VIR	LIB	SCO	SAG
29	CAN	VIR	LIB	—	SAG	AQU	PSC	TAU	GEM	CAN	VIR	LIB	SAG	CAP
30	LEO	VIR	LIB	—	SAG	AQU	PSC	TAU	GEM	LEO	VIR	LIB	SAG	CAP
31	—	VIR	SCO	—	CAP	—	ARI	—	CAN	LEO	—	SCO	—	AQU

A MONTH-BY-MONTH ASTROLOGICAL TIMETABLE FOR 1997

Herewith we provide the following yearlong chart, based on the Moon signs, showing the most favorable times each month for certain activities. BY CELESTE LONGACRE

	JAN.	FEB.	MAR.	APR.	MAY	JUNE	JULY	AUG.	SEPT.	OCT.	NOV.	DEC.
Give up smoking	23, 28	6, 25	24, 29	6, 29	4, 31	23, 27	24, 28	21, 30	17, 26	23, 28	19, 24	8, 31
Begin diet to lose weight	23, 28	6, 25	24, 29	6, 29	4, 31	23, 27	24, 28	21, 30	17, 26	23, 28	19, 24	8, 31
Begin diet to gain weight	10, 14	10, 20	10, 19	15, 20	12, 17	9, 14	6, 11	7, 12	4, 13	1, 6	2, 11	17, 22
Cut hair to encourage growth	16, 17	12, 13	12, 13	8, 9	18, 19	14, 15	11, 12	7, 8	4, 5	1, 2	9, 13	10, 11
Cut hair to discourage growth	29, 30	25, 26	24, 25	4, 5	29, 30	2, 3	26, 27	23, 24	19, 20	28, 29	25, 26	22, 23
Dental care	26, 27	22, 23	21, 22	18, 19	15, 16	11, 12	9, 10	5, 6	1, 2	26, 27	22, 23	19, 20
End old projects	7, 8	5, 6	7, 8	5, 6	4, 5	3, 4	2, 3	1, 2	29, 30	29, 30	28, 29	27, 28
Start a new project	10, 11	8, 9	10, 11	8, 9	7, 8	6, 7	5, 6	4, 5	2, 3	2, 3	1, 2	30, 31
Entertain	23, 24	20, 21	19, 20	15, 16	12, 13	9, 10	6, 7	2, 3	26, 27	23, 24	20, 21	17, 18
Fishing	6, 7	2, 3	29, 30	25, 26	22, 23	19, 20	16, 17	12, 13	9, 10	6, 7	2, 3	27, 28
Breed	4, 5	1, 28	26, 27	23, 24	20, 21	16, 17	14, 15	10, 11	6, 7	3, 4	27, 28	24, 25
Planting above-ground crops	12, 13, 21, 22	8, 9, 17, 18	8, 9, 16, 17, 18	13, 14, 22	10, 11, 20, 21	6, 7, 8, 16, 17, 18	4, 5, 14, 15	10, 11	6, 7, 8, 15, 16	3, 4, 5, 12, 13, 14	1, 9, 10	6, 7
Planting below-ground crops	3, 4, 5, 31	27, 28	26, 27, 28	4, 5, 23, 24	1, 2, 29, 30	25, 26	22, 23, 31	19, 20, 27, 28, 29	23, 24, 25	21, 22	17, 18, 27, 28	15, 16, 24, 25, 26
Destroy pests/weeds	14, 15	10, 11	10, 11	6, 7	4, 5	27, 28	24, 25	21, 22	17, 18	15, 16	11, 12	8, 9
Graft or pollinate	21, 22	17, 18	16, 17	4, 5	10, 11	6, 7	4, 5	19, 20	15, 16	13, 14	9, 10	15, 16
Prune to encourage growth	14, 15	10, 11	10, 11	15, 16	12, 13	9, 10	6, 7	12, 13	9, 10	6, 7	2, 3	8, 9
Prune to discourage growth	24, 25	2, 3	29, 30	25, 26	4, 5	27, 28	24, 25	21, 22	26, 27	23, 24	20, 21	17, 18
Harvest above-ground crops	16, 17	12, 13	12, 13	8, 9	15, 16	11, 12	9, 10	5, 6	1, 2	8, 9	5, 6	10, 11
Harvest root crops	26, 27	4, 5	4, 5	27, 28	24, 25	29, 30	26, 27	23, 24	28, 29	26, 27	22, 23	19, 20
Cut hay	14, 15	10, 11	10, 11	6, 7	4, 5	27, 28	24, 25	21, 22	17, 18	15, 16	11, 12	8, 9
Begin logging	8, 9	4, 5	4, 5	27, 28	24, 25	21, 22	18, 19	15, 16	11, 12	8, 9	5, 6	2, 3
Set posts or pour concrete	8, 9	4, 5	4, 5	27, 28	24, 25	21, 22	18, 19	15, 16	11, 12	8, 9	5, 6	2, 3
Slaughter	4, 5	1, 28	26, 27	23, 24	20, 21	16, 17	14, 15	10, 11	6, 7	3, 4	27, 28	24, 25
Wean	23, 28	6, 25	24, 29	6, 29	4, 31	23, 27	24, 28	21, 30	17, 26	23, 28	19, 24	8, 31
Castrate animals	10, 11	6, 7	6, 7	2, 3	27, 28	23, 24	20, 21	17, 18	13, 14	10, 11	7, 8	4, 5

OVER 2,000 TOMATOES PER PLANT!

Biodynamic Master Gardener L .A. Rotheraine with a 12-foot Selke Biodynamic Cherry Tomato Plant.

The seeds and system for growing this plant bring a new form of lost wisdom from ancient civilizations back to the earth — biodynamic agriculture. Highlands Star Seed has started a scientific revolution.

A plant from our seeds can yield over 2,000 tomatoes per plant, if our planting dates, transplanting dates, and unique organic hilling system are followed. For 12 seeds, planting dates, transplanting dates, and hilling system send $7.00 ($5.00 for seeds and system and $2.00 for postage and handling) to **Highlands Star Seed, P.O. Box 990, Bradford, PA 16701.** With your seed order please list month and approximate date seedlings will be transplanted outside and make checks payable to Highlands Star Seed.

Pennsylvania – Add $0.30 Sales Tax Per Order   Canada – Only a U.S. Postal Money Order Will Be Accepted

SECRETS OF THE ZODIAC

Famous Debowelled Man of the Signs

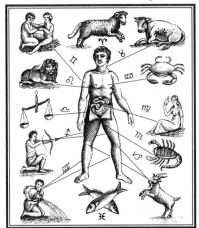

A ncient astrologers associated each of the signs with a part of the body over which they felt the sign held some influence. The first sign of the zodiac — Aries — was attributed to the head, with the rest of the signs moving down the body, ending with Pisces at the feet.

♈	Aries, head. ARI Mar. 21-Apr. 20
♉	Taurus, neck. TAU Apr. 21-May 20
♊	Gemini, arms. GEM May 21-June 20
♋	Cancer, breast. CAN June 21-July 22
♌	Leo, heart. LEO July 23-Aug. 22
♍	Virgo, belly. VIR Aug. 23-Sept. 22
♎	Libra, reins. LIB Sept. 23-Oct. 22
♏	Scorpio, secrets. SCO Oct. 23-Nov. 22
♐	Sagittarius, thighs. SAG Nov. 23-Dec. 21
♑	Capricorn, knees. CAP Dec. 22-Jan. 19
♒	Aquarius, legs. AQU Jan. 20-Feb. 19
♓	Pisces, feet. PSC Feb. 20-Mar. 20

ASTROLOGY AND ASTRONOMY

A strology is a tool we use to time events according to the *astrological* placement of the two luminaries (the Sun and Moon) and eight planets in the 12 signs of the zodiac. Astronomy, on the other hand, is the charting of the actual placement of the planets and constellations, taking into account precession of the equinoxes. As a result, *the placement of the planets in the signs of the zodiac are not the same astrologically and astronomically.* (The Moon's *astronomical* place is given in the Left-Hand Calendar Pages [54-80] and its *astrological* place is given in Gardening by the Moon's Sign, page 161.)

Modern astrology is a study of synchronicities. The planetary movements do not *cause* events. Rather, they explain the "flow" or trajectory that events will tend to follow. Just as with waves or tides in the oceans, your own free will gives you the choice to swim with or against the currents. But those who choose to can plan a schedule in harmony with the flow.

The dates given in the Month-by-Month Astrological Timetable (page 162) have been chosen with particular care to the astrological passage of the Moon. However, since other planets also influence us, it's best to take a look at all indicators before seeking advice on *major* life decisions. A qualified astrologer can study the current relationship of the plan-

ets and your own personal birth chart in order to assist you in the best possible timing for carrying out your plans.

PLANET MERCURY DOES WHAT?

S ometimes when we look out from our perspective here on Earth, the other planets appear to be traveling backward through the zodiac. (They're not actually moving backward, it just looks that way to us.) We call this *retrograde.*

Mercury's retrograde periods, which occur three or four times a year, can cause travel delays and misconstrued communications. Plans have a way of unraveling, too. However, this is an excellent time to be researching or looking into the past. Intuition is high during these periods, and unplanned coincidences can be extraordinary.

When Mercury is retrograde, astrologers advise us to keep plans flexible, allow extra time for travel, and avoid signing contracts. It's OK and even useful to look over projects and plans, because we may see them with different eyes at these times. However, our normal system of checks and balances might not be active, so it's best to wait until Mercury is direct again to make any final decisions. In 1997 Mercury will be retrograde from January 1 to 12, April 15 to May 8, August 17 to September 10, and December 26 to the new year.

To My Very Dearest

On the 150th birthday of America's first official postage stamps, issued on July 1, 1847, we salute those "heart-talkers," as letters were called, that sustain passion, bind families, and record the flow of a person's life.

(P.S. And is it true that a woman will always put her true sentiments in the postscript?)

WITH THE WIDESPREAD USE OF THE FAX MAchine, E-mail, and the Internet, some worry that letter writing may be a dying art. We submit that nothing can substitute for the handwritten letter, composed as if in conversation with an intimate friend and penned in real ink on good rag stationery. As Christopher Morley (1890-1957) said, "It is chiefly — perhaps only — in letters that one gets the mother-of-pearly shimmer inside the oyster of Fact."

WANTED:
SKINNY ORPHANS, NO CUSSING

■ Early on, postage in America was generally paid by the recipient upon delivery, if indeed the letter ever arrived. In 1639 the Richard Fairbanks tavern in Boston was designated the official drop point for mail coming or going between the Colonies and England. From there, overseas mail went by ship, while domestic mail was delivered over "post roads" such as the Boston Post Road, in a relay system from one tavern or coffeehouse to another. Not surprisingly, mail delivery was, at best, uncertain.

In 1860 newspaper ads sought horsemen to carry the mail between St. Joseph, Missouri — the farthest west the railroad and telegraph had reached — and the Pacific coast. The ad read,

by Martha White

"For God's sake, don't give up writing

FARMER'S ALMANAC

from Yours Truly

"Wanted: Young, skinny, wiry fellows not over 18. Must be expert riders willing to risk death daily. Orphans preferred." The pioneer spirit being what it was, willing riders were found, and the Pony Express began. In addition to their courage, the riders had to prove their honesty and integrity by swearing on a Bible that they would not curse, fight, or mistreat their horses.

☞ Return to Sender
ADDRESS UNKNOWN

■ **Depending on the distance a letter had to cover** and the number of relays required, it could prove prohibitively expensive. It was not uncommon for a letter to be refused if it had not been prepaid. Legend has it that Sir Rowland Hill, English postal reformer, found a young girl refusing letters posted to her from her fiancé. The young couple had devised a system whereby he declared his well-being and fond sentiments by means of symbols on the envelope. She examined her mail, then refused to pay, but his message had been delivered. Perceiving that high postage costs were diminishing the numbers and efficiency of letters mailed, Sir Rowland proposed the Uniform Penny Post reform in England, where it passed in 1840; America waited until 1863.

(continued on next page)

> "Letter writing is the only device for combining solitude and good company."
>
> – Lord Byron (1788-1824)

The FOLKLORE and Superstitions of Letters

■ If a moth flies toward you, you will receive a letter.

■ If a bright spark shoots up from a nearby candle, the same.

■ "Sneeze on Wednesday, you sneeze for a letter." (English saying)

■ White spots on your fingernail mean a letter is coming.

■ Lint on your dress spells the initials of the letter writer.

■ To get a letter, hang a found hairpin on a nail.

■ If you and a companion speak at once, have your friend pinch you and you will receive a letter.

■ If your left hand itches, a letter is coming. (Right hand, expect money.)

■ To dream of mailing an unsealed letter means that you fear your secrets are known.

■ If a spider at the end of its thread comes before your eyes, you will receive a letter.

■ Put your lover's letters in a can and throw it into running water to ensure the endurance of that love.

■ Stamp a letter upside down to get a speedy response.

■ Never burn a love letter unless you wish to destroy the love.

■ Burn love letters to ease old, troublesome memories.

to me simply because I don't write to you."
– Robert Frost (1874-1963)

ONLY THE DEAD
NEED APPLY

■ America's first official postage stamps, in 1847, displayed the images of Benjamin Franklin (for 5¢) or George Washington (10¢). With the Ben Franklin you could

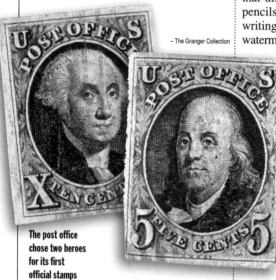

– The Granger Collection

The post office chose two heroes for its first official stamps 150 years ago.

post a one-ounce letter. Conveniently, if you had only an ounce of letter writing in you but were stuck with a two-ounce Washington stamp, you could cut George in half and call it good. The world's first adhesive postage stamps were produced in England in 1840. The "Penny Black" and "Twopence Blue" each showed Queen Victoria. Our Ben Franklin and George Washington followed and established the rule, still in effect, that no living American may be shown on postage stamps.

WHAT'S PROPER
What's Not

■ Many grammar schools have applied themselves to the etiquette of letter writing with some vehemence, teaching such tricky cautions as "Appropriate stationery is stationery that displays good taste." Ruled paper, pencils, unequal margins, uphill handwriting, and cross-outs are all taboo, but watermarked paper evidently shows taste, and "bread and butter" notes are still considered obligatory — at least in etiquette books.

Likewise, the appropriate length of a letter has been hotly debated. Samuel Johnson (1709-1784) believed that "A short letter to a distant friend is, in my opinion, an insult like that of a slight bow or cursory salutation." Lord Byron (1788-1824) liked to read old letters, part of his pleasure being that they needed no answer. Charles Dickens (1812-1870) recommended extreme brevity, saying in his *Pickwick Papers*, "She'll wish there was more, and that's the great art o' letter-writin'."

HOW TO WRITE A
R A T

■ An old New England custom demonstrates our faith in the extraordinary power of letter writing. Some old-timers believed that the best way to relieve a household of rats was to write the rodents a polite letter, inviting them to leave the premises and being sure to specify the exact address where the rats should relocate. Examples of such letters have been found on greased paper, rolled tightly and tucked into the walls of old houses and barns. One example began, "Maine, October 31, 1888, Messrs. Rats & Co.,

> "It has been said of ladies when they write letters, that they put their minds in their postscripts — let out the real objects of their writing, as if it were a second thought, or a thing comparatively indifferent."
>
> – Leigh Hunt (1784-1859)

— Having taken quite a deep interest in your welfare in regard to your winter quarters, I thought I would drop you a few lines. . . ." Folklore has it that these rat letters were far more effective than felines or rat poison, but to our knowledge, an epistolary reply has never been received. Probably the poor rats simply lacked the proper stationery.

> "The public will always give up its dinner to read love letters."
>
> – George Jean Nathan (1882-1958)

– Donald Grant Mitchell ("Ik Marvel," 1822-1908)

P.S.
(POSTAL STATISTICS)

■ In 1993 the United States Post Office delivered 171.2 billion pieces of mail, total (first class and otherwise).

■ The Dead Letter Office receives over 75 million pieces of mail a year.

■ Over 92.2 billion first-class letters go out annually (1993), an estimated 900 million of them valentines.

■ In Venezuela love letters go for half price.

■ In 1985 it was estimated that about half the first-class letters were greeting cards and that 90 percent of those were picked out by women.

■ Christmas cards amount to more than 3 billion pieces of mail annually. Mail order catalogs number over 7 billion.

■ The White House cat, Sox, receives approximately 150 letters a month — rivaling Thomas Jefferson's monthly mail during his presidency.

Dear Sox,

Thomas Jefferson, however, was no slouch: He wrote more than 40,000 letters in his lifetime. Sox, on the other hand, answers his mail with a printed photo postcard signed with his paw print.

■ In 1994 more than 2,700 letter carriers were bitten by dogs. ☐☐

MILLENNIUM COUNTDOWN 1 FOR 997

by Jon Vara

HAPPY NEW YEAR

So When DOES the Millennium Start?
(Are We Being Swayed by the Odometer Syndrome?)

In introducing this department last year, we devoted a good deal of space to what might be called the technical aspects of the coming millennium. We explained, for example, that because of a historical quirk in the system we use for numbering the years — which may stem from the fact that Roman numerals have no character for zero — the traditional date for Christ's birth is not the year 0, but the year 1. As a result, the 2,000th anniversary of that event will take place at the beginning of the year 2001, not the year 2000. Yet we all seem to have an irresistible urge to celebrate the turn from 1999 to 2000.

As historian Hillel Schwartz points out in his book *Century's End*, the question has been the focus of lively debate at least since the close of the 1600s. For instance, on December 31, 1899, novelist Max Halbe observed, "In my life I have seen many people do battle over many things, but over few things with such fanaticism as over the academic question [of when the century would

— H. Armstrong Roberts

end]. . . . Each of the two parties produced for its side the trickiest of calculations and maintained at the same time that it was the simplest matter in the world, one that any child should understand."

What *is* new is the outcome of that debate. In past centuries, once the fussing, complaining, and tricky calculations had run their course, people fell into line — however grudgingly — with the opinion of the pundits, who invariably favored the turn of the century to be New Year's Day of '01. (At the turn of the last century, such people were known as "precisians.") This time around, though, the weight of public opinion is solidly behind the earlier date, and it now seems clear that the major festivities will take place on January 1, 2000.

Why the change? It may be simply that our constant exposure to things like car odometers, electronic scoreboards, and digital clocks means that those of us now awaiting the millennium have a natural tendency to see the event in purely visual terms — all those nines turning over to zeros on New Year's Eve in 1999.

Which brings us to a final point — and an appeal to readers. If most of the celebrations are going to take place at the turn of the year 2000, what, exactly, will we be celebrating? The Big Rollover? The Pre-lennium, perhaps? And how are you going to celebrate? Send us your ideas, and we'll print the best ones in next year's edition of *The Old Farmer's Almanac.*

AND YOU WILL CELEBRATE

At the frayed end of the 1890s — when much of the world was embroiled in a lively debate over the correct starting point of the approaching 20th century — the subjects of Kaiser Wilhelm II of Prussia were plagued by no such doubts. To prevent messy overlap between new-century festivities and the celebration planned around the 200th anniversary of the Prussian monarchy, set for January of 1901, the kaiser simply decreed that the new century would officially begin on New Year's Day of 1900. Prussians loyally followed their leader and welcomed the 20th century a full year before the rest of Europe did.

December 31, 1999:
The PEOPLE'S CHOICE

If advance reservations are any guide, all the action will come on December 31, 1999. (The evening of December 31, 2000, may be pretty dull.)

– H. Armstrong Roberts

The New York Marriott Marquis at Times Square, New York City

■ **New Year's Eve 1999:** One confirmed reservation dating from 1983, two years before the hotel was built; "more than 500" requests for reservations currently on file.

New Year's Eve 2000: "No requests so far."

The Rainbow Room at Rockefeller Center, New York City

■ **New Year's Eve 1999:** Evening's entertainment will cost $1,000 per person, not including drinks and tips; advance deposit of $500 required. Two hundred seats reserved so far, with 600 names on waiting list.

■ **New Year's Eve 2000:** "We've had a lot more inquiries from the media than from people wanting reservations."

(continued on next page)

The Houston Astrodome, Texas

■ **New Year's Eve 1999:** In mid-1995, the 60,000-seat stadium was booked by the Southern Baptist Conference for a celebration to be called "Link 2000."

■ **New Year's Eve 2000:** "No booking so far."

Disney World, Orlando, Florida

■ **New Year's Eve 1999:** Exact figures unavailable, but "all of our accommodations are very heavily booked."

■ **New Year's Eve 2000:** "We do have some advance bookings."

Space Needle, Seattle

■ **New Year's Eve 1999:** Entire 605-foot structure rented by 15 families from Portland, Oregon; 900 invited guests expected to attend.

■ **New Year's Eve 2000:** No special functions planned. "We'll probably have the usual New Year's Eve celebration and fireworks."

From Times Square All the Way to Queens

■ Still no word from the Times Square Business Improvement District on the winner of its 1995 contest to design the perfect millennium celebration. But in the meantime, Times Square has been getting ready for the big night by refurbishing the six-foot time ball that has signaled the arrival of the new year since 1904. It now features a shiny new aluminum skin studded with 1,200 rhinestones and tastefully illuminated by a host of pulsating halogen bulbs and one 10,000-watt xenon lamp. It's now visible, Gretchen Dykstra of the Improvement District says, "from the outermost reaches of Queens."

> "By the year 2020,
> there will be a whole new
> industry built on remembering
> the year 2000."
>
> – Alvin Toffler

HEY,
We've Got to Call It
SOMETHING

Twenty years ago, we were in the midst of a decade we called "the seventies." (Remember?) It was followed by "the eighties" and then "the nineties." And the nineties, of course, will be succeeded by a decade we'll call . . . well, what will we call it?

According to Merriam-Webster Dictionary editor Paul Cappellano, we may find ourselves calling it — as the decade 1900-1909 was called — "the oughts." (It's uncertain, however, whether we will spell it "ought" or "aught.") Noting that "oughts" may sound a bit quaint to postmodern ears — after all, it will be the 21st century — Cappellano suggests two other possibilities as well: "the zeros," or perhaps even "the zips."

But author and language expert Richard Lederer believes that "zeros" and "zips" — along with "noughts," a possible variant of "oughts" — are too negative to gain acceptance. While not ruling out "oughts" or "oughties," he leans toward "the ohs" (which, he points out, can also be spelled "the owes," if the national debt continues to balloon). The standard-setters at National Public Radio are of the same mind; NPR announcers will use "the oughts" or "the ohs," accompanied by the explanatory phrase ". . . the first

OUGHTS
OUGHTIES
AUGHTS
NOUGHTS
OWES
OHS
ZEROS
ZIPS

decade of the 21st century." And who knows? We may even see a revival of a suggestion made by a *New Yorker* columnist back in 1963, that we refer to the decade's opening year as "twenty oh-oh."

Old Checks Soon to
CHECK OUT

Next time you open a new box of blank checks for your checking account, take a look at the space in the top right corner where the date goes, and you may notice a small but significant change. Until now, practically all checks came imprinted with a blank line for the month and day, followed by the number "19" and a short blank for the writer to fill in the last two digits of the year: _____19___.

But because this long-standing format will become obsolete at the end of 1999, check manufacturers have already begun issuing limited numbers of experimental checks that bear a blank line labeled "date," leaving the writer to fill in

all four digits of the year. The new format should be all but universal by the beginning of 1999, to allow stockpiles of old checks to run out before the century's end.

One question, however, remains unanswered: Once the new century is safely under way, will the old-style checks — now updated with a printed "20" — reappear? "We really haven't thought about that yet," says one industry executive.

(Un)Happy No Year

According to technology analyst Peter de Jager, many of the programs used by corporate mainframe computers can recognize only years beginning with "19." When the year 2000 arrives, affected computers will interpret it as 1900, possibly leading to large-scale systems failures and other dire results.

We reported that much in last year's "Millennium Countdown," but since that time there have been some intriguing new developments:

More Consultants
■ The number of computer consultants offering their services to businesses and other institutions anxious to head off possible zero-compatibility problems has skyrocketed. A year ago, de Jager says, there were only a handful; today there are hundreds, with new ones entering the field every week.

More Taxes
■ The state of Nebraska recently placed a two-cent tax on tobacco products in order to generate funds to scrutinize its computer system for zero-compatibility problems.

More Glitches
■ Peter de Jager tells of trying to rent a car from one of the world's largest rental agencies, only to have his application repeatedly rejected by the computer because his driver's license listed an expiration date in the year 2000. "The only way they could give me the car was by falsifying their records and pretending that my license would expire in 1999 instead," he says.

> "Those who are alive at the end of another thousand years will perhaps see the ripe fruits, while we have seen only the blossoms."
>
> – Sylvester II, pope A.D. 999-1003

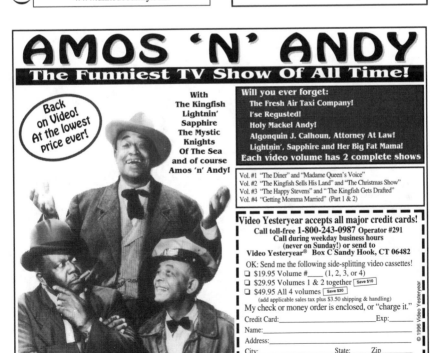

In spite of the ever-increasing amount of weight he had to carry, he was the odds-on favorite to win every race he entered. And, in fact, he <u>did</u> win every race he entered throughout his racing life. Except one. And when you know what happened in that race, you might as well say he went undefeated . . .   by Mel R. Allen

S hortly past noon on a Saturday, November 1, 1947, the most famous redhead of his time died in a barn stall beside the rolling Kentucky pastures where he had lived most of his life. His name was Man o' War, and his death was front-page news across the country.

Even in death, the stallion known around the world as "Big Red" made Thoroughbred history. His age, 30, reportedly made him the longest-lived Thoroughbred

"As Near a Living Flame

Man o' War pulls ahead of John P. Grier in the 1920 Dwyer Stakes — perhaps the greatest

– courtesy Keeneland-Cook

on record. And because he would lie in state while workers prepared his grave, Man o' War became the first horse embalmed for burial. "Mr. Riddle always ordered the best of everything for the horse," explained his Lexington vet.

With a homemade sling, a crew of farm hands raised the great horse's body from his stall and lowered it into an oak casket lined in his yellow and white racing colors. There he lay in the stable for two days, flanked by the stalls of his famous sons, War Admiral and Crusader, while hundreds of grieving horse lovers filed past.

He was buried in his private paddock at the base of a larger-than-life bronze statue. His funeral was covered live by coast-to-coast radio. The local American Legion drum and bugle corps, dressed in yellow and white, sounded taps. At 3 P.M., the moment of his burial, racetracks across America grew silent. The only noise was the stamping and snorting of horses impatient to run.

as Horses Ever Get"

orse race ever run, and the only time his jockey used a whip on "Big Red."

– courtesy Keeneland-Cook

Samuel Riddle *(above)* **bought Man o' War as a yearling for $5,000. Will Harbut** *(opposite)* **began caring for Man o' War in 1930. Horse and man grew old together.**

On June 6, 1919, the two-year-old horse made his debut.... Race watchers knew they had seen something special.

Which is how it should have been. For if any horse was born simply to run, it was Man o' War.

Man o' War's first owner, August Belmont II, had a plan. He would breed his greatest stallion, Fair Play, winner of $86,000, to the daughters of Rock Sand, winner of the English Derby. On March 29, 1917, on a breeding farm just outside Lexington, one of Rock Sand's daughters, Mahubah, who had won but once and earned only $700, produced a chestnut foal with a narrow stripe down his nose. Belmont's wife named the colt Man o' War.

World War I raged then in Europe. Though he was in his sixties, August Belmont II volunteered for duty and shipped out to Paris. He sent word to sell all 20 of his yearlings at the Saratoga, New York, summer auction.

At the auction Man o' War aroused only minor interest, being sold for $5,000 to Samuel Riddle, a Philadelphia carpet manufacturer and horse enthusiast.

On June 6, 1919, the now two-year-old horse made his debut. It was the last race of the day at Belmont Park. On that day race watchers knew they had seen something special. The racing editor of the _New York Morning Telegraph_ wrote: "He made half a dozen high-class youngsters look like $200 horses." From that day on, Man o' War became the odds-on favorite to win every race he entered. Handicappers tried in vain to make his races competitive, assigning ever heavier weights to the precocious horse. Race experts say a pound of extra weight (lead plates placed underneath a saddle) is equal to ⅕ of a second. When Man o' War raced, he spotted his opponents at least ten, sometimes 20 pounds.

Only once did Man o' War ever stare at the back of another horse. The date was August 13, 1919, the Sanford Memorial in Saratoga. It was the seventh race of his career. The undefeated Man o' War carried 130 pounds for this ¾-mile race. The regular race starter that day was ill, and his substitute sent the field off with Man o' War still turned sideways in the gate. By the time Man o' War hit his stride, he was ten lengths behind. When he caught up to the leaders, Golden Broom and Upset, he was pinned on the rail, unable to squeeze through. His jockey swung him wide, conceding two crucial lengths, and though Man o' War pounded furiously toward the finish, a horse named Upset had won by half a length.

Years later, Bill Knapp,

– courtesy Keeneland Library / Skeets Meadors photo

– Culver Pictures

Man o' War touched the lives of these two men: sportswriter Grantland Rice, jockey Clarence Kummer.

– courtesy Keeneland-Cook

Man o' War did much more than win races. He moved people as few athletes ever had.

Upset's jockey, said, "If I'd given so much as an inch, the race would've been as good as over, but jockeys don't ride that way. Sure I won the race all right — it was the biggest thrill of my life — but lookin' back at it now, there's sure one horse which should have retired undefeated. Never was a colt like him! If I'd moved over just an eyelash that day at Saratoga, he'd have beat me from here to Jaloppy. Some-times I'm sorry I didn't do it!"

Six more times Upset would face Man o' War. Six times he finished far behind.

Though famous as a two-year-old, Man o' War's greatest races lay ahead. Samuel Riddle kept his horse out of the 1920 Kentucky Derby, then watched as Man o' War won the Preakness, Withers, Belmont, Stuyvesant Handicap, Dwyer, Miller, Travers, Lawrence Realization,

Jockey Club Stakes, and Potomac Handicap, even outdueling the 1919 Triple Crown winner, Sir Barton, in a memorable match race at Kenilworth, Canada, for a purse of $80,000.

Man o' War broke records in five of his three-year-old starts. In one race, the 1920 Dwyer Stakes at Aqueduct before 25,000 spectators, he competed against another super horse, John P. Grier. It has been called the greatest horse race ever run, and it was the first and last time a jockey ever touched Big Red with a whip.

Here's Grantland Rice, the most famous sportswriter of his time, on that race:

"They were off. Clarence Kummer, riding Man o' War, broke with Big Red's usual thunderbolt rush. But John P. Grier matched this first wild charge to blend the two horses into one picture. . . . They rushed to the five-furlong pole. A handkerchief could have covered both noses. Without a split second's faltering on either side, they came to the six-furlong spot, still head and head, still stride for stride, in the world's record time of 1.09 and 2/5.

(continued on page 182)

Amazing VITASEX ® Formula for MEN & WOMEN

GUARANTEED TO
RENEW VIGOR

REVIVE "YOUR" LOVE LIFE

This amazing formula renews your vigor and may be the fastest, safest, and surest vitamin, mineral tonic and stimulant formula ever released by medical science. Yes, many men and women who have taken these miracle tablets after a tiring working day have found new strength and potency to the point it has made the relationship come alive again. These potent VitaSex tablets are the reason many couples are enjoying a happier home life after years of dragging through each day.

REVITALIZE ENERGY, POTENCY, AND VIGOR

Start today to renew your strength, potency and vigor with the first tablets you take. You don't have to wait days to get results. You get almost immediate new surges of energy because this revolutionary new product is designed to start working instantly. And you won't experience hypertension and jittery energy that accompanies other drugs that you see advertised in certain magazines and newspapers.

AMAZING RESULTS

VITASEX® is a **scientifically formulated** tonic and stimulant that gives you the EXTRA measure of nutrients and stimulant that you may need to revitalize vigor, energy and stamina. Therefore, you'll also experience the exhilarating, rewarding lift of HEALTHY BODY FUNCTION.

Yes, now instead of being left out of the "good times" you can:

• Restore healthy body function . . .
• Improve your desire and performance . . .
• Renew your strength, potency and vigor . . .
• And win the desire of your mate regardless of age, or age differences.

Results with VITASEX have **proven** that it gets guaranteed results! Anyone in good health can renew their strength, stamina and vigor with VITASEX®. **Yes, success in every case.**

RENEW VIGOR WITH THE FASTEST, SUREST, AND SAFEST TONIC AND STIMULANT FORMULA OUR MEDICAL SCIENTISTS HAVE EVER DEVELOPED — ABSOLUTELY GUARANTEED!

In fact, the only way VitaSex® won't work for you is by not using them! It's guaranteed to work for you, even if you've had a problem for years. Even if other formulas have failed you. Even if nothing you've tried in the past had any lasting effect!

That's why we can make this 100% no-risk guarantee. This potent formula must work for you or your money will be refunded (less postage of course), and you can keep the first bottle free. ACT NOW!

For Our Fastest Service
Call 919-554-4014

"Here was the horse race of all horse races. They came to the mile in 1.35 and 3/5, equaling the world's record, still racing as a team, still head and head, eye to eye, stride for stride.

"Before the race, owner Samuel Riddle had given Clarence Kummer just one order: 'Lay alongside of Johnny Grier — use the whip only when you need it. Just once is enough — if you have to.'

"As they came to the sixteenth pole, John P. Grier put his nose in front. . . . And just at that moment Kummer responded to orders. As Kummer struck Big Red, the giant horse took just one great forward leap. Kummer later admitted that Man o' War almost shook him from the saddle. With that one whiplash Man o' War took a full half-length lead. He charged on to beat John P. Grier by almost two lengths, as he raced to a new world record."

Man o' War did much more than win races. He moved people as few athletes ever had. One writer called him "as near a living flame as horses ever get." When Man o' War triumphed at the Travers in Saratoga in 1920, the starter said, "He was so beautiful that it almost made you cry, and so full of fire he made you thank your God you could come close to him."

After Man o' War's match race against an outclassed Sir Barton, the public clamored for him to challenge the great horses of Europe. But Samuel Riddle decided to retire his champion to stud in Lexington. "I was told," Riddle said, "that he would carry more weight than any horse had ever carried before. As much as 145 or 150 pounds. I knew such weight would break down his legs."

He had won 20 of 21 starts, while becoming the first Thoroughbred to earn more than $200,000 on the track. His fame only increased over the years as his offspring included Crusader, winner of the 1926 Belmont Stakes, and War Admiral, winner of the Triple Crown in 1937. He sired foals by 186 mares, and his children won more than $3 million. Racing experts of the time called him the single greatest influence on Thoroughbred racing in the century.

Road markers leading to Lexington advertised the city as the "Home of Man o' War." His 21st birthday celebration, complete with oat and carrot cakes, was broadcast live across the nation. Every day hundreds of horse-struck fans waited outside the black iron gates of Faraway Farm to tour Man o' War's stall, to come close enough to feel his power. Wrote one *New York Times* reporter, "Perhaps it seems a trifle silly and naive for anyone to admit that he actually approached the stall of Man o' War with feelings of awe and humility. But that was the way this observer reacted. It was a genuine thrill to see him, that regal head lifted imperiously and that powerfully built body shimmering aristocratically in the sunlight."

A visit to Man o' War meant a visit, as well, with his groom, Will Harbut. Will, who began caring for Man o' War in 1930, opened the gates to visitors at 9:00 A.M. and shut them at 4:00 P.M. He tended first to his horse, then to the horse's public. He was tour guide to a national monument, and in time, people came to hear Will as much as to see the famed stallion.

"And here he is, MannieWah himself," Will would say, throwing open his arms. "Few years ago a man offered Mr. Riddle a million dollars for him and Mr. Riddle say, 'No.' Say any man could have a million dollars, but only one man could have MannieWah. . . . Stand still, Red. . . . He broke all the records, and he broke down all the horses. So there wasn't nothin' for him to do but retire. He's got everything a horse ought to have and he's got it where a horse ought to have it. Stand still, Red. He's just the mostest hoss."

Lord Halifax, the British ambassador, once listened to Will's tour and said, "It

was worth coming halfway around the world to hear that."

Groom and horse grew old together. In 1942 Man o' War hemorrhaged and was retired from stud. Four years later Will Harbut suffered a stroke and ended his personal tours. And in the spring of 1947 Samuel Riddle closed the gates of Faraway Farm to spare the energies of his horse. That October, Will Harbut died from a heart attack. *The Blood Horse,* the official publication of the Thoroughbred industry, concluded his obituary, "Among his survivors are his wife, six sons, three daughters, and Man o' War." Less than a month later, a heart attack also took Man o' War.

For 30 years Man o' War's body lay beneath his paddock at Faraway Farm. But on a September day in 1976, his body and the four-ton statue were taken to the Kentucky Horse Park in Lexington. There he stands alone, greeting over 200,000 visitors yearly, nearly 80 years after his final race, still the most famous horse in the world. □ □

– courtesy Kentucky Horse Park

Larger than life, Man o' War presides over the grounds of the Kentucky Horse Park, a monument to Thoroughbred excellence.

WIND/BAROMETER TABLE

Barometer (Reduced to Sea Level)	Wind Direction	Character of Weather Indicated
30.00 to 30.20, and steady	westerly	Fair, with slight changes in temperature, for one to two days.
30.00 to 30.20, and rising rapidly	westerly	Fair, followed within two days by warmer and rain.
30.00 to 30.20, and falling rapidly	south to east	Warmer, and rain within 24 hours.
30.20, or above, and falling rapidly	south to east	Warmer, and rain within 36 hours.
30.20, or above, and falling rapidly	west to north	Cold and clear, quickly followed by warmer and rain.
30.20, or above, and steady	variable	No early change.
30.00, or below, and falling slowly	south to east	Rain within 18 hours that will continue a day or two.
30.00, or below, and falling rapidly	southeast to northeast	Rain, with high wind, followed within two days by clearing, colder.
30.00, or below, and rising	south to west	Clearing and colder within 12 hours.
29.80, or below, and falling rapidly	southeast to northeast	Severe storm of wind and rain imminent. In winter, snow or cold wave within 24 hours.
29.80, or below, and falling rapidly	east to north	Severe northeast gales and heavy rain or snow, followed in winter by cold wave.
29.80, or below, and rising rapidly	going to west	Clearing and colder.

Note: A barometer should be adjusted to show equivalent sea-level pressure for the altitude at which it is to be used. A change of 100 feet in elevation will cause a decrease of 1/10th inch in the reading.

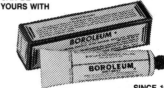

HOMEMADE PIZZA

BY JAMES HALLER

*"As a Midwesterner who had known melted cheese only as something called 'American'
between two slices of Wonder bread, I was wide-eyed with amazement to be eating this strange cheese
that made strings like glue. . . ."*

*Fifty years later this culinary expert reveals how to make delicious pizza with
whatever you happen to have around the house . . .*

....

I first ate pizza in 1947 at my neighbor Mrs. Persino's house. Mrs. Persino's "pizza" was like a bread, two or three inches high with a thick herbed tomato sauce on the top. I don't recall any cheese. It was a simple and delicious dish.

The second time I ate pizza was a few months later at a restaurant called Mama Schiavoni's on Taylor and Carpenter Streets in the "old neighborhood" of Chicago. Mama Schiavoni's made a paper-thin crust rolled gently in cornmeal, then spun in the air until stretched thin and light. After the dough was put onto the long-handled wooden paddles, it was lightly coated with a tomato sauce made with oregano, rosemary, and Italian sausage, sprinkled with a thin mixture of mozzarella, provolone, and fontina cheeses, then baked in a brick oven until the dough crisped up and the cheese began to melt, bubble, and just barely toast. The pizza was then shoveled out onto a platter, cut into two-inch squares, and served hot dripping with pure olive oil. Pizza!

As a Midwesterner who had known melted cheese only as something

called "American" between two slices of Wonder bread, I was wide-eyed with amazement to be eating this strange cheese that made strings like glue when you tried to lift a piece of it onto your plate. They called it a pie, but it wasn't sweet, and it was cut into squares, not wedges, and you ate it with your fingers!

That pizza seems to me the prototype of pizza made in Chicago. Even now, when I go back, I find places that still make it with the thin crust, cooked and herbed sauce, mixture of cheeses, and dripping with olive oil.

There are many different styles of pizza from the various regions of Italy and Sicily. All of them are correct. Some are made with a yeasted bread dough, some with a short crust, and some with focaccia, a Genovese bread made with water, olive oil, and rolled in cornmeal.

Using any of these crusts and toppings or fillings or your own ideas, you can make pizza with whatever you happen to have around the house. Mrs. Persino used bread dough and leftover tomato sauce. Mama Schiavoni's used three cheeses and a boiled-down sauce. My mother, by 1950, used the phone and ordered out. Here is a sampling of the most traditional varieties.

FOCACCIA CRUST

When using focaccia as a crust and not a bread, let the dough rise only once, then punch it down and roll it (or toss, if you know how) as thin as possible.

1 packet (1 scant tablespoon) active dry yeast
1 tablespoon sugar
3 tablespoons warm water
1 tablespoon salt
2 cups warm water
4-1/2 to 5 cups all-purpose flour
4 to 5 tablespoons olive oil

■ Dissolve yeast and sugar in 3 tablespoons warm water. Stir in salt and 2 cups warm water and let mixture begin to foam. Blend in flour and olive oil to make a smooth dough and knead into a ball. Place in an oiled bowl, cover, and let rise for about 45 minutes, until doubled. Roll out and place in greased pizza pans.

Makes 2 large pizza crusts.

PIZZA ALLA FRANCESCANA

PIZZA WITH MUSHROOM, HAM, TOMATO, AND CHEESE

Crust: **Use 1 focaccia crust, above.**

Topping:
2 tablespoons olive oil
1 cup sliced mushrooms
1 cup julienned ham strips
1 cup chopped plum tomatoes
2 tablespoons chopped fresh garlic
1/4 cup chopped fresh basil
2 tablespoons chopped fresh oregano
1 cup grated mozzarella cheese

■ Heat olive oil in a large frying pan and add all ingredients except cheese. Sauté for about 10 minutes, then spread on top of focaccia dough and cover with cheese. Bake at 400° F for 20 to 30 minutes, until cheese is bubbling.

Makes 1 large pizza.

PIZZA ALLA LIGURIA

ANCHOVY PIZZA

Crust: **Use 1 focaccia crust, above.**

Topping:
2 tablespoons olive oil
1/2 cup sliced onion
2 tablespoons chopped fresh garlic
1 cup chopped plum tomatoes
2 tablespoons chopped fresh marjoram
1 tin (2 ounces) anchovies, drained
about a dozen ripe black olives, halved

■ Heat olive oil in a frying pan and cook onion, garlic, tomatoes, and marjoram until onion is limp. Spread topping on the dough. Crisscross anchovies across the top and place olive halves in the center of each diamond-shaped opening. Bake at 400° F for 20 to 30 minutes.

Makes 1 large pizza.

(Recipes continued on next page)

PIZZA ALLA NAPOLETANA

PIZZA WITH TOMATOES AND MOZZARELLA

The secret to this pizza is to cook the topping mixture long enough so that it becomes a sauce.

Crust: **Use 1 focaccia crust on page 187.**

Topping:
4 tablespoons olive oil
3 tablespoons chopped garlic
3 cups chopped plum tomatoes
1/4 cup chopped fresh basil
1/4 cup chopped fresh marjoram
salt and pepper to taste
2 cups grated mozzarella cheese

■ In a large frying pan heat olive oil and sauté garlic, tomatoes, and herbs, stirring often as the juices evaporate. Turn down the heat a little if it looks precarious. Simmer for about 20 minutes, until the mixture looks like a good sauce to you. Roll out the focaccia dough and spread the sauce on top. Sprinkle with the mozzarella. Bake at 400° F for about 20 minutes.

Makes 1 large pizza.

PIZZA ALLA ROMANA

ONION PIZZA

I'm certain there are scores of other recipes for pizza in Rome, but this one seemed to me to be the most traditional. I like the fact that there are no tomatoes or cheese in this interpretation.

Crust: **Use 1 focaccia crust on page 187.**

Topping:
4 tablespoons olive oil
4 tablespoons chopped fresh garlic
1/2 cup chopped fresh marjoram
3 cups thinly sliced onions (Vidalias are really wonderful on this pizza)

■ Heat the olive oil in a large frying pan over low heat and sauté all ingredients until onions are limp. Roll out the focaccia. Spread the onions evenly around the dough and bake at 400° F for about 30 minutes.

Makes 1 large pizza.

PIZZA AL TEGAME

PIZZA WITH TOMATOES AND ANCHOVIES

The crust for this is made with baking powder and is "fried" on both sides in olive oil, then topped and baked.

Crust:
1 cup flour
1 teaspoon baking powder
1/4 cup plus 2 tablespoons water
1 teaspoon salt
3 tablespoons olive oil for frying

■ Combine the crust ingredients (except olive oil) to pull dough into a ball, then roll it on a floured surface until it is about 12 inches in diameter. Heat olive oil in a frying pan and fry the dough on both sides until it is done. *(continued)*

Topping:
2 cups chopped plum tomatoes
2 tablespoons olive oil
1/4 cup chopped fresh basil
1/4 cup chopped fresh marjoram
1 tin (2 ounces) anchovies, drained
2 tablespoons sliced black olives

■ Cook tomatoes in olive oil until soft; add the herbs. Spread mixture on the crust and crisscross anchovies on the top. Put a slice of black olive in each diamond-shaped opening. Bake at 400° F for about 15 minutes.

Makes 1 medium pizza.

PIZZETTE

LITTLE PIZZAS

These are tiny pizzas, about 4 to 6 inches in diameter. They say that the best ones are made in Parma. I like to use a bread dough, one made with milk and butter, unlike the focaccia. This recipe makes a lot — they are great to serve at parties, or for a lot of kids, or for any occasion where you are feeding more than yourself and a pal.

Crust:
7 cups flour
1 cup (2 sticks) ice-cold butter, cubed
1/4 cup warm water
2 packets (about 5 teaspoons) active dry yeast
2 teaspoons sugar
1 tablespoon salt
2-3/4 cups warm milk

■ Work the flour and butter together, either by hand or using the chopping blade on a food processor, until the mixture is mealy. Mix together the water, yeast, sugar, and salt, and stir until dissolved. Mix it into the warm milk, and slowly add the milk and yeast mix-ture to the flour and butter, working it into a ball of dough. (If using the food processor, stop as soon as the mixture forms a ball.) If mixing by hand, knead for about 10 minutes. Put the dough into an oiled bowl and let rise, covered, for about an hour, until doubled. Punch down and put into the refrigerator. Let rest for several hours or overnight.

Cut the chilled dough into pieces about the size of a golf ball, and keep the pieces chilled until you begin to roll them out. Roll into circles 4 to 6 inches in diameter. (Of course, if the dimensions vary, the world of cooking will not come to a complete standstill!)

Topping:
4 tablespoons olive oil
4 tablespoons chopped garlic
6 cups chopped fresh plum tomatoes
1 cup chopped fresh marjoram
salt and pepper to taste
thin slices Bel Paese cheese
1 tin (2 ounces) anchovies, drained (optional)

■ In a large frying pan heat the olive oil and sauté the garlic, tomatoes, and marjoram until tomatoes are soft-ened. Add salt and pepper to taste. Spoon the sauce over the little pizzas to cover them. Add thin slices of Bel Paese and crisscross anchovies over the top if desired. Bake at 400° F for about 10 minutes. Serve piping hot.

Makes about 24 to 30 pizzettes.

This article is from James Haller's manuscript, "Food from the Breast to the Grave: A Culinary Auto-biography." He is the author of several other cookbooks, including *The Blue Strawbery Cookbook* (2 vols., Harvard Common Press); *Cooking in the Shaker Spirit* (with Jeffrey Paige), *What to Eat When You Don't Feel Like Eating,* and with Rich Ferreira, *Food and Fitness: A Chef and Fitness Trainer's Primer to Improved Health at Any Age.* The last three are available from Three Hills Distribution, P.O. Box 110, S. Berwick, ME 03908.

□□

WINNING RECIPES

in the 1996 RECIPE CONTEST

Salads

Asian Wild Rice and Chicken Salad

Dressing
1/4 cup olive oil
3 tablespoons roasted sesame oil
3 tablespoons lemon juice
3 tablespoons soy sauce
1 tablespoon sugar
1 teaspoon ginger juice *or* 1/2 teaspoon
    ground ginger

Whisk dressing ingredients until sugar is dissolved. Let stand at room temperature for 15 to 20 minutes to allow flavors to blend.

Salad
1-1/2 cups cooked wild rice, cooled to
    room temperature
1-1/2 cups cooked, chopped chicken or turkey
1 small can sliced water chestnuts, drained
1/2 cup coarsely chopped onion
2 stalks celery, chopped with tops
1-1/2 cups fresh snow pea pods, lightly steamed;
    or frozen, thawed, and drained
1 cup crisp Chinese noodles
lemon slices, for garnish

Place first 6 salad ingredients in a large salad bowl and toss gently. Pour dressing over salad and toss again. Refrigerate for 1 or 2 hours. Just before serving, toss once more and cover top with Chinese noodles. Garnish with lemon slices. **Makes about 6 cups of salad.**

Ron Glassburn, Tenino, Washington

Second Prize

Poppy Seed Potato Salad

Dressing
1/4 cup olive oil
6 tablespoons frozen apple-juice concentrate,
    thawed
1 tablespoon cider vinegar
1 large clove garlic, pressed
1 tablespoon currants
1 tablespoon diced red onion
2 teaspoons poppy seeds
1/2 teaspoon grated lemon peel
1/2 teaspoon ground cinnamon
1/2 teaspoon coarsely ground black pepper

Salad
3 bunches watercress, coarse stems removed,
    torn into bite-size pieces
1 head radicchio, torn into bite-size pieces
1/3 cup chopped fresh parsley
6 medium red-skinned potatoes, cooked, each cut
    into 6 wedges
2 red-skinned apples, cored and sliced
3 strips bacon, cooked until crisp, crumbled
1/4 cup sliced almonds
lemon twists for garnish (optional)

Combine dressing ingredients; mix until well blended. Combine the watercress, radicchio, and parsley with half the dressing. Arrange on 6 salad plates. Toss the potatoes and apples with the rest of the dressing. Place on top of greens. Top with bacon and nuts. Garnish with lemon twists, if desired. **Makes 6 servings.**

Roxanne E. Chan, Albany, California

Third Prize
Indonesian Red Lentil Salad

Vinaigrette Dressing
3/4 cup corn oil
1/2 cup red-wine vinegar
2 tablespoons sugar
2 teaspoons salt
2 teaspoons pepper
1 teaspoon ground cumin
1 teaspoon dry mustard
1/2 teaspoon turmeric
1/2 teaspoon mace
1/2 teaspoon coriander
1/2 teaspoon cardamom
1/4 teaspoon cayenne pepper
1/4 teaspoon ground cloves
1/4 teaspoon nutmeg
1/4 teaspoon cinnamon

Salad
1 pound dried red lentils
1 cup currants
1/3 cup capers
1-1/2 cups finely chopped onion

W ash lentils and cook in boiling water, testing after only 2 minutes; cook no longer than 5 minutes. Rinse and drain. Combine dressing ingredients and pour over lentils. Refrigerate overnight. Two hours before serving, add currants, capers, and onion. Keeps in refrigerator for 1 month. **Makes 6 to 8 servings.**

Ginger Harrison, Idaho Falls, Idaho

Honorable Mention
Southwestern Black Bean Salad with Fresh Cilantro Dressing

Salad
3 cups black beans, cooked and drained
2 medium red onions, thinly sliced
3 red peppers, seeded and thinly sliced
2 green peppers, seeded and coarsely diced
2 tomatoes, diced
8 ounces mild cheddar cheese, julienned

8 ounces jalapeño Monterey Jack cheese, julienned
12 red lettuce leaves

Fresh Cilantro Dressing
1 cup mayonnaise
1/4 cup chopped, fresh cilantro leaves
1/2 teaspoon dried basil
1/2 teaspoon dried dillweed
1 tablespoon sugar
1/4 cup sour cream

C ombine all salad ingredients except lettuce leaves, saving half the cheeses for garnish. In food processor combine all dressing ingredients until emulsified. Pour over salad, tossing well to blend. To serve, line 12 salad plates with lettuce leaves, top with salad, and garnish with remaining cheeses. **Makes 12 large servings.**

Wolfgang H. M. Hanau, West Palm Beach, Florida

– Carol Varin

ANNOUNCING
The 1997 RECIPE CONTEST
APPETIZERS

F or 1997, cash prizes (first prize, $50; second prize, $25; third prize, $15) will be awarded for the best original recipes for appetizers. All entries become the property of Yankee Publishing Incorporated, which reserves all rights to the materials submitted. Winners will be announced in the 1998 edition of *The Old Farmer's Almanac*. Deadline is March 1, 1997. Address: Recipe Contest, *The Old Farmer's Almanac*, P.O. Box 520, Dublin, NH 03444.

WINNING ESSAYS

in the **1996 ESSAY CONTEST**

My Best Summer Memory as a Child

First Prize

We needed eight; we had seven. Up at 5 A.M., after the Sun but before the other bottle scavengers, we waded through the ankle-deep ivy, looking for soda bottles. The heavy dew coating the large green leaves soaked our pant legs and thin canvas shoes. My feet ached with the moist morning chill, even though it was late July.

Suddenly something hard beneath my feet: "Got it!" I yelled, picking up a stubby Coca-Cola bottle and smacking out the ants against my palm. "That's eight! Let's go!"

We hurried across Mission to Ranson's, where the smell of fresh-baked bread assailed our nostrils, and we dizzied at the rich, full aroma. "One loaf of buttercrust," I beamed, "fresh and unsliced." We paid with cola bottles: one loaf, 24 cents . . . eight bottles.

We walked outside, mouths watering, and sat at the curb, balancing the hot loaf on our knees. Our fingers pierced the light brown crust, almost burning us as we broke off steamy chunks and popped them into our mouths. No butter, nor jam, nor honey. Just the two of us, my sister and me, devouring our breakfast in a hard-won, weekly rite of summer.

Jeffrey Paul Jones, Vista, California

Second Prize

My best summer memory as a child was an unplanned, yet much anticipated tradition at my house. When the mercury hit 100° F, we knew it was coming. It was the one day out of the year when my father would put on short pants.

The station wagon would be loaded with a cold supper of grinders and lemonade. We'd all put on our best serious faces and wait for the telltale creak of Dad's white legs descending the stairs. You see, those legs, all 38-inch-inseam of them, saw the light of day only on this one day out of the year. It was an event not to be missed.

We'd pile into the wagon and snicker all the way to the beach. Dad wouldn't crack a smile until he hit the water. He'd walk out at low tide and then he'd keep walking. He'd walk forever, yet the water would never get much past his knees. I can still hear the rusted teeter-totter; I can smell the seaweed washing up at the shoreline; and I can see the smile on Dad's face, and the silhouette of his white legs as the Sun set behind him at low tide.

Ann Boyd Ivancie, Denver, Colorado

Third Prize

The "best" by any standard is my memory of Six Bs: Bad Boys' Bare-Bottomed Bathing Beach.

Along the curve in a slow-moving stream hidden in the woods about a mile from our elementary school, each June a group of boys would dig out the bottom to create a pond. We removed debris, twigs, leaves, and small branches. This permitted the water to puddle and form a pool approximately four feet deep, eight feet across.

As soon as school officially ended, we gathered at Six Bs. Off came all our clothing and into the water we went. It always seemed

icy cold and forced us to climb out almost as quickly as we had gone in. Finally, after several rapid dips, our bodies could tolerate the chill of our old swimming hole.

A lookout would alert us to any approaching police car. This enabled us to jump into our pants and sit innocently on the riverbank.

Girls, of course, were a problem. We boys realized that girls "knew" about Six Bs. The girls would slip into the woods upstream and quietly sneak toward our oasis. We also realized that they would break into uncontrollable giggling as soon as they spotted any Bare-Bottomed Bad Boy. It became a game for both sexes to play. And the memory lingers on and on.

George W. Nordham, Waldwick, New Jersey

Honorable Mention

I grew up in Jersey City, New Jersey, a piece of unspectacular urbanization bordering the Hudson River, due west of New York City. During my youthful summers in the late 1960s and early 1970s, my friends and I would hike the two miles from our neighborhood to the shore of the river to fish and crab for "Jersey Blues."

There was an old wooden pier — the longest pier I've ever seen — on which we set up our rods and crab traps. Because people believed that the river was dead from pollution, we would have nearly the entire pier to ourselves.

We spent many a summer day on that pier, in the shadow of the Statue of Liberty, with the lower-Manhattan skyline as our backdrop, listening to the latest Motown hits on our transistor radio. The cool breeze coming off the water insulated us from the oppressive urban heat; the salty air made the neighborhood auto fumes a distant memory. In the midst of the most densely populated area of the country, we were worlds away from any city life, on the biggest fishin' hole in the world.

You know, I never did eat the crabs.

Louis Corio, Mount Airy, Maryland

My best summer memory as a child was a tadpole, a water tank, and the wrath of Jonah. Of course, it wasn't funny at the time, but it is now.

When I was about 12, I thought I had the call, like Joan of Arc, only I was going to be an evangelist. So I was trying to live a proper and pious life and thought all my friends should, too.

One summer afternoon six of us kids were watching the tadpoles swim in the cow's watering tank behind Thompson's barn, when Chancey Thompson swore. On target, I said, "Chancey, don't you know it's a sin?"

Chancey erupted. "If we don't do something, we're gonna get preached at from now 'til doomsday," he bellowed. Suddenly Chancey, Lyle, and Will Biggs grabbed me, and though their sisters Minnie and Lily tried to help me, the boys were quick to heft me up and dump me into that slimy tank, where I sank to the bottom like a rock.

When I rose up out of that impromptu christening, my language told me and everybody else that my evangelizing days had died in the baptism.

Charlene Taylor, Brighton, Michigan

A NNOUNCING
The **1997 ESSAY CONTEST**

BEST CURES FOR PICKY EATERS

For 1997, cash prizes (first prize, $50; second prize, $25; third prize, $15) will be awarded for the best 200-word essay on this topic: "Best Cures for Picky Eaters." All entries become the property of Yankee Publishing Incorporated, which reserves all rights to the materials submitted. Winners will be announced in the 1998 edition of *The Old Farmer's Almanac.* Deadline is March 1, 1997. Address: Essay Contest, *The Old Farmer's Almanac,* P.O. Box 520, Dublin, NH 03444.

GESTATION AND MATING TABLE

	Proper age for first mating	Period of fertility, in years	No. of females for one male	Period of gestation in days Range	Average
Ewe	90 lbs. or 1 yr.	6		142-154	147 / 151[8]
Ram	12-14 mos., well matured	7	50-75[2] / 35-40[3]		
Mare	3 yrs.	10-12		310-370	336
Stallion	3 yrs.	12-15	40-45[4] / Record 252[5]		
Cow	15-18 mos.[1]	10-14		279-290[6] 262-300[7]	283
Bull	1 yr., well matured	10-12	50[4] / Thousands[5]		
Sow	5-6 mos. or 250 lbs.	6		110-120	115
Boar	250-300 lbs.	6	50[2] / 35-40[3]		
Doe goat	10 mos. or 85-90 lbs.	6		145-155	150
Buck goat	Well matured	5	30		
Bitch	16-18 mos.	8		58-67	63
Male dog	12-16 mos.	8			
She cat	12 mos.	6		60-68	63
Doe rabbit	6 mos.	5-6		30-32	31
Buck rabbit	6 mos.	5-6	30		

[1]Holstein & beef: 750 lbs.; Jersey: 500 lbs. [2]Handmated. [3]Pasture. [4]Natural. [5]Artificial. [6]Beef; 8-10 days shorter for Angus. [7]Dairy. [8]For fine wool breeds.

Bird and Poultry Incubation Periods, in Days

Chicken......21	Goose 30-34	Guinea........26-28
Turkey........28	Swan 42	Canary.......14-15
Duck 26-32	Pheasant ..22-24	Parakeet.......18-20

Gestation Periods, Wild Animals, in Days

Black bear 210	Seal 330
Hippo....................225-250	Squirrel, gray 44
Moose....................240-250	Whale, sperm 480
Otter......................270-300	Wolf......................60-63
Reindeer 210-240	

Maximum Life Spans of Animals in Capitivity, in Years

Ant (queen) ......18+	Eagle 55	Mussel
Badger 26	Elephant 75	(freshwater) ... 70-80
Beaver ....15+	Giraffe 36	Monarch butterfly .. 1+
Box turtle	Goat (domestic) 20	Octopus 2-3
(Eastern) 138	Goldfish 41	Quahog 150
Camel ....35+	Goose (domestic) .. 20	Rabbit ....18+
Cat (domestic) 34	Gorilla ....50+	Squirrel, gray 23
Chicken (domestic) 25	Horse 62	Tiger 26
Chimpanzee 51	Housefly .... .04	Toad 40
Coyote ....21+	(17 days)	Tortoise
Dog (domestic) 29	Kangaroo 30	(Marion's) .... 152+
Dolphin 25	Lion 29	Turkey (domestic) .. 16
Duck (domestic) ... 23	Mouse (house) 6	

	Recurs if not bred	Estrual cycle incl. heat period (days)		In heat for		Usual time of ovulation
	Days	Avg.	Range	Avg.	Range	
Mare	21	21	10-37	5-6 days	2-11 days	24-48 hours before end of estrus
Sow	21	21	18-24	2-3 days	1-5 days	30-36 hours after start of estrus
Ewe	16½	16½	14-19	30 hours	24-32 hours	12-24 hours before end of estrus
Goat	21	21	18-24	2-3 days	1-4 days	Near end of estrus
Cow	21	21	18-24	18 hours	10-24 hours	10-12 hours after end of estrus
Bitch	pseudo-pregnancy	24		7 days	5-9 days	1-3 days after first acceptance
Cat	pseudo-pregnancy		15-21	3-4 if mated	9-10 days in absence of male	24-56 hours after coitus

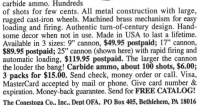

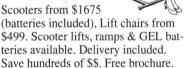

TIME CORRECTION TABLES

The times of sunrise/sunset, moonrise/ moonset, and the rising and setting times of the planets and bright stars are given for **Boston only** on pages 54-80, 46-47, and 50. Use the **Key Letter** shown to the right of each time on those pages with these tables to find the number of minutes that should be added to or subtracted from Boston time to give the correct time for your city. (Because of the complexities of calculation for different locations, times may not be precise to the minute.) If your city is not listed, find the city closest to you in both latitude and longitude and use those figures. **Boston's latitude is 42° 22' and longitude is 71° 03'.** Canadian cities appear at the end of the list. For a more complete explanation of the usage of Key Letters and these tables, see "How to Use This Almanac," page 34.

Time Zone Code: Atlantic Std. is -1; Eastern Std. is 0; Central Std. is 1; Mountain Std. is 2; Pacific Std. is 3; Alaska Std. is 4; Hawaii-Aleutian Std. is 5.

City	North Latitude ° '		West Longitude ° '		Time Zone Code	Key Letters				
						A min.	B min.	C min.	D min.	E min.
Aberdeen, SD	45	28	98	29	1	+37	+44	+49	+54	+59
Akron, OH	41	5	81	31	0	+46	+43	+41	+39	+37
Albany, NY	42	39	73	45	0	+ 9	+10	+10	+11	+11
Albert Lea, MN	43	39	93	22	1	+24	+26	+28	+31	+33
Albuquerque, NM	35	5	106	39	2	+45	+32	+22	+11	+ 2
Alexandria, LA	31	18	92	27	1	+58	+40	+26	+ 9	− 3
Allentown-Bethlehem, PA	40	36	75	28	0	+23	+20	+17	+14	+12
Amarillo, TX	35	12	101	50	1	+85	+73	+63	+52	+43
Anchorage, AK	61	10	149	59	4	−46	+27	+71	+122	+171
Asheville, NC	35	36	82	33	0	+67	+55	+46	+35	+27
Atlanta, GA	33	45	84	24	0	+79	+65	+53	+40	+30
Atlantic City, NJ	39	22	74	26	0	+23	+17	+13	+ 8	+ 4
Augusta, GA	33	28	81	58	0	+70	+55	+44	+30	+19
Augusta, ME	44	19	69	46	0	−12	− 8	− 5	− 1	0
Austin, TX	30	16	97	45	1	+82	+62	+47	+29	+15
Bakersfield, CA	35	23	119	1	3	+33	+21	+12	+ 1	− 7
Baltimore, MD	39	17	76	37	0	+32	+26	+22	+17	+13
Bangor, ME	44	48	68	46	0	−18	−13	− 9	− 5	− 1
Barstow, CA	34	54	117	1	3	+27	+14	+ 4	− 7	−16
Baton Rouge, LA	30	27	91	11	1	+55	+36	+21	+ 3	−10
Beaumont, TX	30	5	94	6	1	+67	+48	+32	+14	0
Bellingham, WA	48	45	122	29	3	0	+13	+24	+37	+47
Bemidji, MN	47	28	94	53	1	+14	+26	+34	+44	+52
Berlin, NH	44	28	71	11	0	− 7	− 3	0	+ 3	+ 7
Billings, MT	45	47	108	30	2	+16	+23	+29	+35	+40
Biloxi, MS	30	24	88	53	1	+46	+27	+11	− 5	−19
Binghamton, NY	42	6	75	55	0	+20	+19	+19	+18	+18
Birmingham, AL	33	31	86	49	1	+30	+15	+ 3	−10	−20
Bismarck, ND	46	48	100	47	1	+41	+50	+58	+66	+73
Boise, ID	43	37	116	12	2	+55	+58	+60	+62	+64
Brattleboro, VT	42	51	72	34	0	+ 4	+ 5	+ 5	+ 6	+ 7
Bridgeport, CT	41	11	73	11	0	+12	+10	+ 8	+ 6	+ 4
Brockton, MA	42	5	71	1	0	0	0	0	0	− 1
Brownsville, TX	25	54	97	30	1	+91	+66	+46	+23	+ 5
Buffalo, NY	42	53	78	52	0	+29	+30	+30	+31	+32
Burlington, VT	44	29	73	13	0	0	+ 4	+ 8	+12	+15
Butte, MT	46	1	112	32	2	+31	+39	+45	+52	+57
Cairo, IL	37	0	89	11	1	+29	+20	+12	+ 4	− 2
Camden, NJ	39	57	75	7	0	+24	+19	+16	+12	+ 9
Canton, OH	40	48	81	23	0	+46	+43	+41	+38	+36
Cape May, NJ	38	56	74	56	0	+26	+20	+15	+ 9	+ 5
Carson City–Reno, NV	39	10	119	46	3	+25	+19	+14	+ 9	+ 5

City	North Latitude ° '	West Longitude ° '	Time Zone Code	Key Letters A min.	B min.	C min.	D min.	E min.
Casper, WY	42 51	106 19	2	+19	+19	+20	+21	+22
Charleston, SC	32 47	79 56	0	+64	+48	+36	+21	+10
Charleston, WV	38 21	81 38	0	+55	+48	+42	+35	+30
Charlotte, NC	35 14	80 51	0	+61	+49	+39	+28	+19
Charlottesville, VA	38 2	78 30	0	+43	+35	+29	+22	+17
Chattanooga, TN	35 3	85 19	0	+79	+67	+57	+45	+36
Cheboygan, MI	45 39	84 29	0	+40	+47	+53	+59	+64
Cheyenne, WY	41 8	104 49	2	+19	+16	+14	+12	+11
Chicago-Oak Park, IL	41 52	87 38	1	+ 7	+ 6	+ 6	+ 5	+ 4
Cincinnati-Hamilton, OH	39 6	84 31	0	+64	+58	+53	+48	+44
Cleveland-Lakewood, OH	41 30	81 42	0	+45	+43	+42	+40	+39
Columbia, SC	34 0	81 2	0	+65	+51	+40	+27	+17
Columbus, OH	39 57	83 1	0	+55	+51	+47	+43	+40
Cordova, AK	60 33	145 45	4	−55	+13	+55	+103	+149
Corpus Christi, TX	27 48	97 24	1	+86	+64	+46	+25	+ 9
Craig, CO	40 31	107 33	2	+32	+28	+25	+22	+20
Dallas-Fort Worth, TX	32 47	96 48	1	+71	+55	+43	+28	+17
Danville, IL	40 8	87 37	1	+13	+ 9	+ 6	+ 2	0
Danville, VA	36 36	79 23	0	+51	+41	+33	+24	+17
Davenport, IA	41 32	90 35	1	+20	+19	+17	+16	+15
Dayton, OH	39 45	84 10	0	+61	+56	+52	+48	+44
Decatur, AL	34 36	86 59	1	+27	+14	+ 4	− 7	−17
Decatur, IL	39 51	88 57	1	+19	+15	+11	+ 7	+ 4
Denver-Boulder, CO	39 44	104 59	2	+24	+19	+15	+11	+ 7
Des Moines, IA	41 35	93 37	1	+32	+31	+30	+28	+27
Detroit-Dearborn, MI	42 20	83 3	0	+47	+47	+47	+47	+47
Dubuque, IA	42 30	90 41	1	+17	+18	+18	+18	+18
Duluth, MN	46 47	92 6	1	+ 6	+16	+23	+31	+38
Durham, NC	36 0	78 55	0	+51	+40	+31	+21	+13
Eastport, ME	44 54	67 0	0	−26	−20	−16	−11	− 8
Eau Claire, WI	44 49	91 30	1	+12	+17	+21	+25	+29
El Paso, TX	31 45	106 29	2	+53	+35	+22	+ 6	− 6
Elko, NV	40 50	115 46	3	+ 3	0	− 1	− 3	− 5
Ellsworth, ME	44 33	68 25	0	−18	−14	−10	− 6	− 3
Erie, PA	42 7	80 5	0	+36	+36	+35	+35	+35
Eugene, OR	44 3	123 6	3	+21	+24	+27	+30	+33
Fairbanks, AK	64 48	147 51	4	−127	+ 2	+61	+131	+205
Fall River– New Bedford, MA	41 42	71 9	0	+ 2	+ 1	0	0	− 1
Fargo, ND	46 53	96 47	1	+24	+34	+42	+50	+57
Flagstaff, AZ	35 12	111 39	2	+64	+52	+42	+31	+22
Flint, MI	43 1	83 41	0	+47	+49	+50	+51	+52
Fort Myers, FL	26 38	81 52	0	+87	+63	+44	+21	+ 4
Fort Scott, KS	37 50	94 42	1	+49	+41	+34	+27	+21
Fort Smith, AR	35 23	94 25	1	+55	+43	+33	+22	+14
Fort Wayne, IN	41 4	85 9	0	+60	+58	+56	+54	+52
Fresno, CA	36 44	119 47	3	+32	+22	+15	+ 6	0
Gallup, NM	35 32	108 45	2	+52	+40	+31	+20	+11
Galveston, TX	29 18	94 48	1	+72	+52	+35	+16	+ 1
Gary, IN	41 36	87 20	1	+ 7	+ 6	+ 4	+ 3	+ 2
Glasgow, MT	48 12	106 38	2	− 1	+11	+21	+32	+42
Grand Forks, ND	47 55	97 3	1	+21	+33	+43	+53	+62
Grand Island, NE	40 55	98 21	1	+53	+51	+49	+46	+44
Grand Junction, CO	39 4	108 33	2	+40	+34	+29	+24	+20
Great Falls, MT	47 30	111 17	2	+20	+31	+39	+49	+58
Green Bay, WI	44 31	88 0	1	0	+ 3	+ 7	+11	+14
Greensboro, NC	36 4	79 47	0	+54	+43	+35	+25	+17

City	North Latitude ° '	West Longitude ° '	Time Zone Code	Key Letters A min.	B min.	C min.	D min.	E min.
Hagerstown, MD	39 39	77 43	0	+35	+30	+26	+22	+18
Harrisburg, PA	40 16	76 53	0	+30	+26	+23	+19	+16
Hartford-New Britain, CT	41 46	72 41	0	+ 8	+ 7	+ 6	+ 5	+ 4
Helena, MT	46 36	112 2	2	+27	+36	+43	+51	+57
Hilo, HI	19 44	155 5	5	+94	+62	+37	+ 7	−15
Honolulu, HI	21 18	157 52	5	+102	+72	+48	+19	− 1
Houston, TX	29 45	95 22	1	+73	+53	+37	+19	+ 5
Indianapolis, IN	39 46	86 10	0	+69	+64	+60	+56	+52
Ironwood, MI	46 27	90 9	1	0	+ 9	+15	+23	+29
Jackson, MI	42 15	84 24	0	+53	+53	+53	+52	+52
Jackson, MS	32 18	90 11	1	+46	+30	+17	+ 1	−10
Jacksonville, FL	30 20	81 40	0	+77	+58	+43	+25	+11
Jefferson City, MO	38 34	92 10	1	+36	+29	+24	+18	+13
Joplin, MO	37 6	94 30	1	+50	+41	+33	+25	+18
Juneau, AK	58 18	134 25	4	−76	−23	+10	+49	+86
Kalamazoo, MI	42 17	85 35	0	+58	+57	+57	+57	+57
Kanab, UT	37 3	112 32	2	+62	+53	+46	+37	+30
Kansas City, MO	39 1	94 20	1	+44	+37	+33	+27	+23
Keene, NH	42 56	72 17	0	+ 2	+ 3	+ 4	+ 5	+ 6
Ketchikan, AK	55 21	131 39	4	−62	−25	0	+29	+56
Knoxville, TN	35 58	83 55	0	+71	+60	+51	+41	+33
Kodiak, AK	57 47	152 24	4	0	+49	+82	+120	+154
LaCrosse, WI	43 48	91 15	1	+15	+18	+20	+22	+25
Lake Charles, LA	30 14	93 13	1	+64	+44	+29	+11	− 2
Lanai City, HI	20 50	156 55	5	+99	+69	+44	+15	− 6
Lancaster, PA	40 2	76 18	0	+28	+24	+20	+17	+13
Lansing, MI	42 44	84 33	0	+52	+53	+53	+54	+54
Las Cruces, NM	32 19	106 47	2	+53	+36	+23	+ 8	− 3
Las Vegas, NV	36 10	115 9	3	+16	+ 4	− 3	−13	−20
Lawrence-Lowell, MA	42 42	71 10	0	0	0	0	0	+ 1
Lewiston, ID	46 25	117 1	3	−12	− 3	+ 2	+10	+17
Lexington-Frankfort, KY	38 3	84 30	0	+67	+59	+53	+46	+41
Liberal, KS	37 3	100 55	1	+76	+66	+59	+51	+44
Lihue, HI	21 59	159 23	5	+107	+77	+54	+26	+ 5
Lincoln, NE	40 49	96 41	1	+47	+44	+42	+39	+37
Little Rock, AR	34 45	92 17	1	+48	+35	+25	+13	+ 4
Los Angeles incl. Pasadena and Santa Monica, CA	34 3	118 14	3	+34	+20	+ 9	− 3	−13
Louisville, KY	38 15	85 46	0	+72	+64	+58	+52	+46
Macon, GA	32 50	83 38	0	+79	+63	+50	+36	+24
Madison, WI	43 4	89 23	1	+10	+11	+12	+14	+15
Manchester-Concord, NH	42 59	71 28	0	0	0	+ 1	+ 2	+ 3
McAllen, TX	26 12	98 14	1	+93	+69	+49	+26	+9
Memphis, TN	35 9	90 3	1	+38	+26	+16	+ 5	− 3
Meridian, MS	32 22	88 42	1	+40	+24	+11	− 4	−15
Miami, FL	25 47	80 12	0	+88	+57	+37	+14	− 3
Miles City, MT	46 25	105 51	2	+ 3	+11	+18	+26	+32
Milwaukee, WI	43 2	87 54	1	+ 4	+ 6	+ 7	+ 8	+ 9
Minneapolis-St. Paul, MN	44 59	93 16	1	+18	+24	+28	+33	+37
Minot, ND	48 14	101 18	1	+36	+50	+59	+71	+81
Moab, UT	38 35	109 33	2	+46	+39	+33	+27	+22
Mobile, AL	30 42	88 3	1	+42	+23	+ 8	− 8	−22
Monroe, LA	32 30	92 7	1	+53	+37	+24	+ 9	− 1
Montgomery, AL	32 23	86 19	1	+31	+14	+ 1	−13	−25
Muncie, IN	40 12	85 23	0	+64	+60	+57	+53	+50
Nashville, TN	36 10	86 47	1	+22	+11	+ 3	− 6	−14
New Haven, CT	41 18	72 56	0	+11	+ 8	+ 7	+ 5	+ 4

City	North Latitude ° '		West Longitude ° '		Time Zone Code	Key Letters A min.	B min.	C min.	D min.	E min.
New London, CT	41	22	72	6	0	+ 7	+ 5	+ 4	+ 2	+ 1
New Orleans, LA	29	57	90	4	1	+52	+32	+16	− 1	−15
New York, NY	40	45	74	0	0	+17	+14	+11	+ 9	+ 6
Newark–Irvington– East Orange, NJ	40	44	74	10	0	+17	+14	+12	+ 9	+ 7
Norfolk, VA	36	51	76	17	0	+38	+28	+21	+12	+ 5
North Platte, NE...............	41	8	100	46	1	+62	+60	+58	+56	+54
Norwalk-Stamford, CT.....	41	7	73	22	0	+13	+10	+ 9	+ 7	+ 5
Oakley, KS.......................	39	8	100	51	1	+69	+63	+59	+53	+49
Ogden, UT	41	13	111	58	2	+47	+45	+43	+41	+40
Ogdensburg, NY...............	44	42	75	30	0	+ 8	+13	+17	+21	+25
Oklahoma City, OK	35	28	97	31	1	+67	+55	+46	+35	+26
Omaha, NE	41	16	95	56	1	+43	+40	+39	+37	+36
Orlando, FL......................	28	32	81	22	0	+80	+59	+42	+22	+ 6
Ortonville, MN	45	19	96	27	1	+30	+36	+40	+46	+51
Oshkosh, WI....................	44	1	88	33	1	+ 3	+ 6	+ 9	+12	+15
Palm Springs, CA	33	49	116	32	3	+28	+13	+ 1	−12	−22
Parkersburg, WV	39	16	81	34	0	+52	+46	+42	+36	+32
Paterson, NJ	40	55	74	10	0	+17	+14	+12	+ 9	+ 7
Pendleton, OR..................	45	40	118	47	3	− 1	+ 4	+10	+16	+21
Pensacola, FL...................	30	25	87	13	1	+39	+20	+ 5	−12	−26
Peoria, IL	40	42	89	36	1	+19	+16	+14	+11	+ 9
Philadelphia-Chester, PA..	39	57	75	9	0	+24	+19	+16	+12	+ 9
Phoenix, AZ.....................	33	27	112	4	2	+71	+56	+44	+30	+20
Pierre, SD........................	44	22	100	21	1	+49	+53	+56	+60	+63
Pittsburgh-McKeesport, PA..	40	26	80	0	0	+42	+38	+35	+32	+29
Pittsfield, MA	42	27	73	15	0	+ 8	+ 8	+ 8	+ 8	+ 8
Pocatello, ID	42	52	112	27	2	+43	+44	+45	+46	+46
Poplar Bluff, MO	36	46	90	24	1	+35	+25	+17	+ 8	+ 1
Portland, ME....................	43	40	70	15	0	− 8	− 5	− 3	− 1	0
Portland, OR	45	31	122	41	3	+14	+20	+25	+31	+36
Portsmouth, NH...............	43	5	70	45	0	− 4	− 2	− 1	0	0
Presque Isle, ME..............	46	41	68	1	0	−29	−19	−12	− 4	+ 2
Providence, RI	41	50	71	25	0	+ 3	+ 2	+ 1	0	0
Pueblo, CO......................	38	16	104	37	2	+27	+20	+14	+ 7	+ 2
Raleigh, NC	35	47	78	38	0	+51	+39	+30	+20	+12
Rapid City, SD.................	44	5	103	14	2	+ 2	+ 5	+ 8	+11	+13
Reading, PA.....................	40	20	75	56	0	+26	+22	+19	+16	+13
Redding, CA	40	35	122	24	3	+31	+27	+25	+22	+19
Richmond, VA..................	37	32	77	26	0	+41	+32	+25	+17	+11
Roanoke, VA	37	16	79	57	0	+51	+42	+35	+27	+21
Roswell, NM....................	33	24	104	32	2	+41	+26	+14	0	−10
Rutland, VT	43	37	72	58	0	+ 2	+ 5	+ 7	+ 9	+11
Sacramento, CA................	38	35	121	30	3	+34	+27	+21	+15	+10
Salem, OR........................	44	57	123	1	3	+17	+23	+27	+31	+35
Salina, KS........................	38	50	97	37	1	+57	+51	+46	+40	+35
Salisbury, MD..................	38	22	75	36	0	+31	+23	+18	+11	+ 6
Salt Lake City, UT	40	45	111	53	2	+48	+45	+43	+40	+38
San Antonio, TX...............	29	25	98	30	1	+87	+66	+50	+31	+16
San Diego, CA..................	32	43	117	9	3	+33	+17	+ 4	− 9	−21
San Francisco incl. Oak- land and San Jose, CA ...	37	47	122	25	3	+40	+31	+25	+18	+12
Santa Fe, NM	35	41	105	56	2	+40	+28	+19	+ 9	0
Savannah, GA...................	32	5	81	6	0	+70	+54	+40	+25	+13
Scranton–Wilkes Barre, PA.	41	25	75	40	0	+21	+19	+18	+16	+15
Seattle-Tacoma- Olympia, WA.................	47	37	122	20	3	+ 3	+15	+24	+34	+42

City	North Latitude ° '	West Longitude ° '	Time Zone Code	Key Letters A min.	B min.	C min.	D min.	E min.
Sheridan, WY	44 48	106 58	2	+14	+19	+23	+27	+31
Shreveport, LA	32 31	93 45	1	+60	+44	+31	+16	+ 4
Sioux Falls, SD	43 33	96 44	1	+38	+40	+42	+44	+46
South Bend, IN	41 41	86 15	0	+62	+61	+60	+59	+58
Spartanburg, SC	34 56	81 57	0	+66	+53	+43	+32	+23
Spokane, WA	47 40	117 24	3	–16	– 4	+ 4	+14	+23
Springfield, IL..................	39 48	89 39	1	+22	+18	+14	+10	+ 6
Springfield-Holyoke, MA.	42 6	72 36	0	+ 6	+ 6	+ 6	+ 5	+ 5
Springfield, MO...............	37 13	93 18	1	+45	+36	+29	+20	+14
St. Johnsbury, VT	44 25	72 1	0	– 4	0	+ 3	+ 7	+10
St. Joseph, MI	42 5	86 26	0	+61	+61	+60	+60	+59
St. Joseph, MO.................	39 46	94 50	1	+43	+38	+35	+30	+27
St. Louis, MO	38 37	90 12	1	+28	+21	+16	+10	+ 5
St. Petersburg, FL	27 46	82 39	0	+87	+65	+47	+26	+10
Syracuse, NY	43 3	76 9	0	+17	+19	+20	+21	+22
Tallahassee, FL	30 27	84 17	0	+87	+68	+53	+35	+22
Tampa, FL........................	27 57	82 27	0	+86	+64	+46	+25	+ 9
Terre Haute, IN	39 28	87 24	0	+74	+69	+65	+60	+56
Texarkana, AR	33 26	94 3	1	+59	+44	+32	+18	+ 8
Toledo, OH	41 39	83 33	0	+52	+50	+49	+48	+47
Topeka, KS	39 3	95 40	1	+49	+43	+38	+32	+28
Traverse City, MI.............	44 46	85 38	0	+49	+54	+57	+62	+65
Trenton, NJ	40 13	74 46	0	+21	+17	+14	+11	+ 8
Trinidad, CO	37 10	104 31	2	+30	+21	+13	+ 5	0
Tucson, AZ......................	32 13	110 58	2	+70	+53	+40	+24	+12
Tulsa, OK........................	36 9	95 60	1	+59	+48	+40	+30	+22
Tupelo, MS	34 16	88 34	1	+35	+21	+10	– 2	–11
Vernal, UT	40 27	109 32	2	+40	+36	+33	+30	+28
Walla Walla, WA..............	46 4	118 20	3	– 5	+ 2	+ 8	+15	+21
Washington, DC	38 54	77 1	0	+35	+28	+23	+18	+13
Waterbury-Meriden, CT ...	41 33	73 3	0	+10	+ 9	+ 7	+ 6	+ 5
Waterloo, IA	42 30	92 20	1	+24	+24	+24	+25	+25
Wausau, WI	44 58	89 38	1	+ 4	+ 9	+13	+18	+22
West Palm Beach, FL	26 43	80 3	0	+79	+55	+36	+14	– 2
Wichita, KS.....................	37 42	97 20	1	+60	+51	+45	+37	+31
Williston, ND..................	48 9	103 37	1	+46	+59	+69	+80	+90
Wilmington, DE...............	39 45	75 33	0	+26	+21	+18	+13	+10
Wilmington, NC	34 14	77 55	0	+52	+38	+27	+15	+ 5
Winchester, VA	39 11	78 10	0	+38	+33	+28	+23	+19
Worcester, MA	42 16	71 48	0	+ 3	+ 2	+ 2	+ 2	+ 2
York, PA	39 58	76 43	0	+30	+26	+22	+18	+15
Youngstown, OH..............	41 6	80 39	0	+42	40	+38	+36	+34
Yuma, AZ	32 43	114 37	2	+83	+67	+54	+40	+28
CANADA								
Calgary, AB	51 5	114 5	2	+13	+35	+50	+68	+84
Edmonton, AB	53 34	113 25	2	– 3	+26	+47	+72	+93
Halifax, NS	44 38	63 35	– 1	+21	+26	+29	+33	+37
Montreal, PQ....................	45 28	73 39	0	– 1	+ 4	+ 9	+15	+20
Ottawa, ON	45 25	75 43	0	+ 6	+13	+18	+23	+28
Peterborough, ON	44 18	78 19	0	+21	+25	+28	+32	+35
Saint John, NB	45 16	66 3	– 1	+28	+34	+39	+44	+49
Saskatoon, SK..................	52 10	106 40	1	+37	+63	+80	+101	+119
Sydney, NS	46 10	60 10	– 1	+ 1	+ 9	+15	+23	+28
Thunder Bay, ON.............	48 27	89 12	0	+47	+61	+71	+83	+93
Toronto, ON.....................	43 39	79 23	0	+28	+30	+32	+35	+37
Vancouver, BC	49 13	123 6	3	0	+15	+26	+40	+52
Winnipeg, MB	49 53	97 10	1	+12	+30	+43	+58	+71

THE TWILIGHT ZONE

How to Determine the Length of Twilight and the Times of Dawn and Dark

Twilight begins (or ends) when the Sun is about 18 degrees below the horizon, and the latitude of a place, together with the time of year, determines the length of the twilight. To find the latitude of your city or the city nearest you, consult the **Time Correction Tables,** page 200. Check the figures against the chart at right for the appropriate date, and you will have the length of twilight in your area.

It is also possible to determine the times dawn will break and darkness descend by applying the length of twilight, taken from the chart at right, to the times of sunrise and sunset at any specific place. (Follow the instructions given in "How to Use This Almanac," page 34, to determine sunrise/sunset times for a given locality.) **Subtract** the length of twilight from the time of sunrise for dawn. **Add** the length of twilight to the time of sunset for dark.

Latitude	25° N to 30° N	31° N to 36° N	37° N to 42° N	43° N to 47° N	48° N to 49° N
	H M	H M	H M	H M	H M
Jan. 1 to Apr. 10	1 20	1 26	1 33	1 42	1 50
Apr. 11 to May 2	1 23	1 28	1 39	1 51	2 04
May 3 to May 14	1 26	1 34	1 47	2 02	2 22
May 15 to May 25	1 29	1 38	1 52	2 13	2 42
May 26 to July 22	1 32	1 43	1 59	2 27	—
July 23 to Aug. 3	1 29	1 38	1 52	2 13	2 42
Aug. 4 to Aug. 14	1 26	1 34	1 47	2 02	2 22
Aug. 15 to Sept. 5	1 23	1 28	1 39	1 51	2 04
Sept. 6 to Dec. 31	1 20	1 26	1 33	1 42	1 50

	Boston, MA (latitude 42° 22')	Biloxi, MS (latitude 30° 24')
Sunrise, August 1	4:37 A.M.	5:23 A.M.
Length of twilight	−1:52	−1:29
Dawn breaks	2:45 A.M., EST	3:54 A.M., CST
Sunset, August 1	7:04 P.M.	6:59 P.M.
Length of twilight	+1:52	+1:29
Dark descends	8:56 P.M., EST	8:28 P.M., CST

TIDAL GLOSSARY

Apogean Tide: A monthly tide of decreased range that occurs when the Moon is farthest from the Earth (at apogee).

Diurnal: Applies to a location that normally experiences one high water and one low water during a tidal day of approximately 24 hours.

Mean Lower Low Water: The arithmetic mean of the lesser of a daily pair of low waters, observed over a specific 19-year cycle called the National Tidal Datum Epoch.

Neap Tide: A tide of decreased range occurring twice a month when the Moon is in quadrature (during the first and last quarter Moons, when the Sun and Moon are at right angles to each other relative to the Earth).

Perigean Tide: A monthly tide of increased range that occurs when the Moon is closest to the Earth (at perigee).

Semidiurnal: Having a period of half a tidal day. East Coast tides, for example, are semidiurnal, with two highs and two lows in approximately 24 hours.

Spring Tide: Named not for the season of spring, but from the German *springen* (to leap up). This tide of increased range occurs at times of syzygy (q.v.) each month. A spring tide also brings a lower low water.

Syzygy: Occurs twice a month when the Sun and Moon are in conjunction (lined up on the same side of the Earth at the new Moon) and when they are in opposition (on opposite sides of the Earth at the full Moon, though usually not so directly in line as to produce an eclipse). In either case, the gravitational effects of the Sun and Moon reinforce each other and tidal range is increased.

Vanishing Tide: A mixed tide of considerable inequality in the two highs or two lows, so that the "high low" may become indistinguishable from the "low high" or vice versa. The result is a vanishing tide, where no significant difference is apparent.

TIDE CORRECTIONS

Many factors affect the time and height of the tides: the coastal configuration, the time of the Moon's southing (crossing the meridian) at the place, and the phase of the Moon. This table of tidal corrections is a sufficiently accurate guide to the times and heights of the high water at the places shown. (Low tides occur approximately 6.25 hours before and after high tides.) No figures are shown for the West Coast or the Gulf of Mexico, since the method used in compiling this table does not apply there. National Ocean Service tide tables for the East, West, and Caribbean regions are available from Reed's Nautical Almanacs, Thos. Reed Publications, Inc., 13A Lewis St., Boston, MA 02113; telephone 800-995-4995.

The figures for Full Sea on the Left-Hand Calendar Pages 54-80 are the times of high tide at Commonwealth Pier in Boston Harbor. (Where a dash is shown under Full Sea, it indicates that time of high water has occurred after midnight and so is recorded on the next date.) The heights of these tides are given on the Right-Hand Calendar Pages 55-81. The heights are reckoned from Mean Lower Low Water, and each day listed has a set of figures — upper for the morning, lower for the evening. To obtain the time and height of high water at any of the following places, apply the time difference to the daily times of high water at Boston (pages 54-80) and the height difference to the heights at Boston (pages 55-81).

	Time Difference: Hr. Min.	Height Feet
MAINE		
Bar Harbor	−0 34	+0.9
Belfast	−0 20	+0.4
Boothbay Harbor	−0 18	−0.8
Chebeague Island	−0 16	−0.6
Eastport	−0 28	+8.4
Kennebunkport	+0 04	−1.0
Machias	−0 28	+2.8
Monhegan Island	−0 25	−0.8
Old Orchard	0 00	−0.8
Portland	−0 12	−0.6
Rockland	−0 28	+0.1
Stonington	−0 30	+0.1
York	−0 09	−1.0
NEW HAMPSHIRE		
Hampton	+0 02	−1.3
Portsmouth	+0 11	−1.5
Rye Beach	−0 09	−0.9

	Time Difference: Hr. Min.	Height Feet
MASSACHUSETTS		
Annisquam	−0 02	−1.1
Beverly Farms	0 00	−0.5
Boston	0 00	0.0
Cape Cod Canal:		
East Entrance	−0 01	−0.8
West Entrance	−2 16	−5.9
Chatham Outer Coast	+0 30	−2.8
Inside	+1 54	*0.4
Cohasset	+0 02	−0.07
Cotuit Highlands	+1 15	*0.3
Dennis Port	+1 01	*0.4
Duxbury – Gurnet Pt.	+0 02	−0.3
Fall River	−3 03	−5.0
Gloucester	−0 03	−0.8
Hingham	+0 07	0.0
Hull	+0 03	−0.2
Hyannis Port	+1 01	*0.3
Magnolia – Manchester	−0 02	−0.7
Marblehead	−0 02	−0.4
Marion	−3 22	−5.4
Monument Beach	−3 08	−5.4
Nahant	−0 01	−0.5
Nantasket	+0 04	−0.1
Nantucket	+0 56	*0.3
Nauset Beach	+0 30	*0.6
New Bedford	−3 24	−5.7
Newburyport	+0 19	−1.8
Oak Bluffs	+0 30	*0.2
Onset – R.R. Bridge	−2 16	−5.9
Plymouth	+0 05	0.0
Provincetown	+0 14	−0.4
Revere Beach	−0 01	−0.3
Rockport	−0 08	−1.0
Salem	0 00	−0.5
Scituate	−0 05	−0.7
Wareham	−3 09	−5.3
Wellfleet	+0 12	+0.5
West Falmouth	−3 10	−5.4
Westport Harbor	−3 22	−6.4
Woods Hole:		
Little Harbor	−2 50	*0.2
Oceanographic Inst.	−3 07	*0.2
RHODE ISLAND		
Bristol	−3 24	−5.3
Sakonnet	−3 44	−5.6
Narrangansett Pier	−3 42	−6.2
Newport	−3 34	−5.9
Pt. Judith	−3 41	−6.3
Providence	−3 20	−4.8
Watch Hill	−2 50	−6.8
CONNECTICUT		
Bridgeport	+0 01	−2.6

	Time Difference: Hr. Min.	Height Feet		Time Difference: Hr. Min.	Height Feet
Madison............................	−0 22	−2.3	Hatteras:		
New Haven........................	−0 11	−3.2	Ocean	−4 26	−6.0
New London......................	−1 54	−6.7	Inlet	−4 03	−7.4
Norwalk............................	+0 01	−2.2	Kitty Hawk....................	−4 14	−6.2
Old Lyme			**SOUTH CAROLINA**		
Highway Bridge	−0 30	−6.2	Charleston	−3 22	−4.3
Stamford...........................	+0 01	−2.2	Georgetown......................	−1 48	*0.36
Stonington	−2 27	−6.6	Hilton Head	−3 22	−2.9
NEW YORK			Myrtle Beach....................	−3 49	−4.4
Coney Island	−3 33	−4.9	St. Helena		
Fire Island Lt....................	−2 43	*0.1	Harbor Entrance	−3 15	−3.4
Long Beach	−3 11	−5.7	**GEORGIA**		
Montauk Harbor...............	−2 19	−7.4	Jekyll Island	−3 46	−2.9
New York City – Battery ..	−2 43	−5.0	Saint Simon's Island	−2 50	−2.9
Oyster Bay........................	+0 04	−1.8	Savannah Beach:		
Port Chester......................	−0 09	−2.2	River Entrance	−3 14	−5.5
Port Washington...............	−0 01	−2.1	Tybee Light..................	−3 22	−2.7
Sag Harbor	−0 55	−6.8	**FLORIDA**		
Southampton			Cape Canaveral	−3 59	−6.0
Shinnecock Inlet...........	−4 20	*0.2	Daytona Beach...................	−3 28	−5.3
Willets Point.....................	0 00	−2.3	Fort Lauderdale.................	−2 50	−7.2
NEW JERSEY			Fort Pierce Inlet................	−3 32	−6.9
Asbury Park	−4 04	−5.3	Jacksonville		
Atlantic City.....................	−3 56	−5.5	Railroad Bridge...........	−6 55	*0.10
Bay Head – Sea Girt	−4 04	−5.3	Miami Harbor Entrance	−3 18	−7.0
Beach Haven	−1 43	*0.24	St. Augustine.....................	−2 55	−4.9
Cape May	−3 28	−5.3	**CANADA**		
Ocean City........................	−3 06	−5.9	Alberton, P.E.I.	−5 45**	−7.5
Sandy Hook.......................	−3 30	−5.0	Charlottetown, P.E.I..........	−0 45**	−3.5
Seaside Park	−4 03	−5.4	Halifax, N.S......................	−3 23	−4.5
PENNSYLVANIA			North Sydney, N.S.	−3 15	−6.5
Philadelphia......................	+2 40	−3.5	Saint John, N.B.	+0 30	+15.0
DELAWARE			St. John's, Nfld.................	−4 00	−6.5
Cape Henlopen..................	−2 48	−5.3	Yarmouth, N.S.	−0 40	+3.0
Rehoboth Beach	−3 37	−5.7			
Wilmington	+1 56	−3.8			

* Where the difference in the "Height/Feet" column is so marked, height at Boston should be multiplied by this ratio.

** Varies widely; accurate only within 1½ hours. Consult local tide tables for precise times and heights.

MARYLAND

Annapolis	+6 23	−8.5
Baltimore...........................	+7 59	−8.3
Cambridge..........................	+5 05	−7.8
Havre de Grace...............+11 21		−7.7
Point No Point...................	+2 28	−8.1
Prince Frederick		
Plum Point	+4 25	−8.5

Example: The conversion of the times and heights of the tides at Boston to those of Miami, Florida, is given below:

Sample tide calculation July 1, 1997:

High tide Boston (p. 70)	8:15 A.M., EST
Correction for Miami	−3:18 hrs.
High tide Miami	4:57 A.M., EST
Tide height Boston (p. 71)	9.5 ft.
Correction for Miami	−7.0 ft.
Tide height Miami	2.5 ft.

VIRGINIA

Cape Charles	−2 20	−7.0
Hampton Roads..................	−2 02	−6.9
Norfolk..............................	−2 06	−6.6
Virginia Beach	−4 00	−6.0
Yorktown	−2 13	−7.0

NORTH CAROLINA

Cape Fear	−3 55	−5.0
Cape Lookout....................	−4 28	−5.7
Currituck	−4 10	−5.8

CLASSIFIED ADVERTISING

ALTERNATIVE ENERGY

BUILD SUN-, WATER-, WIND-powered appliances. Thirty plans. Details $2. MCO, 3203D Bordero, Thousand Oaks CA 91362.

ASTROLOGY/OCCULT

BIORHYTHMS. Your physical, emotional, intellectual cycles charted in color. Interpretation guide. Six months ($12). Twelve months ($18). Send name, birth date. CYCLES, Dept. FAB, 2251 Berkely Ave., Schenectady NY 12309.

FREE OCCULT CATALOG! Over 5,000 books, jewelry, incense, music etc. Abyss, 48-OFA Chester Rd., Chester MA 01011. 413-623-2155.

BEST LIVE PSYCHICS. Accurate and powerful. Fast answers! 18+ from 85¢/min. 800-207-6338, 900-745-0118. Tarot 011-592-580-330.

WICCACRAFT: HARNESS its unique powers. Free protective pentacle: PO Box 1502-OP, New Bern NC 28563.

LIVE PSYCHIC READINGS. Romance, success, difficult decisions. $3.95/min. 24 hrs, 18+. 900-288-1277, ext. 412. Ttone Avalon Comm. 305-525-0800.

AMAZING WITCHCRAFT POWERS for protection, success, happiness. Home study. Learn now. Seminary of Wicca, Box 1366, Nashua NH 03061. 603-880-7237.

ASTROLOGY FORECAST: Six months, $20. One year, $35. Natal horoscope (character analysis) and birth chart, 25-30 pages, $20. Send birth date, birth time, birthplace. Astral Vision, Box 2217, Liverpool NY 13089.

NEEDFUL THINGS. Love, money, success. Occult products catalog. SASE. Archimage, PO Box 606, Tarrytown NY 10591-0606.

LOVE, LUCK, AND MONEY can be yours. Over 5,000 spiritual items. Send $1 for catalog. Church Goods, Dept. F, 801 W. Jackson, Chicago IL 60607.

WHEEL OF LIFE provides a confidential yearly biorhythm diary for $10. Birth date only: Gemfield Association, PO Box 1414, Miami Shores FL 33153-1414.

FREE LUCKY NUMBERS. Send birth date, self-addressed stamped envelope. Mystic, Box 2009-R, Jamestown NC 27282.

BEST TAROT PSYCHICS talk personally with you. Learn secrets. Have your destiny revealed. Free birth chart! 24 hours; VISA/MC, $3.99/min. 18+. 900-868-0300, 800-345-4659.

ASTROLOGY. Personalized, comprehensive natal chart ($12). Progressed chart for current year ($12). Both ($18). Send name, birth date, birth time, birthplace. CYCLES, Dept. FAA, 2251 Berkely Ave., Schenectady NY 12309.

WORLD'S LARGEST OCCULT, New Age, psychic, witchcraft, voodoo. Thousands of fascinating curios, gifts. 1997 issue. $2. By airmail, $3. Worldwide Curio House, Box 17095A, Minneapolis MN 55417.

MOONSTONE CANYON READINGS 'N' RITUAL. Enchanting cassette tarot reading with glowing moonstone talisman. Spellbindingly accurate! Send $17, birth date: Salamandre West, PO Box 80, Trabuco Canyon CA 92678.

THE MOST COMPLETE metaphysical, magical, psychic-power correspondence course ever. Become a recognized professional. Earn unlimited income with our university doctoral degree program. Reasonable rates. Priesthood, 2401 Artesia Blvd. 12-188 FA, Redonda Beach CA 90278.

FREE! One black or white magic spell! Tell me what you need! EKSES, PO Box 9315(B), San Bernardino CA 92427-9315.

ASTROLOGICAL PERSONALITY REPORT, annual forecast, $30. Biorhythms, $20/year. Send birth date, time, place. Angelica, PO Box 402, Grand River OH 44045.

PERSONALIZED ASTROLOGY CHARTS. Natal, transits, compatibility, horoscopes, biorhythms. Free info: APD, PO Box 10104, Bedford NH 03110-0104.

AMAZING OCCULT discoveries develop supernatural powers safely, easily! Free experiments. Williamsburg, Box 3483-FZL, New York NY 10008.

POWERFUL ROOTDOCTOR'S HOTLINE. Gain love, luck, success, remove evil eye. $2.99/min. 18+. Box 87409-F, College Park GA 30337. 900-263-7500, ext. 33.

CATALOG. Complete spiritual, occult needs. Oils, incense, herbs, books, etc. $2. Power Products, Box 442, Mars Hill NC 28754.

FREE METAPHYSICAL BOOK LIST. Hundreds of classic titles. Sunbooks, Box 5588 (OFA), Santa Fe NM 87502-5588 USA.

FREE ZODIAC BIRTH CHART (your astrological birth certificate). Call for details and special offer 800-979-6628.

AUTOMOTIVE

CARS FOR $100. Trucks, boats, four-wheelers, motorhomes, furniture, electronics, computers, etc., by FBI, IRS, DEA. Available your area now. Call 800-513-4343, ext. S-2838.

AUTOMOBILE/TRUCK/MOTORCYCLE literature wanted: 1900-1975. I buy sales brochures, manuals, toys, racing memorabilia, etc. Walter Miller, 6710 Brooklawn, Syracuse NY 13211. 315-432-8282. Fax 315-432-8256.

ALTERNATOR/GENERATOR REBUILDING BOOK. Details: HV, Box 26054, Las Vegas NV 89126. www:http//www.bluehawk.com/~d.hulet/repair.htm. E-mail: hvhedeng@ix.netcom.com.

SAVE GAS! Cut engine wear 50%. Reduce dry starts and repair cost. Used by NASA. Free info. MaGee Group, 39155 Aldieb, Aldie VA 22001.

BEER & WINE MAKING

WINEMAKERS-BEERMAKERS. Free illustrated catalog. Fast service. Since 1967. Kraus, Box 7850-YB, Independence MO 64054. 816-254-0242.

FREE CATALOG full of everything for the home brewer. Homebrew, 1500 Jackson, Minneapolis MN 55413. 800-234-0685.

HOME BREWERS. The Keg and Barrel has quality ingredients, kits for beginners and advanced brewers. Expert help. Call for catalog toll-free 888-BRU-BEER.

BOOKS/MAGAZINES/CATALOGS

WARMAN'S ILLUSTRATED AMERICANA GUIDE lists over 20,000 prices in 250 categories of American collectibles. Invaluable reference for collectors, flea-market shoppers, etc. Send $15 plus $2.50 s/h. The O'Learys, 30 Independence Green, Montpelier VT 05602.

HEMP SOURCE DIRECTORY and 48-page information book. Seed, oil, fabric, clothing, foods, books, paper. Eco-friendly, nondrug products from a renewable resource. $6.50. Terraco, 231 Ululani Rd., Kula HI 97690.

"DRIBBLE," the raccoon, tells values-oriented children's stories! Three books per '95-'96. Call: Dribbleworks, 719-593-7322.

FREE CATALOG of Minnetonka Moccasins, America's favorite. Satisfaction guaranteed. Made in U.S.A. Call toll-free 800-835-2246, ext. 40.

FREE FOR KIDS. Sixty-four-page book with over 350 free things kids can write away for. $4. Alpha Omega, 858 Collingwood Ave., Maywood NJ 07607.

"BOYHOOD ON A FARM." Delightful story of author's early life on a large farm. You will laugh and cry to a lifestyle long gone. $18, hardcover. 800-662-2354.

FREE BOOKLETS: Life, death, soul, resurrection, pollution crisis, hell, Judgment Day, restitution. Bible Standard (OF), PO Box 67, Chester Springs PA 19425-0067.

GOODRIDGE'S GUIDES to flea markets. List over 6,000 U.S. locations in four regional editions. Gulf Books, Box 263484, Tampa FL 33685-3484.

FREE COLOR CATALOG. Distinctive gifts by mail. Personal and unique ideas. Write Leisure Shopping Center, 6964 Schuyler Dr., Derby NY 14047.

CONTENTED CAT LOVER'S catalog. Unique, handcrafted, quality gifts, $1 for postage, 185-911 Yates St. Ste. 307, Victoria BC Canada V8V 4Y9.

ATTENTION, MOOSE LOVERS! Free catalog of fine handcrafted items with "mostly moose" in mind. Call or write: Mostly Moose, 3544 Bakerstown Rd., Bakerstown PA 15007. 800-488-6674.

POETRY COMPETITION. $2,000 in awards. All poets welcome. Submit original poems to: World Art Publishings, PO Box 8340, Kirkland WA 98034.

WHERE TO FIND GRACE LIVINGSTON HILL books? Hundreds in stock. List free. Arnold Publications-A, 2440 Bethel Rd., Nicholasville KY 40356. 800-854-8571.

BUSINESS OPPORTUNITY

THE WORLD'S MOST VALUABLE PHONE NUMBER!™ 800-228-8193, ext. 24019, ID# 278702. Send $1 to Box 912-OF, Silver Springs MD 20910.

WE BUY magazine/newspaper clippings. $781.23 weekly. Send stamped envelope. Edwards, Box 467159FA, Atlanta GA 31146.

EARN $1,000 WEEKLY stuffing envelopes at home. Money never stops. Rush SASE: Lightning Quik Mail Distributors, PO Box 18027, Philadelphia PA 19147.

BUNK BEDS. Clear $300 per day making bunk beds. Start at home in spare time and expand the business at your own pace. Free information. Bunks, 7713 Morgan, Dept. 1043, Minneapolis MN 55423.

PET-SITTING BUSINESS instructions offer. SASE required. APS-Dept. OFA, 909 Marina Village #140, Alameda CA 94501.

$27,000 IN BACKYARD growing new specialty plants. Start with $60. Free booklet. Growers, Box 2010-FA, Port Townsend WA 98368.

WATKINS PRODUCTS since 1868. Has sincere ways to have a successful home-based business. 800-828-1868.

LET THE GOVERNMENT FINANCE your small business. Grants/loans to $800,000. Free recorded message: 707-448-0270 (KE1).

LIFETIME STREAMS OF INCOME! Limitless income and time to enjoy it. Recorded message: 800-211-3181.

NATIONAL DIRECTORY lists over 100 companies seeking home workers. Good pay. Easy work. Free information. Gulf Books, Box 263484, Tampa FL 33685-3484.

ALLIGATOR, KANGAROO, buffalo, ostrich, venison jerky. Route sales with protected territory. Low start-up costs, free information. Buffalo Bob's, 7713 Morgan, Dept. 270, Minneapolis MN 55423.

COMPANY DOWNSIZING? Worried? Stressed out? Self-determined enterpreneurial type? PT/FT 800-927-2527, ext. 7262 (CT096171).

$575 WEEKLY! Complete dealership. Mailing "list advertisements" from home. Superior (FA-97), Box 7, Bedford Park IL 60499.

BIG DEMAND. LOW START-UP. Home based. Part-time. $500-$10,000 plus weekly potential. Eliminate long-distance phone bills. Risk-free. Simple. Tremendous support. Prepaid calling cards. T4C. 800-731-4612.

MAKE $25 PER POUND from free aluminum scrap? Yes! Free report! Ameriscrap-FA97, Alexandria Bay NY 13607-0127.

TURN YOUR SEWING into marketable merchandise. Guide reveals buyers, sellers, advertising, 36 business sources and 9 business plans. Helps you get started fast. $4.50. Kibler Publications, Box 550987, Jacksonville FL 32255-0987.

SLOT BUSTERS! Disarm the bandits consistently. Free slots guide! No obligation. Write: JSA Pub, Box 919, N. Arlington NJ 07031.

MAKE REAL MONEY selling fake tattoos at fairs and festivals. Free sample and color brochure. 507-956-2024.

PERFECT OPPORTUNITY to earn up to $80,000/year restocking our unique gourmet nut-warming machines placed in key locations around your community. Full-time, part-time. Blue Ribbon Nuts, 7713 Morgan, Dept. 813, Richfield MN 55423.

DEBT FREE! Excellent network-marketing business opportunity for the average person. Anyone can experience true success! Free copy 800-856-7112.

JOIN HOME-WORKER'S ASSOCIATION. Get "guaranteed legitimate" home-employment offers! Many choices! Write: Association-FA97, Alexandria Bay NY 13607-0250.

RECORD VIDEOTAPES. At home. $5,000 monthly possible. No pornography. Free details. Write: CMS Video Co., 210 Lorna Sq. #163FA, Birmingham AL 35216.

$80,000 FROM ONE ACRE! Grow ginseng, sell $60 pound. Information $1, LSASE. Leeland's, Box 68276-FM, New Augusta IN 46268.

MAKE TWO TO THREE times your cost. Thirty-five hundred products. Drop shipping available. Free info: Southwest Distribution/FA97, 4312 W. Romero Cir., Prescott Valley AZ 86314.

FREE GOVERNMENT GRANTS for any small business. Start-up bonus: we'll incorporate you free. 202-842-1434, ext. 2500; 800-935-5171, ext. 2500; 24 hrs.

SPECTACULAR MAIL ORDER HOME BUSINESS. We drop-ship 3,500 best-selling products. Lowest below-wholesale prices. Immediate delivery. Free book, tape. SMC, 9401 De Soto Ave. Dept. 358-93, Chatsworth CA 91311-4991.

CHEESEMAKING SUPPLIES

CHEESEMAKING! Make delicious, creamy soft cheese at home. Complete kit $16.95 ppd. Free catalog: New England Cheese Making, Box 85FA, Ashfield MA 01330.

COLLECTIBLES/NOSTALGIA

COLLECT WORLDWIDE STAMPS. All different, starter lot $10. Mint lot $15. Scarce specimen/imperforate lot $25. John Somma, Box 621, Wyandotte MI 48192.

UNIQUE ARTWORK from Ferry-Morse, established 1856. Old seed ads, tin boxes, calendars, and more. Free catalog. #96570. Call 800-283-3400.

ALADDIN LAMPS and parts. Kerosene lamps, beautiful, collectible. Catalog $1. MGS Co., Box 11, Mitchellville TN 37119.

CRAFTS

TEDDY BEAR SWEATERS. Two knitting books. $7 each, CA res. include sales tax. U.S. funds only. Betty Lampen, 2930 Jackson St. Dept. FA, San Francisco CA 94115-1007.

CRAFTS, BUILD AND DECORATE birdhouses for extra money! Information $1. Dorett Marketing, RR #1 Box 223, Browerville MN 56438.

WOODEN CHRISTMAS POST-CARDS. Mail and use as tree ornament. Free brochure: Fischer Woodwork, PO Box 131F, Stillwater NJ 07875.

INDIAN CRAFTS. Free brochure showing materials used. Recommended to Indian Guides, Scout troops, etc. Cleveland Leather, 2629 Lorain Ave., Cleveland OH 44113.

EXOTIC/TROPICAL PLANTS

CARNIVOROUS (insect-eating) plants, seeds, supplies, and books. Peter Paul's Nurseries, Canandaigua NY 14424-8713.

EDUCATION/INSTRUCTION

VETERINARY ASSISTANT/ANIMAL CARE careers. Home study. P.C.D.I., Atlanta, Georgia. Free literature. 800-362-7070, Dept. CCK554.

LEARN SEWING/DRESSMAKING at home. Latest factory shortcuts and methods. Free information. Call 800-326-9221, or write Lifetime Career Schools, Dept. 0B0317, 101 Harrison St., Archbald PA 18403.

LEARN PC REPAIR, troubleshooting, servicing. Home study. Free literature. P.C.D.I., Atlanta, Georgia. 800-362-7070, Dept. JJK554.

COLLEGE DEGREE BY MAIL. Accredited. CBC, Station Square, Ste. 227, Rocky Mount NC 27804. 919-442-1211.

HIGH SCHOOL AT HOME, diploma awarded. Low tuition and accredited. Est. 1897. Information free. Phone 800-228-5600, or write American School®, Dept. #348, 2200 E. 170th St., Lansing IL 60438.

LEARN FLOWER ARRANGING. Start business or hobby. Free brochure on home-study program. Lifetime Career Schools, Dept. 0B0217, 101 Harrison St., Archbald PA 18403.

BECOME A MEDICAL TRANSCRIPTIONIST. Home study. Free career literature. P.C.D.I., Atlanta, Georgia. 800-362-7070, Dept. YYK554.

DAVID'S GUIDE TO HOME GARDENING and mechanical marvels. Catalog $1. D. Chandler, PO Box 691, Milton NH 03851.

LEARN TAX PREPARATION. Approved home study. Free career literature. P.C.D.I., Atlanta, Georgia. 800-362-7070, Dept. TPK554.

BECOME A HOME INSPECTOR. Approved home study. Free literature. P.C.D.I., Atlanta, Georgia. 800-362-7070, Dept. PPK554.

UNIVERSITY DEGREES without classes! Accredited bachelor's, master's, doctorate. Free revealing facts! Thorson-FA7, Box 470886, Tulsa OK 74147.

LEARN LANDSCAPING at home. Free brochure. Call 800-326-9221, or write Lifetime Career Schools, Dept. 0B0117, 101 Harrison St., Archbald PA 18403.

BECOME A PARALEGAL. Attorney-instructed home study. P.C.D.I., Atlanta, Georgia. Free catalog. 800-362-7070, Dept. LKK554.

EARN YOUR HIGH SCHOOL diploma. Home study. P.C.D.I., Atlanta, Georgia. Free literature. 800-362-7070, Dept. JMK554.

LEARN TO BARTEND. For booklet send $12 to: Home-Study Bartenders Course, PO Box 1413, Hightown NJ 08520.

BECOME A PROFESSIONAL LOCKSMITH. Home study. Free career literature. P.C.D.I., Atlanta, Georgia. 800-362-7070, Dept. LKK554.

FARM AND GARDEN

TROYBILT OWNERS. Discount parts catalog. Send stamp. Replacement tines $57. Kelley's, Manilla IN 46150. 317-398-9042.

FREE CATALOG. Ninety-eight pages of flower, herb, and vegetable seed. Burrell, PO Box 150-FA, Rocky Ford CO 81067.

TOMATOES WEEKS EARLIER! Details, send SASE $2 to: Tim Phillips, 2844 Phillipstown Rd., Bremen KY 42325.

HYDROELECTRIC SYSTEMS since 1973. Free brochure, guide, U.S. $15. WPM, c/o Box 9723, Midland TX 79708. 915-697-6955.

SUPERB HOME WATER-PRESSURE booster from common materials. Plans $15 check or $10 cash. Efficiency Research, Box 102, Hartley TX 79044.

FOOD-PRESERVATION SUPPLIES. Complete selection. Dryers, canners, pectin, tools, ingredients, books, and more! Free catalog. Kitchen Krafts, Box 805-FA1, Mt. Laurel NJ 08054-0805. 800-776-0575.

FREE GARDENING CATALOG — 4,000 items! Seeds, trees, shrubs, supplies, greenhouses, beneficial insects. Mellinger's, Dept. 720L Range Rd., North Lima OH 44452-9731.

THE TOMATO CLUB newsletter. Fabulous tips on America's #1 backyard crop. Double your harvest! Grow the biggest, tastiest, and best. Delicious recipes. Six issues/year $15.95 and free trial seeds. Sample copy $3. TTCN, PO Box 418, Bogota NJ 07603.

BIG DISCOUNTS on seeds, bulbs, and garden supplies. Free catalog. #96571. Call Ferry-Morse at 800-283-3400.

FINANCIAL/LOANS BY MAIL

DID YOU SELLER-FINANCE the sale of your property? Tired of receiving payments? Need cash? We buy mortgages, land contracts, trust deeds, nationwide! 800-839-YESS.

SMALL BUSINESS government loans available nationwide! It's easy when you know how. Call 800-226-3601, BF8440.

GOVERNMENT LOANS for home buyers/investors. Your dream, their money! Available nationwide. Call now: 800-434-5977, ext. GH8440.

FLAGS

FLAGS, FLAGS! American, state, NASCAR, MIA/POW, Confederate, historical. For color catalog send $2 to: Flags & Things, PO Box 356, Dillsburg PA 17019.

FREE FLAG information sheets. Foreign, states, Confederate, rainbow, USA, boat, custom. Toll-free 800-774-3524.

FLOWERING PLANTS

AUSTRALIAN, WESTERN NATIVE PLANTS. Write for free catalog to: Seascape, PO Box 2981-FA, Salt Lake City UT 84110.

CHRYSANTHEMUMS. Footballs, spiders, garden types, every kind imaginable. Largest selection. Color catalog $2 deductible. King's, Box 368A, Clements CA 95227.

FOR THE HOME

WEATHER VANES $29.95. DINNERBELLS rugged steel. Free brochure. Americana Ironworks, PO Box 35525, Tulsa OK 74158. 918-492-2834.

CUCKOO, CUCKOO: Handcarved wooden cuckoo clocks. Catalog $1. Terre Celeste, Box 4125, Kenmore NY 14217.

HURRICANE WINDPROOFING, harnessing wind energy, and more. Free newsletter. Gustbusters Design, Box 160205, San Antonio TX 78280.

DRINKING-WATER PROBLEMS? Large or small, we solve them all with a pure water distillation system. Dealer inquiries are also welcome. Call us at 800-875-5915.

WEATHER HOUSE. Deluxe wooden chalet 5.5"x7.5" made in Black Forest, Germany. Maiden steps out in fair weather, man in wet. $25 ppd. N.Y. add tax. To order, call 800-632-8105.

GENEALOGY

ENHANCE FADED FAMILY PHOTOGRAPHS. Archival copies and restoration. Just Black & White, Box 4628, Portland ME 04112.

ALL THINGS HERALDIC! Coat-of-arms on parchment, bookplates, plaques, stationery, needlework, etc. Catalog $1. Crest Studios, Box 24890, Rochester NY 14624-0890.

ANCESTOR HUNTING? Trace your family roots the easy way. Save time, effort, money. Details $1. Lokadex Library, Box 19630, Rochester NY 14619-0630.

GINSENG AND HERBS

GINSENG. First-year roots $20/100, stratified seed $12/ounce. Complete information $1. Ginseng OFAG, Flagpond TN 37657.

HEALTH/HEALTH-CARE PRODUCTS

FREE, OLD, HARD-to-find herbal and patent-medicine brochures. Send long stamped envelope. Champion's Rx-Herb Store, 2369 Elvis Presley, Memphis TN 38106-7744. 800-936-6662.

"RED GINSENG." The very best in the world — 1 box $9.99, 2 boxes $17 plus $3 s/h. Leonard, PO Box 43138, Detroit MI 48243.

HERPES COLD SORES. Reduce or even eliminate outbreaks. Complete program. Confidential. $19.95 N.C.T.C.L., Box 5826, Stn.-L, Edmonton AB Canada T6C 4G3.

OZONE GENERATORS — medical grade, multipurpose. Treat a wide spectrum of illnesses. Purify air or water. 604-524-4062.

COMMON HOUSEHOLD items harmless, when used will stop groin and rectum itch. Also will stop radiator leaks. Send self-addressed stamped envelope and $3 to: 85 Bishop St., Waterbury CT 06704-3306. No stamps please. Will send information.

MEDICINES. Safe, natural for your common ailments. Homeopathic medicines have no side effects. Free catalog. Luyties, Box 8080 Dept. F7, St. Louis MO 63156. 800-325-8080.

ARTHRITIS, RHEUMATIC PAINS. Successful program designed by doctors practicing nutritional medicine. $19.95 N.C.T.C.L., Box 5826, Stn. -L, Edmonton AB Canada T6C 4G3.

HELP IMPOTENCY. Five million customers. Increase size and firmness. Cat. #71FA Pump. Instructional video, magazine, shipping $29.95. METCO, Dept. 71FA, Box 7020, Tarzana CA 91357. VISA/MC/AMEX 800-378-4689.

AVOID A BAD COLD. Guaranteed results. Send $4 to Dept. CFC, PO Box 3168, Spring TX 77373.

COLLOIDAL SILVER HEALS! An elemental microsolution that kills viruses, bacteria, and fungi on contact and prevents 650 diseases! Free brochures. Pro II Products. Distributorship available. 800-646-6779.

DEATH BEGINS IN THE COLON. Headaches, indigestion, constipation, diarrhea, heartburn, fatigue, irritable bowel, gas, big stomach, all have been directly attributed to a toxic colon. Raw dietary fiber and enzymes are the answer. Call 800-610-1958, ext. 3100, to reclaim your health.

EAR CANDLING. An old home remedy. "How-to Book & Video" $24.95. Helps enhance hearing, dry sinuses, plus more. Free catalog. Order ear candles $2 each. 800-309-3277.

MAGNETIC PRODUCTS. Free information reports and catalog. Dealer inquiries welcome. American Health Service Magnetics 800-544-7521.

FREE CATALOG! NATURAL EDGAR CAYCE health/beauty products. The Heritage Store, PO Box 444-FA, Virginia Beach VA 23458. 804-428-0100.

HEARING-AID REPAIRS. Guaranteed! Only $69. New, rebuilt aids. Batteries. Save! Reber, Box 51, York PA 17405.

VERY DRY SKIN? Alpha-hydroxy acid removes dead skin. Revolutionary moisturizers bring new skin to life. Comfortable Choices, 800-971-2002, ext. FA900.

DISCOVER THE SECRET to longevity and better health! Tape by Nobel prize nominee reveals startling facts that doctors won't tell. Tape and information $3. D. Schrock, 4029 Bee Ridge Rd., Ste. 5018, Sarasota FL 34232.

FREE CATALOG! National-brand vitamins up to 60% off! Kal, Schiff, Twinlab, and more! 800-858-2143.

HELP WANTED

EXCELLENT EXTRA INCOME! Assemble simple craft products at home. Program guaranteed. Call now! 800-377-6000, ext. 8440.

HOME TYPISTS, PC users needed. $45,000 income potential. Call 800-513-4343, ext. B-2838.

HERBS & SPICES

HERBS, HERBS, HERBS — 278 of them. Culinary, medicinal, ornamental. Perennials & scented geraniums, too. Catalog $2.50. Wrenwood, Rte. 4 Box 361, Berkeley Springs WV 25411.

INVENTION/PATENTS

INVENTIONS, IDEAS, new products! Presentation to industry/exhibition at national innovation exposition. Patent services. 800-288-IDEA.

PATENT IT ECONOMICALLY! Free details. Licensed since 1958. Near Washington, D.C. Ph.D. Associates, 800-546-2649.

JEWELRY

COPPER BRACELETS: Solid copper chain link. Beautifully hand polished. Specify eight-, nine-, or ten-inch length. $12.50 each. Touch of Excellence, 75 Forest Ridge Dr., Columbus OH 43235-1410.

KITS/PLANS

OOOUCH! Don't get scalded in the shower again. Complete plans. $12.95. Oooouch!, PO Box 97026, Pittsburgh PA 15229-0026.

LOTTERY/LOTTERY PRODUCTS

1997 LOTTERY PLAYER'S CALENDAR. Free details. Send #10 SASE. Ms. Mabel, Box 1694-FA7, Mabelton GA 30059. Hot numbers forecast, $2.49/min. 18+. 900-622-3579, ext. 41.

RED-HOT POWERBALL NUMBERS (Wed./Sat.). $10/call. 18+. Bro. Élé, PO Box 11482-F, Atlanta GA 30310. 900-772-7462, ext. 18.

MUSIC/RECORDS/TAPES

LED ZEPPELIN WANTED. Interested in contacting anybody that personally taped Led Zeppelin in concert from 1969 to 1977. Also interested in memorabilia. Paul 412-339-4276.

ACCORDIONS, CONCERTINAS, button boxes. New, used, buy, sell, trade, repair. Hohners, Martin guitars, lap harps, hammer dulcimers. Catalog $5. Castiglione, Box 40-B, Warren MI 48090. 810-755-6050.

CASH FOR OLD RECORDS! Illustrated 72-page catalog, showing thousands of specific prices we pay for 78s on common labels (Columbia, Decca, Victor, etc.). Information about scarce labels, shipping instruction, etc. Send $2 (refundable). Discollector, Box 691035(FA), San Antonio TX 78269.

FIDDLING, FOLK MUSIC instruction, recordings, free catalog. Captain Fiddle, 4 Elm Court, Newmarket NH 03857. 603-659-2658.

NURSERY STOCK

EVERGREEN TREE SEEDLINGS. Direct from grower. Free catalog. Carino Nurseries, Box 538, Dept. AL, Indiana PA 15701.

GINSENG! GOLDENSEAL! Profitable, good demand. Quality planting stock. Comfrey. Information $1. William Collins, Viola IA 52350

WILDFLOWERS — NURSERY PROPAGATED woodland and prairie plants. Free catalog. Contact Cattail Meadows Ltd., PO Box 39391 Dept. OL, Solon OH 44139.

OF INTEREST TO ALL

PRAISE GOD with Lisa Jackson's inspirational albums. Glorious, uplifting experience. Free sample tape/catalog: $1 p&h. Ruth Music, Box 19630-A, Rochester NY 14619.

EXPLORE YOUR INNER SELF. Charted biorhythm will give you insight into your emotional, physical, and intellectual self. Sample package, low intro price $12.88. Call 888-8RH-YTHM. Biorhythms by Monica, 2810 B St., McKeesport PA 15133.

GIFTS BY MAIL. For all occasions. Send $1 for colorful catalog. V.P. Enterprise, PO Box 1196, Highstown NJ 08520.

TWELVE-MONTH BIORHYTHM CHARTS $6. Send birth date and year. John Morgan, 1208 Harris, Bartlesville OK 74006.

TELL & SELL MAGAZINE. Three-issue subscription $15. Send your single-again ad. Entreprenueur, 6150 Michigan Rd., Indianapolis IN 46228.

WHISPERING ORACLE™. New Age readings and more. Catalog $1. PO Box 691, Milton NH 03851.

NO MORE LEMONS! Video helps save $$ buying used cars. Only $12.95. Fountain Rock, 2546 S. Dupont Blvd., Smyrna DE 19977.

SWISS ARMY-STYLE KNIFE. Burgundy. Customized with your state name and map in gold ink. Designs for all 50 states available. Fully guaranteed. $15 each. Brochure $5. Armu Products-FA97, 8322 Dalesford, PO Box 10980, Baltimore MD 21234.

FIND YOUR SECRET KEY to success. Learn meditation at home. "Safe, natural, effective." HLD, Box 85464-L, Seattle WA 98145. 800-739-2885.

KNOW YOUR MEDICAL RIGHTS. Information packet $1. Resource Finders, PO Box 535, Plymouth CA 95669.

PERSONALS

SISTER RUBY gives advice on love, business, all problems. Removes suffering and bad luck. 912-776-3069.

MOTHERLY, SISTERLY, BEST FRIEND. Talk it out: chatting, confusion, indecision, questions. Live. Call now! $3.99/min. Must be 18+. 900-388-2500, ext. 5382.

MEET LATIN LADIES! America's #1 friendship/marriage agency. Videos, tours, free photo brochure! TLC, PO Box 924994AC, Houston TX 77292-4994. 713-896-9224.

JAPANESE, ASIAN, European pen pals seek correspondence! All ages. Information: Inter-Pacific, Box 304-K, Birmingham MI 48012.

WONDERING ABOUT TOMORROW? Find out today! Let Sister Hope help you with love, marriage, business, good luck. Whatever your problem may be, call today, for tomorrow may be too late. 706-548-8598.

PERFECT DINNER COMPANION, romance, or friend is looking for you also! Call now! $2.99/min. Must be 18+. 900-329-5000, ext. 1635.

LONELY? UNLUCKY? UNHAPPY? Lost nature? Lost love? Linda solves all problems, quickly. Free readings, 912-995-3611.

MOTHER DORA can influence others. Bring luck. Help with all problems. Right, wrongs. Results! 912-888-5999.

PRAYER & EXTRAORDINARILY gifted psychics clarify your love, money, health! Call now! $3.99/min. Must be 18+. 900-825-3800, ext. 5363.

RUSSIAN LADIES, truly beautiful, educated, seek companionship. Beautiful color photo catalogs, live videos, Moscow tours. Free color photo brochure. Russia182, PO Box 888851, Atlanta GA 30356. 770-458-0909.

NEW AGE contacts, occultists, circles, wicca, companionship, love, etc. America/worldwide. Dollar bill: Dion, Golden Wheel, Liverpool L15 3HT England.

THAI ASIAN worldwide ladies desire correspondence, marriage. Free brochure! TAWL, Box 937(FA), Kailua-Kona HI 96745. 808-329-5559.

LATIN, ORIENTAL LADIES seek friendship, marriage. Free photo brochure. "Latins," Box 740116, San Diego CA 92174.

ATTENTION: SISTER LIGHT, Spartanburg, S.C. One free reading when you call. I will help in all problems. 864-576-9397.

NEED HELP DESPERATELY? Mrs. Stevens, astrologer, helps all. Lonely? Unlucky? Unhappy? Marriage, love, business, health, stress. I will give you options you never considered, never dreamed of. Immediate results. Call or write now. Mrs. Stevens, PO Box 207, Lauren SC 29360. 864-682-3669.

READINGS BY SIRENA. Can help in all problems. Call now for one free reading. 407-844-3419.

SISTER JOSIE can solve all problems in life such as love, business, health, marriage, financial. 706-353-9259.

MOTHER DOROTHY, reader and adviser. Advice on all problems — love, marriage, health, business, and nature. Gifted healer, she will remove your sickness, sorrow, pain, bad luck. ESP. Results in three days. Write or call about your problems. 1214 Gordon St., Atlanta GA 30310. 404-755-1301.

BEAUTIFUL ASIAN LADIES overseas seek love, marriage. Lowest rates! Free brochure: PR, Box 1245FA, Benicia CA 94510. 707-747-6926.

FREE INFORMATION! Pen pals, singles, all ages. America, Britain, Scandinavia, France, worldwide. Inexpensive. Fascinating! 24 hours 717-370-3564.

ASIAN WOMEN desire marriage! Overseas. $2 for details, photos! Sunshine International, Box 5500-YH, Kailua-Kona, HI 96745-5500. http://sunshine-girls.com.

NICE SINGLES with Christian values. Free magazine. Send age, interests. Singles, Box 310-OFA, Allardt TN 38504.

CALL PSYCHIC ANDERSON no matter what your trouble may be. Years of helpful and proven experience. 334-281-1116.

SISTER SHAWNEE wants to help you with all your problems, large or small. 65 years' experience. 305-248-1988.

PSYCHIC WINSTON helps in all problems. Specializes in reuniting lovers immediately. Guaranteed results. 817-589-9118/817-536-9033.

UNMARRIED CATHOLICS! Unlimited choice, large membership. Established 1980. Sparks, Box 872-F, Troy NY 12181.

PET AND PET SUPPLIES

AMERICAN PIT BULL. Breed information, collectibles, belt buckles, books, old magazines, photos, watches, etc. $1. Y.F.&M., PO Box 1522, Ramona CA 92065-1522.

MAKE PETS VISIBLE AT NIGHT. Reflective collar for cats and dogs. Sizes 8"-10", 10"-15", 14"-20", $12 includes shipping. VISA/MC, check to Visuwear, RR #3, Brantford ONT Canada N3T 5L6.

PHOTOGRAPHY

8"x10" COLOR GLOSSY FROM your home video, $19.95. Free information. Send SASE. CCG, Dept. FA, Box 234, E. Northport NY 11731-0234.

UFO NIGHT FLYERS, 8"x10" color photo print. Fantastic! Send $10 and return address to: Night Flyers, PO Box 105, Thompson Ridge NY 10985-0105.

POULTRY

NEW BOOK: POULTRY OF THE WORLD, over 400 color pictures. Baby peacocks, incubators, wild turkeys — "Everything. You name it." Free catalog. Strombergs, Pine River 45, Minnesota MN 56474. 800-720-1134.

GOSLINGS, DUCKLINGS, CHICKS, guineas, turkeys, bantams, pheasants, quail, swans. Books, medications. Hoffman Hatchery, Gratz PA 17030.

AMERICAN POULTRY ASSOCIATION, promoting all breeds domestic poultry and waterfowl. $10/year, $25/3 years. Free brochure. Karen Porr, 72 Springer Ln., Dept. OF, New Cumberland PA 17070.

VISIT NATIONAL POULTRY MUSEUM. Most interesting. Free information. Contributions welcome. Bonner Springs KS 66012.

GOSLINGS, DUCKLINGS, CHICKS, turkeys, guineas, books. Picture catalog $1, deductible. Pilgrim Goose Hatchery, OF-97, Williamsfield OH 44093.

REAL ESTATE

GOVERNMENT LAND now available for claim. Up to 160 acres/person. Free recorded message 707-448-1887 (4KE1).

BARGAIN HOMES. Foreclosed, HUD, VA, S&L bailout properties. Low down. Fantastic savings. Call 800-513-4343, ext. H-2838, for list.

LET THE GOVERNMENT PAY for your new or existing home. Over 100 different programs available. Free recorded message: 707-448-3210 (8KE1).

OZARK MOUNTAIN OR LAKE ACREAGES. From $30/month, nothing down, environmental protection codes, huge selection. Free catalog. Woods & Waters, Box 1-FA, Willow Springs MO 65793. 417-889-8006.

ARKANSAS — FREE CATALOG. Natural beauty. Low taxes. The good life for families and retirement. Fitzgerald-Olsen Realtors, PO Box 237-A, Booneville AR 72927. Call toll-free 800-432-4595, ext. 641A.

ARKANSAS LAND. Free lists! Recreational, investment, retirement homes, acreages. Gatlin's, Box 790, Waldron AR 72958. Toll-free 800-562-9078, ext. OFA.

RECIPES

REALE MCCOYS CHILI, SALSA, BEANS. Spicy, ranch recipes. SASE. $2 ea./all $5. Box 21572, Oklahoma City OK 73156.

FREE POSTAGE/HANDLING 25 Creekhouse cookin' recipes. $5. Name/address. Creekhouse, Box 2005, Murrells Inlet SC 29576.

HEARTY SOUP RECIPES. Beefy vegetable/hearty chili. Send $2. SASE. Recipes, PO Box 502, Eaton OH 45320.

NEVER BUY STORE PICKLES AGAIN! Baba's sweet, dill, refrigerator pickles. Recipe: Fast, simple, delicious! No canning. SASE & $2 to L. Garrahan, 13 Thompson-OFA, Washingtonville NY 10992.

FIVE ABSOLUTELY PERFECT unique bread recipes and primer, from my kitchen to yours. Please send $3 to: Cindy, PO Box 367, Goffstown NH 03045.

DANISH EBLESKIVER plus 30 family-heritage recipes. $4 add $1 S&H. Heartland Direct, Dept. FA97, 321 56 St., Des Moines IA 50312.

FAT-FREE CHEESECAKES, chocolate marble, raspberry swirl, others. Send SASE/$3 to: 1155 Newland Hollow, Ashland City TN 37015.

IMPORTANT MESSAGE — This could be the most important phone call you ever make! 100% USDA beefalo, tender and great tasting, 1/5 the fat of USDA beef, less cholesterol than chicken. Lose weight and feel great! $99 sample pack: 5 pounds ground beefalo; 2 N.Y. strips; 2 sirloins; 2 rib eyes. 100% natural — be heart smart! VISA/MC/DISC. Write: Babb's Healthy Heart Farms, PO Box 1164, Dalton GA 30722. Call: Shahn Babb, 770-773-2663; fax 706-226-1723.

MOCK DUCK with oyster dressing $2. Lemon Schaum Torte $1.50. Both $3. To: 3352 R.O. Peach Rd., Columbia TN 38401.

GOURMET CHEESECAKE RECIPE. $3 cash. SASE. Kate, PO Box 2095, Largo FL 34649.

ALLIGATOR, OSTRICH, beefalo, elk, venison, buffalo, game meat snack sticks/$18 per dozen plus $2.95 s/h. Babb's Heathy Heart Farms, PO Box 1164, Dalton GA 30722. 770-773-2663.

RELIGION

FREE: Three booklets of Bible verses: Vernon-OFA, 11613 N. 31st Dr., Phoenix AZ 85029-3201.

REVELATION: HOW TO STUDY IT and have it make sense. Historic/prophetic. Two hundred definitions unlocking its symbols. Eighty-page booklet $1. Clearwater Bible Students, PO Box 8216, Clearwater FL 34618.

FREE BIBLE COURSE: An enlightening study of God's word. Write to: Correspondence Studies, Box 283, Plainview TX 79073.

FREE ADULT OR CHILDREN Bible-study courses. Project Philip, Box 35-A, Muskegon MI 49443.

BEGINNING OF THE END TIMES? Seventy Bible lessons $1. Danna, 33227 Bainbridge, Cleveland OH 44139.

SEEDS

RARE HILARIOUS peter, female, and squash pepper seeds. $3 per pkg. Any two $5. All three $7.50. Over 100 rare peppers. Seeds, 2119 Hauss Nursery Rd., Atmore AL 36502.

ENDANGERED/HEIRLOOM vegetable, herb, flower seeds. Catalog $1. Greenseeds-FA, 4N381 Maple Ave., Bensenville IL 60106.

BIG DISCOUNTS on seeds, bulbs, and garden supplies. Free catalog #96572. Call Ferry-Morse at 800-283-3400.

WANTED

BOY SCOUT: Order of the Arrow items, medals, world and national jamboree items, etc. Wanted! Doug Bearce, Box 4742, Salem OR 97302. 503-399-9872.

WANTED: AUTOGRAPHS, signed photos, letters, documents of famous people. Gray, Box 5084, Cochituate MA 01778, or 617-426-4912.

OLD FIRECRACKER packs, labels, boxes, catalogs (pre-1969) wanted by preservationist. Brian Zompanti, PO Box 3193, New Britain CT 06050. 860-225-5137.

CASH BY RETURN MAIL, send for free recycling kit for your dental pieces, rings, old coins, chains, wristwatches, and pocket watches. In any condition. Laidnear Corporation, 7501 W. Devon Ave., Chicago IL 60631. 312-594-1702.

WE BUY ROYALTIES and minerals in producing oil and gas wells. Please write Marienfeld Royalty Corp., PO Box 25914, Houston TX 77265 or call 800-647-2580.

KNIFE COLLECTIONS WANTED. Cash paid. Sensitive to private and estate situations. Small or large quantities. Send list and price. Reference available. Bill Penley, Box 818-OFA, Fletcher NC 28732. 704-891-5800.

WORK CLOTHES

WORK CLOTHES. Save 80%. Shirts, pants, coveralls. Free folder. Write: Galco, 4004 East 71st St., Dept. OF-4, Cleveland OH 44105.

MISCELLANEOUS

LET THE GOVERNMENT FINANCE your career in writing or the arts. Free recorded message: 707-448-0200 (5KE1).

FIFTEEN PERCENT off on Watkins great products with a great name. Free call 800-354-0386.

FREE DEGREES! Counseling, metaphysics, theology, hypnotherapy, parapsychology! Ministerial license. P.U.L.C., Box 276265-FA, Sacramento CA 95827.

INDIAN ARTIFACTS: CASH for arrowheads, stone tools, beadwork, baskets, moccasins, pipes, clothing, anything Indian. Highest prices paid. Please contact Derek, Box 1115, Afton NY 13730. 607-639-2052.

HYDRO-SIL — SAVE up to 50% on heating and never use oil, gas, wood, or kerosene again. 800-627-9276 (MC/VISA). See display ad, page 131.

BURIED TREASURE, water, mineral deposits. Sensitive equipment allows locating from distance. Brochure free. Simmon Scientific, Box 10057PA, Wilmington NC 28405.

ANECDOTES *and* PLEASANTRIES

A motley collection of useful (and useless) facts, stories, advice, and observations compiled mostly from reader correspondence received over the past 12 months.

The Most Famous Editorial in the History of American Journalism

In 1897 a little girl named Virginia O'Hanlon wrote the following letter to the editor of *The New York Sun:* "Dear Editor, I am eight years old. Some of my little friends say there is no Santa Claus. Papa says, 'If you see it in *The Sun,* it's so.' Please tell me the truth, is there a Santa Claus?"

The reply, appearing as an unsigned editorial in the September 21, 1897, edition of *The Sun,* was written by editor Francis Pharcellus Church and soon became the most famous — certainly the most reprinted — editorial in the history of American journalism. Here is what he wrote . . .

"Yes, Virginia, there is a Santa Claus. He exists as certainly as love and generosity and devotion exist, and you know that they abound and give to your life its highest beauty and joy. Alas! how dreary would be the world if there were no Virginias. There would be no childlike faith then, no poetry, no romance to make tolerable this existence. We should have no enjoyment. . . . The eternal light with which childhood fills the world would be extinguished. . . .

"Not believe in Santa Claus! You might as well not believe in fairies. . . . Nobody sees Santa Claus, but that is no sign that there is no Santa Claus. The most real things in the world are those that neither children nor men can see. Did you ever see fairies dancing on the lawn? Of course not, but that's no proof that they are not there. Nobody can conceive or imagine all the wonders there are unseen and unseeable in the world.

"No Santa Claus! Thank God he lives and he lives forever. A thousand years from now, Virginia, nay, ten times ten thousand years from now, he will continue to make glad the heart of childhood."

Epilogue: Editor Francis Church died nine years later and only then, in his obituary, did he receive credit for his famous editorial. *The New York Sun* went out of business almost 50 years ago. Little Virginia O'Hanlon became a teacher in New York working with handicapped children and was always a popular subject for Christmas retrospectives. To her dying day she answered questions about Santa Claus by saying, "Yes, I still believe."

Editor's Note: Since 1984 Almanac friend and contributor Richard Church Thompson of Gaithersburg, Maryland (whose Michigan mother knew Francis Church as "Cousin Frank"), has been working to have the United States Postal Service create a commemorative "Yes, Virginia . . . " stamp for the 1997

Francis Church

Christmas season — a labor of love culminating, we are happy to say, in success. The stamp will, indeed, be out with much hoopla and fanfare for Christmas 1997. Not only that, but Thompson's son, well-known artist Richard Thompson Jr., will be the artist.

(Yes, Virginia, some stories do have happy endings.)

... and a Half Dozen Other Things That Happened 100 Years Ago

■ Although gelatin is older, Jell-O wasn't introduced until 1897. In that year a carpenter named Pearl B. Wait of Le Roy, New York, created a flavored gelatin and began peddling it door-to-door as Jell-O, a name thought up by his wife, May.

■ On May 31 a chess match was played by telegraph between members of the United States House of Representatives and the British House of Commons.

■ Proposed amendments to their state constitutions allowing women the right to vote were defeated in the state legislatures of California, Connecticut, Massachusetts, Montana, Nebraska, Nevada, and Oklahoma. (It wasn't until 23 years later that all adult Americans could vote.)

■ A French scientist, M. Villedieu Chassagne, invented a method for taking photographs in color.

■ There were 250,000 "telephone subscribers" in the United States, and the telephone business provided 15,000 jobs. (Today around 96,000,000 households in the United States have one or more phones, and telephone companies employ close to a million people.)

■ Dr. John Kellogg served the world's first cornflakes to his patients at a mental hospital in Battle Creek, Michigan.

Dr. John Kellogg

(continued)

Omigosh, Mondays Are Even Worse Than We Thought
(But Sundays Are Better)

Probably most people are aware that the most common day of the week for a heart attack to occur is a Monday. Now scientists at the Framingham Study and Boston University School of Medicine tell us it's the worst day of the week for strokes, too. Over a period of 40 years, there were 637 strokes among about 5,000 men and women, ages 30 to 62, all free of heart and blood disease, who comprised the study group. Sev-

enteen percent of those strokes occurred on Mondays. They also found that working men were twice as likely as working women or retirees to have strokes.

One theory for this phenomenon is that the physical change from a weekend schedule to the hurly-burly workweek causes subtle changes in blood pressure and heart rate.

The least likely day of the week to have a stroke? Sunday.

Submitted by Arnold McTaish, Los Angeles, and courtesy of Better Homes and Gardens, November 1995.

Drawing a Bead on How We Talk

Lest anyone think hunting and shooting are dying sports, we became aware recently of just what a hold they have on all of us. For instance, most people are aware that "lock, stock, and barrel" means everything, but how many are aware that these are the basic parts of a gun? Everyone also knows someone who is "hair-triggered" or "goes off half-cocked" and who "shoots from the hip." Such a person may "give 'em both barrels," possibly "right between the eyes." If he tends to do something, he's going to "take a shot at it" and will "give it his best shot." Of course, he'll "zero in" first and then perhaps have to "raise his sights" before he can "draw a bead" on his target.

He'll have to decide whether to give it "a rifle or shotgun approach." And he'll want to "cover the field," because "a bird in the hand is worth two in the bush." If he rushed in, he'll be "in full cry," but he might be more successful if he "stalks his prey" before it "goes to ground." If he's successful, it'll be "in the bag."

Those terms are pretty much self-explanatory, but others are more obscure.

It's in the bag

We know what's meant by "a flash in the pan," though we may not know the origin of the expression. It refers to a flintlock gun, which is set off by powder in a pan alongside the barrel. If the pan goes off without firing the gun, it's a flash in the pan, or ineffectual. The old phrase "keep your powder dry" referred to black powder, which was useless if wet, but today means, "be prepared for any emergency."

A "shot in the dark" obviously is not going to be very effective, possibly dangerous. And we have a general idea of what is meant by "half shot." But how many know that the "whip" in political organization refers back to the person in a fox hunt — the whipper-in — whose job it was to urge the dogs into the chase?

Shot your wad? Now let's start working on angling. Let's see, there's "hook, line, and sinker," "hooked," "swallow the bait," "give him enough line," "fishing for a compliment," "set the hook" . . .

Submitted by Gordon McQuade, St. Louis. Condensed from an article by James F. Keefe in the Missouri Conservationist, *copyright 1985 by the Conservation Commission of the State of Missouri. Reprinted by permission.*

Why Did Kamikaze Pilots Wear Helmets?

. . . and other unanswerable questions gleaned over the past year from the World Wide Web

1. Why are there interstate highways in Hawaii?

2. If nothing ever sticks to TEFLON, how do they make TEFLON stick to the pan?

3. Why do we drive on parkways and park on driveways?

4. If you're in a vehicle going the speed of light, what happens when you turn on the headlights?

5. Have you ever imagined a world with no hypothetical situations?

6. Why do "fat chance" and "slim chance" mean the same thing?

7. Why isn't "phonetic" spelled the way it sounds?

(continued on page 218)

8. Why does your nose run and your feet smell?

9. If 75 percent of all accidents happen within five miles of home, why not move ten miles away?

10. Why is it called a TV "set" when you get only one?

11. Shouldn't there be a shorter word for *monosyllabic*?

12. Why does an alarm clock "go off" when it begins to ring?

13. Why do we sing "Take Me Out to the Ball Game" when we're already there?

14. If *pro* is the opposite of *con*, then is *progress* the opposite of *congress*?

15. What is another word for *thesaurus*?

27 Words to Test Your Memory

Harry Pillsbury (1872-1906) of Somerville, Massachusetts, one of the world's greatest chess players, was once shown the following list of 27 words just prior to his participation in a chess exhibition. Pillsbury proceeded to quickly read through the list and put it away. He then rattled off all 27 words in their actual order, perfectly. When he finished, he said them in reverse order, again flawlessly. The next day, without having seen the list again, he did the same thing without a hitch. Want to try it?

Here are those 27 words . . .

antiphlogistine	Freiheit	Piet Potgelter's
periosteum	Philadelphia	rost
taka-diastase	Cincinnati	salmagundi
plasmon	athletics	oomisillecootsi
Threlkeld	no war	Bangmamvate
streptococcus	Etchenberg	Schlechter's Nek
micrococcus	American	theosophy
plasmodium	Russian	catechism
Mississippi	philosophy	Madjescomalops

Courtesy of Patrick J. Leonard, Braintree, Massachusetts

The Best Ways to Get Rid of Roaches, Moles, and the Smell of Skunk
(Reader Wisdom from Georgia, Missouri, and New Hampshire)

ROACHES ■ **Thought you might find this** of interest for your 1997 Almanac. Here's a sure way to rid one's household of those critters called cockroaches. It's an old family recipe that's been handed down for generations. Never fails.

9 ounces boric acid powder
1/2 cup flour
1/4 cup sugar
1/4 cup cooking oil
1/2 cup grated onion
Mix well. Add water if it dries out.

Keep out of reach of children and pets.

Kenneth Rotch, Decatur, Georgia

MOLES ■ **I would like to share my** way of getting rid of moles. I have had no luck with either traps or chemicals and I am not inclined to chase them over to my neighbors. But this method works.

Remove the muffler on your power lawn mower and then add a piece of bent or fitted metal pipe in its place

to reach from mower to the diggings. Run the mower a minute or so in each opening. Presto! The moles are dead and buried.

Be sure to wear heavy gloves when handling the pipe because it gets very hot. Also, plug up the holes afterward because the mole runs make good breeding nests for mice and snakes. *George Kvaternik, Trimble, Missouri*

THE SMELL OF SKUNK ■ Paul Krebaum, a chemist, has used an alkaline hydrogen peroxide compound to remove hydrogen sulfide from waste-gas streams in his laboratory. This compound also destroys a class of chemicals called thiols, which are the major constituents of skunk spray.

One evening a neighbor's cat had an encounter with a skunk and was exiled from the house. The neighbors tried the usual remedies (tomato juice, etc.) without success. Krebaum suggested they bathe the cat in a modified version of the laboratory reagent. It worked, and the cat was allowed back into the house.

Here is the formula for pets: 1 quart 3% hydrogen peroxide (from a drug store), 1/4 cup baking soda (sodium bicarbonate), and 1 teaspoon liquid soap. Thoroughly bathe the animal, working the soapy solution well into the fur and taking care to avoid the eyes.

This remedy may also work for cleaning the front bumper of your car should you hit a skunk.

Stephen H. Taylor, Commissioner, Dept. of Agriculture, New Hampshire

It's Not Always Easy to Put Excitement into a Long, Comfortable Marriage

Here's a gentle case in point . . .

I've been stargazing since I was 11 years old, but I never thought anything like this would happen to me," said British amateur astronomer George Sallit after he discovered a tiny new planet 400 million miles from Earth, to be named Sallit One, and had his remarkable discovery verified by professional astronomers at Harvard University and the Smithsonian Institution.

Sallit said he found the planet, only 20 miles in diameter, between Mars and Jupiter quite by chance when he was scouring the Universe, as he has been doing for years, through a powerful telescope set up out in his garden shed. In fact, at first he thought it might merely be a scratch on his lens.

In talking to reporters, he said he's grateful to his wife, Jennifer, for her patience throughout his years of stargazing and for all the thousands of cups of tea she has delivered to him out in the shed. As she set the tea down beside him on the night of his historic discovery and he excitedly told her he'd found a new planet, she reportedly replied, "That's nice, dear."

Courtesy of Gordon Peery, Nelson, New Hampshire

If It's Greek to You, What Is It to a Greek?

So what does a Greek say to confess to total noncomprehension? Well, apparently a Greek says, "Stop talking Chinese."

OK, so what does a Chinese person say under similar circumstances? Actually, he's likely to say, "Your words are like Buddha's attendant: 12 feet tall, whose head I cannot reach!"

When Polish people, on the other hand, are unable to understand, they are apt to blurt, "I am hearing a sermon in Turkish!"

(continued)

French people, when irritated by incomprehensibility, murmur, "Pray stop talking Hebrew!"

And Jews dismiss ensnarled or foolish statements with "Stop knocking a teapot!"

Courtesy of Hoorah for Yiddish *by Leo Rosten, published by Simon & Schuster*

Never (Ever!) Play Dominoes in the Cow Barn in Canada

Most of the following cattle laws were passed long ago in various Canadian towns and then, sooner or later, pretty much forgotten or ignored. But they're still on the books . . .

■ In L'Ardoise, Nova Scotia, a farmer is not allowed to walk behind his bull without singing to him.

la-a-a-a la la la

sigh!

■ In Sebringville, Ontario, it's unlawful for a cattleman "to wink at any female person with whom he is unacquainted."

■ In Alonsa, Manitoba, no farmer and his wife and members of his immediate family are allowed to attend a livestock auction within four hours after eating garlic.

■ No farmer can legally trade any livestock before the Sun comes up in Rexton, New Brunswick.

■ Playing dominoes while in a barn with cattle is forbidden in Kennetcook, Nova Scotia. (This was to prevent the farmer from "acquiring a taste for gambling.")

■ It's illegal in Orangeville, Ontario, for a farmer to work around cattle while wearing socks with holes in the toes.

■ In Raymond, Alberta, there's a $1 fine for a farmer who lets his cow run into a church. For a bull doing the same thing, the fine is doubled.

■ In Cottonwood, British Columbia, no cattleman can legally leave his new bride alone on his wedding day in order to go fishing.

■ It's against the law in Bladworth, Saskatchewan, for a farmer to "frown" at any of his cows.

■ Lingerie cannot legally be hung on a clothesline around cattle in the town of Winkler, Manitoba, but an exception to the law can be made if the lingerie is hidden from the cattle by a high fence or a "suitable screen."

■ Citizens of Finnegan, Alberta, cannot legally make "ugly faces" at cattle who are found to be "freely roaming" the community.

■ In Jasmin, Saskatchewan, it's against the law for a cow to moo within 300 feet of a private home.

■ No female wearing a nightgown in Summerside, Prince Edward Island, can be seen feeding cattle.

by Robert Pelton, courtesy of Mark F. Kihn and adapted from the Canadian Hereford Digest

For a Final Thought, Contemplate What Hamlet Told His Mother . . .

"Assume a virtue if you have it not . . . for use almost can change the stamp of nature."

Vinegar . . .
Mother Nature's Liquid Gold

CANTON (Special)- Research from the U.S. to Asia reports that VINEGAR-- *Mother Nature's Liquid Gold--* is one of the most powerful aids for a healthier, longer life.

Each golden drop is a natural storehouse of vitamins and minerals to help fight ailments and extend life. In fact:
- Studies show it helps boost the immune system to help prevent cancer, ease arthritic pain, and fight cholesterol build-up in arteries.

And that's not all!

Want to control Your weight?

Since ancient times a teaspoon of apple cider vinegar in water at meals has been the answer. Try it.

Worried about age spots? Troubled by headaches? Aches and pain?

You'll find a vinegar home remedy for your problem among the 308 researched and available for the first time in the exclusive *"The Vinegar Book,"* by natural health author Emily Thacker.

As *The Wall Street Journal* wrote in a vinegar article: "Have a Problem? Chances are Vinegar can help solve it."

This fascinating book shows you step by step how to mix *inexpensive* vinegar with kitchen staples to help:
- Lower blood pressure
- Speed up your metabolism
- Fight pesky coughs, colds
- Relieve painful leg cramps
- Soothe aching muscles
- Fade away headaches
- Gain soft, radiant skin
- Help lower cholesterol
- Boost immune system in its prevention of cancer
- Fight liver spots

- Natural arthritis reliever
- Use for eye and ear problems
- Destroy bacteria in foods
- Relieve itches, insect bites
- Skin rashes, athlete's foot
- Heart and circulatory care, and so much more

You'll learn it's easy to combine vinegar and herbs to create tenderizers, mild laxatives, tension relievers.

Enjoy bottling your own original and delicious vinegars. And tasty pickles and pickling treats that win raves!

You'll discover vinegar's amazing history through the ages *PLUS easy-to-make cleaning formulas that save you hundreds of dollars every year.*

"The Vinegar Book" is so amazing that you're invited to use and enjoy its wisdom on a **90 day No-Risk Trial basis. If not delighted simply tear off and return** *the cover only* **for a prompt refund.** To order right from the publisher at the introductory low price of $12.95 plus $2 postage & handling do this now:

Write "Vinegar Preview" on a piece of paper and send it with your check or money order to: "The Vinegar Book," 718 - 12th St. N.W., Dept. F6039, Canton, Ohio 44703.

Save even more and order two books for only $20 postpaid. It's a great gift!

VISA/MasterCard holders can charge by mail-- include card number and expire date-- or by phoning Toll-Free 1-800-772-7285, Ext. F6039 for even faster service. Either way order today and get:

SPECIAL BONUS of Brain Health Power Foods booklet FREE with your trial order. ©1996 TRESCO TF512-2

1 9 9 6

JANUARY
S	M	T	W	T	F	S
	1	2	3	4	5	6
7	8	9	10	11	12	13
14	15	16	17	18	19	20
21	22	23	24	25	26	27
28	29	30	31			

FEBRUARY
S	M	T	W	T	F	S
				1	2	3
4	5	6	7	8	9	10
11	12	13	14	15	16	17
18	19	20	21	22	23	24
25	26	27	28	29		

MARCH
S	M	T	W	T	F	S
					1	2
3	4	5	6	7	8	9
10	11	12	13	14	15	16
17	18	19	20	21	22	23
24	25	26	27	28	29	30
31						

APRIL
S	M	T	W	T	F	S
	1	2	3	4	5	6
7	8	9	10	11	12	13
14	15	16	17	18	19	20
21	22	23	24	25	26	27
28	29	30				

MAY
S	M	T	W	T	F	S
			1	2	3	4
5	6	7	8	9	10	11
12	13	14	15	16	17	18
19	20	21	22	23	24	25
26	27	28	29	30	31	

JUNE
S	M	T	W	T	F	S
						1
2	3	4	5	6	7	8
9	10	11	12	13	14	15
16	17	18	19	20	21	22
23	24	25	26	27	28	29
30						

JULY
S	M	T	W	T	F	S
	1	2	3	4	5	6
7	8	9	10	11	12	13
14	15	16	17	18	19	20
21	22	23	24	25	26	27
28	29	30	31			

AUGUST
S	M	T	W	T	F	S
				1	2	3
4	5	6	7	8	9	10
11	12	13	14	15	16	17
18	19	20	21	22	23	24
25	26	27	28	29	30	31

SEPTEMBER
S	M	T	W	T	F	S
1	2	3	4	5	6	7
8	9	10	11	12	13	14
15	16	17	18	19	20	21
22	23	24	25	26	27	28
29	30					

OCTOBER
S	M	T	W	T	F	S
		1	2	3	4	5
6	7	8	9	10	11	12
13	14	15	16	17	18	19
20	21	22	23	24	25	26
27	28	29	30	31		

NOVEMBER
S	M	T	W	T	F	S
					1	2
3	4	5	6	7	8	9
10	11	12	13	14	15	16
17	18	19	20	21	22	23
24	25	26	27	28	29	30

DECEMBER
S	M	T	W	T	F	S
1	2	3	4	5	6	7
8	9	10	11	12	13	14
15	16	17	18	19	20	21
22	23	24	25	26	27	28
29	30	31				

1 9 9 7

JANUARY
S	M	T	W	T	F	S
			1	2	3	4
5	6	7	8	9	10	11
12	13	14	15	16	17	18
19	20	21	22	23	24	25
26	27	28	29	30	31	

FEBRUARY
S	M	T	W	T	F	S
						1
2	3	4	5	6	7	8
9	10	11	12	13	14	15
16	17	18	19	20	21	22
23	24	25	26	27	28	

MARCH
S	M	T	W	T	F	S
						1
2	3	4	5	6	7	8
9	10	11	12	13	14	15
16	17	18	19	20	21	22
23	24	25	26	27	28	29
30	31					

APRIL
S	M	T	W	T	F	S
		1	2	3	4	5
6	7	8	9	10	11	12
13	14	15	16	17	18	19
20	21	22	23	24	25	26
27	28	29	30			

MAY
S	M	T	W	T	F	S
				1	2	3
4	5	6	7	8	9	10
11	12	13	14	15	16	17
18	19	20	21	22	23	24
25	26	27	28	29	30	31

JUNE
S	M	T	W	T	F	S
1	2	3	4	5	6	7
8	9	10	11	12	13	14
15	16	17	18	19	20	21
22	23	24	25	26	27	28
29	30					

JULY
S	M	T	W	T	F	S
		1	2	3	4	5
6	7	8	9	10	11	12
13	14	15	16	17	18	19
20	21	22	23	24	25	26
27	28	29	30	31		

AUGUST
S	M	T	W	T	F	S
					1	2
3	4	5	6	7	8	9
10	11	12	13	14	15	16
17	18	19	20	21	22	23
24	25	26	27	28	29	30
31						

SEPTEMBER
S	M	T	W	T	F	S
	1	2	3	4	5	6
7	8	9	10	11	12	13
14	15	16	17	18	19	20
21	22	23	24	25	26	27
28	29	30				

OCTOBER
S	M	T	W	T	F	S
			1	2	3	4
5	6	7	8	9	10	11
12	13	14	15	16	17	18
19	20	21	22	23	24	25
26	27	28	29	30	31	

NOVEMBER
S	M	T	W	T	F	S
						1
2	3	4	5	6	7	8
9	10	11	12	13	14	15
16	17	18	19	20	21	22
23	24	25	26	27	28	29
30						

DECEMBER
S	M	T	W	T	F	S
	1	2	3	4	5	6
7	8	9	10	11	12	13
14	15	16	17	18	19	20
21	22	23	24	25	26	27
28	29	30	31			

1 9 9 8

JANUARY
S	M	T	W	T	F	S
				1	2	3
4	5	6	7	8	9	10
11	12	13	14	15	16	17
18	19	20	21	22	23	24
25	26	27	28	29	30	31

FEBRUARY
S	M	T	W	T	F	S
1	2	3	4	5	6	7
8	9	10	11	12	13	14
15	16	17	18	19	20	21
22	23	24	25	26	27	28

MARCH
S	M	T	W	T	F	S
1	2	3	4	5	6	7
8	9	10	11	12	13	14
15	16	17	18	19	20	21
22	23	24	25	26	27	28
29	30	31				

APRIL
S	M	T	W	T	F	S
			1	2	3	4
5	6	7	8	9	10	11
12	13	14	15	16	17	18
19	20	21	22	23	24	25
26	27	28	29	30		

MAY
S	M	T	W	T	F	S
					1	2
3	4	5	6	7	8	9
10	11	12	13	14	15	16
17	18	19	20	21	22	23
24	25	26	27	28	29	30
31						

JUNE
S	M	T	W	T	F	S
	1	2	3	4	5	6
7	8	9	10	11	12	13
14	15	16	17	18	19	20
21	22	23	24	25	26	27
28	29	30				

JULY
S	M	T	W	T	F	S
			1	2	3	4
5	6	7	8	9	10	11
12	13	14	15	16	17	18
19	20	21	22	23	24	25
26	27	28	29	30	31	

AUGUST
S	M	T	W	T	F	S
						1
2	3	4	5	6	7	8
9	10	11	12	13	14	15
16	17	18	19	20	21	22
23	24	25	26	27	28	29
30	31					

SEPTEMBER
S	M	T	W	T	F	S
		1	2	3	4	5
6	7	8	9	10	11	12
13	14	15	16	17	18	19
20	21	22	23	24	25	26
27	28	29	30			

OCTOBER
S	M	T	W	T	F	S
				1	2	3
4	5	6	7	8	9	10
11	12	13	14	15	16	17
18	19	20	21	22	23	24
25	26	27	28	29	30	31

NOVEMBER
S	M	T	W	T	F	S
1	2	3	4	5	6	7
8	9	10	11	12	13	14
15	16	17	18	19	20	21
22	23	24	25	26	27	28
29	30					

DECEMBER
S	M	T	W	T	F	S
		1	2	3	4	5
6	7	8	9	10	11	12
13	14	15	16	17	18	19
20	21	22	23	24	25	26
27	28	29	30	31		

A Reference Compendium

compiled by Sarah Hale and Mare-Anne Jarvela

Is It Raining, Drizzling, or Misting?

	Drops (per sq. ft. per second)	Diameter of Drops (mm)	Intensity (in. per hr.)
Cloudburst	113	2.85	4.00
Excessive Rain	76	2.40	1.60
Heavy Rain	46	2.05	.60
Moderate Rain	46	1.60	.15
Light Rain	26	1.24	.04
Drizzle	14	.96	.01
Mist	2,510	.10	.002
Fog	6,264,000	.01	.005

A Table Foretelling the Weather Through All the Lunations of Each Year (Forever)

This table is the result of many years' actual observation and shows what sort of weather will probably follow the Moon's entrance into any of its quarters. For example, the weather for the week following May 22, 1997, would be rainy because the Moon becomes full that day at 4:13 A.M., EST. (See Left-Hand Calendar Pages 54-80 for Moon phases.)

Editor's note: *While the data in this table is taken into consideration in the yearlong process of compiling the annual long-range weather forecasts for* The Old Farmer's Almanac, *we rely far more on our projections of solar activity.*

Time of Change	Summer	Winter
Midnight to 2 A.M.	Fair	Hard frost, unless wind is south or west
2 A.M. to 4 A.M.	Cold, with frequent showers	Snow and stormy
4 A.M. to 6 A.M.	Rain	Rain
6 A.M. to 8 A.M.	Wind and rain	Stormy
8 A.M. to 10 A.M.	Changeable	Cold rain if wind is west; snow if east
10 A.M. to noon	Frequent showers	Cold with high winds
Noon to 2 P.M.	Very rainy	Snow or rain
2 P.M. to 4 P.M.	Changeable	Fair and mild
4 P.M. to 6 P.M.	Fair	Fair
6 P.M. to 10 P.M.	Fair if wind is northwest; rain if south or southwest	Fair and frosty if wind is north or northeast; rain or snow if wind is south or southwest
10 P.M. to midnight	Fair	Fair and frosty

This table was created more than 160 years ago by Dr. Herschell for the Boston Courier; *it first appeared in* The Old Farmer's Almanac *in 1834.*

Windchill Table

A s wind speed increases, the air temperature against your body falls. The combination of cold temperatures and high winds creates a cooling effect so severe that exposed flesh can freeze. (Inanimate objects, such as cars, do not experience windchill.)

To gauge wind speed: at 10 miles per hour you can feel wind on your face; at 20 small branches move, and dust or snow is raised; at 30 large branches move and wires whistle; at 40 whole trees bend. *– courtesy Mount Washington Observatory*

Wind Velocity (MPH)	Temperature (° F)												
	50	41	32	23	14	5	–4	–13	–22	–31	–40	–49	–58
	Equivalent Temperature (° F) (Equivalent in Cooling Power on Exposed Flesh under Calm Conditions)												
5	48	39	28	19	10	1	–9	–18	–27	–36	–51	–56	–65
10	41	30	18	7	–4	–15	–26	–36	–49	–60	–71	–81	–92
20	32	19	7	–6	–18	–31	–44	–58	–71	–83	–96	–108	–121
30	28	14	1	–13	–27	–40	–54	–69	–81	–96	–108	–123	–137
40	27	12	–2	–17	–31	–45	–60	–74	–89	–103	–116	–130	–144
50	25	10	–4	–18	–33	–47	–62	–76	–90	–105	–119	–134	–148
	Little Danger			Increasing Danger				Great Danger					
	Danger from Freezing of Exposed Flesh (for Properly Clothed Person)												

Heat Index

A s humidity increases, the air temperature feels hotter to your skin. The combination of hot temperature and high humidity reduces your body's ability to cool itself. For example, the heat you feel when the actual temperature is 90 degrees Fahrenheit with a relative humidity of 70 percent is 106 degrees.

Humidity (%)	Temperature (° F)										
	70	75	80	85	90	95	100	105	110	115	120
	Equivalent Temperature (° F)										
0	64	69	73	78	83	87	91	95	99	103	107
10	65	70	75	80	85	90	95	100	105	111	116
20	66	72	77	82	87	93	99	105	112	120	130
30	67	73	78	84	90	96	104	113	123	120	148
40	68	74	79	86	93	101	110	123	137	135	
50	69	75	81	88	96	107	120	135	150		
60	70	76	82	90	100	114	132	149			
70	70	77	85	93	106	124	144				
80	71	78	86	97	113	136					
90	71	79	88	102	122						
100	72	80	91	108							

Average Monthly Temperatures for Selected U.S. Cities

Daily maximum (**bold numbers**) and minimum averages in degrees Fahrenheit

	JAN.	FEB.	MAR.	APR.	MAY	JUNE	JULY	AUG.	SEPT.	OCT.	NOV.	DEC.
Mobile,	**59.7**	**63.6**	**70.9**	**78.5**	**84.6**	**90.0**	**91.3**	**90.5**	**86.9**	**79.5**	**70.3**	**62.9**
Alabama	40.0	42.7	50.1	57.1	64.4	70.7	73.2	72.9	68.7	57.3	49.1	43.1
Anchorage,	**21.4**	**25.8**	**33.1**	**42.8**	**54.4**	**61.6**	**65.2**	**63.0**	**55.2**	**40.5**	**27.2**	**22.5**
Alaska	8.4	11.5	18.1	28.6	38.8	47.2	51.7	49.5	41.6	28.7	15.1	10.0
Phoenix,	**65.9**	**70.7**	**75.5**	**84.5**	**93.6**	**103.5**	**105.9**	**103.7**	**98.3**	**88.1**	**74.9**	**66.2**
Arizona	41.2	44.7	48.8	55.3	63.9	72.9	81.0	79.2	72.8	60.8	48.9	41.8
Little Rock,	**49.0**	**53.9**	**64.0**	**73.4**	**81.3**	**89.3**	**92.4**	**91.4**	**84.6**	**75.1**	**62.7**	**52.5**
Arkansas	29.1	33.2	42.2	50.7	59.0	67.4	71.5	69.8	63.5	50.9	41.5	33.1
San Francisco,	**55.6**	**59.4**	**60.8**	**63.9**	**66.5**	**70.3**	**71.6**	**72.3**	**73.6**	**70.1**	**62.4**	**56.1**
California	41.8	45.0	45.8	47.2	49.7	52.6	53.9	55.0	55.2	51.8	47.1	42.7
Denver,	**43.2**	**46.6**	**52.2**	**61.8**	**70.8**	**81.4**	**88.2**	**85.8**	**76.9**	**66.3**	**52.5**	**44.5**
Colorado	16.1	20.2	25.8	34.5	43.6	52.4	58.6	56.9	47.6	36.4	25.4	17.4
Hartford,	**33.2**	**36.4**	**46.8**	**59.9**	**71.6**	**80.0**	**85.0**	**82.7**	**74.8**	**63.7**	**51.0**	**37.5**
Connecticut	15.8	18.6	28.1	37.5	47.6	56.9	62.2	60.4	51.8	40.7	32.8	21.3
Washington,	**42.3**	**45.9**	**56.5**	**66.7**	**76.2**	**84.7**	**88.5**	**86.9**	**80.1**	**69.1**	**58.3**	**47.0**
D.C.	26.8	29.1	37.7	46.4	56.6	66.5	71.4	70.0	62.5	50.3	41.1	31.7
Miami,	**75.2**	**76.5**	**79.1**	**82.4**	**85.3**	**87.6**	**89.0**	**89.0**	**87.8**	**84.5**	**80.4**	**76.7**
Florida	59.2	60.4	64.2	67.8	72.1	75.1	76.2	76.7	75.9	72.1	66.7	61.5
Atlanta,	**50.4**	**55.0**	**64.3**	**72.7**	**79.6**	**85.8**	**88.0**	**87.1**	**81.8**	**72.7**	**63.4**	**54.0**
Georgia	31.5	34.5	42.5	50.2	58.7	66.2	69.5	69.0	63.5	51.9	42.8	35.0
Honolulu,	**80.1**	**80.5**	**81.6**	**82.8**	**84.7**	**86.5**	**87.5**	**88.7**	**88.5**	**86.9**	**84.1**	**81.2**
Hawaii	65.6	65.4	67.2	68.7	70.3	72.2	73.5	74.2	73.5	72.3	70.3	67.0
Boise,	**36.4**	**44.2**	**52.9**	**61.4**	**71.0**	**80.9**	**90.2**	**88.1**	**77.0**	**64.6**	**48.7**	**37.7**
Idaho	21.6	27.5	31.9	36.7	43.9	52.1	57.7	56.7	48.2	39.0	31.1	22.5
Chicago,	**29.0**	**33.5**	**45.8**	**58.6**	**70.1**	**79.6**	**83.7**	**81.8**	**74.8**	**63.3**	**48.4**	**34.0**
Illinois	12.9	17.2	28.5	38.6	47.7	57.5	62.6	61.6	53.9	42.2	31.6	19.1
Indianapolis,	**33.9**	**38.2**	**50.0**	**62.4**	**73.2**	**82.3**	**85.6**	**83.8**	**78.0**	**65.8**	**52.2**	**39.2**
Indiana	17.2	20.3	30.9	41.2	51.6	61.1	65.4	62.9	55.8	43.4	34.4	23.1
Des Moines,	**28.1**	**33.7**	**46.9**	**61.8**	**73.0**	**82.2**	**86.7**	**84.2**	**75.6**	**64.3**	**48.0**	**32.6**
Iowa	10.7	15.6	27.6	40.0	51.5	61.2	66.5	63.6	54.5	42.7	29.9	16.1
Wichita,	**39.8**	**45.9**	**57.2**	**68.3**	**76.9**	**86.8**	**92.8**	**90.7**	**81.4**	**70.6**	**55.3**	**43.0**
Kansas	19.2	23.7	33.6	44.5	54.3	64.6	69.9	67.9	81.4	46.6	33.9	23.0
Louisville,	**40.3**	**44.8**	**56.3**	**67.3**	**76.0**	**83.5**	**87.0**	**85.7**	**80.3**	**69.2**	**56.8**	**45.1**
Kentucky	23.2	26.5	36.2	45.4	54.7	62.9	67.3	65.8	58.7	45.8	37.3	28.6
New Orleans,	**61.3**	**64.5**	**71.8**	**78.7**	**84.5**	**89.4**	**90.8**	**90.5**	**87.1**	**80.0**	**71.5**	**64.8**
Louisiana	44.1	47.1	54.2	60.9	67.5	73.0	74.9	74.8	71.7	61.8	54.1	47.6
Portland,	**30.3**	**33.1**	**41.4**	**52.3**	**63.2**	**72.7**	**78.8**	**77.4**	**69.3**	**58.7**	**47.0**	**35.1**
Maine	11.4	13.5	24.5	34.1	43.4	52.1	58.3	57.1	48.9	38.3	30.4	17.8
Boston,	**35.7**	**37.5**	**45.8**	**55.9**	**66.6**	**76.3**	**81.8**	**79.8**	**72.8**	**62.7**	**52.2**	**40.4**
Massachusetts	21.6	23.0	31.3	40.2	49.8	59.1	65.1	64.0	56.8	46.9	38.3	26.7
Detroit,	**30.3**	**33.3**	**44.4**	**57.7**	**69.6**	**78.9**	**83.3**	**81.3**	**73.9**	**61.5**	**48.1**	**35.2**
Michigan	15.6	17.6	27.0	36.8	47.1	56.3	61.3	59.6	52.5	40.9	32.2	21.4
Minneapolis-	**20.7**	**26.6**	**39.2**	**56.5**	**69.4**	**78.8**	**84.0**	**80.7**	**70.7**	**58.8**	**41.0**	**25.5**
St. Paul, Minnesota	2.8	9.2	22.7	36.2	47.6	57.6	63.1	60.3	50.3	38.8	25.2	10.2

	JAN.	FEB.	MAR.	APR.	MAY	JUNE	JULY	AUG.	SEPT.	OCT.	NOV.	DEC.
Jackson,	55.6	60.1	69.3	77.4	84.0	90.6	92.4	92.0	88.0	79.1	69.2	59.5
Mississippi	32.7	35.7	44.1	51.9	60.0	67.1	70.5	69.7	63.7	50.3	42.3	36.1
St. Louis,	37.7	42.6	54.6	66.9	76.1	85.2	89.3	87.3	79.9	68.5	54.7	41.7
Missouri	20.8	25.1	35.5	46.4	56.0	65.7	70.4	69.7	60.5	48.3	37.7	26.0
Butte,	28.5	33.9	39.9	50.4	60.3	70.2	80.1	78.4	66.4	55.5	39.3	29.4
Montana	5.0	10.0	16.7	25.9	34.0	41.7	45.7	44.0	35.1	26.4	16.0	5.5
Omaha,	29.7	35.0	47.6	62.4	72.8	82.4	86.5	84.0	74.9	64.0	47.7	32.9
Nebraska	11.2	16.6	27.8	40.3	51.8	61.4	66.5	63.8	54.7	43.0	29.7	15.9
Reno,	45.1	51.7	56.3	63.7	72.9	83.1	91.9	89.6	79.5	68.6	53.8	45.5
Nevada	20.7	24.2	29.2	33.3	40.1	46.9	51.3	49.6	41.3	32.9	26.7	19.9
Albuquerque,	46.8	53.5	61.4	70.8	79.7	90.0	92.5	89.0	81.9	71.0	57.3	47.5
New Mexico	21.7	26.4	32.2	39.6	48.6	58.3	64.4	62.6	55.2	43.0	31.2	23.1
Buffalo,	30.2	31.6	41.7	54.2	66.1	75.3	80.2	77.9	70.8	59.4	47.1	35.3
New York	17.0	17.4	25.9	36.2	47.0	56.5	61.9	60.1	53.0	42.7	33.9	22.9
Charlotte,	49.0	53.0	62.3	71.2	78.3	85.8	88.9	87.7	81.9	72.0	62.6	52.3
North Carolina	29.6	31.9	39.4	47.5	56.4	65.6	69.6	68.9	62.9	50.6	41.5	32.8
Bismarck,	20.2	26.4	38.5	54.9	67.8	77.1	84.4	82.7	70.8	58.7	39.3	24.5
North Dakota	-1.7	5.1	17.8	31.0	42.2	51.6	56.4	53.9	43.1	32.5	17.8	3.3
Columbus,	34.1	38.0	50.5	62.0	72.3	80.4	83.7	82.1	76.2	64.5	51.4	39.2
Ohio	18.5	21.2	31.2	40.0	50.1	58.0	62.7	60.8	54.8	42.9	34.3	24.6
Tulsa,	45.4	51.0	62.1	73.0	79.7	87.7	93.7	92.5	83.6	73.8	60.3	48.8
Oklahoma	24.9	29.5	39.1	49.9	58.8	67.7	72.8	70.6	63.0	50.7	39.5	28.9
Portland,	45.4	51.0	56.0	60.6	67.1	74.0	79.9	80.3	74.6	64.0	52.6	45.6
Oregon	33.7	36.1	38.6	41.3	47.0	52.9	56.5	56.9	52.0	44.9	39.5	34.8
Philadelphia,	37.9	41.0	51.6	62.6	73.1	81.7	86.1	84.6	77.6	66.3	55.1	43.4
Pennsylvania	22.8	24.8	33.2	42.1	52.7	61.8	67.2	66.3	58.7	46.4	37.6	28.1
Charleston,	57.8	61.0	68.6	75.8	82.7	87.6	90.2	89.0	84.9	77.2	69.5	61.6
South Carolina	37.7	40.0	47.5	53.9	62.9	69.1	72.7	72.2	67.9	56.3	47.2	40.7
Huron,	24.1	29.7	42.1	58.6	70.4	80.3	87.1	84.8	74.2	61.5	43.0	28.3
South Dakota	2.3	9.1	21.7	34.0	44.8	55.5	61.7	58.8	47.3	35.4	21.8	7.8
Nashville,	45.9	50.8	61.2	70.8	78.8	86.5	89.5	88.4	82.5	72.5	60.4	50.2
Tennessee	26.5	29.9	39.1	47.5	56.6	64.7	68.9	67.7	61.1	48.3	39.6	30.9
Houston,	61.0	65.3	71.1	78.4	84.6	90.1	92.7	92.5	88.4	81.6	72.4	64.7
Texas	39.7	42.6	50.0	58.1	64.4	70.6	72.4	72.0	67.9	57.6	49.6	42.2
Salt Lake City,	36.4	43.6	52.2	61.3	71.9	82.8	92.2	89.4	79.2	66.1	50.8	37.8
Utah	19.3	24.6	31.4	37.9	45.6	55.4	63.7	61.8	51.0	40.2	30.9	21.6
Burlington,	25.1	27.5	39.3	53.6	67.2	75.8	81.2	77.9	69.0	57.0	44.0	30.4
Vermont	7.5	8.9	22.0	34.2	45.4	54.6	59.7	57.9	48.8	38.6	29.6	15.5
Richmond,	45.7	49.2	59.5	70.0	77.8	85.1	88.4	87.1	80.9	70.7	61.3	50.2
Virginia	25.7	28.1	36.3	44.6	54.2	62.7	67.5	66.4	59.0	46.5	37.9	29.9
Seattle-Tacoma,	45.0	49.5	52.7	57.2	63.9	69.9	75.2	75.2	69.3	59.7	50.5	45.1
Washington	35.2	37.4	38.5	41.2	46.3	51.9	55.2	55.7	51.9	45.8	40.1	35.8
Charleston,	41.2	45.3	56.7	66.8	75.5	83.1	85.7	84.4	78.8	68.2	57.3	46.0
West Virginia	23.0	25.7	35.0	42.8	51.5	59.8	64.4	63.4	56.5	44.2	36.3	28.0
Madison,	24.8	30.1	41.5	56.7	68.9	78.2	82.4	79.6	71.5	59.9	44.0	29.8
Wisconsin	7.2	11.1	23.0	34.1	44.2	54.2	59.5	56.9	48.2	37.7	26.7	13.5
Cheyenne,	37.7	40.5	44.9	54.7	64.6	74.4	82.2	80.0	71.1	60.0	46.8	38.8
Wyoming	15.2	18.1	22.1	30.1	39.4	48.3	54.6	52.8	43.7	33.9	23.7	16.7

(courtesy Dr. Richard Head and National Climatic Data Center)

Winter Weather Terms

Winter Storm Watch
■ Possibility of a winter storm. Be alert to changing weather conditions. Unnecessary travel should be avoided.

Winter Storm Warning
■ A severe winter storm has started or is about to begin in the forecast area. You should stay indoors during the storm. If you must go outdoors, wear several layers of lightweight clothing, which will keep you warmer than a single heavy coat. In addition, wearing gloves or mittens and a hat will prevent loss of body heat. Cover your mouth to protect your lungs.

Heavy Snow Warning
■ Snow accumulations are expected to approach or exceed 6 inches in 12 hours but will not be accompanied by significant wind. This warning could also be issued if 8 inches or more of accumulation are expected in a 24-hour period.

Also during a heavy snow warning, freezing rain and sleet are not expected.

Blizzard Warning
■ Sustained winds or frequent gusts of 35 miles per hour or greater will occur in combination with considerable falling and/or blowing snow for a period of at least 3 hours. Visibility will often be reduced to less than ¼ mile in a blizzard.

Ice Storm Warning
■ A significant coating of ice, ½ inch thick or more, is expected.

Windchill Warning
■ Windchills reach life-threatening levels of minus 50 degrees Fahrenheit or lower.

Windchill Advisory
■ Windchill factors fall between minus 35 and minus 50 degrees Fahrenheit.

Beaufort's Scale of Wind Speeds

"Used Mostly at Sea but of Help to all who are interested in the Weather"

A scale of wind velocity was devised by Admiral Sir Francis Beaufort of the British Navy in 1806. The numbers 0 to 12 were arranged by Beaufort to indicate the strength of the wind from a calm, force 0, to a hurricane, force 12. This adaptation of Beaufort's scale is used by the U.S. National Weather Service.

Force	Description	Statute Miles per Hour
0	Calm	less than 1
1	Light air	1 to 3
2	Light breeze	4 to 7
3	Gentle breeze	8 to 12
4	Moderate breeze	13 to 18
5	Fresh breeze	19 to 24
6	Strong breeze	25 to 31
7	Moderate gale	32 to 38
8	Fresh gale	39 to 46
9	Strong gale	47 to 54
10	Whole gale	55 to 63
11	Storm	64 to 72
12	Hurricane	73 or more

1997 Atlantic and Caribbean Hurricane Names

Ana	Erika	Juan	Nicholas	Teresa
Bill	Fabian	Kate	Odette	Victor
Claudette	Grace	Larry	Peter	Wanda
Danny	Henri	Mindy	Rose	
	Isabel		Sam	

Temperature Conversion Formulas

Fahrenheit to Celsius

To convert temperatures in degrees Fahrenheit to Celsius, subtract 32 and multiply by .5556 (or 5/9).

Example: (50° F - 32) x .5556 = 10° C

Celsius to Fahrenheit

To convert temperatures in degrees Celsius to Fahrenheit, multiply by 1.8 (or 9/5) and add 32.

Example: 30° C x 1.8 + 32 = 86° F

Cricket Chirps to Temperature

To convert cricket chirps to degrees Fahrenheit, count number of chirps in 14 seconds then add 40 to get temperature.

Example: 30 chirps + 40 = 70° F

To convert cricket chirps to degrees Celsius, count number of chirps in 25 seconds, divide by 3, then add 4 to get temperature.

Example: 48 chirps ÷ 3 + 4 = 20° C

A Defining Moment

Sleet: frozen or partially frozen rain in the form of ice pellets that hit the ground so fast they bounce off with a sharp click.

Freezing rain: rain that falls as a liquid but turns to ice on contact with a frozen surface to form a smooth ice coating called glaze.

1" Water = How Much Snow?

	Water	Average snow	Heavy, wet snow	Dry, powdery snow
Inches	1	10	4-5	15
Centimeters	2.5	25	10-13	38

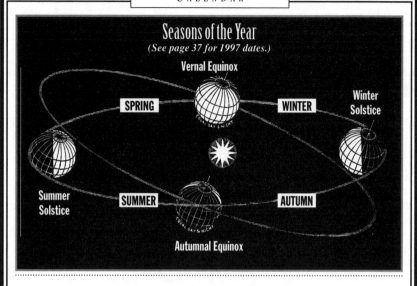

Seasons of the Year
(See page 37 for 1997 dates.)

Vernal Equinox

SPRING   WINTER   Winter Solstice

Summer Solstice

SUMMER   AUTUMN

Autumnal Equinox

☞ Glossary of Almanac Oddities

Many readers have expressed puzzlement over the rather obscure notations that appear on our Right-Hand Calendar Pages (pages 55-81). These "oddities" have long been fixtures in the Almanac, and we are pleased to provide some definitions. (Once explained, it would seem that they are not so odd after all!)

■ Ember Days (Movable)

The four periods set apart by the Roman Catholic and Anglican churches for special prayer and fasting and the ordination of clergy. The Ember Weeks are the complete weeks following 1) the First Sunday in Lent; 2) Pentecost (Whitsunday); 3) the Feast of the Holy Cross (September 14); and 4) the Feast of St. Lucy (December 13). The Wednesdays, Fridays, and Saturdays of these weeks are the Ember Days — days marked for fasting. (The word *ember* is thought to derive from an Old English term that refers to the revolution of time.)

Folklore has it that the weather on each of the three days foretells weather for three successive months — that is, in September Ember Days, Wednesday forecasts weather for October, Friday for November, and Saturday for December.

■ Plough Monday (January)

The first Monday after the Epiphany (January 6); so called because it was the end of the Christmas holidays when men returned to their plough — or daily work. It was customary for farm laborers to draw a plough through the village, soliciting money for a "plough-light," which was kept burning in the parish church all year. In some areas, the custom of blessing the plough is maintained.

■ Three Chilly Saints (May)

Pancratius, Mammertius, and Gervatius, three early Christian saints, whose feast days occur on May 11, 12, and 13, respectively. Because these days are traditionally cold (an old French saying goes: "St. Mammertius, St. Pancras, and St. Gervais do not pass without a frost"), they have come to be known as the Three Chilly Saints.

■ **Midsummer Day (June 24)**

While it occurs near the summer solstice, to the farmer it is the midpoint of the growing season, halfway between planting and harvest, and an occasion for festivity. The English church considered it a "Quarter Day," one of the four major divisions of the liturgical year. It also marks the feast day of St. John the Baptist.

■ **Cornscateous Air (July)**

A term first used by the old almanac makers signifying warm, damp air. While it signals ideal climatic conditions for growing corn, it also poses a danger to those affected by asthma, pneumonia, and other respiratory problems.

■ **Dog Days (July-August)**

The hottest and most unhealthy days of the year. Also known as "Canicular Days," the name derives from the Dog Star, Sirius. The Almanac lists the traditional timing of Dog Days: The 40 days beginning July 3 and ending August 11, coinciding with the heliacal (at sunrise) rising of Sirius.

■ **Cat Nights Begin (August)**

The term harks back to the days when people believed in witches. An old Irish legend has it that a witch could turn herself into a cat eight times and then regain herself, but on the ninth time — August 17 — she couldn't change back.

Hence the saying, "A cat has nine lives." Since August is a "yowly" time for cats, this may have prompted the speculation about witches on the prowl in the first place.

■ **Harvest Home (September)**

In both Europe and Britain, the conclusion of the harvest each autumn was once marked by great festivals of fun, feasting, and thanksgiving known as "Harvest Home." It was also a time to hold elections, pay workers, and collect rents. These festivals usually took place around the time of the autumnal equinox. Certain ethnic groups in this country, particularly the Pennsylvania Dutch, have kept the tradition alive.

■ **St. Luke's Little Summer (October)**

A spell of warm weather occurring about the time of the saint's feast day, October 18. This period is sometimes referred to as "Indian Summer."

■ **Indian Summer (November)**

A period of warm weather following a cold spell or a hard frost. While there are differing dates for the time of occurrence, for 205 years the Almanac has adhered to the saying, "If All Saints brings out winter, St. Martin's brings out Indian Summer." Accordingly, Indian Summer can occur between St. Martin's Day, November 11, and November 20. As for the origin of the term, some say it comes from the early Indians who believed the condition was caused by a warm wind sent from the court of their southwestern God, Cautantowwit.

■ **Halcyon Days (December)**

A period (about 14 days) of calm weather, following the blustery winds of autumn's end. The ancient Greeks and Romans believed them to occur around the time of the winter solstice when the halcyon, or kingfisher, was brooding. In a nest floating on the sea, the bird was said to have charmed the wind and waves so the waters were especially calm during this period.

■ **Beware the Pogonip (December)**

The word *pogonip* is a meteorological term used to describe an uncommon occurrence — frozen fog. The word was coined by American Indians to describe the frozen fogs of fine ice needles that occur in the mountain valleys of the western United States. According to Indian tradition, breathing the fog is injurious to the lungs.

Month Names

JANUARY	Named for the Roman god Janus, protector of gates and doorways. Janus is depicted with two faces, one looking into the past, the other into the future.
FEBRUARY	From the Latin word *februare*, to cleanse. The Roman Februalia was a month of purification and atonement.
MARCH	Named for the Roman god of war, Mars. This was the time of year to resume military campaigns that had been interrupted by winter.
APRIL	From the Latin word *aperire*, to open (bud), because plants begin to grow in this month.
MAY	Named for the Roman goddess Maia, who oversaw the growth of plants. Also from the Latin word *maiores*, meaning elders, who were celebrated during this month.
JUNE	Named for the Roman goddess Juno, patroness of marriage and the well-being of women. Also from the Latin word *juvenis*, young people.
JULY	Named to honor Roman dictator Julius Caesar (100 B.C.- 44 B.C.). In 63 B.C. Julius Caesar made one of his greatest contributions to history: With the help of Sosigenes he developed the Julian calendar, the precursor to the Gregorian calendar we use today.
AUGUST	Named to honor the first Roman emperor (and grand-nephew of Julius Caesar), Augustus Caesar (63 B.C. - 14 B.C.)
SEPTEMBER	From the Latin word *septem*, seven, because this had been the seventh month of the early Roman calendar.
OCTOBER	From the Latin word *octo*, eight, because this had been the eighth month of the early Roman calendar.
NOVEMBER	From the Latin word *novem*, nine, because this had been the ninth month of the early Roman calendar.
DECEMBER	From the Latin word *decem*, ten, because this had been the tenth month of the early Roman calendar.

Phases of the Moon

NEW   FIRST   FULL   LAST   NEW

W a x i n g ⟶ | ⟶ W a n i n g ⟶

Full Moon Names

Historically the Indians of what are now the northern and eastern United States kept track of the seasons by giving a distinctive name to each recurring full Moon, this name being applied to the entire month in which it occurred. With some variations, the same Moon names were used throughout the Algonquin tribes from New England to Lake Superior.

Name	Month	Other Names Used
Full Wolf Moon	**January**	Full Old Moon
Full Snow Moon	**February**	Full Hunger Moon
Full Worm Moon	**March**	Full Crow Moon, Full Crust Moon, Full Sugar Moon, Full Sap Moon
Full Pink Moon	**April**	Full Sprouting Grass Moon, Full Egg Moon, Full Fish Moon
Full Flower Moon	**May**	Full Corn Planting Moon, Full Milk Moon
Full Strawberry Moon	**June**	Full Rose Moon, Full Hot Moon
Full Buck Moon	**July**	Full Thunder Moon, Full Hay Moon
Full Sturgeon Moon	**August**	Full Red Moon, Full Green Corn Moon
Full Harvest Moon*	**September**	Full Corn Moon
Full Hunter's Moon	**October**	Full Travel Moon, Full Dying Grass Moon
Full Beaver Moon	**November**	Full Frost Moon
Full Cold Moon	**December**	Full Long Nights Moon

* The Harvest Moon is always the full Moon closest to the autumnal equinox. If the Harvest Moon occurs in October, the September full Moon is usually called the Corn Moon.

How to Find the Day of the Week for Any Given Date

To compute the day of the week for any given date as far back as the mid-18th century, proceed as follows:

Add the last two digits of the year to one-quarter of the last two digits (discard any remainder if it doesn't come out even), the given date, and the month key from the key-box below. Divide the sum by seven; the number left over is the day of the week (one is Sunday, two is Monday, and so on). If it comes out even, the day is Saturday. If you go back before 1900, add two to the sum before dividing; before 1800, add four. Don't go back before 1753. From 2000 to 2099, subtract one from the sum before dividing.

Example: **The Dayton Flood was on Tuesday, March 25, 1913.**

Last two digits of year:	....	13
One-quarter of these two digits:	....	3
Given day of month:	....	25
Key number for March:	....	4
	Sum:	45

45/7=6, with a remainder of 3. The flood took place on Tuesday, the third day of the week.

	KEY
January	1
leap year	0
February	4
leap year	3
March	4
April	0
May	2
June	5
July	0
August	3
September	6
October	1
November	4
December	6

Dining by the Calendar: Traditional Foods for Feasts and Fasts

JANUARY

Feast of the Circumcision: Black-eyed peas and pork (United States); oat-husk gruel or oatmeal porridge (Scotland).

Epiphany: Cake with a lucky bean baked in it; the one who finds the bean is the king or queen of the feast, in memory of the three wise men (France).

Robert Burns Day: Haggis — sheep's stomach stuffed with suet, chopped organ meat (heart, lungs, liver), onions, oatmeal, and seasonings (Scotland). Haggis is a traditional Scottish delicacy served on all holidays of national importance.

FEBRUARY

Candlemas Day: Pancakes eaten today will prevent hemorrhoids for a full year (French American).

St. Agatha: Round loaves of bread blessed by a priest (southern Europe).

Shrove Tuesday: Pancakes (England); oatcakes (Scotland); rabbit (Ireland). Rich foods are eaten to usher in the Lenten fast; pancakes use up the last of the eggs and butter.

Lent: Simnel, a large fruitcake baked so hard it has sometimes been mistaken by recipients for a hassock or footstool (Great Britain).

MARCH

St. David: Leeks, to be worn (Wales) or eaten raw (England). Recalls a Welsh victory over the Saxons in A.D. 640; the Welsh wore leeks in their hats to distinguish them from the enemy.

St. Benedict: Nettle soup (ancient monastic practice). Picking nettles, which irritate the skin, was a penance in keeping with the spirit of the monastic rule of St. Benedict.

Purim: Strong drink and three-cornered cookies flavored with poppy seed (Jewish). These cookies, called hamantaschen, are said to represent the three-cornered hat of Haman,

the enemy of the Jewish people, whose downfall is celebrated on this holiday.

Maundy Thursday: Green foods or foods colored green (southern Europe). The medieval liturgical observance called for green vestments; in some parts of Europe, it is still called Green Thursday.

Good Friday: Hot cross buns. If made properly on this day, they will never get moldy (England).

APRIL

Easter: Lamb as symbol of sacrifice; ham.

Beltane, May Day Eve: Strong ale (England); oatcakes with nine knobs to be broken off one by one and offered to each of nine supernatural protectors of domestic animals (Scotland).

MAY

Ascension Day: Fowl, or pastries molded in the shape of birds, to commemorate the taking of Jesus into the skies (medieval Europe).

Whitsunday (Pentecost): Dove or pigeon in honor of the Holy Spirit (southern Europe); strong ale (England).

St. Dunstan: Beer. Cider pressed today will go bad (England).

Corpus Christi: Orange peel dipped in chocolate, chicken stuffed with sauerkraut (Basque Provinces).

JUNE

St. Anthony of Padua: Liver, possibly based on pre-Christian custom of eating liver on the summer solstice.

Feast of St. John the Baptist: First fruits of spring harvest eaten.

JULY

St. Swithin: Eggs, because the saint miraculously restored intact a basket of eggs that had been broken by a poor woman taking them to market; he also looks after apples (medieval England).

St. James: Oysters, because James was a fisherman (England).

AUGUST

Lammas Day: Oatcakes (Scotland); loaves made from new grain of the season (England); toffee; seaweed pudding. Blueberries in baskets as an offering to a sweetheart are the last vestige of this holiday as a pagan fertility festival (Ireland).

St. Lawrence of Rome: Because the saint was roasted to death on a gridiron, it is courteous to serve only cold meat today (southern Europe).

Feast of the Assumption: Onions, possibly because they have always been considered wholesome and potent against evil (Polish American).

SEPTEMBER

St. Giles: Tea loaf with raisins (Scotland).

Nativity of Mary: Blackberries, possibly because the color is reminiscent of depiction of the Virgin's blue cloak (Brittany).

Michaelmas Day: New wine (Europe); goose, originally a sacrifice to the saint (Great Britain); cake of oats, barley, and rye (Scotland); carrots (Ireland).

OCTOBER

Rosh Hashanah: Sweet foods; honey; foods colored orange or yellow to represent a bright, joyous, and sweet new year (Jewish).

Yom Kippur: Fast day; the day before, eat kreplach (filled noodles), considered by generations of mothers to be good and filling (Jewish).

St. Luke: Oatcakes flavored with anise and cinnamon (Scotland).

Sts. Simon and Jude: Dirge cakes, simple fried buns made for distribution to the poor. Also apples or potatoes, for divination (Scotland and England). Divination with apples is accomplished by peeling the fruit in one long strip and tossing the peel over one's shoulder. The letter formed by the peel is then interpreted.

All Hallows Eve: Apples and nuts for divination (England); buttered oat-husk gruel (Scotland); bosty, a mixture of potatoes, cabbage, and onions (Ireland).

NOVEMBER

All Saints Day: Chestnuts (Italy); gingerbread and oatcakes (Scotland); milk (central Europe); doughnuts, whose round shape indicates eternity (Tyrol).

All Souls Day: Skull-shaped candy (Mexico); beans, peas, and lentils, considered food of the poor, as penance for souls in purgatory (southern Europe).

St. Martin: Last religious feast day before the beginning of the Advent fast. Goose, last of fresh-killed meat before winter; blood pudding (Great Britain).

St. Andrew: Haggis — stuffed sheep's stomach (Scotland).

DECEMBER

St. Nicholas: Fruit, nuts, candy for children (Germany). Commemorates, in part, the miracle by which the saint restored to life three young boys who had been murdered by a greedy innkeeper.

St. Lucy: Headcheese; cakes flavored with saffron or cardamom, raisins, and almonds (Sweden). The saffron imparts a yellow color to the cakes, representing sunlight, whose return is celebrated at the solstice.

Christmas: Boar's head or goose, plum pudding, nuts, oranges (England); turkey (United States); spiced beef (Ireland).

St. John the Evangelist: Small loaves of bread made with blessed wine (medieval Europe). This is a feast on which wine is ritually blessed in memory of the saint, who drank poisoned wine and miraculously survived.

Chanukah: Latkes — potato pancakes (Jewish).

Holy Innocents Day: Baby food, pablum, Cream of Wheat, in honor of the children killed by King Herod of Judea (monastic observance).

St. Sylvester: Strong drink (United States); haggis, oatcakes and cheese, oat-husk gruel or porridge (Scotland). — *E. Brady*

Day Names

The Romans named the days of the week after the Sun, the Moon, and the five known planets. These names have survived in European languages, but English names also reflect an Anglo-Saxon influence.

Latin	French	Italian	Spanish	Saxon	English
Solis (Sun)	dimanche	domenica	domingo	Sun	Sunday
Lunae (Moon)	lundi	lunedì	lunes	Moon	Monday
Martis (Mars)	mardi	martedì	martes	Tiw (the Anglo-Saxon god of war, equivalent to the Norse Tyr or the Roman Mars)	Tuesday
Mercurii (Mercury)	mercredi	mercoledì	miércoles	Woden (the Anglo-Saxon equivalent to the Norse Odin, or the Roman Mercury)	Wednesday
Jovis (Jupiter)	jeudi	giovedì	jueves	Thor (the Norse god of thunder, equivalent to the Roman Jupiter)	Thursday
Veneris (Venus)	vendredi	venerdì	viernes	Frigg (the Norse god of love and fertility, the equivalent of the Roman Venus)	Friday
Saturni (Saturn)	samedi	sabato	sábado	Saterne (Saturn, the Roman god of agriculture)	Saturday

Easter Sunday (1997-2001)

Christian churches that follow the Gregorian calendar (Eastern Orthodox churches follow the Julian calendar) celebrate Easter on the first Sunday after the full Moon that occurs on or just after the vernal equinox.

In ...	Easter will fall on ...
1997	March 30
1998	April 12
1999	April 4
2000	April 23
2001	April 15

Chinese Zodiac

The animal designations of the Chinese zodiac follow a 12-year cycle and are always used in the same sequence. The Chinese year of 354 days begins three to seven weeks into the western 365-day year, so the animal designation changes at that time, rather than on January 1.

RAT

Ambitious and sincere, you can be generous with your financial resources. Compatible with the dragon and the monkey. Your opposite is the horse.

1900	1960
1912	1972
1924	1984
1936	1996
1948	2008

RABBIT (HARE)

Talented and affectionate, you are a seeker of tranquility. Compatible with the sheep and the pig. Your opposite is the rooster.

1903	1963
1915	1975
1927	1987
1939	1999
1951	2011

HORSE

Physically attractive and popular, you like the company of others. Compatible with the tiger and the dog. Your opposite is the rat.

1906	1966
1918	1978
1930	1990
1942	2002
1954	2014

ROOSTER (COCK)

Seeking wisdom and truth, you have a pioneering spirit. Compatible with the snake and the ox. Your opposite is the rabbit.

1909	1969
1921	1981
1933	1993
1945	2005
1957	2017

OX (BUFFALO)

A leader, you are bright and cheerful. Compatible with the snake and the rooster. Your opposite is the sheep.

1901	1961
1913	1973
1925	1985
1937	1997
1949	2009

DRAGON

Robust and passionate, your life is filled with complexity. Compatible with the monkey and the rat. Your opposite is the dog.

1904	1964
1916	1976
1928	1988
1940	2000
1952	2012

SHEEP (GOAT)

Aesthetic and stylish, you enjoy being a private person. Compatible with the pig and the rabbit. Your opposite is the ox.

1907	1967
1919	1979
1931	1991
1943	2003
1955	2015

DOG

Generous and loyal, you have the ability to work well with others. Compatible with the horse and the tiger. Your opposite is the dragon.

1910	1970
1922	1982
1934	1994
1946	2006
1958	2018

TIGER

Forthright and sensitive, you possess great courage. Compatible with the horse and the dog. Your opposite is the monkey.

1902	1962
1914	1974
1926	1986
1938	1998
1950	2010

SNAKE

Strong-willed and intense, you display great wisdom. Compatible with the rooster and the ox. Your opposite is the pig.

1905	1965
1917	1977
1929	1989
1941	2001
1953	2013

MONKEY

Persuasive and intelligent, you strive to excel. Compatible with the dragon and the rat. Your opposite is the tiger.

1908	1968
1920	1980
1932	1992
1944	2004
1956	2016

PIG (BOAR)

Gallant and noble, your friends will remain at your side. Compatible with the rabbit and the sheep. Your opposite is the snake.

1911	1971
1923	1983
1935	1995
1947	2007
1959	2019

Planning Your Garden

Sow or plant in cool weather	Beets/chard, cabbage, broccoli, brussels sprouts, lettuce, onions, parsley, peas, radishes, spinach, turnips
Sow or plant in warm weather	Beans, carrots, corn, cucumbers, eggplant, peppers, squash tomatoes, melons, okra
One crop per season	Corn, eggplant, melons, leeks, peppers, tomatoes, summer squash, winter squash, New Zealand spinach, potatoes
Resow for additional crops	Beans, beets, carrots, cabbage family, kohlrabi, lettuce, radishes, rutabagas, spinach, turnips

Herb Companions in Garden and Kitchen

Herbs are great companions to food in your culinary masterpieces, and they are great companions in the garden, too.

Anise

In the garden: Plant with coriander, which promotes its germination and growth.

In the kitchen: Use in cookies, cakes, fruit fillings, and breads, or with cottage cheese, shellfish, and spaghetti dishes.

Basil

In the garden: Plant with tomatoes. Repels flies and mosquitoes.

In the kitchen: Use in tomato dishes, pesto, sauces, and salad dressings.

Borage

In the garden: Plant with tomatoes, squash, and strawberries. Deters tomato worm.

In the kitchen: Use leaves in salads; flowers in soups and stews.

Caraway

In the garden: Plant here and there. Loosens soil.

In the kitchen: Use in rye breads, cheese dips and rarebits, soups, applesauce, salads, coleslaw, and over pork or sauerkraut.

Chervil

In the garden: Plant with radishes.

In the kitchen: Use with soups, salads, sauces, eggs, fish, veal, lamb, and pork.

Chives

In the garden: Plant with carrots.

In the kitchen: Related to the onion, chives enliven vegetable dishes, dressings, casseroles, rice, eggs, cheese dishes, sauces, gravies, and dips.

Dill

In the garden: Plant with cabbages. Keep away from carrots.

In the kitchen: Use seed for pickles and also to add aroma and taste to strong vegetables like cauliflower, cabbage, and turnips. Use fresh with green beans, potato dishes, cheese, soups, salads, seafood, and sauces.

Fennel

In the garden: Plant away from other herbs and vegetables.

In the kitchen: Use to flavor pastries, confectionery, sweet pickles, sausages, tomato dishes, soups, and to flavor vinegars and oils. Gives warmth and sweetness to curries.

Garlic

In the garden: Plant near roses and raspberries. Deters Japanese beetle.

In the kitchen: Use in tomato dishes, garlic bread, soups, dips, sauces, marinades, or with meats, poultry, fish, and vegetables.

Lovage

In the garden: Plant here and there to improve the health and flavor of other plants.

In the kitchen: It's a great flavoring for soups, stews, and salad dressings. Goes well with potatoes. The seeds can be used on breads and biscuits.

Marjoram

In the garden: Good companion to all vegetables.

In the kitchen: Excellent in almost any meat, fish, dairy, or vegetable dish that isn't sweet. Add near the end of cooking.

Mint

In the garden: Plant near cabbage and tomatoes. Deters white cabbage moth.

In the kitchen: It is common in Middle Eastern dishes. Use with roast lamb or fish and in salads, jellies, or teas.

Oregano

In the garden: Good companion to all vegetables.

In the kitchen: Of Italian origin, its taste is zesty and strong, good in any tomato dish. Try oregano with summer squash and potatoes, mushroom dishes, beans, or in a marinade for lamb or game.

Parsley

In the garden: Plant near asparagus, corn, and tomatoes.

In the kitchen: Use fresh parsley in soups, sauces, and salads. It lessens the need for salt in soups. You can fry parsley and use it as a side dish with meat or fish. It is, of course, the perfect garnish.

Rosemary

In the garden: Plant near cabbage, beans, carrots, and sage. Deters cabbage moth, bean beetles, and carrot fly.

In the kitchen: Use for poultry, lamb, and tomato dishes, stews, soups, and vegetables. Try it finely chopped in breads and custards.

Sage

In the garden: Plant near rosemary, cabbage, and carrots; away from cucumbers. Deters cabbage moth and carrot fly.

In the kitchen: Use in cheese dishes, stuffings, soups, pickles, with beans and peas, and in salads. Excellent for salt-free cooking.

Summer Savory

In the garden: Plant with beans and onions to improve growth and flavor.

In the kitchen: Popular in soups, stews, stuffings, and with fish, chicken, green beans, and eggs.

Tarragon

In the garden: Good companion to most vegetables.

In the kitchen: Great with meat, eggs, poultry, seafood, and in salad dressings, marinades, and sauces.

Thyme

In the garden: Plant near cabbage. Deters cabbage worm.

In the kitchen: Use in casseroles, stews, soups, ragouts, and with eggs, potatoes, fish, and green vegetables.

Herbs to Plant in Lawns

Choose plants that suit your soil and your climate. All these can withstand mowing and consider-able foot traffic.

- Ajuga or bugleweed *(Ajuga reptans)*
- Roman chamomile *(Chamaemelum nobile)*
- Dwarf cinquefoil *(Potentilla tabernaemontani)*
- Corsican mint *(Mentha requienii)*
- English pennyroyal *(Mentha pulegium)*
- Thyme *(Thymus serpyllum)*
- Pearly everlasting *(Anaphalis margaritacea)*
- Rupturewort *(Herniaria glabra)*
- Speedwell *(Veronica officinalis)*
- White clover *(Trifolium repens)*
- Wild strawberries *(Fragaria virginiana)*
- Sweet violets *(Viola odorata* or *tricolor)*
- Wintergreen or partridgeberry *(Mitchella repens)*
- Green Irish moss *(Sagiona subulata)*
- Stonecrop *(Sedum ternatum)*

Symbolic Meanings of Herbs and Plants

Aloe . . . . . . Healing, protection, affection	**Morning glory** . . . . Affectation
Angelica . . . . Inspiration	**Nasturtium** . . . . Patriotism
Arbor vitae . . . . Unchanging friendship	**Oak** . . . . Strength
Bachelor's button . . . . . . Single blessedness	**Oregano** . . . . Substance
Basil . . . . Good wishes, love	**Pansy** . . . . Thoughts
Bay . . . . Glory	**Parsley** . . . . Festivity
Black-eyed Susan . . . . Justice	**Pine** . . . . Humility
Carnation . . . . Alas for my poor heart	**Poppy, Red** . . . . Consolation
Chamomile . . . . Patience	**Rose** . . . . Love
Chives . . . . Usefulness	**Rosemary** . . . . Remembrance
Clover, White . . . . Think of me	**Rue** . . . . Grace, clear vision
Coriander . . . . Hidden worth	**Sage** . . . . Wisdom, immortality
Cumin . . . . Fidelity	**Salvia, Blue** . . . . I think of you
Fennel . . . . Flattery	**Salvia, Red** . . . . Forever mine
Fern . . . . Sincerity	**Savory** . . . . Spice, interest
Geranium, oak-leaved . . . . . True friendship	**Sorrel** . . . . Affection
Goldenrod . . . . Encouragement	**Southernwood** . . . . Constancy, jest
Heliotrope . . . . Eternal love	**Sweetpea** . . . . Pleasures
Holly . . . . Hope	**Sweet woodruff** . . . . Humility
Hollyhock . . . . Ambition	**Tansy** . . . . Hostile thoughts
Honeysuckle . . . . Bonds of love	**Tarragon** . . . . Lasting interest
Horehound . . . . Health	**Thyme** . . . . Courage, strength
Hyssop . . . . Sacrifice, cleanliness	**Valerian** . . . . Readiness
Ivy . . . . Friendship, continuity	**Violet** . . . . Loyalty, devotion
Lady's mantle . . . . Comforting	**Violet, Blue** . . . . Faithfulness
Lavender . . . . Devotion, virtue	**Violet, Yellow** . . . . Rural happiness
Lemon balm . . . . Sympathy	**Willow** . . . . Sadness
Marjoram . . . . Joy, happiness	**Zinnia** . . . . Thoughts of absent friends
Mint . . . . Eternal refreshment	

General Rules for Pruning

What	When	How
Apple	Early spring	Prune moderately. Keep tree open with main branches well spaced. Avoid sharp V-shaped crotches.
Cherry	Early spring	Prune the most vigorous shoots moderately.
Clematis	Spring	Cut weak growth. Save as much old wood as possible.
Flowering dogwood	After flowering	Remove dead wood only.
Forsythia	After flowering	Remove old branches at ground. Trim new growth.
Lilac	After flowering	Remove diseased, scaly growth, flower heads, and suckers.
Peach	Early spring	Remove half of last year's growth. Keep tree headed low.
Plum	Early spring	Cut dead, diseased branches; trim rank growth moderately.
Rhododendron	After flowering	Prune judiciously. Snip branches from weak, leggy plants to induce growth from roots.
Roses (except climbers)	Spring, after frosts	Cut dead and weak growth; cut branches or canes to four or five eyes.
Roses, climbers	After flowering	Cut half of old growth; retain new shoots for next year.
Rose of Sharon	When buds begin	Cut all winter-killed wood to swell growth back to live wood.
Trumpet vine	Early spring	Prune side branches severely to main stem.
Virginia creeper	Spring	Clip young plants freely. Thin old plants and remove dead growth.
Wisteria	Spring, summer	Cut new growth to spurs at axils of leaves.

Spring-Flowering Bulbs

These bulbs, planted in the fall, will be welcome heralds of spring.

	Planting Depth (inches)	Flower Height (inches)		Planting Depth (inches)	Flower Height (inches)
Early Spring Blooms			**Mid-Spring Blooms**		
Galanthus (snowdrop)	5	6	Daffodil	8	20
			Darwin hybrid tulip	8	28
Crocus	5	6	Fritillaria imperialis	8	40
Anemone blanda	5	6	**Late Spring Blooms**		
Muscari (grape hyacinth)	5	10			
			Spanish bluebell	5	10
Greigii tulip	8	14	Dutch iris	8	24
Fosteriana	8	14	Late tulip	8	32
Hyacinth	8	14	Allium giganteum	8	50

Manure Guide

Type of Manure	Water Content	Primary Nutrients (pounds per ton)		
		Nitrogen	Phosphate	Potash
Cow, horse	60%-80%	12-14	5-9	9-12
Sheep, pig, goat	65%-75%	10-21	7	13-19
Chicken: Wet, sticky, and caked	75%	30	20	10
Moist, crumbly to sticky	50%	40	40	20
Crumbly	30%	60	55	30
Dry	15%	90	70	40
Ashed	none	none	135	100

Type of Garden	Best Type of Manure	Best Time to Apply
Flower	cow, horse	early spring
Vegetable	chicken, cow, horse	fall, spring
Potato or root crop	cow, horse	fall
Acid-loving plants (blueberries, azaleas, mountain laurel, rhododendrons)	cow, horse	early fall or not at all

Houseplant Harmonies

Experiments conducted in a controlled environment during the 1960s and 1970s suggest that you may want to consider the health and well-being of your houseplants when making musical selections.

Type of Music / Effect on Plant Growth

Classical	Lush and abundant growth; good root development
Indian devotional	Lush and abundant growth; good root development
Country	No abnormal growth reaction
Silence	No abnormal growth reaction
Jazz	Abundant growth
Rock 'n' Roll	Poor growth; roots scrawny and sparse
White Noise	Plants died quickly

Forcing Indoor Blooms

Here is a list of shrubs and some trees that can be forced to flower indoors. (The trees tend to be stubborn, and their blossoms may not be as rewarding as those of the shrubs.) The numbers indicate the approximate number of weeks they will take to flower.

Buckeye	5	Lilac	4
Cherry	4	Magnolia	3
Cornelian dogwood	2	Pussy willow	2
Crabapple	4	Red maple	2
Deutzia	3	Redbud	2
Flowering almond	3	Red-twig dogwood	5
Flowering dogwood	5	Spicebush	2
Flowering quince	4	Spirea	4
Forsythia	1	Wisteria	3
Honeysuckle	3		
Horse chestnut	5		

Source: Purdue University Cooperative Extension Service

Flowers That Attract Hummingbirds

Beard tongue	*Penstemon*	Foxglove	*Digitalis*
Bee balm	*Monarda*	Lily	*Lilium*
Butterfly bush	*Buddleia*	Lupine	*Lupinus*
Catmint	*Nepeta*	Petunia	*Petunia*
Clove Pink	*Dianthus*	Pincushion flower	*Scabiosa*
Columbine	*Aquilegia*	Red-hot poker	*Kniphofia*
Coral bells	*Heuchera*	Scarlet sage	*Salvia splendens*
Daylily	*Hemerocallis*	Scarlet trumpet	
Larkspur	*Delphinium*	honeysuckle	*Lonicera sempervirens*
Desert candle	*Yucca*	Soapwort	*Saponaria*
Flag	*Iris*	Summer phlox	*Phlox paniculata*
Flowering tobacco	*Nicotiana alata*	Verbena	*Verbena*
		Weigela	*Weigela*

Note: Choose varieties in red and orange shades.

Plants That Attract Butterflies

Allium	*Allium*	Helen's flower	*Helenium*	Purple coneflower	
Aster	*Aster*	Hollyhock	*Alcea*		*Echinacea*
Bee balm	*Monarda*	Honeysuckle	*Lonicera*	Purple loosestrife	*Lythrum*
Butterfly bush	*Buddleia*	Lavender	*Lavendula*	Rock cress	*Arabis*
Catmint	*Nepeta*	Lilac	*Syringa*	Sage	*Salvia*
Clove Pink	*Dianthus*	Lupine	*Lupinus*	Sea holly	*Eryngium*
Cornflower	*Centaurea*	Lychnis	*Lychnis*	Shasta daisy	*Chrysanthemum*
Daylily	*Hemerocallis*	Mallow	*Malva*	Snapdragon	*Antirrhinum*
False indigo	*Baptisia*	Milkweed	*Asclepias*	Stonecrop	*Sedum*
Fleabane	*Erigeron*	Mint	*Mentha*	Sweet alyssum	*Lobularia*
Floss flower	*Ageratum*	Pansy	*Viola*	Sweet rocket	*Hesperis*
Globe thistle	*Echinops*	Phlox	*Phlox*	Tickseed	*Coreopsis*
Goldenrod	*Solidago*	Privet	*Ligustrum*	Zinnia	*Zinnia*

Fall Palette

TREE	COLOR
Sugar maple and sumac	Flame red and orange
Red maple, dogwood, sassafras, and scarlet oak	Dark red
Poplar, birch, tulip tree, willow	Yellow
Ash	Plum purple
Oak, beech, larch, elm, hickory, and sycamore	Tan or brown
Locust	Stays green (until leaves drop)
Black walnut and butternut	Drops leaves before turning color

How to Speak Plant Latin

by Mary Cornog

You don't have to delve very deeply into gardening to realize that those mysterious Latin (and latinized Greek) names that appear in italics in catalogs and on plant labels are as important in identifying specific plants as your own name is in identifying you.

The translation of the scientific name of a familiar plant gives clues to the history and original uses of the plant. *Paeonia officinalis,* a member of the large peony family, is an old-fashioned single red peony that has long been in cultivation and once had medicinal (*officinalis*) applications.

Carl Linnaeus, the Swedish naturalist, began the modern system of classification and Latin nomenclature in the 18th century. Linnaeus gave each plant a permanent set of names drawn from early Greek and Latin efforts (some as old as Aristotle) that indicate genus, species, and sometimes variety.

In 1867 scientists began to formulate an International Code of Botanical Nomenclature, an intricate set of rules for identifying and naming all living things. The scientific name of even the most modern genetically engineered variety has this highly structured code and centuries of precedence behind it.

The list that follows is no substitute for a schooling in the classics, but will help gardeners decipher catalogs and make good choices about plants. All terms are Latin unless followed by a (G) for Greek.

How to Pronounce Botanical Latin and Wow Your Local Plant Supplier

Pronunciation of Latin plant names follows general English pronunciation, with few exceptions. To give a few examples:

Senecio cineraria =
seh-né-see-oh sĭ-ne-rá-ri-a (dusty miller)

Salvia officinalis =
sál-vi-a of-fi-shi-ná-lis (common sage)

Cardiocrinum giganteum =
car-di-o-crí-num ji-gán-te-um
(giant Himalayan lily)

Centaurea cyanus =
sen-táur-e-a si-á-nus (cornflower)

-ae = long e
ch = k
c = s before i, e, y; = k before a, o, u
g = hard before a, o, u; = soft (j) before i, e, y

Accent: In two-syllable words, the accent falls on the first syllable. For longer words, it generally falls, as in English, on the second-last (penultimate) syllable of the word, if that syllable is long (e.g., for-mó-sus), and on the third-last (antepenultimate) syllable if the second-last is short (e.g., fló-ri-dus).

A Brief Glossary of Terms Commonly Used in Plant Names

acanthus thorn (G)
aestivalis summer
alatus winged
altus tall
amoenus harmless, charming
angustifolius narrow-leaved
arborenscens treelike
asper rough
aureus golden
australis southern
autumnalis of autumn
baccatus berry- or pearl-like
barbatus bearded or barbed
bellus beautiful
borealis northern (G)
brevis short
caeruleus blue
campanulatus bell-shaped
campestris growing in fields
candidus white
canescens grayish
capillaris hairlike
cardinalis bright red
carneus flesh-colored
caudatus tailed
cinnamomeus cinnamon brown
coccineus scarlet
cordatus heart-shaped
coriaceus leathery
corniculatus horned
cuneifolius wedge-shaped
   leaves
cyaneus blue (G)
dactyloides finger-shaped (G)
didymus in pairs (G)
digitatus finger-shaped
dulcis sweet
echinatus spiny, bristly (G)
edulis edible
elatus tall
erythrocarpus red-fruited (G)
esculentus edible
fasciculatus clustered, bundled
ferrugineus rust-colored
flavens yellowish

fulvus brownish yellow
germinatus twin
gibbosus humped, swollen
   on one side
glabratus smooth
glaucescens becoming bluish-
   or greenish-gray (G)
hastatus spear-shaped
heterophyllus with leaves of
   several shapes (G)
hirsutus hairy or shaggy
humifusus sprawling
humilis dwarf
inodorus without odor
junceus rushlike
kewensis relating to Kew
   Gardens
labiatus lipped
lacteus milky
laevigatus smooth
lanosus woolly
latiflorus broad-flowered
laxiflorus loose-flowered
leucanthus white-flowered (G)
lignosus like wood
limosus of muddy places
lucidus shiny
luteus muddy yellow
macrophyllus large-leaved (G)
maculatus spotted
microcarpus small-fruited (G)
mirabilis wonderful
nanus dwarf (G)
natans floating
nemoralis growing in woods
niger black
nitens shining
niveus snow-white
noctiflorens night-flowering
nyctagineus night-flowering (G)
occidentalis western
officinalis a formerly
   recognized medicinal
oleraceus from a vegetable
   garden

pallens pale
paludosus marshy
parviflorens small-flowering
patens spreading
pauciflorus few-flowered
pratensis growing in meadows
pubens downy
pumilus dwarf, small
puniceus reddish-purple
quadrifolius four-leaved
quinquefolius five-leaved
radicans rooting
regalis royal
repens creeping
reptans crawling
reticulans netlike
riparius growing near a river
roseus rose-colored
rubens red
ruderalis growing among
   rubbish
rugosus wrinkled
sativus cultivated
scandens climbing
sericeus silky
setosus bristly
speciosus beautiful
spinosus with spines
stellatus starlike
stramineus straw-colored
strigosus stiff-bristled
tenuis slender
tinctorius used for dyeing
tomentosus like felt
tuberosus with tubers
urens stinging
vacillans swaying
velutinus velvety
vernalis spring-flowered
verus true
villosus with soft hairs
violaceus violet
viridis green
vulgaris common
xanthinus yellow (G)

How Much Water Is Enough?

When confronted with a dry garden and the end of a hose, many gardeners admit to a certain insecurity about just how much water those plants really need. Here's a guide to help you estimate when and how much to water, assuming rich, well-balanced soil. Increase frequency during hot, very dry periods.

Vegetable	Critical time(s) to water
■ **Beets**	Before soil gets bone-dry.
● **Beans**	When flowers form and during pod-forming and picking.
■ **Broccoli**	Don't let soil dry out for 4 weeks after transplanting.
■ **Brussels sprouts**	Don't let soil dry out for 4 weeks after transplanting.
▲ **Cabbage**	Water frequently in dry weather for best crop.
■ **Carrots**	Before soil gets bone-dry.
▲ **Cauliflower**	Water frequently for best crop.
▲ **Celery**	Water frequently for best crop.
● **Corn**	When tassels form and when cobs swell.
▲ **Cucumbers**	Water frequently for best crop.
▲ **Lettuce/Spinach**	Water frequently for best crop.
■ **Onions**	In dry weather water in early stage to get plants going.
■ **Parsnips**	Before soil gets bone-dry.
● **Peas**	When flowers form and during pod-forming and picking.
● **Potatoes**	When the size of marbles.
▲ **Squash (all types)**	Water frequently for best crop.
● **Tomatoes**	For 3 to 4 weeks after transplanting and when flowers and fruit form.

▲ Needs a lot of water during dry spells.   ● Needs water at

Number of gallons of water needed for a 5-foot row	Comments
1 at early stage; 2 every 2 weeks	Water sparingly during early stages to prevent foliage from becoming too lush at the expense of the roots; increase water when round roots form.
2 per week depending on rainfall	Dry soil when pods are forming will adversely affect quantity and quality.
1 to 1-1/2 per week	Best crop will result with no water shortage.
1 to 1-1/2 per week	Plants can endure dry conditions once they are established. Give 2 gallons the last 2 weeks before harvest for most succulent crop.
2 per week	If crop suffers some dry weather, focus efforts on providing 2 gallons 2 weeks before harvest. (Too much water will cause heads to crack.)
1 at early stage; 2 every 2 weeks as roots mature	Roots may split if crop is watered after soil has become too dry.
2 per week	Give 2 gallons before harvest for best crop.
2 per week	If conditions are very dry, water daily.
2 at important stages (left)	Cob size will be smaller if plants do not receive water when ears are forming.
1 per week	Water diligently when fruits form and throughout growth; give highest watering priority.
2 per week	Best crop will result with no water shortage.
1/2 to 1 per week if soil is very dry	Withhold water from bulb onions at later growth stages to improve storage qualities; water salad onions anytime soil is very dry.
1 per week in early stages	Water when dry to keep plants growing steadily. Too much water will encourage lush foliage and small roots.
2 per week	To reduce excess foliage and stem growth, do not water young seedlings unless wilting.
2 per week	In dry weather give 2 gallons throughout the growing season every 10 days. Swings from very dry to very wet produce oddly shaped and cracked tubers.
1 per week	Water diligently when fruits form and throughout their growth; give highest watering priority.
1 twice a week or more	Frequent watering may increase yield but adversely affect flavor.

critical stages of development.   ■ Does not need frequent watering.

Animal Terminology

Animal	Male	Female	Young
Ant	Male-ant (reproductive)	Queen (reproductive), worker (nonreproductive)	Antling
Antelope	Ram	Ewe	Calf, fawn, kid, yearling
Ass	Jack, jackass	Jenny	Foal
Bear	Boar, he-bear	Sow, she-bear	Cub
Beaver	Boar	Sow	Kit, kitten
Bee	Drone	Queen or queen bee, worker (nonreproductive)	Larva
Buffalo	Bull	Cow	Calf, yearling, spike-bull
Camel	Bull	Cow	Calf, colt
Caribou	Bull, stag, hart	Cow, doe	Calf, fawn
Cat	Tom, tomcat, gib, gibcat, boarcat, ramcat	Tabby, grimalkin, malkin, pussy, queen	Kitten, kit, kitling, kitty, pussy
Cattle	Bull	Cow	Calf, stot, yearling, bullcalf, heifer
Chicken	Rooster, cock, stag, chanticleer	Hen, partlet, biddy	Chick, chicken, poult, cockerel, pullet
Deer	Buck, stag	Doe	Fawn
Dog	Dog	Bitch	Whelp
Duck	Drake, stag	Duck	Duckling, flapper
Elephant	Bull	Cow	Calf
Fox	Dog	Vixen	Kit, pup, cub
Giraffe	Bull	Cow	Calf
Goat	Buck, billy, billie, billie-goat, he-goat	She-goat, nanny, nannie, nannie-goat	Kid
Goose	Gander, stag	Goose, dame	Gosling
Horse	Stallion, stag, horse, stud	Mare, dam	Colt, foal, stot, stag, filly, hog-colt, hogget
Kangaroo	Buck	Doe	Joey
Leopard	Leopard	Leopardess	Cub
Lion	Lion, tom	Lioness, she-lion	Shelp, cub, lionet
Moose	Bull	Cow	Calf
Partridge	Cock	Hen	Cheeper
Quail	Cock	Hen	Cheeper, chick, squealer
Reindeer	Buck	Doe	Fawn
Seal	Bull	Cow	Whelp, pup, cub, bachelor
Sheep	Buck, ram, male-sheep, mutton	Ewe, dam	Lamb, lambkin, shearling, yearling, cosset, hog
Swan	Cob	Pen	Cygnet
Swine	Boar	Sow	Shoat, trotter, pig, piglet, farrow, suckling
Termite	King	Queen	Nymph
Walrus	Bull	Cow	Cub
Whale	Bull	Cow	Calf
Zebra	Stallion	Mare	Colt, foal

Collective

Colony, nest, army, state, swarm

Herd

Pace, drove, herd

Sleuth, sloth

Family, colony

Swarm, grist, cluster, nest, hive, erst

Troop, herd, gang

Flock, train, caravan

Herd

Clowder, clutter (kindle or kendle of kittens)

Drove, herd

Flock, run, brood, clutch, peep

Herd, leash

Pack (cry or mute of hounds, leash of greyhounds)

Brace, team, paddling, raft, bed, flock, flight

Herd

Leash, skulk, cloud, troop

Herd, corps, troop

Tribe, trip, flock, herd

Flock (on land), gaggle, skein (in flight), gaggle or plump (on water)

Haras, stable, remuda, stud, herd, string, field, set, pair, team

Mob, troop, herd

Leap

Pride, troop, flock, sawt, souse

Herd

Covey

Bevy, covey

Herd

Pod, herd, trip, rookery, harem

Flock, drove, hirsel, trip, pack

Herd, team, bank, wege, bevy

Drift, sounder, herd, trip (litter of pigs)

Colony, nest, swarm, brood

Pod, herd

Gam, pod, school, herd

Herd

More Animal Collectives

army of caterpillers, frogs

bale of turtles

band of gorillas

bed of clams, oysters

brood of jellyfish

business of flies

cartload of monkeys

cast of hawks

cete of badgers

charm of goldfinches

chatter of budgerigars

cloud of gnats, flies, grasshoppers, locusts

colony of penguins

congregation of plovers

convocation of eagles

crash of rhinoceri

descent of woodpeckers

dole of turtles

down of hares

dray of squirrels

dule of turtle doves

exaltation of larks

family of sardines

flight of birds

flock of lice

gang of elks

hatch of flies

horde of gnats

host of sparrows

hover of trout

husk of hares

knab of toads

knot of toads, snakes

murder of crows

murmuration of starlings

mustering of storks

nest of vipers

nest or nide of pheasants

pack of weasels

pladge of wasps

plague of locusts

scattering of herons

sedge or siege of cranes

smuck of jellyfish

span of mules

spring of teals

steam of minnows

tittering of magpies

troop of monkeys

troubling of goldfish

volery of birds

watch of nightingales

wing of plovers

yoke of oxen

Dogs: Gentle, Fierce, Smart, Popular

GENTLEST BREEDS	FIERCEST BREEDS	SMARTEST BREEDS	MOST POPULAR BREEDS
Golden retriever	Pit bull	Border collie	Labrador retriever
Labrador retriever	German shepherd	Poodle	Rottweiler
Shetland sheepdog	Husky	German shepherd	Cocker spaniel
Old English	Malamute	(Alsatian)	German shepherd
sheepdog	Doberman pinscher	Golden retriever	Poodle
Welsh terrier	Rottweiler	Doberman pinscher	Golden retriever
Yorkshire terrier	Great Dane	Shetland sheepdog	Beagle
Beagle	Saint Bernard	Labrador retriever	Dachshund
Dalmatian		Papillon	Shetland sheepdog
Pointer		Rottweiler	Chow chow
		Australian cattle dog	

How Old Is Your Dog?

Multiplying your dog's age by seven is easy, but it doesn't always hold true. The more carefully graded system below has the human equivalency years piled onto a dog's life more quickly during the dog's rapid growth to maturity, after which each year for a dog becomes the equivalent of four human years, and after age 13 it slows down to 2½ years.

Dog Age	Equivalent Human Age	Dog Age	Equivalent Human Age
6 months	10 years	16	75½
1 year	15	17	78
2 years	24	18	80½
3	28	19	83
4	32	20	85½
5	36	21	88
6	40	22	90½
7	44	23	93
8	48	24	95½
9	52	25	98
10	56	26	100½
11	60	27	103
12	64	28	105½
13	68	29	108
14	70½	30	110
15	73		

Don't Poison Your Pussycat!

Certain common houseplants are poisonous to cats. They should not be allowed to eat the following:

- *Caladium* (elephant's ears)
- *Dieffenbachia* (dumb cane)
- *Euphorbia pulcherrima* (poinsettia)
- *Hedera* (true ivy)
- *Rhododendron* (azalea)
- Mistletoe

- Oleander
- Philodendron
- *Prunus laurocerasus* (common or cherry laurel)
- *Solanum capiscastrum* (winter or false Jerusalem cherry)

Ten Most Intelligent Animals
(Besides Humans)

According to Edward O. Wilson, behavioral biologist, professor of zoology, Harvard University, they are:

1. Chimpanzee (two species)
2. Gorilla
3. Orangutan
4. Baboon (seven species, including drill and mandrill)
5. Gibbon (seven species)
6. Monkey (many species, especially the macaques, the patas, and the Celebes black ape)
7. Smaller toothed whale (several species, especially killer whale)
8. Dolphin (many of the approximately 80 species)
9. Elephant (two species)
10. Pig

Night Eyes

Who goes there? You may have only a pair of gleaming eyes to go on, so it's best to know whose are whose.

Bear ...... Bright orange eyes, close together
Raccoon .. Bright yellow eyes, low to the ground
Dog or fox .... Bright white eyes
Bobcat .... Yellowish white eyes
Porcupine ...... Bright white eyes, up in a tree

A Defining Moment

Ape: Any of various large, tailless Old World primates of the family Pongidae, including the chimpanzee, gorilla, gibbon, and orangutan.

Monkey: Any of various long-tailed, medium-size members of the order Primates, including the macaques, baboons, guenons, capuchins, marmosets, and tamarins and excluding the anthropoid apes (Primate family Pongidae) and the prosimians (suborder of primates that includes lemurs, lorises, and tarsiers).

For the Birds

	Sunflower seeds	Millet (white proso)	Niger (thistle seeds)	Safflower seeds	Corn, cracked	Corn, whole	Peanuts	Peanut butter	Suet	Raisins	Apples	Oranges and grapefruits
Blue jay	■			■	■	■	■			■		
Bunting	■	■	■	■	■							
Cardinal	■	■		■	■					■	■	■
Catbird										■	■	■
Cedar waxwing											■	■
Chickadee	■	■		■	■		■	■	■			
Cowbird		■										
Crossbill	■	■		■				■				
Duck		■			■	■						
Finch	■	■	■	■	■		■	■				■
Flicker							■	■	■			
Goldfinch	■		■									
Goose					■	■						
Grackle	■											
Grosbeak	■	■		■			■			■	■	■
Junco	■	■	■	■	■							
Mockingbird										■	■	
Mourning dove	■	■		■	■	■	■					
Nuthatch	■	■		■			■	■	■			
Oriole												■
Pheasant					■							
Pine siskin	■	■	■	■			■			■		■
Redpoll	■	■	■	■								
Sparrow	■	■		■	■							
Starling					■							
Tanager												■
Thrasher					■		■			■	■	
Thrush										■	■	
Titmouse	■	■		■	■		■	■	■			
Towhee		■										
Warbler							■					■
Woodpecker							■	■	■			

What Counts as a Serving?

Bread Group
1 slice of bread
1 ounce of ready-to-eat cereal
½ cup of cooked cereal, rice, or pasta

Vegetable Group
1 cup of raw leafy vegetable
½ cup of other vegetables, cooked or
    chopped raw
¾ cup of vegetable juice

Fruit Group
1 medium apple, banana, orange
½ cup of chopped, cooked, or canned fruit
¾ cup of fruit juice

Milk Group
1 cup of milk or yogurt
1½ ounces of natural cheese
2 ounces of processed cheese

Meat Group
2 to 3 ounces of cooked lean meat,
    poultry, or fish
½ cup of cooked dry beans, 1 egg, or 2
    tablespoons of peanut butter count as
    1 ounce of meat (about ⅓ serving)

Fats, Oils, and Sweets (use sparingly)

Milk Group — 2 - 3 SERVINGS
Meat Group — 2 - 3 SERVINGS
Vegetable Group — 3 - 5 SERVINGS
Fruit Group — 2 - 4 SERVINGS
Bread Group — 6 - 11 SERVINGS

Suggested Daily Servings

The best Dietary Guidelines for a healthful diet from the USDA (United States Department of Agriculture) and HHS (Department of Health and Human Services) are:

❤ Eat a variety of foods

❤ Maintain healthy weight

❤ Choose a diet low in fat, saturated fat, and cholesterol

❤ Choose a diet with plenty of vegetables, fruits, and grain products

❤ Use sugars only in moderation

❤ Use salt only in moderation

❤ If you drink alcoholic beverages, do so in moderation

Food for Thought

☞ A piece of pecan pie = 580 calories
☞ Grilled cheese sandwich = 440 calories
☞ A chocolate shake = 364 calories
☞ Bagel with cream cheese = 361 calories
☞ 20 potato chips = 228 calories
☞ 10 french fries = 214 calories
☞ Half a cantaloupe = 94 calories
☞ Corn on the cob = 70 calories (no butter)
☞ One carrot = 30 calories

Don't Freeze These

Bananas
Canned hams
Cream fillings and
    puddings
Cooked eggs
Cooked potatoes
Custards
Fried foods
Gelatin dishes
Mayonnaise

Raw vegetables, such
    as cabbage, celery,
    green onions,
    radishes, and salad
    greens
Soft cheeses, cottage
    cheese
Sour cream
Yogurt

Substitutions for Common Ingredients

ITEM	QUANTITY	SUBSTITUTION
Allspice	1 teaspoon	½ teaspoon cinnamon plus ⅛ teaspoon ground cloves
Arrowroot, as thickener	1½ teaspoons	1 tablespoon flour
Baking powder	1 teaspoon	¼ teaspoon baking soda plus ⅝ teaspoon cream of tartar
Bread crumbs, dry	¼ cup	1 slice bread
soft	½ cup	1 slice bread
Buttermilk	1 cup	1 cup plain yogurt
Chocolate, unsweetened	1 ounce	3 tablespoons cocoa plus 1 tablespoon butter or fat
Cracker crumbs	¾ cup	1 cup bread crumbs
Cream, heavy	1 cup	¾ cup milk plus ⅓ cup melted butter (this will not whip)
Cream, light	1 cup	⅞ cup milk plus 3 tablespoons melted butter
Cream, sour	1 cup	⅞ cup buttermilk or plain yogurt plus 3 tablespoons melted butter
Cream, whipping	1 cup	⅔ cup well-chilled evaporated milk, whipped; **or** 1 cup nonfat dry milk powder whipped with 1 cup ice water
Egg	1 whole	2 yolks
Flour, all-purpose	1 cup	1⅛ cups cake flour; **or** ⅝ cup potato flour; **or** 1¼ cups rye or coarsely ground whole grain flour; **or** 1 cup cornmeal
Flour, cake	1 cup	1 cup minus 2 tablespoons sifted all-purpose flour
Flour, self-rising	1 cup	1 cup all-purpose flour plus 1¼ teaspoons baking powder plus ¼ teaspoon salt
Garlic	1 small clove	⅛ teaspoon garlic powder; **or** ½ teaspoon instant minced garlic
Herbs, dried	½ to 1 teaspoon	1 tablespoon fresh, minced and packed
Honey	1 cup	1¼ cups sugar plus ½ cup liquid

Measuring Vegetables

Asparagus: 1 pound = 3 cups chopped

Beans (string): 1 pound = 4 cups chopped

Beets: 1 pound (5 medium) = 2-1/2 cups chopped

Broccoli: 1/2 pound = 6 cups chopped

Cabbage: 1 pound = 4-1/2 cups shredded

Carrots: 1 pound = 3-1/2 cups sliced or grated

Celery: 1 pound = 4 cups chopped

Cucumbers: 1 pound (2 medium) = 4 cups sliced

Eggplant: 1 pound = 4 cups chopped (6 cups raw, cubed = 3 cups cooked)

Garlic: 1 clove = 1 teaspoon chopped

Leeks: 1 pound = 4 cups chopped (2 cups cooked)

Mushrooms: 1 pound = 5 to 6 cups sliced = 2 cups cooked

Onions: 1 pound = 4 cups sliced = 2 cups cooked

Parsnips: 1 pound unpeeled = 1-1/2 cups cooked, pureed

Peas: 1 pound whole = 1 to 1-1/2 cups shelled

Potatoes: 1 pound (3 medium) sliced = 2 cups mashed

Pumpkin: 1 pound = 4 cups chopped = 2 cups cooked and drained

Spinach: 1 pound = 3/4 to 1 cup cooked

ITEM	QUANTITY	SUBSTITUTION
Lemon	1	1 to 3 tablespoons juice, 1 to 1½ teaspoons grated rind
Lemon juice	1 teaspoon	½ teaspoon vinegar
Lemon rind, grated	1 teaspoon	½ teaspoon lemon extract
Milk, skim	1 cup	⅓ cup instant nonfat dry milk plus about ¾ cup water
Milk, whole	1 cup	½ cup evaporated milk plus ½ cup water; **or** 1 cup skim milk plus 2 teaspoons melted butter
Milk, to sour	1 cup	Add 1 tablespoon vinegar or lemon juice to 1 cup milk minus 1 tablespoon. Stir and let stand 5 minutes.
Molasses	1 cup	1 cup honey
Mustard, prepared	1 tablespoon	1 teaspoon dry or powdered mustard
Onion, chopped	1 small	1 tablespoon instant minced onion; **or** 1 teaspoon onion powder; **or** ¼ cup frozen chopped onion
Sugar, granulated	1 cup	1 cup firmly packed brown sugar; **or** 1¾ cups confectioners' sugar (do not substitute in baking); **or** 2 cups corn syrup; **or** 1 cup superfine sugar
Tomatoes, canned	1 cup	½ cup tomato sauce plus ½ cup water; **or** 1⅓ cups chopped fresh tomatoes, simmered
Tomato juice	1 cup	½ cup tomato sauce plus ½ cup water plus dash each salt and sugar; **or** ¼ cup tomato paste plus ¾ cup water plus salt and sugar
Tomato ketchup	½ cup	½ cup tomato sauce plus 2 tablespoons sugar, 1 tablespoon vinegar, and ⅛ teaspoon ground cloves
Tomato purée	1 cup	½ cup tomato paste plus ½ cup water
Tomato soup	1 can (10¾ oz.)	1 cup tomato sauce plus ¼ cup water
Vanilla	1-inch bean	1 teaspoon vanilla extract
Yeast	1 cake (⅗ oz.)	1 package active dried yeast (1 scant tablespoon)
Yogurt, plain	1 cup	1 cup buttermilk

Squash (summer): 1 pound = 4 cups grated = 2 cups salted and drained

Squash (winter): 2 pounds = 2-1/2 cups cooked, pureed

Sweet Potatoes: 1 pound = 4 cups grated = 1 cup cooked, pureed

Swiss Chard: 1 pound = 5 to 6 cups packed leaves = 1 to 1-1/2 cups cooked

Tomatoes: 1 pound (3 or 4 medium) = 1-1/2 cups seeded pulp

Turnips: 1 pound = 4 cups chopped = 2 cups cooked, mashed

Measuring Fruits

Apples: 1 pound (3 or 4 medium) = 3 cups sliced

Bananas: 1 pound (3 or 4 medium) = 1-3/4 cups mashed

Berries: 1 quart = 3-1/2 cups

Dates: 1 pound = 2-1/2 cups pitted

Lemon: 1 whole = 1 to 3 tablespoons juice; 1 to 1-1/2 teaspoons grated rind

Lime: 1 whole = 1-1/2 to 2 tablespoons juice

Orange: 1 medium = 6 to 8 tablespoons juice; 2 to 3 tablespoons grated rind

Peaches: 1 pound (4 medium) = 3 cups sliced

Pears: 1 pound (4 medium) = 2 cups sliced

Rhubarb: 1 pound = 2 cups cooked

Strawberries: 1 quart = 4 cups sliced

Beef Cuts

RIB
Rib Roast, large end
Rib Roast, small end
Rib Steak, small end
Rib Eye Steak
Rib Eye Roast
Back Ribs

SHORT LOIN *
Top Loin Steak, boneless
T-Bone Steak
Porterhouse Steak
Tenderloin Roast / Steak

SIRLOIN *
Top Sirloin Steak
Sirloin Steak
Tenderloin Roast / Steak
Beef Tri-Tip

The tri-tip roast is a boneless cut from the bottom sirloin. It is also called a "triangle" roast because of its shape.

ROUND *
Round Steak
Top Round Roast
Top Round Steak
Bottom Round Roast
Tip Roast Cap Off
Eye Round Roast
Tip Steak
Boneless Rump Roast

FLANK *
Flank Steak
Flank Steak Rolls

PLATE
Skirt Steak

SHANK
Shank Crosscut

BRISKET
Whole Brisket
Brisket, point half, corned
Brisket, flat half

CHUCK
Chuck Eye Roast, boneless
Top Blade Steak, boneless
Arm Pot Roast
Shoulder Pot Roast, boneless
Mock Tender Roast
Blade Roast
Under Blade Pot Roast
7-Bone Pot Roast
Short Ribs
Flanken-Style Ribs
Cross Rib Pot Roast

Diagram labels: ROUND, SHANK, SIRLOIN, Tenderloin, Top Sirloin, Bottom Sirloin, SHORT LOIN, FLANK, RIB, PLATE, CHUCK, BRISKET, SHANK

* Beef primals that feature cuts lowest in fat.

– courtesy the Beef Industry Council

Basic Kitchen Equipment

FOOD PREPARATION
Measuring cups
  Dry measure: set
    of 4 cups
  Wet measure:
    1-cup; 2-cup
Measuring spoons
Ruler
Thermometers
  Meat
  Candy/frying
  Freezer
Timer
Mixing bowls (3 sizes)
Chopping board
Knives
  Chef's knife
  Paring knife
  Bread knife
    (serrated edge)
  Carving knife
Knife sharpener
Kitchen shears
Vegetable parer

Openers
  Bottle opener
  Corkscrew
  Jar opener
  Can opener
Pepper grinder
Rotary egg beater
Nutcracker
Funnel
Grater
Colander
Strainer
Juicer

COOKING
Pots, Skillets, and Pans
  Saucepans: 1- to
    2-cup, 1-quart,
    2-quart, and 8-
    quart
  Skillets/frying
    pans: 7-inch,
    10-inch, 12-inch
  Griddle

Flameproof
  casserole or
  Dutch oven
Casseroles and
  baking dishes
Roasting pan
  (with rack)
Double boiler
Steamer

Kettle
Coffeepot
Wooden spoons
Rubber spatula
Metal utensils
  Metal spatula
  Slotted spoon
  Cooking fork
  Ladle
  Potato masher
  Tongs
  Whisk

Skewers
Bulb baster
Brush

BAKING
Pastry blender
Rolling pin
Sifter
Cake pans
  Pair of 8 (and/or 9)
    x1-1/2-inch
    round
  8- or 9-inch
    square
  9x12-inch
    rectangular
  10-inch tube
Loaf pans
Cookie sheets (at least 2)
Jelly-roll pan
Muffin tins
Pie pans
Custard cups
Cooling racks

Appetizing Amounts

Occasion	Number of bites per person
Hors d'oeuvres (with meal following)	4
Cocktail party	10
Grand affair, no dinner following (e.g., wedding reception)	10-15

Pass the Pasta

All pastas, when cooked, are not created equal. Four ounces of dried pasta, the usual serving size, yields different amounts depending on the pasta shape.

Type of pasta, 4 ounces uncooked	Cooked yield (in cups)
Spaghetti, vermicelli, capellini, linguine	2
Elbow macaroni, conchiglie (seashells), rotini, ruote (cartwheels), mostaccioli, ziti, penne	2-1/2
Medium egg noodles, tagliatelle	3

A Defining Moment

Pot: Any of various usually domestic containers made of pottery, metal, or glass, as: **a.**) A round, fairly deep cooking vessel with a handle and often a lid. **b.**) A short, round container for storing or serving food: a jam pot; a mustard pot. **c.**) A coffeepot. **d.**) A teapot.

Pan: A shallow, wide, open container, usually of metal and without a lid, used for holding liquids, cooking, and other domestic purposes.

Fruit: The product of a seed-bearing plant that contains the seeds, usually refers to such a product that is edible. In a non-seed-bearing plant, the fruit is the fertile, spore-bearing structure of the plant. Some "fruit vegetables" include: pumpkin, squash, eggplant, tomato, cucumber, sweet pepper, hot pepper, green bean, and zucchini.

Vegetable: a.) A plant cultivated for an edible part, such as the root of the beet, the leaf of spinach, or the flower buds of broccoli or cauliflower. **b.**) The edible part of such a plant.

Unexpected Uses for Household Items

SALT

■ **Rub salt on fruit stains while still wet, then put them in the wash.**

■ For mildew spots, rub in salt and some buttermilk, and then let dry in the sun.

■ **If you spill wine or fruit juice on your tablecloth, pour salt on the spot at once to absorb the stain.**

■ Apply a paste of salt and olive oil to ugly heat rings on your table. Let sit for about an hour and then wipe off with a soft cloth.

■ **To catch a wild bird easily, first sprinkle some salt on its tail.**

■ Sprinkle salt on a piece of paper and run your sticky iron over it a few times while the iron is hot. You should notice a big improvement next time you use the iron.

■ **To restore some of the color to faded fabric, soak it in a strong solution of salt and water.**

■ You can get rid of an evil spell by throwing a pinch of salt over your left shoulder.

■ **Mix a tablespoon of salt into the water of a vase of cut flowers to keep them fresh longer.**

VINEGAR

■ Bring a solution of 1 cup vinegar and 4 tablespoons baking soda to a boil in teapots and coffeepots to rid them of mineral deposits.

■ **A solution of vinegar and baking soda will easily remove cooking oil from your stovetop.**

■ Clean the filter on your humidifier by removing it and soaking it in a pan of white vinegar until all the sediment is off.

■ **Vinegar naturally breaks down uric acid and soapy residue, leaving baby clothes and diapers soft and fresh. Add a cup of vinegar to each load during the rinse cycle.**

■ Saturate a cloth with vinegar and sprinkle with baking soda, then use it to clean fiberglass tubs and showers. Rinse well and rub dry for a spotless shine.

■ **To remove chewing gum, rub it with full-strength vinegar.**

■ For a clean oven, combine vinegar and baking soda, then scrub.

■ **Soak paint stains in hot vinegar to remove them.**

BAKING SODA

■ Add baking soda to your bath water to relieve sunburned or itchy skin.

■ **Make a paste of baking soda and water, and apply to a burn or an insect bite for relief.**

■ Clean your refrigerator with a solution of 1 teaspoon baking soda to 1 quart of warm water.

■ **Pour a cup of baking soda into the opening of your clogged drain and then add a cup of hot vinegar. After a few minutes, flush the drain with a quart of boiling water.**

■ To remove perspiration stains, make a thick paste of baking soda and water. Rub paste into the stain, let sit for an hour, then launder as usual.

■ **If you crave sweets, rinse your mouth with 1 teaspoon baking soda dissolved in a glass of warm water. Don't swallow the mixture; spit it out. Your craving should disappear at once.**

■ Tough meat can be tenderized by rubbing it with baking soda. Let stand for several hours before rinsing and cooking.

How Long Household Items Last

ITEMS	YEARS (Approx. Averages)
Electric shavers	4
Personal computers	6
Lawn mowers	6
Automatic coffee makers	6
VCRs	6
Food processors	7
Electric can openers	7
CD players	7
Camcorders	7
Toasters	8
Stereo receivers	8
Color TV sets	8
Blenders	8
Room air conditioners	9
Vacuum cleaners	10
Microwave ovens	10
Dishwashers	11
Dehumidifiers	12
Washing machines	13
Electric dryers	13
Refrigerators	14
Gas dryers	14
Electric ranges	15
Gas ranges	18

The life span of a product depends not only on its actual durability but also on your desire for some new convenience found only on a new model.

– courtesy Consumer Reports

How Much Electricity Is Used?

The table below indicates the annual estimated energy consumption for various household electrical products. Note: One kilowatt equals 1,000 watts; a kilowatt-hour is the work done by one kilowatt in an hour.

Appliance	Estimated kilowatt-hours
Water heater (standard)	4,219
Refrigerator (frost free)	1,591-1,829
Freezer (frost free)	1,820
Air conditioner (room)	1,389
Range (self-cleaning oven)	1,205
Clothes dryer	993
Television (color)	502
Computer	25-400
Dehumidifier	377
Dishwasher	165-363
Microwave oven	300
Fan (attic)	291
Frying pan	186
Iron	144
Coffee maker	106
Clothes washer	103
Broiler	100
Radio	86
Videocassette recorder (VCR)	10-70
Vacuum cleaner	46
Fan (circulating)	43
Garbage disposal	30
Clock	17
Blender	15
Hair dryer	14
Food mixer	13

How Much Water Is Used ?

	Gallons
To brush your teeth (water running)	1-2
To flush a toilet	5-7
To run a dishwasher	9-12
To shave (water running)	10-15
To wash dishes by hand	20
To take a shower	15-30
By an average person daily	123
In the average residence during a year	110,000

Source: American Water Works

Homeowner's Tool Kit

THE ESSENTIALS

Butt chisel
Putty knife
Adjustable wrench
Slip-joint pliers
Needle-nose pliers
Block plane
Four-in-one rasp
Hacksaw
Crosscut saw
Retractable steel ruler
Drain auger
C-clamp
Nail set
Curved-claw hammer
Push drill and drill point

3 standard screwdrivers
  (3 sizes)
2 Phillips screwdrivers
  (2 sizes)
Combination square
Level
Utility knife
Toilet plunger
Screws and nails

OTHER SUPPLIES

Machine oil
Penetrating lubricant
Pencils
Bolts & nuts, hollow-wall
  fasteners, etc.
Adhesives
Sandpaper and steel wool

Sharpening stone
Wire brush
Paintbrushes
Dustpan and brush
Lint-free rags or
  cheesecloth
Clip-on light
Grounded extension cord
Single-edge razor blades
  with holder
Scissors
Toolbox
Stepladder

Cost of a Load of Laundry

Electric Water Heater (8¢/kWh)			Gas Water Heater (60¢/therm)		
Wash/rinse settings	kWh used	Average cost per load (cents)	Wash/rinse settings	Therms used	Average cost per load (cents)
Water-heater thermostat set at 140° F					
Hot/Hot	8.3	66	Hot/Hot	.329	20
Hot/Warm	6.3	50	Hot Warm	.247	15
Hot/Cold	4.3	34	Hot/Cold	.164	10
Warm/Warm	4.3	34	Warm/Warm	.164	10
Warm/Cold	2.3	18	Warm/Cold	.082	5
Cold/Cold	0.4	3	Cold/Cold	—	3
Water-heater thermostat set at 120° F					
Hot/Hot	6.5	52	Hot/Hot	.248	15
Hot/Warm	4.9	39	Hot/Warm	.186	10
Hot/Cold	4.3	27	Hot/Cold	.124	7
Warm/Warm	3.4	27	Warm/Warm	.124	7
Warm/Cold	1.9	15	Warm/Cold	.062	4
Cold/Cold	0.4	3	Cold/Cold	—	3

Paper Clutter — Save, Stash, or Scrap?

SAVE For a While or Forever

- Canceled checks that substantiate tax deductions (file with tax material) or major purchases (file with product warranties)
- Purchase and sale documents (including tax form 2119) for every home you've owned
- Documents relating to capital home-improvement expenditures (new roofs, remodeled kitchen/bath, landscaping, etc.)
- Credit-card records (for six years)
- Health records (forever)
- Contracts (for seven years past expiration date)
- Loan papers (for three years after final payment)
- Records of all contributions to non-deductible IRAs, including form 8606
- Current will (copy — leave original with your attorney)
- Tax returns (for six years, in individual folders)

STASH In a Safe Deposit Box

- Valuable, hard-to-replace papers (keep photocopies at home)
- Deeds and other records of ownership (inventory, appraisals, photos, receipts)
- Birth and marriage certificates
- Passports
- Stock and bond certificates
- List of all insurance policies and agents (store original documents at home)
- Adoption papers
- Divorce decrees
- Custody agreements

SCRAP What You Can Safely Throw Away (When in doubt, consult your CPA or lawyer)

- Expired insurance policies (with no possibility of claim)
- Nontax-related checks more than three years old
- Records for items you no longer own (cars, boats)
- Pay stubs going back more than two years

Heat Values of Fuels
(approximate)

Fuel	BTU	Unit of measure
Oil	141,000	gallon
Coal	31,000	pound
Natural gas	1,000	cubic foot
Steam	1,000	cubic foot
Electricity	3,413	kilowatt-hour
Gasoline	124,000	gallon

Stovewood — Best Heat Value

You will pay more for these hardwoods, but you will get more heat for your dollar.

Ash, white	Locust, black
Beech	Maple, sugar
Birch, yellow	Oak, red
Hickory, shagbark	Oak, white
Hop hornbeam	

A Few Clues About Cords

1. A cord of wood is a pile of logs 4 feet wide by 4 feet high by 8 feet long.
2. A cord of wood may contain from 77 to 96 cubic feet of wood.
3. The larger the unsplit logs, the larger the gaps, with fewer cubic feet of wood actually in the cord.

The Right Wood for the Job

Doors	Birch, oak
Cabinet doors	Maple, oak, birch, cherry
Shelving	Ash, birch, maple, oak, walnut, poplar, Douglas fir, redwood, ponderosa pine, sugar pine, Idaho white pine
Paneling	Oak, redwood, cypress, walnut, cedar, ash, birch, pine
Stairways	Oak, birch, maple, walnut, beech, ash, cherry
Interior trim, natural finish	Oak, birch, maple, cypress, cherry, sycamore, beech, walnut. Knotty surface: cedar, ponderosa pine, spruce, sugar pine, gum, lodgepole pine
Interior trim, painted finish	Northern and Idaho white pine, ponderosa pine, sugar pine, poplar
Exterior trim	Cedar, cypress, redwood, northern and Idaho white pine, ponderosa pine, sugar pine
Frames and sash	Cypress, cedar, redwood, northern and Idaho white pine, ponderosa pine, sugar pine
Siding	Western red cedar, cypress, redwood
Decking and outdoor steps	White oak, locust, walnut
Exposed platforms and porches	Redwood, locust, white oak
Shingles	Cedar, cypress, redwood
Plank roof decking	Southern yellow pine, Douglas fir, or other softwood
Fence posts	Black locust, Osage orange, white oak, cedar, cypress, redwood, catalpa, chestnut
Gates and fences	Douglas fir, western larch, southern yellow pine, redwood, white oak
Roof sheathing	Douglas fir, western larch, southern yellow pine
Wall sheathing	Cedar, hemlock, northern and Idaho white pine, redwood, aspen, spruce, balsam, white fir, basswood, lodgepole pine, poplar, sugar pine, ponderosa pine
Subfloors	Douglas fir, western larch, southern yellow pine, ash, oak

Guide to Lumber and Nails

Lumber Widths and Thickness in Inches

NOMINAL SIZE	ACTUAL SIZE Dry or Seasoned
1 x 3	¾ x 2½
1 x 4	¾ x 3½
1 x 6	¾ x 5½
1 x 8	¾ x 7¼
1 x 10	¾ x 9¼
1 x 12	¾ x 11¼
2 x 3	1½ x 2½
2 x 4	1½ x 3½
2 x 6	1½ x 5½
2 x 8	1½ x 7¼
2 x 10	1½ x 9¼
2 x 12	1½ x 11¼

Nail Sizes

The nail on the left is a 5d (penny) finish nail; on the right, 20d common. The numerals below the nail sizes indicate the approximate number of common nails per pound.

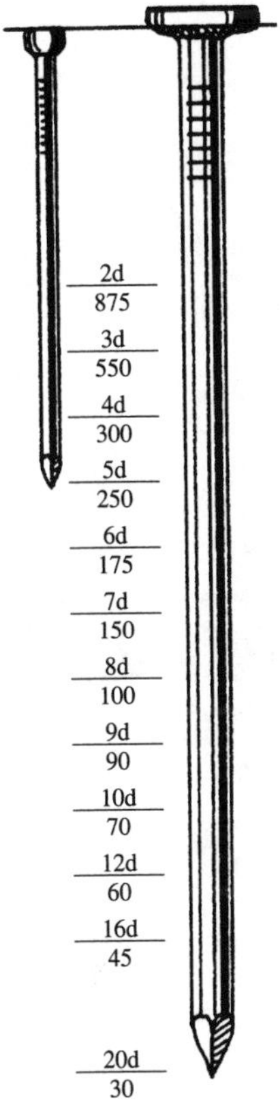

Size	Nails per lb.
2d	875
3d	550
4d	300
5d	250
6d	175
7d	150
8d	100
9d	90
10d	70
12d	60
16d	45
20d	30

Lumber Measure in Board Feet

LENGTH Size in Inches	12 ft.	14 ft.	16 ft.	18 ft.	20 ft.
1 x 4	4	4⅔	5⅓	6	6⅔
1 x 6	6	7	8	9	10
1 x 8	8	9⅓	10⅔	12	13⅓
1 x 10	10	11⅔	13⅓	15	16⅔
1 x 12	12	14	16	18	20
2 x 3	6	7	8	9	10
2 x 4	8	9⅓	10⅔	12	13⅓
2 x 6	12	14	16	18	20
2 x 8	16	18⅔	21⅓	24	26⅔
2 x 10	20	23⅓	26⅔	30	33⅓
2 x 12	24	28	32	36	40
4 x 4	16	18⅔	21⅓	24	26⅔
6 x 6	36	42	48	54	60
8 x 8	64	74⅔	85⅓	96	106⅔
10 x 10	100	116⅔	133⅓	150	166⅔
12 x 12	144	168	192	216	240

Daily Caloric Requirements

These hypothetical examples demonstrate changing caloric requirements at different times of life.

Age range	MALE Weight in pounds	MALE Calories needed	FEMALE Weight in pounds	FEMALE Calories needed
1	24	1,100	24	1,100
2-3	31	1,300	31	1,300
4-6	40	1,800	40	1,800
7-9	55	2,200	55	2,200
10-12	75	2,500	79	2,200
13-15	110	2,800	106	2,200
16-18	136	3,200	117	2,100
19-24	156	3,000	128	2,100
25-49	163	2,700	130	1,900
50-74	161	2,300	139	1,800

PLEASE NOTE: If pregnant or nursing, add 300 to 500 calories.

Prescription-ese

Abbreviation	Latin	Meaning
ac	ante cibum	before meals
ad lib	ad libitum	at pleasure
bid	bis in die	twice a day
cum	cum	with
disp #50		pharmacist should dispense 50 pills
et	et	and
gtt	guttae	drops
hs	hora somni	at bedtime
npo	nihil per os	nothing by mouth
pc	post cibum	after meals
po	per os	by mouth
prn	pro re nata	as needed
qd	quaque die	every day
qh	quaque hora	every hour
qid	quater in die	four times a day
Rx	recipe	take
semis	semis	a half
Sig	signetur	let it be labeled
sine	sine	without
stat	statim	immediately
tid	ter in die	three times a day

Health Hot Lines

Aging
National Council on Aging
800-424-9046

AIDS
CDC National AIDS Hot Line
800-342-AIDS (2437)

Alcohol and Drug Abuse
National Clearinghouse for
Alcohol and Drug Information
800-729-6686

Cancer
Cancer Information Service
800-4-CANCER (422-6237)

Child Abuse
National Child Abuse Hot Line
800-422-4453

Food and Drug Safety
Food and Drug Administration,
Office of Consumer Affairs
301-443-3170

Heart, Lung, and Blood Diseases
National Heart, Lung, and
Blood Institute Education
Programs Center
301-251-1222

Maternal and Child Health
National Maternal and Child
Health Clearinghouse
703-821-8955, ext. 254

Mental Health
National Mental Health
Association
800-969-6642

Occupational Safety and Health
National Institute for
Occupational Safety and Health
800-35-NIOSH (356-4674)

Physical Activity and Fitness
Aerobic and Fitness
Foundation
800-BE FIT 86 (233-4886)

Safety and Injury Prevention
Consumer Product Safety
Commission
800-638-CPSC (2772)

National Highway Traffic
Safety Administration,
Auto Safety Hot Line
800-424-9393

Sexually Transmitted Diseases
CDC National STD Hot Line
800-227-8922

What Should You Weigh?

Women (Medium Frame)		Men (Medium Frame)	
Height	Weight	Height	Weight
5' 0"	113 - 126 lbs.	5' 2"	131 - 141 lbs.
5' 2"	118 - 132 lbs.	5' 4"	135 - 145 lbs.
5' 4"	124 - 138 lbs.	5' 6"	139 - 151 lbs.
5' 6"	130 - 144 lbs.	5' 8"	145 - 157 lbs.
5' 8"	136 - 150 lbs.	5' 10"	151 - 163 lbs.
5' 10"	142 - 156 lbs.	6' 0"	157 - 170 lbs.
6' 0"	148 - 162 lbs.	6' 2"	164 - 178 lbs.

pho·bi·a (fō-bē-ə) *noun*

1.   A persistent, abnormal, or irrational fear of a specific thing or situation that compels one to avoid the feared stimulus.

2.   A strong fear, dislike, or aversion.

PHOBIA SUBJECT	PHOBIA TERM
Air, drafts	Aerophobia
Animals	Zoophobia
Beards	Pogonophobia
Books	Bibliophobia
Cats	Ailurophobia
Churches	Ecclesiaphobia
Crowds	Ochlophobia
Dirt, contamination	Mysophobia
Dreams	Oneirophobia
England, the English	Anglophobia
Flowers	Anthophobia
Food	Sitophobia
Foreign persons or things; strangers	Xenophobia
Gay or homosexual people or their lifestyle or culture	Homophobia
Graves	Taphophobia
Great height, being near something of (e.g., skyscraper, mountain)	Batophobia
High places	Acrophobia
Infection	Nosemaphobia
Lakes	Limnophobia
Leaves	Phyllophobia
Lightning and thunder	Astraphobia
Men	Androphobia
Mites, small insects, worms	Acarophobia
Money	Chrometophobia
Music	Musicophobia
Narrow or enclosed places, being in	Claustrophobia
Newness	Cainotophobia
Night, darkness	Nyctophobia
Number 13	Triskaidekaphobia
Open or public places	Agoraphobia
Sex	Genophobia
Shadows	Sciophobia
Sharply pointed objects, esp. needles	Belonephobia
Spiders	Arachnophobia
Sun	Heliophobia
Touch	Haptophobia
Trees	Dendrophobia
Walking	Basiphobia
Water	Hydrophobia
Women	Gynophobia
Work	Ergophobia
Writing	Graphophobia

First-Aid Essentials

Cuts and Abrasions

+ Antibacterial soap
+ Adhesive bandages (Band-Aids) of various sizes
+ Roll of adhesive tape
+ Sterile dressings (esp. 4"x 4" gauze pads)
+ Roll of 4" gauze (to hold dressings)
+ Pair of blunt-end scissors

Eye Injuries

+ Prepared eyewash and eyecup

Burns (minor)

+ Burn ointment or spray

Skin Problems

+ Hydrocortisone cream or calamine lotion (itches & rashes)
+ Petroleum jelly
+ Antifungal powder or spray for athlete's foot
+ Sunscreen and sunburn spray for relief
+ Insect repellent

Poison (swallowed)

+ Syrup of ipecac (to induce vomiting, after consulting physician or poison-control center)
+ Activated charcoal (to absorb poisons that shouldn't be regurgitated)
+ Epsom salts (to speed excretion of poison)

Heat exhaustion

+ Sodium bicarbonate (mix a pinch with ¼ teaspoon salt in quart of water, and drink)

Pain relief

+ Aspirin or other over-the-counter pain reliever

Miscellaneous

+ Surgical tweezers for removing splinters
+ Cotton balls
+ Elastic bandage for sprains
+ Ice bag to reduce swellings
+ Hot-water bottle and heating pad for aches and pains
+ Aspirin and/or acetaminophen for pain relief and fever reduction
+ Thermometer
+ Sodium bicarbonate for bee, ant, and wasp stings

EMERGENCY CAR KIT

- Battery-powered radio, flashlight, and extra batteries
- Blanket
- Booster cables
- Fire extinguisher (5-lb., A-B-C type)
- First-aid kit and manual
- Bottled water and nonperishable high-energy foods such as granola bars, raisins, and peanut butter
- Maps, shovel, flares
- Tire repair kit and pump

Calorie Burning

If you hustle through your chores to get to the fitness center, relax. You're getting a great workout already. The left-hand column lists "chore" exercises, the middle column shows number of calories you burn per minute per pound of your body weight, the right-hand column lists comparable "recreational" exercises. For example, a 150-pound person forking straw bales burns 9.45 calories per minute, the same workout he/she would get playing basketball.

Chore	Calories	Recreational
Ax chopping, fast	0.135	Skiing, cross country — up hill (0.125)
Climbing hills, with 44-pound load	0.066	Swimming, crawl — fast (0.071)
Digging trenches	0.065	Skiing, cross country — steady walk
Forking straw bales	0.063	Basketball
Chopping down trees	0.060	Football
Climbing hills, with 9-pound load	0.058	Swimming, crawl — slow
Sawing by hand	0.055	Skiing, cross country, moderate
Lawn mowing	0.051	Horseback riding, trotting (0.050)
Scrubbing floors	0.049	Tennis
Shoveling coal	0.049	Aerobic dance, medium
Hoeing	0.041	Weight training, circuit training (0.042)
Stacking firewood	0.040	Weight lifting, free weights (0.039)
Shoveling grain	0.038	Golf
House painting	0.035	Walking, normal pace — asphalt road
Weeding	0.033	Table tennis (0.031)
Food shopping	0.028	Cycling, 5.5 mph (0.029)
Mopping floors	0.028	Fishing
Window cleaning	0.026	Croquet
Raking	0.025	Dancing, ballroom (0.023)
Driving a tractor	0.016	Drawing, in standing position

How Fat Are You?

More accurate than a standard height/weight table is the body mass index (BMI), which measures the percentage of fat in the body. This formula is a quick way to determine your BMI:

1. Convert your weight to kilograms: Divide your weight in pounds (no clothes) by 2.2. _____ kilograms

2. Convert your height to meters: Divide your height in inches (no shoes) by 39.4, then square it (multiply it by itself). _____ meters

3. Divide (1) by (2). This is your BMI. _____

Men: Desirable BMI: 22-24
Overweight: 28.5 and over
Seriously overweight: Above 33

Women: Desirable BMI: 21-23
Overweight: 27.5 and over
Seriously overweight: Above 31.5

Pitches

CURVEBALL
Veers or breaks to the left when thrown with the right hand and to the right when thrown with the left hand.

KNUCKLEBALL
A slow, randomly fluttering pitch thrown by gripping the ball with the tips or nails of two or three fingers.

SLIDERBALL
A fast pitch that breaks in the same direction as a curveball at the last moment.

FASTBALL
A pitch thrown at the pitcher's maximum speed.

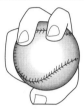

FORKBALL
A pitch with the ball placed between the index and middle fingers so that the ball takes a sharp dip near home plate.

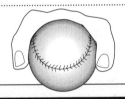

The Most Landed-on Spaces on the Monopoly Game Board

1. Illinois Avenue
2. Go
3. B&O Railroad
4. Free Parking
5. Tennessee Avenue
6. New York Avenue
7. Reading Railroad
8. St. James Place
9. Water Works
10. Pennsylvania Railroad

The Rank of Poker Hands (without wild cards)

1. **Royal flush** — ace, king, queen, jack, ten of the same suit
2. **Straight flush** — five cards, same suit, in sequence
3. **Four of a kind** — four cards, same rank
4. **Full house** — three cards, same rank, and a pair of another rank
5. **Flush** — five cards, same suit
6. **Straight** — five cards in sequence (different suits)
7. **Three of a kind** — three cards, same rank
8. **Two pairs** — two of the same rank, and two cards of a different rank
9. **One pair** — two cards, same rank
10. **High card** — highest rank of five unmatched cards

Origins of Sports

Badminton: Probably originated in China. The first badminton club was formed in the United States in 1878.

Baseball: Early 19th century; derived from the English games of cricket and rounders.

Basketball: Originated 1891 in Springfield, Massachusetts, by Dr. James Naismith of the YMCA.

Billiards: Various games played in England and France in the 15th and 16th centuries.

Bowling: Originated in ancient Germany; introduced in America in the 17th century by the Dutch.

Boxing: One of the oldest forms of competition known. After the fall of Rome, boxing declined but was revived in England in the early 18th century. Modern boxing is based on a code of rules introduced in 1867 by the Marquess of Queensberry. Boxing was illegal in the United States until 1896, when New York became the first state to legalize it.

Checkers: Popular game in Europe since the 16th century; similar to a game played in ancient times.

Chess: Probably originated in India. Popular throughout Europe by the 15th century. First modern international chess tournament was held in London in 1851.

Croquet: Developed in France in the 17th century. The modern form of the game was devised in England in 1857.

Field hockey: Of ancient origin. Played in England for centuries before spreading to other countries.

Football: Developed from English games of soccer and rugby. American football evolved slowly in the 19th century.

Golf: Origin unknown, played in Scotland as early as 1457. The British Open Tournament was established in 1860. May have been played in the American colonies in the 17th century; first United States club organized 1888.

Ice Hockey: Originated in Canada in the mid-19th century. It later spread to the United States and other countries. The first formal hockey game was played in Kingston, Ontario, in 1855.

Lacrosse: Of Native American origin. Developed in Canada and introduced into the United States in the 1870s.

Polo: Probably originated in ancient Persia about 600 B.C. Played in India in the 19th century by British officers and thereafter spread to England and the United States.

Rodeo: Based on the riding and roping skills of the Western cowboy. Prescott, Arizona, held first formal rodeo in 1888.

Rugby: Originated at the Rugby School in England ca. 1840.

Soccer: Earliest recorded game played in England in A.D. 217. By the 12th century, it was a regular Shrove Tuesday event. Refined in the 19th century to emphasize only the kicking aspects. It arrived in the United States in the late 19th century. Today soccer is played in more than 140 countries, making it the most popular international sport.

Softball: Invented in Chicago in 1888. International rules were established in 1933.

Swimming: Swimming contests were organized in Japan as early as the first century B.C. It became organized as an amateur sport in the late 19th century.

Table tennis: Originated in England in the late 19th century. The first world championships were held in London in 1926.

Tennis: Englishman Major Walter C. Wingfield borrowed from older forms of the game to found the sport of modern tennis in 1873. The first United States tennis championship was held in 1881.

Volleyball: Originated in Holyoke, Massachusetts, 1895. It was invented by YMCA physical-fitness director William G. Morgan. The International Volleyball Federation was formed in 1947.

Sports Quiz

Can you match each term with its correct sport? We bet even the most savvy fan will be stumped by some of these. (Answers below.)

1.	Basket		A.	Bowling
2.	Belly		B.	Rugby
3.	Engaged		C.	Fencing
4.	Kiss		D.	Billiards
5.	Hooker		E.	Skiing
6.	Lip		F.	Archery
7.	Turkey		G.	Weight lifting
8.	Jerk		H.	Golf

Answers: 1. E; 2. F; 3. C; 4. D; 5. B; 6. H; 7. A; 8. G

Artificial Fly

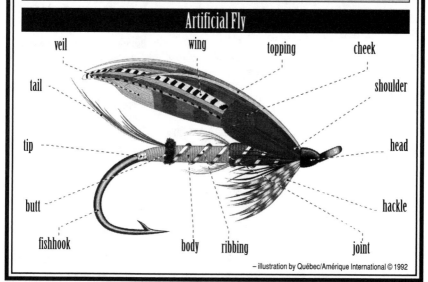

veil · wing · topping · cheek · tail · shoulder · tip · head · butt · hackle · fishhook · body · ribbing · joint

– illustration by Québec/Amérique International © 1992

Safe Ice Thickness *

Ice Thickness	Permissible load
2 inches	one person on foot
3 inches	group in single file
7½ inches	passenger car (2-ton gross)
8 inches	light truck (2½-ton gross)
10 inches	medium truck (3½-ton gross)
12 inches	heavy truck (8-ton gross)
15 inches	10 tons
20 inches	25 tons
30 inches	70 tons
36 inches	110 tons

* Solid clear blue/black pond and lake ice

☞ Slush ice has only one-half strength of blue ice.

☞ Strength value of river ice is 15 percent less.

Source: American Pulpwood Association

Sports Halls of Fame

Association of Sports Museums and Halls of Fame
101 West Sutton Place
Wilmington, DE 19810

Pro Football Hall of Fame
2121 George Halas Dr. N.W.
Canton, OH 44708
216-456-8207

National Football Foundation and Hall of Fame
1865 Palmer Ave.
Larchmont, NY 10538
914-834-0474

National Soccer Hall of Fame
5-11 Ford Ave.
Oneonta, NY 13820
607-432-3351

Pro Rodeo Hall of Fame
101 Pro Rodeo Dr.
Colorado Springs, CO 80919
719-528-4764

International Boxing Hall of Fame
P.O. Box 425
Canastota, NY 13032
315-697-7095

National Baseball Hall of Fame and Museum
P.O. Box 590
Cooperstown, NY 13326
607-547-7200

Naismith Memorial Basketball Hall of Fame
1150 W. Columbus Ave.
Springfield, MA 01101
413-781-6500

National Softball Hall of Fame
2801 N.E. 50th St.
Oklahoma City, OK 73111
405-424-5266

Hockey Hall of Fame and Museum
Yonge & Front Sts.
Toronto, Ontario
Canada M5E 1X8
416-360-7765

National Tennis Foundation and Hall of Fame
100 Park Ave.
New York, NY 10017
212-880-4179

International Swimming Hall of Fame
1 Hall of Fame Dr.
Fort Lauderdale, FL 33316
305-462-6536

Bowling Hall of Fame and Museum
111 Stadium Plaza
St. Louis, MO 63102
314-231-6340

International Checker Hall of Fame
220 Lynn Ray Rd.
(P.O. Box 365)
Petal, MS 39465
601-582-7090

National Freshwater Fishing Hall of Fame
1 Hall of Fame Dr.
(P.O. Box 33)
Hayward, WI 54843
715-634-4440

Abbreviations Approved by the U.S. Postal Service to Be Used in Addressing Mail

Alabama	AL	North Dakota	ND	East	E
Alaska	AK	North Mariana Islands	MP	Estates	EST
American Samoa	AS	Ohio	OH	Expressway	EXPY
Arizona	AZ	Oklahoma	OK	Extension	EXT
Arkansas	AR	Oregon	OR	Freeway	FWY
California	CA	Pennsylvania	PA	Gardens	GDNS
Colorado	CO	Puerto Rico	PR	Grove	GRV
Connecticut	CT	Rhode Island	RI	Heights	HTS
Delaware	DE	South Carolina	SC	Highway	HWY
District of Columbia	DC	South Dakota	SD	Island	IS
Florida	FL	Tennessee	TN	Junction	JCT
Georgia	GA	Texas	TX	Lake	LK
Guam	GU	Trust Territory	TT	Lane	LN
Hawaii	HI	Utah	UT	Manor	MNR
Idaho	ID	Vermont	VT	Mountain	MTN
Illinois	IL	Virgin Islands, U.S.	VI	North	N
Indiana	IN	Virginia	VA	Park	PK
Iowa	IA	Washington	WA	Parkway	PKY
Kansas	KS	West Virginia	WV	Place	PL
Kentucky	KY	Wisconsin	WI	Plaza	PLZ
Louisiana	LA	Wyoming	WY	Point	PT
Maine	ME			Road	RD
Maryland	MD	Alley	ALY	Room	RM
Massachusetts	MA	Apartment	APT	Rural	R
Michigan	MI	Arcade	ARC	South	S
Minnesota	MN	Avenue	AVE	Square	SQ
Mississippi	MS	Boulevard	BLVD	Station	STA
Missouri	MO	Branch	BR	Street	ST
Montana	MT	Bypass	BYP	Suite	STE
Nebraska	NE	Causeway	CSWY	Terrace	TER
Nevada	NV	Center	CTR	Trail	TRL
New Hampshire	NH	Circle	CIR	Turnpike	TPKE
New Jersey	NJ	Court	CT	Viaduct	VIA
New Mexico	NM	Courts	CTS	Vista	VIS
New York	NY	Crescent	CRES	Valley	VLY
North Carolina	NC	Drive	DR	West	W

Canadian Province and Territory Postal Codes

Alberta	AB	Northwest Territories	NT
British Columbia	BC	Ontario	ON
Manitoba	MB	Prince Edward Island	PE
New Brunswick	NB	Quebec	PQ
Newfoundland	NF	Saskatchewan	SK
Nova Scotia	NS	Yukon Territory	YT

Presidential Libraries

Office of Presidential Libraries
National Archives and Records Administration
Washington, DC 20408
PHONE: 202-501-5700
FAX: 202-501-5709

Herbert Hoover Library
211 Parkside Dr., P.O. Box 488
West Branch, IA 52358-0488
PHONE: 319-643-5301
FAX: 319-643-5825
E-MAIL: library@hoover.nara.gov

Franklin D. Roosevelt Library
511 Albany Post Rd.
Hyde Park, NY 12538-1999
PHONE: 914-229-8114
FAX: 914-229-0872
E-MAIL: library@roosevelt.nara.gov

Harry S. Truman Library
500 West U.S. Highway 24
Independence, MO 64050-1798
PHONE: 816-833-1400
FAX: 816-833-4368
E-MAIL: library@truman.nara.gov

Dwight D. Eisenhower Library
200 SE 4th St., Abilene, KS 67410-2900
PHONE: 913-263-4751
FAX: 913-263-4218
E-MAIL: library@eisenhower. nara.gov

John Fitzgerald Kennedy Library
Columbia Point, Boston, MA 02125-3398
PHONE: 617-929-4500
FAX: 617-929-4538
E-MAIL: library@kennedy.nara.gov

Lyndon Baines Johnson Library
2313 Red River St., Austin, TX 78705-5702
PHONE: 512-916-5137
FAX: 512-478-9104
E-MAIL: library@johnson.nara.gov

Nixon Presidential Materials Staff
National Archives at College Park
8601 Adelphi Rd.
College Park, MD 20740-6001
PHONE: 301-713-6950
FAX: 301-713-6916
E-MAIL: nixon@arch2.nara.gov

Richard Nixon Library and Birthplace (private)
18001 Yorba Linda Blvd.
Yorba Linda, CA 92686
PHONE: 714-993-3393

Gerald R. Ford Library
1000 Beal Ave., Ann Arbor, MI 48109-2114
PHONE: 313-741-2218
FAX: 313-741-2341
E-MAIL: library@fordlib.nara.gov

Gerald R. Ford Museum
303 Pearl St., NW
Grand Rapids, MI 49504-5353
PHONE: 616-451-9263
FAX: 616-451-9570
E-MAIL: information.museum@fordmus.nara.gov

Jimmy Carter Library
1 Copenhill Ave. NE, Atlanta, GA 30307-1406
PHONE: 404-331-3942
FAX: 404-730-2215
E-MAIL: library@carter.nara.gov

Ronald Reagan Library
40 Presidential Dr.
Simi Valley, CA 93065-0666
PHONE: 805-522-8444
FAX: 805-522-9621
E-MAIL: library@reagan.nara.gov

George Bush Presidential Materials Project
701 University Dr. East, Suite 300
College Station, TX 77840-9554
PHONE: 409-260-9551
FAX: 409-260-9557
E-MAIL: library@bush.nara.gov

Presidents of the United States — Service

1. George Washington (1732-1799) 1789-1797
2. John Adams (1735-1826) 1797-1801
3. Thomas Jefferson (1743-1826) 1801-1809
4. James Madison (1751-1836) 1809-1817
5. James Monroe (1758-1831) 1817-1825
6. John Quincy Adams (1767-1848) 1825-1829
7. Andrew Jackson (1767-1845) 1829-1837
8. Martin Van Buren (1782-1862) 1837-1841
9. William Henry Harrison (1773-1841) 1841
10. John Tyler (1790-1862) 1841-1845
11. James K. Polk (1795-1849) 1845-1849
12. Zachary Taylor (1784-1850) 1849-1850
13. Millard Fillmore (1800-1874) 1850-1853
14. Franklin Pierce (1804-1869) 1853-1857
15. James Buchanan (1791-1868) 1857-1861
16. Abraham Lincoln (1809-1865) 1861-1865
17. Andrew Johnson (1808-1875) 1865-1869
18. Ulysses S. Grant (1822-1885) 1869-1877
19. Rutherford B. Hayes (1822-1893) 1877-1881
20. James A. Garfield (1831-1881) 1881
21. Chester A. Arthur (1830-1886) 1881-1885
22. Grover Cleveland (1837-1908) 1885-1889
23. Benjamin Harrison (1833-1901) 1889-1893
24. Grover Cleveland (1837-1908) 1893-1897
25. William McKinley (1843-1901) 1897-1901
26. Theodore Roosevelt (1858-1919) 1901-1909
27. William H. Taft (1857-1930) 1909-1913
28. Woodrow Wilson (1856-1924) 1913-1921
29. Warren G. Harding (1865-1923) 1921-1923
30. Calvin Coolidge (1872-1933) 1923-1929
31. Herbert C. Hoover (1874-1964) 1929-1933
32. Franklin D. Roosevelt (1882-1945) 1933-1945
33. Harry S. Truman (1884-1972) 1945-1953
34. Dwight D. Eisenhower (1890-1969) 1953-1961
35. John F. Kennedy (1917-1963) 1961-1963
36. Lyndon B. Johnson (1908-1973) 1963-1969
37. Richard M. Nixon (1913-1994) 1969-1974
38. Gerald R. Ford (1913-) 1974-1977
39. James (Jimmy) Carter (1924-) 1977-1981
40. Ronald Reagan (1911-) 1981-1989
41. George Bush (1924-) 1989-1993
42. William (Bill) Clinton (1946-) 1993-

America's Seacoasts

STATE	LENGTHS IN STATUTE MILES	
	1. General Coastline	2. Tidal Shoreline
Atlantic Coast		
Maine	228	3,478
New Hampshire	13	131
Massachusetts	192	1,519
Rhode Island	40	384
Connecticut	–	618
New York	127	1,850
New Jersey	130	1,792
Pennsylvania	–	89
Delaware	28	381
Maryland	31	3,190
Virginia	112	3,315
North Carolina	301	3,375
South Carolina	187	2,876
Georgia	100	2,344
Florida (Atlantic)	580	3,331
Total	**2,069**	**28,673**
Gulf Coast		
Florida (Gulf)	770	5,095
Alabama	53	607
Mississippi	44	359
Louisisana	397	7,721
Texas	367	3,359
Total	**1,631**	**17,141**
Pacific Coast		
California	840	3,427
Oregon	296	1,410
Washington	157	3,026
Hawaii	750	1,052
Alaska (Pacific)	5,580	31,383
Total	**7,623**	**40,298**
Arctic Coast		
Alaska (Arctic)	1,060	2,521
Total	**1,060**	**2,521**
UNITED STATES TOTAL	**12,383**	**88,633**

1. Figures are lengths of general outline of seacoast. Measurements made with unit measure of 30 minutes of latitude on charts as near scale of 1:1,200,000 as possible. Coastline of bays and sounds is included to point where they narrow to width of unit measure, and distance across at such point is included.

2. Figures obtained in 1939-1940 with recording instrument on largest-scale maps and charts then available. Shoreline of outer coast, offshore islands, sounds, bays, rivers, and creeks is included to head of tidewater or to point where tidal waters narrow to width of 100 feet.

Source: Department of Commerce, National Oceanic and Atmospheric Administration, National Ocean Service

The Sequence of Presidential Succession

1. Vice President
2. Speaker of the House
3. President Pro Tempore of the Senate
4. Secretary of State
5. Secretary of the Treasury
6. Secretary of Defense
7. Attorney General
8. Secretary of the Interior
9. Secretary of Agriculture
10. Secretary of Commerce
11. Secretary of Labor
12. Secretary of Health and Human Services
13. Secretary of Housing and Urban Development
14. Secretary of Transportation
15. Secretary of Energy
16. Secretary of Education

Top 10 Ancestries of the U.S. Population
According to 1990 U.S. Census*

Ancestry Group	Number
1. German	57,947,873
2. Irish	38,735,539
3. English	32,651,788
4. African	23,777,098
5. Italian	14,644,550
6. American	12,395,999
7. Mexican	11,586,983
8. French	10,320,935
9. Polish	9,366,106
10. American Indian	8,708,220

*Survey asked people to identify the ancestry group to which they believed themselves to belong.

Dear Congressman...

Address a letter to your senator or representative as follows:

[Senator's name]
United States Senate
Washington, DC 20510

[Representative's name]
United States House of Representatives
Washington, DC 20515

Federal Agencies

Advisory Council on Historic Preservation	202-254-3974
Consumer Product Safety Commission	800-638-2772
Environmental Protection Agency	202-260-2090
Farm Credit Administration	703-883-4000
Federal Communications Commission	202-418-0200
Federal Maritime Commission	202-523-5707
General Services Administration	202-708-5082
National Science Foundation	703-306-1234
Peace Corps	800-424-8580
Small Business Administration	800-827-5722
Smithsonian Institution	202-357-1300
U.S. Information Agency	202-619-4700
U.S. Postal Service	202-268-2000

Federal Information Center

If you have a question about the federal government, but don't know whom to call, start with the Federal Information Center. Following is a list of numbers for major metropolitan areas. If you are outside the areas listed, call **301-722-9000.**

800-347-1997

Connecticut: Hartford, New Haven

Florida: Fort Lauderdale, Jacksonville, Miami, Orlando, St. Petersburg, Tampa, West Palm Beach

Georgia: Atlanta

Indiana: Indianapolis

Kentucky: Louisville

Maryland: Baltimore

Massachusetts: Boston

Michigan: Detroit, Grand Rapids

New Jersey: Newark, Trenton

New York: Albany, Buffalo, New York, Rochester, Syracuse

North Carolina: Charlotte

Ohio: Akron, Cinncinnati, Cleveland, Columbus, Dayton, Toledo

Pennsylvania: Philadelphia,

Pittsburgh

Rhode Island: Providence

Tennessee: Chattanooga

Virginia: Norfolk, Richmond, Roanoke

800-366-2998

Alabama: Birmingham, Mobile

Arkansas: Little Rock

Illinois: Chicago

Indiana: Gary

Louisiana: New Orleans

Minnesota: Minneapolis

Missouri: St. Louis

Nebraska: Omaha

Oklahoma: Oklahoma City, Tulsa

Tennessee: Memphis, Nashville

Texas: Austin, Dallas, Fort Worth, Houston, San Antonio

Wisconsin: Milwaukee

800-359-3997

Arizona: Phoenix

Colorado: Colorado Springs, Denver, Pueblo

New Mexico: Albuquerque

Utah: Salt Lake City

800-726-4995

California: Los Angeles, Sacramento, San Diego, San Francisco, Santa Ana

Oregon: Portland

Washington: Seattle, Tacoma

800-733-5996

Hawaii: Honolulu

800-729-8003

Alaska: Anchorage

800-735-8004

Iowa: all locations

Kansas: all locations

A Defining Moment

Ocean: 1.) The entire body of salt water that covers more than 70 percent of the Earth's surface. **2.)** Any of the principal divisions of the ocean, including the Atlantic, Pacific, and Indian oceans, their southern extensions in Antarctica, and the Arctic Ocean.

Sea: 1.) The continuous body of salt water covering most of the Earth's surface, especially this body regarded as a geophysical entity distinct from earth and sky. **2.)** A tract of water within an ocean. **3.)** A relatively large body of salt water completely or partially enclosed by land. **4.)** A relatively large landlocked body of fresh water.

Copyright: The legal right granted to an author, a composer, a playwright, a publisher, or a distributor to exclusive publication, production, sale, or distribution of a literary, musical, dramatic, or artistic work.

Patent: A grant made by a government that confers upon the creator of an invention the sole right to make, use, and sell that invention for a set period of time.

The New York Public Library's "Books of the Century"

To commemorate the centennial of the New York Public Library, librarians from both the Branch and Research libraries identified books that played defining roles in society during the first 100 years of the library (1895-1995). Titles were grouped in 11 categories: Landmarks of Modern Literature; Nature's Realm; Protest & Progress; Colonialism & Its Aftermath; Mind & Spirit; Popular Culture & Mass Entertainment; Women Rise; Economics & Technology; Utopias & Dystopias; War, Holocaust, Totalitarianism; and Optimism, Joy & Gentility.

Here are the book lists from three categories:

NATURE'S REALM

Maurice Maeterlinck. *La vie des abeilles [The Life of the Bee]* (1901)

Marie Sklodowska Curie. *Traité de radioactivité [Treatise on Radioactivity]* (1910)

Albert Einstein. *The Meaning of Relativity* (1922)

Roger Tory Peterson. *A Field Guide to the Birds* (1934)

Aldo Leopold. *A Sand County Almanac* (1949)

Konrad Z. Lorenz. *Er redete mit dem Vieh, den Vögeln und Fischen: King Solomon's Ring [King Solomon's Ring: New Light on Animal Ways]* (1949)

Rachel Carson. *Silent Spring* (1962)

Smoking and Health (known as *The Surgeon General's Report*) (1964)

James Watson. *The Double Helix: A Personal Account of the Discovery of the Structure of DNA* (1968)

Edward O. Wilson. *The Diversity of Life* (1992)

POPULAR CULTURE & MASS ENTERTAINMENT

Bram Stoker. *Dracula* (1897)

Henry James. *The Turn of the Screw* (1898)

Arthur Conan Doyle. *The Hound of the Baskervilles* (1902)

Edgar Rice Burroughs. *Tarzan of the Apes* (1912)

Zane Grey. *Riders of the Purple Sage* (1912)

Agatha Christie. *The Mysterious Affair at Styles* (1920)

Dale Carnegie. *How to Win Friends and Influence People* (1936)

Margaret Mitchell. *Gone with the Wind* (1936)

Raymond Chandler. *The Big Sleep* (1939)

Nathanael West. *The Day of the Locust* (1939)

Grace Metalious. *Peyton Place* (1956)

Dr. Seuss. *The Cat in the Hat* (1957)

Robert A. Heinlein. *Stranger in a Strange Land* (1961)

Joseph Heller. *Catch-22* (1961)

Truman Capote. *In Cold Blood: A True Account of a Multiple Murder and Its Consequences* (1965)

Jim Bouton. *Ball Four: My Life and Hard Times Throwing the Knuckleball in the Big Leagues* (1970)

Stephen King. *Carrie* (1974)

Tom Wolfe. *The Bonfire of the Vanities* (1987)

OPTIMISM, JOY & GENTILITY

Sarah Orne Jewett. *The Country of the Pointed Firs* (1896)

Helen Keller. *The Story of My Life* (1903)

G. K. Chesterton. *The Innocence of Father Brown* (1911)

Juan Ramón Jimenez. *Platero y yo [Platero and I: An Andalusian Elegy]* (1914)

George Bernard Shaw. *Pygmalion* (1914)

Emily Post. *Etiquette in Society, in Business, in Politics, and at Home* (1922)

P. G. Wodehouse. *The Inimitable Jeeves* (1925)

A. A. Milne. *Winnie-the-Pooh* (1926)

Willa Cather. *Shadows on the Rock* (1931)

Irma S. Rombauer. *The Joy of Cooking: A Compilation of Reliable Recipes with a Casual Culinary Chat* (1931)

J. R. R. Tolkien. *The Hobbit* (1937)

Margaret Wise Brown. *Goodnight Moon* (1947)

Harper Lee. *To Kill a Mockingbird* (1960)

Langston Hughes. *The Best of Simple* (1961)

Elizabeth Bishop. *The Complete Poems, 1927-1979* (1983)

Tips on Tipping

LOCATION	PERSON	AMOUNT
Airport	skycaps	$1 or more for full baggage cart
	in-flight personnel	none
Barbershop	haircutter	15% of the cost, generally a minimum of $1
Beauty salon	one beautician	15% of bill
	several operators	10% of bill to person who sets hair; 10% divided among others
	manicurist	$1 or more, depending on cost
Cruise ship	cabin steward	2.5%-4% of total fare, paid at end of each week
	dining-room steward	2.5%-4% of total fare, paid at end of each week
	cabin boy, bath steward, bar steward, wine steward	5%-7.5% of total fare divided among them, paid at the end of each week
Hotel	chambermaid	$1 a night or $5-$10 a week for longer stays
	room-service waiter	15% of bill
	bellhop	$1 per bag for taking you to your room with luggage; 50¢ for opening and showing the room
	lobby attendant	none for opening door and calling taxi from stand; $1 or more for help with luggage or finding a taxi on the street
	desk clerk	none unless special service is given during long stay; then $5
Restaurant	waiter or waitress	15% of bill
	headwaiter/maître d'	none, unless special services are provided; then about $5
	wine steward	15% of wine bill
	bartender	10%-15% of bar bill
	busboy	none
	servers at counter	15% of bill
	coat-check attendant	$1 for one or two coats
	restroom attendant	50¢
	car park attendant	$1
Sports arena	usher	50¢-$1 per party if shown to your seat
Taxi	driver	15% of fare, no less than 50¢
Train	dining-car waiter	15% of bill
	stewards/bar-car waiters	15% of bar bill
	redcaps	posted rate plus $1

Greatest Hits

The top ten songs represented by BMI (Broadcast Music Incorporated), based on the most American radio and television broadcasts.

Title	Composer(s)
"Yesterday"	John Lennon & Paul McCartney
"Never My Love"	Donald & Richard Addrisi
"By the Time I Get to Phoenix"	Jim Webb
"Gentle on My Mind"	John Hartford
"You've Lost That Lovin' Feelin'"	Phil Spector, Barry Mann & Cynthia Weil
"More"	Norman Newell, Nino Oliviero, Riz Ortalani & Marcello Ciorcioloni
"Georgia on My Mind"	Hoagy Carmichael & Stuart Gorrell
"Bridge over Troubled Water"	Paul Simon
"Something"	George Harrison
"Mrs. Robinson"	Paul Simon

Car Dollars

Figures are given in cents per mile (average) and are based on suburban driving conditions.

	LARGE (weight more than 3,500 pounds)	INTERMEDIATE (weight less than 3,500 pounds)	COMPACT (weight less than 3,000 pounds)	SUBCOMPACT (weight less than 2,500 pounds)	PASSENGER VAN (weight less than 5,000 pounds)
Depreciation	9.6	8.6	7.3	5.9	10.7
Maintenance	6.0	5.2	4.6	5.1	6.9
Gas and oil	7.0	5.7	4.6	4.4	9.1
Parking and tolls	0.9	0.9	0.9	0.9	0.9
Insurance	4.9	5.6	4.3	5.0	8.9
Taxes	2.2	1.8	1.6	1.4	2.7
Total costs	30.6	27.8	23.3	22.7	39.2

Richter Scale for Measuring Earthquakes

MAGNITUDE	POSSIBLE EFFECTS
1	Detectable only by instruments
2	Barely detectable, even near the epicenter
3	Felt indoors
4	Felt by most people; slight damage
5	Felt by all; damage minor to moderate
6	Moderately destructive
7	Major damage
8	Total and major damage

Devised by American geologist Charles W. Richter in 1935 to measure the magnitude of an earthquake.

Knots

overhand knot   figure-eight knot   granny knot   square knot

common whipping   cow hitch   clove hitch   fisherman's knot

sheet bend   double sheet bend   running bowline   bowline

bowline on a bight   sheepshank   heaving line knot

INCHES   1   2   3   4

CENTIMETERS   1   2   3   4   5   6   7   8   9   10

Makeshift Measurers

When you don't have a measuring stick or tape, use what is at hand. To this list, add any other items that you always (or nearly always) have handy.

Credit card: 3-3/8" x 2-1/8"
Business card (standard): 3-1/2" x 2"
Floor tile: 12" square
Dollar bill: 6-1/8" x 2-5/8"
Quarter (diameter): 1"
Penny (diameter): 3/4"
Sheet of paper: 8-1/2" x 11"
   (legal size: 8-1/2"x 14")

Your foot/shoe: _____

Your outstretched arms, fingertip to fingertip:

   _____

Your shoelace: _____

Your necktie: _____

Your belt: _____

Decibels

Decibels (dB) are used to measure the loudness or intensity of sounds. One decibel is the smallest difference between sounds detectable by the human ear. Intensity varies exponentially: A 20 dB sound is 10 times louder than a 10 dB sound; a 30 dB sound is 100 times louder than a 10 dB sound; a 40 dB sound is 1,000 times louder than a 10 dB sound; and so on. A 120-decibel sound is painful.

10 decibels	light whisper
20	quiet conversation
30	normal conversation
40	light traffic
50	typewriter, loud conversation
60	noisy office
70	normal traffic, quiet train
80	rock music, subway
90	heavy traffic, thunder
100	jet plane at takeoff

Metric Conversion

	CONVENTIONAL TO METRIC, MULTIPLY BY		METRIC TO CONVENTIONAL, MULTIPLY BY	
inch	2.54	centimeter	0.39	inch
foot	30.48	centimeter	0.033	foot
yard	0.91	meter	1.09	yard
mile	1.61	kilometer	0.62	mile
square inch	6.45	square centimeter	0.15	square inch
square foot	0.09	square meter	10.76	square foot
square yard	0.8	square meter	1.2	square yard
square mile	0.84	square kilometer	0.39	square mile
acre	0.4	hectare	2.47	acre
ounce	28.0	gram	0.035	ounce
pound	0.45	kilogram	2.2	pound
short ton (2,000 pounds)	0.91	metric ton	1.10	short ton
ounce	30.0	milliliter	0.034	ounce
pint	0.47	liter	2.1	pint
quart	0.95	liter	1.06	quart
gallon	3.8	liter	0.26	gallon

If you know the conventional measurement and want to convert it to metric, multiply it by the numbers in the first column (example: 1 inch equals 2.54 centimeters). If you know the metric measurement, multiply it by the numbers in the second column (example: 2 meters equals 2.18 yards).

Know Your Angels

I.	First Group — nearest to God	Seraphim
		Cherubim
		Thrones

II.	Second Group — receives the reflection of Divine Presence from the first group	Dominions
		Virtues
		Powers

III.	Angelic Group — ministers directly to human beings	Principalities
		Archangels
		Angels

Animals in the Bible

In addition to the following list of references to specific animals, there are numerous general references: beast (337), cattle (153), fowl (90), fish (56), and bird (41).

Animal	Old Testament	New Testament	Total
Sheep	155	45	200
Lamb	153	35	188
Lion	167	9	176
Ox	156	10	166
Ram	165	0	165
Horse	137	27	164
Bullock	152	0	152
Ass	142	8	150
Goat	131	7	138
Camel	56	6	62

Best-Bet Wedding Gifts

At a loss for an appropriate gift? Emily Post has a few ready suggestions.

For the couple just starting out:

◆ Set of folding tables on rack
◆ Mirror for entry or hall
◆ Crystal vase
◆ Food processor
◆ Electric hot tray
◆ Lamp
◆ Set of glasses
◆ Carving set
◆ Microwave cookware
◆ Wooden salad bowl
◆ Large pepper grinder or salt-and-pepper set
◆ Framed print or photograph
◆ Wastebasket
◆ Hors d'oeuvres tray
◆ Items of the silver or china selected by the bride
◆ Answering machine

Second-marriage gifts, for couples who have already set up house:

◆ A plant, tree, or shrub
◆ A selection of fine wines or champagnes
◆ If they are collectors, something to add to their collection
◆ A picture frame containing a meaningful photo
◆ Ceramic or copper molds for cooking or decoration
◆ A subscription to a magazine related to their special interests
◆ A gift package of gourmet-food selections
◆ A painting or lithograph (if you know their tastes)
◆ If either one has small children, sitter service for a specified period (either yourself or hired)

Principal Religions of the World

The figures given for membership in each religious affiliation are estimates based on 1991 statistics.

Christians . . . . 1.8 billion
Muslims 1   "
Nonreligious . . . . 900 million
Hindus 750   "
Buddhists 325   "
Atheists 250   "
Chinese folk religionists . . 200   "
New-Religionists 150   "
Tribal religionists 100   "
Sikhs 19   "
Jews 18   "
Shamanists 10   "
Confucians 6   "
Baha'is . . . . .5.5   "
Jains . . . . 3.8   "
Shintoists . . . . 3.2   "
Other religionists 18   "

The Golden Rule
(It's True in All Faiths)

BRAHMANISM:
This is the sum of duty: Do naught unto others which would cause you pain if done to you.   *Mahabharata 5:1517*

BUDDHISM:
Hurt not others in ways that you yourself would find hurtful.   *Udana-Varga 5:18*

CONFUCIANISM:
Surely it is the maxim of loving-kindness: Do not unto others what you would not have them do unto you.   *Analects 15:23*

TAOISM:
Regard your neighbor's gain as your own gain and your neighbor's loss as your own loss.   *T'ai Shang Kan Ying P'ien*

ZOROASTRIANISM:
That nature alone is good which refrains from doing unto another whatsoever is not good for itself.   *Dadistan-i-dinik 94:5*

JUDAISM:
What is hateful to you, do not to your fellowman. That is the entire Law; all the rest is commentary.   *Talmud, Shabbat 31a*

CHRISTIANITY:
All things whatsoever ye would that men should do to you, do ye even so to them; for this is the law and the prophets.
          Matthew 7:12

ISLAM:
No one of you is a believer until he desires for his brother that which he desires for himself.   *Sunnah*

– courtesy Elizabeth Pool

Every Minute Counts

The Tax Foundation gives a breakdown of the amount of time you work in an eight-hour day to pay for certain expenses as follows:

Federal and state taxes	2 hours, 45 minutes	Transportation	39 minutes
Housing	1 hour, 25 minutes	Recreation	25 minutes
Food, tobacco	57 minutes	Other	1 hour, 3 minutes
Medical care	46 minutes		

Rules of Introduction

Countless situations call for introductions. Here are some basic guidelines to help you through. Even if you can't remember the proper order of introduction, forget names, or make another mistake in your introduction, it is a far greater blunder to neglect this social courtesy altogether. To easily carry out a "proper" introduction, just remember to say first the name of the person who is having someone introduced *to* them. For example, you would say: " Mary, this is Tom Smith; Tom, Mary Jones."

A man	TO	a woman
A young person	TO	an older person
A less important person	TO	a more important person
A peer in your own company	TO	a peer in another company
A nonofficial person	TO	an official person
A junior executive	TO	a senior executive
A fellow executive	TO	a customer or client

Having Tea with the Queen?

On the off chance that you may have the honor of conversing with members of the British Royal Family or members of the nobility, use these forms of address:

Your Majesty (to the queen or king)

Your Royal Highness (to the monarch's spouse, children, and siblings)

Your Highness (to nephews, nieces, and cousins of the monarch)

Duke or Duchess (to a duke or duchess if you are also among the nobility)

Your Grace (to a duke or duchess if you are a commoner; to an archbishop of the Church of England)

My Lord (to a peer below a duke; to a bishop of the Church of England)

Lord (to an earl, marquis, or viscount; an earl and marquis is usually "of" somewhere, but you don't say the "of," just Lord

Derby for the Earl of Derby)

Lady (to a marchioness, countess, viscountess, or baroness; as in Lord, you don't say the "of")

Sir (to a baronet or knight, using his first name; i.e., Sir Thomas Lipton)

Lady (to the wife of a baronet or knight; in olden days, the title was Dame)

Appropriate Finger Foods

Asparagus, if crisp.

Bananas. Peel completely, then break pieces off with fingers.

Corn on the cob. Eat the corn "typewriter-style."

Grapes. Break off a small bunch. Then pluck and eat one by one.

Lemon. Squeeze wedges with fingers to trickle juice on food.

Lobster. Crack first with tools provided.

Olives. Remove pits from mouth with fingers.

Spare ribs and rack of lamb. Use knife and fork to get easy meat first.

Steamed clams. Lift each out by its neck, dip in butter, eat in one bite.